THE GREAT

CONVENT CASE

Saurin v. Star & Kennedy

TRIED BEFORE LORD CHIEF JUSTICE COCKBURN
IN THE COURT OF QUEEN'S BENCH
FEBRUARY, 1869.

CONTAINING

The Speeches of Counsel on Both Sides, and the Evidence in
Full of the Various Witnesses, Corrected from the
Short-Hand Writers' Notes.

Together with Copies of the Writ of Action, the Pleadings, Issue,
Record, Names of Jurymen, and OTHER PARTICULARS
ONLY TO BE FOUND IN THIS WORK.

WITH A PREFACE BY JAMES GRANT, ESQ.,
AUTHOR OF "THE RELIGIOUS TENDENCIES OF THE TIMES," ETC.

LONDON:

WARD, LOCK, AND TYLER, Warwick House, Paternoster Row.

AGENTS:

New York: WILLMER & ROGERS. Paris: A. & W. GALIGNANI. Brussels: C. MUQUARDT. Leipsic: BROCKHAUS. Stuttgart: HALLBERGER. Berlin: F. SCHNEIDER & Co. Vienna: W. BRAUMULLER. Antwerp: MAX KORNICKER. Rotterdam: H. A. KRAMERS. Turin and Florence: H. LOESCHER. Stockholm: SAMSON & WALLIN. Athens: C. WILBERG. Constantinople: S. H. WEISS. Madras: GANTZ Brothers. Calcutta: THACKER, SPINK, & Co., G. C. HAY & Co., and R. C. LEPAGE & Co. Bombay: THACKER, VINING, & Co. Kingston, Jamaica: DE CORDOVA, M'DOUGALL, & Co. Melbourne: G. ROBERTSON. Adelaide: W. C. RIGBY. Sydney: W. MADDOCK. Tasmania: J. WALSH & SONS.

1869

LONDON:

PRINTED BY J. OGDEN AND CO.,

172, ST. JOHN STREET, E.C.

Printing Statement:

Due to the very old age and scarcity of this book,
many of the pages may be hard to read due to the
blurring of the original text, possible missing pages,
missing text, dark backgrounds and other issues
beyond our control.

Because this is such an important and rare work, we
believe it is best to reproduce this book regardless of
its original condition.

Thank you for your understanding.

PREFACE.

BELIEVING that the revelations which have been made respecting the nature of Popery in the course of the great Convent Case which has been for so long a time before the Court of Queen's Bench, are eminently adapted to accomplish a vast amount of moral and social good, I have gladly and readily responded to an application made to me to write a Preface to a republication, in the pamphlet form, of all the evidence and leading speeches of counsel, which have appeared day after day in the public journals, while the case was proceeding. Not only was this trial, as the Lord Chief Justice remarked, the most protracted of the kind of which we have any record in the annals of our courts of justice, but it was in some respects the most important ecclesiastical cause that was ever brought before a British tribunal.

The case of Saurin *v.* Star is, therefore, one which deserves to be recorded in a more permanent and more convenient form, than in the ephemeral newspapers of the day. The publishers, sharing in this view, have brought out a full and accurate report of the case, in the shape in which it is now presented to the public. And they cannot doubt that the public will prove, by the reception which the work will meet with, that they have not erred in their anticipations of the welcome with which it will be greeted by the country.

Though the idea of writing this Preface did not originate with me, I feel that the task could not, in some respects, have been more appropriately confided to other hands. In various works, of no small size, and in a daily journal—the *Morning Advertiser*—of which I am Editor, I have for more than thirty years made it an essential part of the business of my life, to do all in my power to expound the true nature of Popery. I, therefore, heartily embrace the opportunity afforded me by the disclosures made in this extraordinary Convent Case, to give whatever additional currency my name can impart to the circulation of the proofs furnished by the recent proceedings in the Court of Queen's Bench, of the darkness in which the professors of Romanism delight to shroud their acts. The whole country has been astounded by the evidence which has been brought forward in the course of this remarkable trial, of the real character of Roman Catholicism. The outer world now see Popery with a clearness of vision with which they never saw it before; and the sight will not, I feel assured, render it more attractive in the eyes of those whose mental perceptions are not obscured. They must, on the contrary, be appalled as well as amazed by the hideousness of the features which Popery presents as exhibited within the last few weeks in Westminster Hall.

I have heard again and again great surprise expressed in the course of this trial, that as nuns are treated with so much harshness they should remain in convents, when they might leave them at any time, if so disposed. It was proved in the most ample manner—it was not, in fact, denied—that Miss Saurin might have quitted the convent at any time she pleased. The Lady Superior, indeed, had for several years been most desirous that she should return to her family, or repair to some other convent. The explanation is this :—A nun who either leaves a convent of her own accord, or is expelled, can never again hold up her head in Roman Catholic society. She is set down as one who has not what is called a "vocation" for conventual life, and this is regarded as a proof that she is destitute of all that the Roman Catholics consider as meritorous in the sight of God and the Church. She is viewed in the same light—as a Roman Catholic lady remarked to me a few days since—as a returned convict is by the rest of the community. Hence many nuns will bear anything rather than expose themselves to this terrible proscription by all their friends and co-religionists. Death itself is, indeed, in their view to be preferred. They feel exactly the same as those do who are "cursed from the Altar," and consequently shunned in the ordinary intercourse of life.

One of the happy results of this publication must inevitably be to deter many well-meaning, amiable, but grievously mistaken young ladies from immuring themselves in the dark and dismal cells of a convent, instead of carrying out their pious purpose of self-consecration to God, and to the holy mission of doing all they can, by their intercourse with their fellow-creatures, to ameliorate the moral, the social, and spiritual condition of suffering and sorrowing humanity.

Another great and immediate good which must of necessity be accomplished by this extraordinary trial, will be the passing of a measure by the Legislature, authorizing and enforcing the periodical inspection of all the convents in Her Majesty's dominions, by a Commission appointed for the purpose, consisting chiefly, if not exclusively, of lay members. For many years I have, in my capacity as a public journalist, laboured most earnestly and assiduously with the view of prevailing on the Legislature to adopt such a measure. The great hindrance to the acquiescence in that course on the part of Parliament has arisen from the difficulty of obtaining authentic information respecting the existence of such abuses as would justify its passing a measure of that nature. That obstacle has been removed out of the way by the trial just ended. All necessary evidence as to the treatment to which nuns are subjected, and the great difficulty they have in the vast majority of cases—indeed, in many cases, the absolute impossibility—of making their wrongs known to even their nearest and dearest of relations, will be found clearly brought out in the recent trial, during the examination of the Sisters themselves, including equally the Superioress and the subordinate nuns. This work will, therefore, be one of inestimable importance to the philosopher in his investigations into the various phases in which human nature presents itself. It will no less be a work which the future Protestant historian will consult with interest, as furnishing him with valuable materials for his illustrations of the nature of Popery, as exemplified in the form of conventual life.

JAMES GRANT.

41, Guildford Street, Russell Square,
February 25, 1869.

THE

GREAT CONVENT CASE,

Saurin v. Star & Kennedy.

COURT OF QUEEN'S BENCH, *Wednesday, February* 3*rd*, 1869.

Before Lord Chief Justice COCKBURN, *and a Special Jury.*

THIS was an action brought by a professed Sister of the Order of Mercy against the Mother Superioress and a professed Sister of the same order in the convent at Hull, to recover damages for assault, and conspiracy to drive her from the convent and have her expelled from the order.

The declaration stated that the defendants on divers occasions assaulted and beat the plaintiff, that they took her clothes and property from her, and imprisoned her for a long time, whereby she was rendered sick and ill, and greatly distressed in body and mind. The second count was a trover for a watch, wearing apparel, books, and papers. The other counts in the declaration alleged that the plaintiff was a member of a religious order of Roman Catholic women called Sisters of Mercy, and of the house or religious establishment of such Sisters of Mercy; that the defendants were members of the same order, and that the defendant Star was the superioress of the same; the plaintiff as such member was legally entitled to certain privileges and advantages, and amongst others to board, lodging, clothing, and maintenance at the expense of the order, and to the right of attending certain services of the Roman Catholic Church in a building attached to the said house; that the defendants wrongfully and maliciously conspired together to compel the plaintiff to cease to be a member by subjecting her to various indignities, persecutions, annoyances, and by depriving her of the food and clothing to which, as a member, she was lawfully entitled, and by imprisoning her and keeping her imprisoned, and by preventing her from attending the services of the said church; and, further, that the defendants unlawfully and maliciously conspired to procure the expulsion of the plaintiff from the said religious house and order by making false charges of disobedience, contempt of authority, and neglect of duty, and other misconduct; that the Roman Catholic bishop, who, by the rules and constitution of the said order, had lawful authority to act in their behalf, did expel the plaintiff. The plaintiff says that, in pursuance of the conspiracy, the defendants did subject her to a long series of indignities, persecution, and

annoyances, and did deprive her of food and clothing, and of divers articles of her property; they also imprisoned the plaintiff to prevent her from attending the services, and made a false charge against her to the bishop, whereby she was expelled from the order, and lost all the benefits accruing from her membership. The fourth count contained the libel complained of, which, it was alleged, was written and published by the defendant Star to the bishop, and was to the following effect: "That she (the plaintiff) is dissatisfied with and complains of her boots and shoes, and the food given to her, and the veil. She is late in her duties. She eats during the hours when eating is prohibited. She has spoken privately to the priest. She has contradicted the superioress, and spoken disrespectfully of her. She met the priest in the convent in disobedience of orders. She converses with externs. She does not scruple to approach the sacraments for the purposes of deception; and that, after she had been guilty of the aforesaid acts, she sent for the Rev. Mr. Armt, and made a false statement to him." The plaintiff claims £5,000 damages.

The defendants paid £5 into court as sufficient to satisfy the count in trover. They pleaded not guilty to other counts, and generally that the plaintiff was not a member of the order, and was not lawfully entitled to the privileges and advantages of the institution; and that, after the accruing of the matters of complaint and cause of action, the same was referred, with all matters in difference, to Dr. Robert Cornthwaite, Roman Catholic Archbishop of Beverley, who duly made and published his award; that the alleged matters of complaint and cause of action had not nor had any of them accrued, and had not, nor had any of them existed. The plaintiff rejoined that the sum paid into court was insufficient, and upon the rest issue was joined.

The Solicitor-General, Mr. Digby Seymour, Q.C., and Mr. Willes, were counsel for the plaintiff; Mr. Hawkins, Q.C., Mr. Mellish, Q.C., and Mr. Charles Russell were counsel for the defendants.

Mr. WILLES opened the pleadings, and

The SOLICITOR-GENERAL stated the plaintiff's case. He said : I have the honour to appear in this case with my learned friends on behalf of the plaintiff, Miss Susan Saurin, and I dare say you will have all gathered from the few sentences of Mr. Willes the case which I have to lay before you, and which will demand more than the ordinary amount of watchful and impartial attention upon the part of the gentlemen of the jury. The facts are strange and painful. They are strange and painful first as a revelation of human nature. They are strange and painful next as a revelation of female nature ; and they are strange and painful as well as a revelation of conventual female nature, showing what women are capable of when they shut themselves up from their kind, and shut out the instincts of their better nature, and what mean and petty cruelties they can wreak upon their sister women, and that in the name of the God of Love, and under the supposed sanction of that blessed religion, the Divine Author of which died on the cross to show his deep tenderness for the world, which was disposed to reject him. This is no common Exeter Hall kind of exposure ; it is no ultra-Protestant revelation ; this is no indiscriminate attack upon the belief and practices of the largest body of Christians in the world. The plaintiff and defendants are Roman Catholics alike. They are alike devoted to the belief and practices of the Roman Catholic Church. They alike believe with a patient and intense devotion in the Divine authority, and the exclusive authority of that branch of the Church Catholic of which Pius IX. is the head. The defendant is the superioress of the Convent of Our Lady of Mercy at Hull. The plaintiff is a person of very good family, and connected with good families in Ireland, herself a person of great devotion, having two sisters nuns in different Roman Catholic orders, having a brother a Jesuit priest, and an uncle a parish priest in Ireland, and brought up amongst Roman Catholic associations and surrounded in every way by Roman Catholic influences of the best sort. Therefore she comes before a jury of Englishmen, not in the least for the purpose of casting any aspersions upon the Church to which she belongs, or upon its religious orders, but to complain of a gross personal wrong inflicted upon her, as she believes, in breach of the rules of those institutions, and contrary to the real intention of the religion to which she is ardently devoted. From early youth she was desirous of entering into religious orders, but she was not permitted to do so prematurely. Two of her sisters had already gone into convents, and her family, although religious, was not desirous that their third daughter should be devoted to conventual life, and for some years they opposed her desire ; but at last she obtained the consent of her mother, and with her uncle, a Roman Catholic priest named Mathews, she visited several convents to see what kind of habit of life she liked best ; and eventually, in November, 1851, she entered the convent of the Sisters of Mercy, in Baggot-street, Dublin, as a postulant. I ought to explain that this body of Sisters of Mercy is not, according to Roman Catholic ideas, what is called an order, strictly speaking, but something different, and less strict. It is an

institution or congregation, and the vows and rules connected with it are not so stringent as if it were what was called an order. For instance, they are allowed a great extent of external usefulness. Nuns are immured ; they never come out of doors ; they give themselves up to praying, contemplation, and other devotions ; but Sisters of Mercy make themselves extremely useful in visiting the sick, instructing the ignorant, and other works of usefulness in the world. On the 5th August, 1851, she took what was called the holy habit, and became a novice in the convent in Dublin. The following are the vows which she took, and the professions which she subscribed :

Do you earnestly desire to become a good and fervent religious member of this institute ?—Yes.

Are you resolved to observe its rules and customs faithfully, as you have been made acquainted with them ?—Yes.

Are you resolved to obey your superiors in all things, whether matters of great or little moment, agreeable or disagreeable ?—Yes.

Are you satisfied to spend your life in any office or employment assigned you, be it ever so disagreeable, laborious, or humiliating ?—Yes.

Are you willing to receive and dispense the profit of public as well as of private reprehension and penance?—Yes.

Are you willing to have your faults made known to your superioress by whoever becomes acquainted with them, and are you ready to make the customary manifestation of conscience whenever you may be required to do so ?—Yes.

Susan M. Saurin, do you find any serious difficulty in the practice of holy poverty or obedience, or in the observance of our holy rule ?—No.

Are you firmly resolved to pass your life in the exact observance of our holy rule and customs, without requiring or seeking any dispensations or particularities in respect of food, clothing, lodging, or the like ?—I am.

Do you esteem and love this institute, and do you find the exercise of its characteristic functions conducive to your own perfection ?—I do.

Is there anything in its rules or constitutions, or in the approved customs of this congregation, to which you find a particular difficulty in submitting your judgment ?—No.

Have you any doubts respecting your vocation of so strong a nature as to warrant a fear that you will hereafter be likely to abandon it ?—No.

Are you willing to go to any of our branch houses and to remain there as your superioress may deem expedient, and are you satisfied to be sent on a foundation to any part of the United Kingdom ?—Yes.

(Signed)
Sister M. SCHOLASTICA JOSEPH SAURIN.

The order of admission is as follows :

In the name of our Lord and Saviour Jesus Christ, and under the protection of his immaculate Mother Mary, ever Virgin, I, Susan Mary Saurin, called in religion Sister Mary Scholastica Joseph, do vow and promise to God poverty, chastity, and obedience, and the service of the poor sick, and ignorant, and to persevere until death in this institute of Our Lady of Mercy, according to its approved rule and constitutions, under the authority and in presence of you, my Lord and Most Reverend Father in God, Paul

Cullen, Archbishop of this diocese, and of our reverend mother, Ellen Whitty, called in religion Mary Vincent, mother superior of this Convent of Mercy, this 3rd day of October, in the year of our Lord 1853.

(Signed)
Susan M. Saurin (called in religion Sister Mary Scholastica Joseph.)
Sister Mary Juliana Dellany, Assistant.
Sister Mary Vincent Whitty, Superioress.
Paul Cullen, Archbishop of Dublin.

Upon that profession having been made in 1853 she became a regular professed sister in this order, when she took the following vows of poverty and obedience :

The sisters shall therefore keep their hearts perfectly disengaged from every affection to the things of this world, content with the food and raiment allowed them, and willing at all times to give up whatever has been allotted for their use. They shall not give or receive any present without permission from the mother superior. When with her permission they receive any present from their relatives or other persons it must be considered as for the use of the community, and not for the particular use of the receiver. Nothing shall appear in their dress but what is grave and modest, nor can they keep in their cells anything superfluous, nor any costly or rich furniture or decoration. All must be suitable to religious simplicity and poverty.

The sisters are always to bear in mind that by the vow of obedience they have for ever renounced their own will, and resigned it to the direction of their superiors. They are to obey the mother superior as holding her authority from God, rather through love than servile fear. They shall love and respect her as their mother, and, in order that she may be able to direct them in the way of the divine service, it is recommended to them to make known to her their penitential works and mortifications, with the advantages derived from them. They shall, without hesitation, comply with all the directions of the mother superior, whether in matters of great or little moment, agreeable or disagreeable. They shall never murmur; but, with humility and spiritual joy, carry the sweet yoke of Jesus Christ. They shall not absent themselves from the common exercises without her leave, except in a case of pressing urgency ; and if they cannot then have access to her, they shall make known the reason of their absence at the earliest opportunity. They shall obey the call of the bell as the voice of God.

In another rule it was directed that the sister should regard the voice of the mother superior as the voice of an angel. The defendants, Mrs. Star and Mrs. Kennedy, joined the convent about the same time as the plaintiff, Mrs. Star taking the religious name of Sister Mary Joseph, and Mrs. Kennedy that of Sister Mary Magdalen. After some time, Mrs. Star was removed to a convent at Clifford, in Yorkshire, of which she became the superioress, when she was joined by the defendant, Mrs. Kennedy, and also, after considerable opposition by her parents, by Miss Saurin, at Mrs. Star's request, and with the special condition, made by her mother, and acquiesced in by Archbishop Cullen, that she should return to Baggot-street, Dublin, if she wished to do so. Things went happily for some time, until,

in the year 1861, the superioress (Mrs. Star) became anxious to know what had passed between Sister Scholastica and her priest at confession. I do not pretend to be an expert in these matters ; but I understand if there is one thing more sacred than another, it is that which passes between priest and penitent under the seal of the confessional. I am, of course, assuming, and I do so heartily, that these things are done honestly, and that nothing passes which savours of immorality or impropriety. Miss Saurin declined to answer questions which she considered immoral, and from that moment she found that the demeanour of the superioress was changed towards her. She was watched by her and the other sisters, and a course of petty annoyances was entered on which was continued down to the final act of expulsion. It was absolutely necessary for her, in the discharge of her duties in teaching children and attending the sick, to speak to those who were outside the walls of the convent ; and yet one accusation against her is that she communicated with externs. The Chinese call us outer barbarians, and the nuns call us externs. She was accused of speaking to the patroness of the schools at Clifford, Mrs. Grimstone, and to the Roman Catholic clergyman, Mr. Pamiston. She was obliged to rise at three o'clock in the morning. One charge was that she had a piece of calico, a pair of scissors, and some cotton in her cell, and all these things were duly recorded against her as offences ; and notwithstanding they were atoned for by penances, they were raked up against her in the final accusations by which she was driven from the community. Her mother became anxious that she should be removed to Dublin, and wrote to that effect, stating she had Archbishop Cullen's permission for her to return ; but Mrs. Star's reply was that the plaintiff could not go at that time, if she ever could, and reminded Mrs. Saurin that her daughter was not under the jurisdiction of the Archbishop of Dublin ; and notwithstanding that Mrs. Saurin had stated that Mr. Saurin was in bad health, and wished to settle his private affairs, as she had expressed by the following letters :—

Garballagh House, Sunday Morning.
My dear Rev. Mother—I am disappointed in not hearing from you. I feel pained in being obliged to obtrude my private affairs on your overtaxed time, but my peculiar difficulties oblige me to do so. I am sorry to inform you that Mr. Saurin is worse, and labouring under a disease that may at any time prove fatal. This is a state of things I would not like to make known to Sister Scholastica, as it might overwhelm her, living at such a distance. Mr. Saurin is most anxious to see her. When will it be in your power to permit her to visit Dublin, where he will be able to see her? Mr. Saurin wishes also to settle his temporal affairs, and you know it was one of the conditions of my giving my consent to her going to England that she should come to Ireland in such circumstances as these, and Dr. Cullen fully sanctioned this arrangement, and you yourself promised me it should be so when I met you in Dublin. I hope to hear from you in a few days.—I am, &c. B. M. Saurin.

This was followed by the following.

Garballagh House, Tuesday Morning.
My dear Rev. Mother—I am in receipt of your letter of the 7th inst., and I must say it is quite

explicit on every point: but either you or Sister Scholastica, or both, are under gross misapprehensions as to Mr. Saurin's intentions as to the final disposal of his property. If he should do anything it will be of his own free will. You are quite mistaken as to the means furnished to the convent at Baggot Street for Sister Scholastica. It was considerably beyond £310. . . . Her going to England to assist in the work of the mission was on the condition, as expressed by his Grace, Dr. Cullen, that she should return whenever it was deemed advisable.

Yours, most respectfully,
B. M. SAURIN.

The letter of her mother and other relations to the plaintiff were intercepted, while in the letters of the mother superioress it was complained of her that she had committed most grave offences, which called for grave punishment; that her vows were no longer the occasion of merit, but the occasion of sin. At length she wrote to her uncle, who is parish priest of Drogheda, and her mother's brother, the following letter. And before I read the letter I should observe that the letters were not written as those often produced at Nisi Prius trials are—for the purpose of producing effect. No one who penned them ever imagined they would see the light, and they are, in fact, produced from the arcana of the convent by the mother superior herself in obedience to a judge's order. The letter which was intercepted and never sent was as follows, and it was plain that the writer was anxious to make things as pleasant as possible:

Convent of Our Lady of Mercy, Clifford,
Thursday.

My ever and very dearest Uncle—It seems a long time since I wrote to you, so I am going to trouble you with a few lines before the holy season of Lent sets in. I trust you continue quite well. When Palk wrote, he told me you were getting young. I do not see the least chance of my going over. I mentioned there might be after Christmas, but as I said in the beginning, reverend mother had no idea of letting me leave—at least for a long time. There were both postulants and novices dismissed from our community. I did not think it would be quite the thing to return with them, so I said nothing about it. Reverend mother does not know I wish to go. She is perfectly afraid of the family altogether. I could see that when I was in Hull last. One time she said anything any of you took into your head, you saw it done. Some one had been telling her. When she was here last she complained of mamma's impertinent letters, &c. She certainly made a great mistake in some things she told mamma I said. When I see mamma I shall explain all to her. Will you kindly tell her so? I do not know what to say, only that I have long since placed the whole affair in the sacred hearts of Jesus and Mary, who, I feel sure, will assist you, my dearest uncle, to do what is best. You must not think I am unhappy. I am far from it, and my health has never been so good. The only thing—I am not settled, nor do I think ever can again here. The only thing I regret, poor mamma knowing anything about it, lest it might not be right. Also she may think I am unhappy, which would be untrue. I must now say good-

bye.—Believe me, dearest uncle, your ever-grateful niece in Jesus Christ,
M. SCHOLASTICA JOSEPH.

To the Rev. T. Matthews, P.P.,
St. Mary's, Drogheda, Ireland.

The learned counsel then entered into a detail of some of the petty persecutions to which this lady had been subjected during her sojourn in the convent, and which, he said, would be more particularly laid before the jury in her evidence. Amongst others was the sending her to a drawer, where a heap of her relatives' intercepted letters were accumulated, without permitting her to read any of them. At other times the giving of letters to her with passages obliterated, and which were snatched away almost instantly and destroyed, without her having the slightest chance of reading them. She was put to work of the most menial character, such as scrubbing the floors and cleaning the stoves. On one occasion her hands were so chapped with the cold and the water that they were in sores. One of the sisters, commiserating her condition and sufferings, advised her to put candle-grease to the chaps in order to alleviate her sufferings, but on its becoming known to Mrs. Star she insisted on her washing the candle-grease off. She was made to lie on the bare boards of the bed, her straw mattrass being removed, and with no covering. She was not allowed to sit down, except on the floor, and she often used to kneel in order to alleviate her sufferings. At length broken down in spirit, and under the strong influences they might all imagine, she wrote the following letter to the mother superioress, Mrs. Star:

Convent of Our Lady of Mercy, Clifford.

My dearest Reverend Mother—I feel really very sorry that I had not my letter with the others; still, I think it was not the will of God the long letter I had should have gone. Sister Mary Agnes seemed very much displeased. I closed it without her telling me to do so. It was one sheet of note-paper put up in a little silver paper, which I had to open again, as sister wished it, I also crossed it a little, which I gave you my reason for. I am always, I believe, to be doing things wrong. I did feel very much indeed, dear reverend mother, to come back to Clifford with Sister Mary Agnes. I knew she looked on me as such a cross. I could not help seeing her feelings towards me. I went, as Father Lands told me, on my knees, begged pardon, and made the most humble apology I could. I well felt how she received it. First she said, "You cannot say now, as you did before, I was unkind to you." I only said I did not deserve, nor did I expect, kindness from any one. If I were dying, dear mother, I could not remember one act of her kindness. I did not say a word when Father Lands told me all the trouble I gave Sister Mary Agnes. All, I will say, I tried my best to please and obey her, though I often failed. Dear reverend mother, when I said Easter was not the same at Clifford, I did not mean to complain in the least. It was only when she herself and Sister Mary Evangelist said the Sunday after we returned. I could not help thinking, dear reverend mother, in my heart, when you were last at Clifford, you said I would never be able to bear all I had to go through. I could never have borne as much as

I have gone through. I can bear so much more now. Much of that horrid pride is broken down. I had a long list written in retreat to read for you, but could not do so. Human respect overcame me. How much I wished, when in the train, I had done so, or that you could have seen all that happened in the past year with your own eyes! But God knows all sister said. I did not mind. Little she knew, when sound asleep, my many wakeful nights. If I had only wet as many handkerchiefs for my sins as for other things, I should have a little off my purgatory. I must say, dear reverend mother, I never felt so happy after a confession in my life as I did after my last with Father Lands. I did my best both in confession and out of it, and let him see the real state of my soul. I do not remember I have ever once mentioned anyone, or I have excused a fault. I really tried to make him think me as bad as I did myself. I could not tell you how bad he thought me. Some of the questions he asked me quite shocked me; but I felt glad, for it proved to me the light he looked on me in, and still he told me he could not account for it, but still felt, notwithstanding all he heard and knew, gave him but little hope. Still, he felt, if I only kept to my rule, and the things worked out of me, he felt I would persevere, and be good yet. I hope God will not let me live to disappoint him; and see, dear reverend mother, how soon I fell to-day! I was leaving Hull. Sister Mary Agnes left the paper for Clifford. I took a sheet, intending to leave a note for you to send mamma. Then I had no ink or pens, and, instead of going to you as soon as I could to acknowledge my fault, which I saw, I said, "I will just leave it back with Sister Mary Agnes when I go to Clifford," which I did; but what I suffered after I did so, I shall never forget. I thought lecture would never end. I went to sister, told her all about it, how sorry I felt, &c. I do feel, reverend mother, I shall never do so again. All my promises to both you and Father Lands rushed to my mind. I thought, was this the way I was to acknowledge every fault? I stayed longer than I had leave—several minutes—with a person in the school; also spoke to a little girl unnecessarily, and allowed her to speak during school time, rang the bells a few minutes late. I did not eat all my food, thought I did not get half what others did. I have been sick every day. I even dread dinner coming, but, please God, next time you will see I will be better. I did so long without. I feel it is the whole cause. Out of the past twelve months I spent nine I never tasted meat. I often thought then, though I did not seem to mind, how unkind sister was not to get other meat besides mutton. Now, dear reverend mother, I feel ashamed, and think it far too good. I also see how wrong and contrary to poverty I have acted. Still only think Sister Mary Agnes has just told me all the trouble I gave her for the past two days. All I can say, I never intended it. I knew she would feel my want of confidence in closing my note. I trust God will reward the charity of Mother Magdalene, M. M. of Mercy, and M. M. Clare for their kindness after you asked them to forgive me. May I beg a little cotton and wool to mend our stockings, a little black and white cotton? I did not know whether, dear reverend mother, you meant to get my winter habit. The other is in complete rags,

but Sister Mary Agnes said one was enough. I felt the cold very much for the past winter. I often had to get M. M. Clare to tie my bonnet and coif strings; but if you wish me to have but one, all right. It is well patched, but looks badly. Dear reverend mother, I have suffered very much from constant pain in my back. If any message is coming I shall feel grateful for something. I have so much more to say, dear reverend mother, but I have to finish. The box is going to be shut. Forgive me, dear reverend mother, this once, for this untidy letter. I shall write the next better, please God. With love to all, your ever attached and obedient child in Jesus Christ.

SISTER M. SCHOLASTICA.

I have no time to read.

I will not comment upon that letter. I would rather let it have its own effect upon your minds. I do not say that in the, as I hold it to be, perverse and wicked cruelty practised towards this poor girl, and which she will fully lay before you, they did not think they were perfectly right. I do not mean to say that they believed themselves in their consciences to be doing wrong. I speak from my point of view; they acted from theirs. Her father was dangerously ill; she was not permitted to know it. The people at home feared that she was wanting in natural affection. But what was the fact? Her letters were kept from her, and she was ordered not to write home oftener than once a year. Passages in the letters of her father were blotted out.

The LORD CHIEF JUSTICE: From her father?

The SOLICITOR-GENERAL: Yes, my lord.

The LORD CHIEF JUSTICE: From or to her father?

The SOLICITOR-GENERAL: From him. Her brother a Jesuit priest, wrote to her, and his letters were not delivered to her. In 1863 another brother died. All knowledge of the fact, although communicated by letter, was kept from her; and when she was told of the painful event months after it occurred, she was immediately sent to work on hearing it. In fact the case would show a fertile ingenuity in the art of persecution and petty cruelty, which I think I may say would not be possible in the other sex. The plaintiff was compelled to make monthly reports of her shortcomings to the Mother Superioress. In October, 1862, she confesses—and I think you will say that confession, extorted under such influences as were exercised in her case, even if they were serious, would have been unworthy of credit—to have been untidy, and to have communicated with externs (the externs being her aunt and nephew). In November she confesses she is "far below the lowest in the community;" and she said she had prayed "never to be looked upon except with the contempt I am regarded with at present." She further confessed she was negligent of the little children; that she had rung the bell two or three minutes late. In her previous letter to the rev. mother she confessed that she had twice in the month showed reluctance to do what she had been told; that she had twice spoken unkindly to the children in the school. In January she said she had prayed for strength to be better. "May God give me grace to receive all at His hands! I forgot to ring the bell once. I spoke to the little children more than was necessary. Sister Mary says I show want of submission and judgment in the school. Please let me have one little leaves out this time"—the little leaves being cotton thread, bits of silk, scissors, pens, books, and such like. In all the remaining monthly confessions she spoke of being late for ringing the bell by a minute or two—of being, as she said, unkind to the little children in school. "I fear," she said in one, "I have tried my best to take mutton. I cannot do so. God only knows how much I wish I could." There was a certain amount of humour about some of these serious confessions. The sources of laughter and tears are very near. In another confession she said, "I wish I could begin over again for the last seven or eight years. All the sins and faults of my life begin from that. Oh! if you could forget the past! May God give me grace to be resigned and to persevere in religion until death." In the year 1864 her brother came to see her. He was only allowed to speak to her for a little over quarter of an hour, and although he requested permission to see her next day he was refused, and wrote to the bishop on the subject. The bishop thereupon wrote to Mrs. Star saying that she had committed an error of judgment. To this Mrs. Star replied, "The presence of Sister Scholastica amongst us is a very heavy cross. She is an enemy living in our midst. She was never formally received in the community, and the omission may have been permitted by Providence to free ourselves of so dangerous a person." (A laugh.) To this letter the bishop replied that he did not speak of rule, he referred to prudence. To interpret the bishop's thoughts freely, they were to this effect, "There are English juries about, and English law prevails, and a free press exists; you ought not to have refused a brother's request to see his sister." I will not detail the delicate manipulations of the torturing screw which were resorted to. They will be spoken of in the evidence. She was unable to get over her dislike to mutton given from day to day.

The LORD CHIEF JUSTICE : Having mutton, and nothing else, might well give a distaste for it.

The SOLICITOR-GENERAL : No doubt, my lord ; and there is good mutton and bad mutton —hot mutton and cold mutton—fat mutton and lean mutton. She had only the bad, the cold, the fat, and—at last—the leavings of the plates of others. At length, after events which will be detailed in evidence, the mother superior wrote to the bishop that either Sister Scholastica should go, or she (the mother) should, and the bishop behaved as people in his position sometimes do ; he stood by the highest authority, he backed up the powers that be.

The LORD CHIEF JUSTICE : Was the absolute authority in the mother superioress?

Mr. HAWKINS : There was an appeal to the bishop.

The LORD CHIEF JUSTICE : But was there no council within the walls of the convent?

Mr. HAWKINS : There was by one of the rules —the superioress, the bursar. I shall have a copy of the rules handed to your lordship.

The SOLICITOR-GENERAL went on to read a letter from the defendant to the Bishop of Beverley, in which she accused plaintiff of having broken her vows of poverty and obedience, and added, " We have long suspected her of stealing. Suspicions are not proofs." She adds:

Within the last year I have discovered that my suspicions were well grounded, and that her offences can be proved by different members of the community, who, through a mistaken idea of charity, kept their knowledge to themselves until by chance I made enquiries on the subject. I believe her late conduct has been occasioned by her vexation at the precautions which have been quietly taken to guard her against indulging this propensity in the convent ; but, like an incurable disease, if healed in one place it breaks out in another with greater malignity. We now fear that she steals from the school children. She is so artful, so dexterous, that it will be impossible for any one to detect her ; but the eyes of the young are piercing, and their tongues ever ready to publish the weaknesses of others, and disgrace may come upon religion and upon us before we are aware of it.

The bishop, in his reply, said :

Springfield House, Leeds,
May 5, 1865.

Dear Rev. Mother—Be calm, patient, and full of trust in God. I go to Ireland on the 11th, and will take steps to settle your difficulty. What convent did S. M. S. come from in Ireland? Where did she spend her noviceship, and where was she professed?—With a blessing, I am, yours in Christ,

✠ ROBERT CORNTHWAITE.

In a subsequent letter, dated August 9, 1865, the bishop wrote :

I hope that you are quite certain about the thefts and other things, and that the facts are proveable. I was unable to move efficaciously in the matter without faculties from the Holy See. I asked for them along ago. They were unfortunately mis-sent, and have only reached me this morning. In case of expulsion, will Baggot-street do anything in the way of dowry?

The reply was to the effect that the Baggot-street convent would at once surrender the dower, and then the bishop wrote, under date August 15 :—

Dear Rev. Mother,—Bear in mind that everything will need to be full proved to render my power of any avail. I send a fervent blessing to you all.

After some time it was resolved, as the result of the correspondence between the reverend mother and the bishop, that an inquiry should take place before commissioners, to be appointed by the latter. Before it could be held, the result which was to be come to was arrived at, and the bishop had obtained from the Holy See powers to absolve the sister from her vows ; to have the ring taken from her finger by which she believed herself married to Our Redeemer ; and to have been expelled and driven out disgraced and degraded upon the world. If it were a less serious case, they might be disposed to be amused at the course that was resolved to be adopted. It was this : she was to be absolved. It was true she did not want to be absolved, but it was determined that, want it or not, she should be. They manage these things well ; and how do you think this was managed? Thus : the absolution was to be pronounced under the authority of the See of Rome, and it was to take effect on the happening of a certain condition. That condition Miss Saurin, as a religious woman, could not by possibility escape fulfilling. It was on her attending ten masses.

The LORD CHIEF JUSTICE : Then the attendance at the tenth mass fulfilled the involuntary condition, and the dispensation from the vows was complete?

The SOLICITOR-GENERAL : Yes, my lord, and complete, notwithstanding the ardent desire of Miss Saurin that it should not be. A correspondence took place between the Rev. Mr. Mathews and the bishop upon the subject of the projected inquiry, or, as my learned friend will endeavour to call it, submission to arbitration, and the bishop endeavoured to obtain from Mr. Mathews a promise that if his niece were found guilty he should take her home, and if she were found innocent he should take her home, as staying amongst those, in that convent, who had accused her, would not be edifying. The Rev. Mr. Mathews suggested there should be a friend of the family on the commission, and he accordingly named Dr. O'Hanlan, Librarian to Maynooth. That was assented to by the bishop, and he accordingly acted as one of the commissioners. When this case was ripe for trial a subpœna was obtained, a few days since, to be served on Dr. O'Hanlan, for the purpose of having his evidence on this occasion, but, strange to say, he cannot be found, nor can any information be obtained of his whereabouts. Where Dr. O'Hanlan is I should very much like to know, and I assure you that if he is within twenty-four hours' distance of London, and we can find him, he shall be put into the witness-box.

The LORD CHIEF JUSTICE : I take it for granted then, that when he hears of that statement he will present himself to be examined ?

Mr. HAWKINS : I can only assure your lordship that I have no more knowledge of Dr. O'Hanlan's whereabouts than my learned friend. I will consent to any adjournment of the case for his attendance. We have not the least desire to keep back his evidence.

The LORD CHIEF JUSTICE : I take it for granted that some accidental circumstances must have kept him away, and that when he hears what has been said to-day he will come and tender his evidence. I have too high an opinion of his sense of duty to think that he will voluntarily absent himself.

Mr. HAWKINS : We will give every assistance to obtain his attendance.

The SOLICITOR-GENERAL : I have not the slightest doubt that Dr. O'Hanlan, so far as he is personally concerned, would not disobey the subpœna of this Court. But please to recollect, there are influences which are perfectly capable of being understood, and the employment of which I must acquit my learned friend, which may fully account for the widowed condition of the books at Maynooth. (Laughter.)

The LORD CHIEF JUSTICE : I do hope, Mr. Solicitor-General, that you are mistaken in your supposition that any authority has been exercised, or any influence brought to bear, to induce him to keep out of the way, when his presence is challenged as being essential to the administration of justice.

Mr. HAWKINS : I have no wish that the plaintiff's case should be prejudged by Dr. O'Hanlan's absence ; and, if he does not come forward after this appeal, I will admit any document in writing of his bearing on the case.

The LORD CHIEF JUSTICE : If he does not come forward after this appeal that has been made to him, not only by the Solicitor-General, but by myself, I shall look upon his absence as a great scandal upon a matter of great public concern.

Mr. HAWKINS : I can only say, my lord, that the defendants equally wish Dr. O'Hanlan's presence.

The SOLICITOR-GENERAL : I intended my words with reference to Dr. O'Hanlan's absence should have the effect and interpretation they have received ; but it is very strange that another circumstance equally curious should have occurred with reference to this case. The plaintiff's brother, as I have already told you, is a Jesuit priest. He seems to have entertained a strong view in favour of his sister's case, and his evidence would be open to the objection, no doubt, that he was her brother ; but, strange to say, we cannot find him either.

The LORD CHIEF JUSTICE : Is he not forthcoming?

The SOLICITOR-GENERAL : No, we cannot find him ; and it may be that he is gone on a party of pleasure to South America. All, however, I can say is, that attempts have been made to subpœna him, but without effect. The learned counsel then proceeded to detail what took place before the commissioners, but before doing so, he stated that he had been informed Dr. O'Hanlan left Maynooth the day after Mr. Willes's application was made to this court, and published in the papers, for permission to subpœna witnesses in .Ireland. I do not, said the learned counsel, charge the bishop with interfering with the members of the commission ; but he put Mrs. Star in communication with Mr. Porter, and she, instead of writing to that gentleman, went to him at Liverpool, and, as the Scotch say, precognosed him—(laughter)—but the plaintiff was left with but a small piece of paper and an old worn-out pen with which to write her defence in the intervals in the discharge of her ordinary duties. At length the commission sat, and the plaintiff was called upon her defence.

The LORD CHIEF JUSTICE : Was no proof given of the charges?

The SOLICITOR-GENERAL : No, my lord. The only proof was the reading of the charges, and they were not the serious charge made in the letter to the bishop of theft, which would have driven her from any station in society, but that she was disobedient to the superioress ; that she had communicated with externs ; that she had eaten buttered toast—(laughter)—that a cake had been discovered in her drawer, and once that she had been seen eating one. And it was arranged that she should be held guilty, unless four-fifths of her judges pronounced her to be innocent. They were deprived of the evidence of Dr. O'Hanlan, in the manner in which the inquiry was conducted ; but they had the letters of Mr. Mathews, himself a priest of the Catholic Church, denouncing the inquiry as an indecent farce, calculated to bring ignominy upon the convent of Hull and upon every convent in the three kingdoms. They found her guilty, and the bishop absolved her. Then commenced a new series, not of petty, but of positive persecutions. She was watched night and day. The ring was taken from her finger ; her secular dress was brought into her cell ; and, when she refused to put it on her, she was left no alternative by her religious dress being taken from her at night. She, was left in the cold of January without fire or clothing. Her food she describes as the washings of the coffee pots and mouldy and mouse-eaten bread, with the leavings of the plates of the sisters. She was not allowed soap, towels, or water ; sisters were constantly with her ; and she was not allowed to leave her cell for any purpose whatever ; the jury could understand what that meant. The object of all this was not, I will say, cruelty, but to drive her from that which she held dearer than life. She was requested to go ; but positively, except by force, she would not leave, and thereby admit she had been properly expelled. For seven months this course of conduct was adopted towards her. During that time the sheets of her wooden bed had not been exchanged, and three times only had she been allowed to change her under-clothing. At length, worn out by this treatment, she wrote to her brother, who came over and took her away. In conclusion, the learned gentleman said : I do not say one word against these institutions, or the principles of the persons who reside in them. I make no attack upon either of them. I make no appeal to feeling, still less to prejudice ; but I only say I earnestly hope you will teach those ladies that, although they may shroud themselves in their seclusion, and seek to shelter themselves under the shade of religion, English justice has eyes that can pierce through all their veils, and English law has power enough to protect their victims.

The following evidence was given :

Miss SUSAN SAURIN, who was attired in black, and wore a heavy veil, which she put aside on entering the box, was first sworn. In reply to Mr. Willes she said: I am daughter of Mr. M. Saurin, of Garballagh, near Drogheda. I was desirous, before 1850, of entering a religious house. My parents opposed it at first, but ulti-mately consented. Baggot-street was selected as the convent into which I should enter, after I had seen several others. I became a postulant on 21st November, 1850, and remained so for more than six months. On the 5th of August, 1851, I became a novice, and on 3rd October, 1853, I made my profession as a regular sister of the order of Mercy. I took the name in religion of Sister Mary Scholastica Joseph. [The act of profession, questions and answers, put in.] When I entered at Baggot-street, the defendant, Mrs. Star, was a postulant. She had entered a few months before I did. She made her act of profession a few months before I did, and took the name of Sister Mary Joseph. Mrs. Kennedy, the other defendant, entered a few months after me, and took her profession a few months after me. She took the name of Mary Magdalene. We were all three thrown very much into each other's society. I became very intimate with Mrs. Star, and attached to her, and she to me. We were associated in the work of education. I was equally attached to Mrs. Kennedy. These happy relations continued all the time we were at Baggot-street together. Mrs. Star left in 1857 to be superioress at the new foundation at Clifford, near Tadcaster, in Yorkshire. I went to Clifford in May, 1858. Mrs. Star wrote to

the superioress at Baggot-street to request that I might be allowed to join her. Mrs. Kennedy had removed to Clifford, and I found her there. Mrs. Delany, Mrs. M'Keon, and a lay sister had gone with Mrs. Star. Mrs. M'Keon was called Sister Mary Agnes. My father and mother offered great opposition to my going, but ulti-mately they gave their consent. During the course of 1858, a convent was founded at Hull, and Mrs. Star went there. I joined her there, and remained a few months. I was sometimes at Hull, sometimes at Clifford, but more fre-quently at Clifford. Mrs. Star was sometimes at Clifford, but stayed the greater part of her time at Hull. She was superioress of both. Mrs. Kennedy remained chiefly at Hull. She was mother assistant part of the time. She be-came so in 1859. The holder of the office of mother assistant was changed from time to time. A local superior was appointed by Mrs. Star for Clifford. Mrs. Delany acted part of the time, and Mrs. M'Keon part of the time. Mrs. Starr and Mrs. Kennedy visited Ireland in August or September, after I came to Clifford. On my return Mrs. Star mentioned she had seen my mother in Jervis-street hospital ; that she had explained to her how I was circumstanced ; that my mother was satisfied at my remaining ; and that I was to write to her once a month. Mrs. Star said she told her that, as I was not strong, she would take every possible care of me. My duties then were to take charge of the in-firmary, of the housekeeping, visitation of the sick, and I had several hours in school, morning and afternoon, as schoolmistress. These duties necessarily brought me in contact with people in the outer world. I was then on excellent terms with Mrs. Star and Mrs. Kennedy. Down to the year 1860 my life passed very happily. Sometime in that year Mrs. Star asked me to tell her my confession—what had passed between me and my father confessor. I said I thought it would be contrary to honour and every regula-tion to do so. She insisted, and I said I did not remember exactly what the priest had said.

The LORD CHIEF JUSTICE : Did she ask what the priest had said to you, as well as your con-fession to him ?—Witness : Yes, my lord.

Examination continued : She told me that she would give me time ; that I should go away and come back next day, and to try and remember in the interval. Next day I still refused to do so, saying I thought it would be a breach of honour to reveal anything that had been said to me in confession. She asked me several times during that day, and said no other sister in the house had refused her. After this I saw a change in her manner to me. She said I had shown great want of confidence in her. She excluded herself from recreation times—that is, times each day when we all used to converse together. She and Mrs. M'Keon would retire, and leave me with the novices and postulants.

The LORD CHIEF JUSTICE : Did she assign any reason for wanting to know your confession? —None, my lord.

Examination continued : Her withdrawal was a matter of daily occurrence. Shortly afterwards the mother superior and some sisters came over from Baggot-street to a public reception at Hull. On one occasion they found me with the novices and postulants, and spoke to me about it.

Shortly after that Mrs. Star told me that I had said to the mother assistant of Baggot-street that she (Mrs. Star) had excluded herself from recreation, and she added that the mother assistant of Baggot-street had reproved her. She did not exclude herself after that so frequently. About this time a branch house was formed at Anleby-road, Hull. I had a good deal to do with the arrangements for the removal, and that necessarily brought me into frequent contact with externs. I was never in the least found fault with at the time for it. Mrs. Star was not so friendly with me then as she had been. Mrs. Kennedy was very friendly with me. Some months afterwards there was a project entertained of giving up the establishment at Clifford, as the school was so much reduced. There was a difference between the priest and the superioress. The establishment was not given up. I was sent to Clifford to try and get the schools up, the attendance having greatly fallen off. I went and devoted myself specially to that task. I was necessarily brought into contact with the parents of the children, and with the visitors of the schools, including Mrs. Grimstone, who with her husband are the principal patrons and supporters of the convent schools. I succeeded in the course of a few months in bringing up the attendance again. Mrs. Star and Mrs. Kennedy came over there to meet the bishop, and it was arranged the establishment should be continued. About May, 1861, Mrs. Star came to Clifford, and remained until the August retreat following.

The LORD CHIEF JUSTICE: What is a retreat? —Witness: Spiritual exercises for ten days.

Examination continued: It is a time when the observances are stricter than usual. At that time Mrs. Kennedy was at Hull. Mrs. Star treated me during her stay at Clifford very unkindly. She seemed dissatisfied with what I was doing. Some work was brought from Hull for me to do, and she obliged me to prepare it and put it out on Sunday. I never saw a nun do such a thing before. The usual time for rising in the convent was half-past five o'clock. We went to bed at ten. Mrs. Star told me to get up and get the work done at three o'clock, and I had to do so for several mornings. One of the sisters offered to get up and help me, and she was allowed to do so at a later hour. I went to Mrs. Star one night, and I said, "What in the world am I doing to give you such displeasure? I am trying my best to please you, and give you satisfaction. If you tell me anything more I can do, I will try and do it." She said, "I have allowed you too much liberty, but I am determined to put you down." On the same day she said she had found a piece of calico in my cell, and asked me where I had got it, and also a pair of scissors. I took the calico and showed her her own name written with a pencil on it. It had been written by myself. I told her it was part of a coif, or head-dress, I was making for her. She was satisfied that it was. She insinuated that I had taken the scissors from her, and I told her I had got them as a present from a sister in Baggot-street, and I told her she had herself given me permission to keep them. At the time of the August retreat I went to Hull with Mrs. Star to the retreat. Her demeanour towards me was then much the same as it had been at Clifford. After the retreat I returned to Clifford. In September I received a visit from my uncle,

the Rev. Mr. Mathews. He is my mother's brother, and parish priest at Drogheda. Mrs. M'Keon was mother assistant at Clifford. I was treated by her with some reserve. I received very few letters from my friends. Those I received I was obliged to return to Mrs. M'Keon.

To the Court: I never knew that to be done except in my case.

Examination continued: I learned from Mrs. M'Keon that it was done by the orders of Mrs. Star. I became anxious to get back to Baggot-street, Dublin. I wrote a letter to my uncle, the Rev. Mr. Mathews, in March, 1862. I left the letter in my cell. Mrs. King, a sister in the convent, found it there. She sent it, as I heard afterwards, to the superioress at Hull. [Letter read.] Some days subsequently, I received a letter from Mrs. Star in reference to what I had done. It was afterwards taken away from me with other things. She said in it she supposed I was aware that my letter had been sent to her, and she said it was contrary to the vow of obedience and rule to have written it. She asked me also in the letter whether I wished to return to Baggot-street; would she write, or should I do so? I wrote an answer to her stating I did wish to return, and, if possible, that night. That I said to express my great wish to go back. I had no reply to that letter. I wrote a second letter to my uncle. I supposed the first had been sent to him; and when I found it had not, I wrote to him a few lines without leave. I sent the letter to the post, but do not know what became of it. Very shortly afterwards I had a visit from my mother and brother Patrick. I was teaching in the school when they arrived, and sent a child to answer the ring at the bell. I had seen them through the window. In a few minutes Mrs. M'Keon came in, and ordered me to go to my cell. She told me my mother and brother had come, but that she could not allow me to see them, as Mrs. Star had given her directions to that effect. As I passed from the school to the chapel—for it is usual to go after school to the chapel, to pay a visit to the Sacraments—I passed the open door of the reception-room, in which my mother and brother were. My mother saw me, came to me, and embraced me. As I had not leave to speak to her, I passed on as quickly as I could disengage myself, without speaking to her. Mrs. M'Keon followed me to my cell. She desired me to close the door of my cell while she sent my mother and brother away. I begged permission to see my mother. She said she could not do so, and I then closed the door. In about five minutes more she came back, and told me my mother had brought an order from Mrs. Star to see me. She then opened the door, and I went out to the corridor where my mother was. My mother clasped me in her arms, and said, "My child, are they going to make a prisoner of you?" I went into the room with my mother, and Mrs. M'Keon tried to excuse herself, saying it was not her fault; that she was obliged to act as she had done, by order of Mrs. Star. My mother and brother stayed some hours with me. My mother told me Mrs. Star had complained of the impertinent note I had written, and that if I had done so I ought to apologize. Accordingly I wrote a long letter to Mrs. Star, apologizing. I showed it to Mrs. M'Keon, and she approved of it.

After that time there was a great change in Mrs. M'Keon's deportment towards me. She took away from me all writing materials, and also letters from my family which were in my desk, which was also taken away. There were several manuscripts also in the desk. I have never had the letters nor the manuscripts back. Mrs. M'Keon was a great deal more reserved towards me at recreation time. She told me she would rather speak before a lay postulant, than before me, any matters she was particular about. The other sister, Mrs. King, seemed to be with me everywhere I went. I was ordered to change my cell to one opposite to Mrs. M'Keon's. The door of my cell was sometimes suddenly opened at night, and Mrs. M'Keon would come in. I found the drawer where my clothes were kept tossed about. There was no fastening on the door of the cell I was removed to.

SECOND DAY.—*Thursday, Feb. 4.*

THE examination of Miss Susan Saurin, the plaintiff, by Mr. Willes was resumed. She said : After my mother visited me I saw no more of my family until the month of May, when my uncle, Father Mathews, came to me. I had a conversation with him, and he advised me to write to the bishop. I wrote to the bishop accordingly. I had an answer from him, but I did not receive it till the following September. Towards the end of July, 1862, I went to Hull for the retreat. The first Saturday I was there the reverend mother sent for me. She desired me to take off my habit, my usual nun's dress, and gave me an old one to put on. I did not know what her motive was for taking it, but she said it required something to be done to it—that there was too much lining in it. She returned it to me in the evening. On the following day (Sunday) she sent for me again, and spoke to me as to the letters I had written to my reverend uncle. She asked me several questions as to them. I got ill during the conversation. Some time after, in the evening, she called me out of the chair, and asked me to write to my uncle to have me removed to St. Mary's, Drogheda. It was not usual to write letters in retreat. She said she wished to have all arranged before retreat. She got a slate and dictated a letter for me to write, and told me I should sit down then and write it. I did so. She made no complaint at that time to me, except about having written the letters. A few days subsequently I had a communication with Father Porter as to the writing of the letters, and in consequence of what passed I saw Mrs. Star again on the subject. I saw her on the day Father Porter advised me to do so. She took me to the library, and I acknowledged having written the two letters, and sent them without permission.

To the Court : That was the first time I ever acknowledged having written them. On the former occasion I said I did not wish to tell whether I had written them.

The LORD CHIEF JUSTICE : Is it contrary to the rules to send a letter to a relative without the superioress seeing it ?—It is contrary to the book of customs, my lord.

Then the superior sees all letters that are sent? —That is the custom, my lord.

Examination continued : The reverend mother told me to write an acknowledgment of having written them, as the bishop might require it. She also told me to write a resolution for the future. I wrote the following acknowledgment : " I acknowledge to have written two notes to my uncle, the Reverend Father Mathews, parish priest of St. Mary's, Drogheda, and sent them without the knowledge of my superior." She embraced me, then told me to go to bed, and to write the resolution the following day. Next day she told me she had mentioned the matter to the other sisters, and that it would raise me considerably in their estimation if I acknowledged it before them. I acknowledged it before Mrs. M'Keon and Mrs. Kennedy on my knees.

The LORD CHIEF JUSTICE : Who told you to go on your knees?—Witness : The rev. mother.

Examination continued : A day or two afterwards she presented me with a second acknowledgment in her own handwriting, and asked me to sign it, as she said the bishop might wish to see it. (Paper produced.) This is the paper. I signed it. It was as follows : " I acknowledge to have written two letters to my uncle, the Rev. Father Mathews, P.P., to obtain his assistance to get me into another community, and that I sent them without the knowledge of my superior." I said I did not write letters—that they were notes. She said it made no difference ; that everything would be arranged and the past forgotten. Next day there was a public chapter for the acknowledgment of faults. I asked Mrs. Star whether I should acknowledge my fault of having written the letters before all the sisters, and she said no; that they were young, and that they might be disedified. I had never been charged up to this time with levity of conduct or any misconduct other than with having sent the letters. I wrote the resolutions as required, and gave them to Mrs. Star.

Mr. WILLES called for the production.

MR. HAWKINS : They were destroyed long since.

MR. MELLISH : We have produced every document in our possession bearing on the case, and on affidavit.

Examination continued : I had not been charged up to that time with " habitual disregard to the rules in minor matters, general levity of conduct, unauthorized intercourse with externs, disregard of the rules of silence, and want of truth."

MR. WILLES : These are the charges made at that time by the defendant to the bishop.

The LORD CHIEF JUSTICE (to witness): You had never been charged with any one of them up to th. time?—No, my lord.

To MR. WILLES : I was not aware that a council, or chapter, had been held as to my conduct. I had no idea that Mrs. Star was proposing to the bishop that I should be released from my vows.

The LORD CHIEF JUSTICE : Is the rule as to

silence enforced?—So far as circumstances permit, my lord.

To Mr. WILLES: I had received no notice whatever of any inquiry being held as to me, or any consideration of my case. After the retreat I returned to Clifford, and supposed that my transgression as to disregard of the rules had been overlooked. Mrs. Star, before I returned to Clifford, told me my father wished to see me— that he had sent money to pay my expenses, but that she had no notion of letting me go. I did not learn till afterwards that he had been dangerously ill. She did not tell me. It was usual to allow the sisters to visit their families when they made a report to that effect. Mrs. Star told me that once a year was often enough to write to my friends. I told her I had not heard from my brother, the Jesuit priest, for a long time. She told me she had received letters from him, but that she would not give them to me. On one occasion she sent me to one of her drawers. I do not know for what purpose. I there saw some letters from my Jesuit brother, addressed to me. There was a parcel of them. Mrs. M'Keon was the local superioress at Clifford on my return, as she had been before. I was subjected to several restrictions.

The LORD CHIEF JUSTICE : Of what sort?

Mr. HAWKINS objected. What occurred at Clifford in the absence of the defendant was not evidence.

The LORD CHIEF JUSTICE said that evidence of the same kind had been received already without objection.

Mr. HAWKINS : Only while Mrs. Star was there, or under her directions.

After some discussion, Mr. Hawkins withdrew his objection.

The LORD CHIEF JUSTICE said the defendant, Mrs. Star, could state in her evidence how far she directed Mrs. M'Keon to act ; and she would be legally and morally responsible only for that which was done by her direction.

Examination continued : Mrs. Star told me that I was to put myself the lowest of the community at Clifford, and that I was to obey the novice ; adding that she had given, or would give, Mrs. M'Keon directions as to the distribution of my time. Mrs. M'Keon gave me a distribution of time. I was put under the novice, Mrs. Ferran.

To the LORD CHIEF JUSTICE : I never had had a distribution of time given me before.

To Mr. WILLES : The "distribution" prescribed what I was to do each hour of the day. I was placed junior to the lay sister and the novice. I had never been so placed before. The lay sister was a servant who did the household work.

The LORD CHIEF JUSTICE : Had you to do the household work, then ?—I had to sweep the schools.

Had you to do so ever before?—No, my lord.

Examination continued : I was restricted from speaking to any stranger who might come to the school. If they spoke to me I was to motion them to Mrs. Ferran, the novice. That had never been so before. I was placed by this restriction in great difficulties in conducting the school. If any one came in I had to make a sign to them to be seated or to go the novice. In November I went to the visitation at Hull and saw the bishop there. I received advice from him.

To the LORD CHIEF JUSTICE : I spoke to him on this subject.

Mr. WILLES : There was no change for the better in my condition at Clifford after I had spoken to the bishop. In August, 1863, I went again to Hull to the retreat. I saw Father Lands, and he spoke to me on the subject of having written the letters to my uncle. While at Hull Mrs. Star told me to write a monthly confession of faults. She told me that I would have to undergo great suffering ; that if I remained in the convent I should wear the cast-off clothes of the lay sister ; that she did not think I would be able to endure the punishment that might be imposed upon me. She told me I was to have no communication with externs. After the retreat I returned to Clifford. Further restrictions were imposed upon me. I was not to speak to Mrs. Grimstone, the patroness of the school, or to the clergymen, nor was I to speak to the novices alone. At that time I was senior of the community at Hull next to Mrs. Star, and senior at Clifford. Further domestic duties were put upon me. I had to brush and polish the boards of the rooms. I had every day to sweep and clean my cell and the corridor.

To the LORD CHIEF JUSTICE : That had been done before by a novice or lay sister.

To Mr. WILLES : I had also to do the stoves and grates in the school, and also to clean the reception-rooms and stairs. I had to polish the floors with wax. I had often to do the steps of the front door. Sometimes I got a little girl to do them for me. There were a couple of flagged areas in front of the convent, and those I had also to clean. There was a closet connected with the school which I had also to clean. I had never known such work put upon a community of sisters. They sometimes chose to do so themselves. I had to teach in the school as well from nine to twelve, and from one till half-past three, and also for two hours in the night school, from six till eight o'clock. I had in addition to get a large quantity of needlework ready for the needlework classes. If I omitted to do any of these things, or if it was improperly done, I was reproved by Mrs. M'Keon before the other sisters severely, and made to acknowledge my fault on my knees afterwards.

The LORD CHIEF JUSTICE : Is it usual in this community when a sister acknowledges a fault to do so on her knees ?—It was a custom introduced by Mrs. Star.

When ?—About 1860.

Examination continued : My food was not the same as that of the other sisters. I got mutton, for which I have a natural dislike. I had been in very delicate health when I entered the convent, and had a difficulty in taking food. I was under medical treatment in 1862. Mrs. Star was aware of my dislike for mutton. Before our relations with each other became unpleasant, she had been considerate to me in the matter of food. On the occasion of fasts she directed me not to observe them on account of my health. She desired me to have other meat than mutton, and other meat was generally in the house. Up to 1862 I had charge of the food, but then Mrs. Star took charge of it. Mrs M'Keon or Mrs. Ferran had charge of the food at Clifford. In 1863 and 1864, I was allowed nothing but mutton.

The LORD CHIEF JUSTICE : Every day ?— Witness : Yes, my lord, every day except fast day.

The LORD CHIEF JUSTICE: Were you obliged to take mutton while the others had other meat?—No, my lord; one joint lasted the week, and it was mutton.

Examination continued: I was unwell in the winter of 1863, and asked for medicine. It was refused by Mrs. M'Keon, by orders, as she said, of Mrs. Star. I was at this time restricted from sitting. I was obliged to stand during school hours by order of Mrs. Star. No other sister was obliged to stand all day. While they were teaching they had leave to sit. I was weakly in health and got tired, sometimes very tired. When holding the children's hands, writing, I tried to kneel on the bench for a few minutes to rest myself. My brother Thomas died on the 18th of February, 1863. I did not hear of his death for two or three weeks afterwards. Mrs. M'Keon told me of it. She gave me a note from my uncle.

The LORD CHIEF JUSTICE: Have you got it? —No, my lord. It was taken away with the other papers when my desk was taken.

Examination continued: I did not get a letter from my father or mother. I was greatly distressed when I heard of my brother's death. I had heard some months before that he was in improving health. I was startled on receiving the intelligence, and went to the chapel, but in a few minutes I was sent to teach the night-school. I had to go. I received not one word of sympathy or kindness. In September, 1863, I received a visit from my mother, two of my uncles, the Rev. Mr. Mathews, his brother James, and my aunt, Mrs. James Mathews. My uncle James is a magistrate. My mother told me the details of my brother's illness and death. I was left alone with my mother while she did so. My mother was very ill at the time. She sent me several times to Mrs. M'Keon with a message desiring to see her.

The LORD CHIEF JUSTICE: Had you made any communication to your mother as to grievances or supposed grievances?—No, my lord.

To Mr. WILLES: It would have been contrary to the rules of the convent to have done so. Mrs. M'Keon refused to see my mother. On former visits my mother had been treated with courtesy and attention. She left without being able to see Mrs. M'Keon. On the following day my uncle, the Rev. Father Mathews, came to say mass and to see me. It was customary when a priest, a relative of a sister, came to the convent that he should say mass. I showed my uncle two letters I received from the bishop. He destroyed them.

The LORD CHIEF JUSTICE: Your uncle did? —Yes, my lord. He said it was better I should not have them, as my other letters had been taken away in my desk.

To Mr. WILLES: I had to go several times to Mrs. M'Keon before she would see my uncle. In October, 1863, the bishop came to visit Clifford, and Mrs. Star came to meet him. The evening before the bishop came Mrs. Star saw me. She spoke to me as to my monthly confessions. She said there was nothing in them that a saint might not have said. (A laugh.) She mentioned some serious fault against the rules and asked me, if I did so and so, why did I not mention it?

The LORD CHIEF JUSTICE: Faults that you had committed?—No, my lord, I had not.

Examination continued: She said other sisters confessed to such faults—naming several faults against the rules—and I said I had not. She said I was not improved.

Had you, in point of fact, put down all your faults?—Yes, every fault. I put down all that Mrs. M'Keon considered a fault, whether I thought it was one or not.

Examination continued: I was kept at work in the community-room the day the bishop came, instead of being over the schools as usual. I was desired not to go to the school. I saw the bishop for a few minutes. He asked to see me in the reception-room. I was given a watch after my profession by my father. There was an inscription on it, "To Susannah Saurin, from her loving father." I had had leave both at Baggot-street and at Clifford to have the use of the watch. On the occasion I allude to at Clifford Mrs. Star asked me for the watch. Mrs. M'Keon had told me before she was going to have a lottery. Mrs. Star did not tell me what she wanted with the watch. I said I should not like it to be disposed of in a lottery, as my father's name was on it—that he had given it on condition that I was not to give it away. I mentioned that to the superioress at Baggot-street when I got it first. Mrs. Star said I had no right to receive it on those conditions. I gave it to her, and did not see it again until a few days before I left the convent, when it was sent in to me on a dinner-plate. In one of my letters I asked for the usual "leaves." The "leaves" are permission to lend or borrow small articles, such as thread, scissors, tapes, pins, and needles, pencils, pens, ink, note-paper, and other things.

To the LORD CHIEF JUSTICE: We could not lend or borrow these things without permission. The community sisters had "leaves" signed once a year; the novices once a month. Mrs. M'Keon, in January, 1864, refused to renew my "leaves," and said I should write to Mrs. Star for a renewal. I did so, and got no answer. I was, in consequence, obliged to apply to Mrs. M'Keon for any of these little matters. I did not get leaves from her. In May, 1864, there was a chapter held in Hull for the purpose of re-electing the superioress. I was entitled to be summoned for the purpose by the rules, and also to the chapter for the resignation. I was not summoned to the latter. I attended the chapter for the re-election of Mrs. Star. I was at Hull on that occasion, a few days. During my stay Mrs. Star called me into the library. She said, I was an unfortunate creature; that I had all the sisters against me. I said, "Reverend mother, what am I doing?" She said "You complained of me to the bishop. That is enough to be put against you." Either then, or later on, she said my life was a martyrdom there, and that it would be worse every day that I stayed; that she herself would go and be a postulant anywhere rather than live as I was living. She said that my uncle, Father Mathews, was my greatest enemy; that if he had only come to her, instead of going to complain to the bishop, she would have settled all long since, but now that she would show him what she would do. She said that she only had to call a chapter of the community, and that the sisters would be with her, and no bishop could go against them. Then she asked me why I did not try to get into some other convent. I returned to Clifford, and remained there until June. My condition was not improved. It continued as it had been. About the middle of June, Mrs. Star, Mrs. Kennedy, and two of the novices came to Clifford. I was not allowed to associate with Mrs. Star, or Mrs. Kennedy, but was left in a room with the novices. On that occasion the bed and bedding were taken out of my cell for the sisters or the novices. An iron bedstead was left in the room, with a quilt or counterpane on it, and a blanket. I believe the sheets I had had were left there. I was left in that way for two days, and then I went to Hull. On former occasions, when extra bed and bedding were required, Mrs. Grimstone always lent it willingly. Mrs. Star, on the day she came, gave me additional duties. They were of a menial character. I was to sweep and clean the stone passages between the convent and the school and other passages. Next day I was in the recreation-room, sewing. Mrs. Star and Mrs. Kennedy came into the room. Mrs. Star took the work I was sewing, and said I was to come to Hull with her. I asked whether I might tell the sister who was to teach what the school duties were. She said "No ; you must come at once." I was not allowed to go downstairs for my boots. They were sent to my cell, into which she saw me, and where I was to dress. Mrs. Kennedy came into my cell. She threw my cloak over me. I asked Mrs. Star whether I might change my coif for the end of the week, and she said "No." I had changed one stocking, and was not allowed to put on the other. When putting on my boots, Mrs. Kennedy said I was not hurrying, and she attempted to push on my boot. Her manner was very rough. I asked to be allowed to pack up some clothes to take with me, but was not permitted to do so. Mrs. Star stuffed some of my clothes—a change of linen—into a basket. There were a great many other things in the basket. I had to carry it, by Mrs. Star's direction. From the time I received notice that I was to go to Hull till I was out of the house could not have been more than four or five minutes. I had not even time to button my boots, or to say "Good-bye" to any one. Mrs. Kennedy pushed me down the back steps.

The LORD CHIEF JUSTICE: Pushed you down? —Yes, my lord.

Did she say anything?—That I would be late for the train.

To Mr. WILLES : It was a very wet night. I had to carry, besides the basket, a large umbrella. It was more to protect Mrs. Star than myself. I carried both to the station—about a mile and a half or two miles' distance. She walked very fast. I was exhausted when about half way, and asked Mrs. Star to hold the umbrella until I changed the basket. When I had done so she handed me the umbrella back. We had nearly an hour at the station waiting for the train. I was very wet. I was not able to shelter myself from the wet. Mrs. Star told me two or three times I was holding it badly. On other occasions luggage was sent by a school child, or in Mrs. Grimstone's carriage. We got to Hull about ten o'clock at night. It was still raining heavily. I had to carry the basket and umbrella as before, to the convent, about half a mile. I had a little tea, and then went to my cell. The skirts of my dress were wet next morning. They continued wet about three days. I had no dry ones with me.

Mrs. M'Keon was then at Hull. Mrs. Kennedy remained at Clifford until the following August, when she came to Hull. There were about eleven or twelve sisters there, most of them comparative strangers to me. I was senior member of the convent, excepting Mrs. Star. The day of my removal to Hull was on the 17th. On the following Sunday, the 19th, Mrs. Star sent for me to her own room. She had a slate before her, with something written on it. It was a distribution of time for me. I was told to copy it, and took out my tablet for the purpose. There was something written on the tablet. Mrs. Star took it out of my hand, read what was on it, and asked me the meaning of it.

The LORD CHIEF JUSTICE: What was it ?— I told her part of it was matter for my confession, and that I did not wish it to be read by any one. She told me there were things against sisters and her that I intended telling the bishop. I said, "No," that I did not intend to tell the bishop. She asked me the meaning of one particular sentence, and I told her it was a remark on Mrs. M'Keon remaining for several hours on the top of the tower outside of the enclosure of the convent with Mr. Collins, the secular, which I believed to be contrary to custom. I do not remember what Mrs. Star said, but she was displeased I had made the remark. Mrs. Star took the tablet, and I do not remember having seen it again.

Mr. WILLES called for its production. [Tablet produced by defendants' attorney.]

Mr. HAWKINS : There is nothing on it now.

Mr. WILLES : It is a *tabula rasa* now.

Examination continued : When Mrs. Star took the tablet from me, I believe there was a great deal written on it.

The LORD CHIEF JUSTICE : But you must know whether there was or not.—Witness : There was, my lord.

The LORD CHIEF JUSTICE (having examined the tablet) : You are sure there was writing on it? —I am, my lord.

The LORD CHIEF JUSTICE : There is none now, certainly.

Examination continued : Mrs. Star asked me had I anything else in my pocket. I said I had some thread, a silver thimble, part of a copy of the rules, the silver top of a pen-holder, and a paper on which faults were written. Mrs. Star put her hand in my pockets, searched them, and took the things I have named out. I never saw them afterwards. She got me to bring her the coifs and guimps, or capes, I had brought with me. She left me two—just a change—and kept the others. From that time forward I had only the two. Shortly afterwards I was again sent for. Mrs. Kennedy was present. Mrs. Star gave me a letter from my brother Palk to read.

To the LORD CHIEF JUSTICE : He is not the Jesuit priest.

To Mr. WILLES : My brother said in the letter my friends were coming to England, and he wished to know whether I was at Hull or Clifford. Before I had finished reading the letter Mrs. Star took it out of my hand and tore it up. She gave me a scrap of soiled paper, and told me to kneel down and write.

The LORD CHIEF JUSTICE : To kneel down ? —Yes, my lord.

To Mr. LEWIS : She told me to write "Sister

B

Scholastica is still at Hull." I did so. I did not know what she wanted this for. (Letter of plaintiff's brother produced.) This letter I never saw before. Mrs. Star said as the superioress of Baggot-street was changed she thought I could get back there again, and that she would send a sister with me. I said I could not do anything of the kind without consulting my mother. I left the room then. About this time I was directed by Mrs. Star not to speak to any of the sisters ; that they had all directions to tell her everything I said to them. She said if she had gone through one-half of what I had gone through she would have been in her grave long ago. I told her I had done everything in my power to give her satisfaction. She said I had complained to the bishop. At Hull I had three corridors to sweep, and to dust the three altars, fourteen stations of the cross, to clean the closets, the stone hall, two pairs of stairs, the sink, and the doors and windows generally. I was also called upon to empty a large dust-box. I had, further, to sweep the walls and do needlework. On several times Mrs. Star called me from mass and chapel to clean the closet. She had a window in it blocked up, because she said I had gone there to sew in strings and write down what was said. Some of these duties had to be performed in the dark in winter. I was not allowed the extra hour on Saturdays. Frequently I was unable to get the work done on Saturdays, and I had to finish it on Sunday. I had to carry the dust-box across the yard, and was exposed to the children and externs. The sisters are not allowed to go out on wet days. On one occasion I did not, and I had to hold the box the following Sunday morning in my hand as a penance during lecture time, at the end of the table, in the presence of all the community. I was directed to wear a duster over my head. Mrs. Star thought I had not sufficiently dusted some chairs in the community-room. She took the duster to put over my head. I told her it was wet. She sent Mrs. Ker to dry it, and then Mrs. Star put it over my veil, and I was obliged to wear it all day, in the chapel and at meal times. It was a soiled duster. The corridor was covered with cocoa matting, and required three to carry it. I was directed to take it into the yard by myself and dust it. It had been swept in the corridor up to that time. I had to drag it down stairs and then get it up again without any assistance. The community-room matting was much longer, and I was directed to take that down into the yard also. I said I was not able to do it. She insisted that I was, and assisted me with it out of the door. A sister would have assisted me if she dared. Mrs. Star had forbidden it. I was also required to sweep up the spot in the yard where I dusted the matting. The custom was to take the matting of the corridor up once a quarter. I had to do it once a fortnight. I suffered very much from this very heavy work. I had to take into the yard and shake the ordinary foot mats. A change was made in cleaning the boots and cloaks, and, instead of their being done in the scullery, they were cleaned in one of the passages I had to keep in order. The lay and community sisters both used it, and I had to clean after them. When mass was not celebrated at the convent, the sisters spent their time in doing things that they had left undone ; but I was appointed to do needle-

work under Mrs. Kennedy. If I was late in my duties, I had to acknowledge it as a fault before the sisters. I was not supplied with proper materials for all this cleaning. I was only allowed one duster. I washed a duster in the sink by Mrs. Star's orders, and it was made a charge against me before the commission. Mrs. Star was sometimes late in the mornings, and then she was represented by Mrs. Kennedy. If I failed in my tasks I was reproved, and had to acknowledge the fault. At recreation time the sisters were allowed to hold general intercourse. Mrs. Star directed I should sit next to her on those occasions, but she never spoke to me except in reproof and to give me directions. I spent the time in silence. When Mrs. Star was absent I had to sit beside Mrs. Kennedy. Mrs. Star gave me one day some little pictures to frame. I asked one of the sisters if the picture was straight. Mrs. Star afterwards told me I had broken the rule of silence, and asked me why I did not acknowledge it. By her directions I did so, and she said to the other sisters that I was a wicked creature, and warned all the others against me. She said I was a murmurer, and did not observe my rule.

To the LORD CHIEF JUSTICE : I never knew the rule of silence to be enforced, so as to prevent a sister from asking another for advice or assistance about work, except in my case.

Examination continued : I was required to repair a number of the school books every Sunday from the time I last went to Hull, until I left the convent. It was the duty of Mrs. Kennedy, who was in charge of the school, to repair them. I never knew it done before on a Sunday. I don't know that a little such work on a Sunday would have been objectionable. I often had work given to me that kept me standing, but I was not prohibited from sitting down. Sometimes the work required that I should stand to do it, and at others sitting on the floor, making carpets. I never saw the other sisters employed on this class of work. I was at times deprived of going near the fire, whilst others were permitted to do so. I had on those occasions to do work that could be better done at the tables. I was told to sit there to do the work. I had to paper the crevices in the floor of the community-room on Sundays. It occupied several Sundays. Lay sisters were in the room at the time at recreation. One offered to assist me, but Mrs. Star called her away. One Sunday I was shown some rusty iron bedsteads, and I was ordered to clean them with grease and a cloth ; it occupied several hours ; a novice and lay sister assisted me for a short time, but Mrs. Star sent them away. I had to cut out and prepare needlework on Sundays. On Easter Sunday, the matting having been taken off the community-room, I had to wash the paper off the crevices with water and a cloth. I had to scrape the paper off with my nails. Mrs. Kennedy said it would make the work easier for the lay sisters, who had to wash the room the next day. A novice and a lay postulant offered to help me, but Mrs. Star called them away. On the feast of Corpus Christi the other sisters had recreation nearly the whole of the day, but I had to dry rub the corridor, and brighten the boards with a very heavy brush. I had to clean my cell by six o'clock, the other sisters were allowed until nine or ten. At meals Mrs. Star or Mrs. Kennedy presided. I frequently saw I had not the same food as the other sisters. I generally had a small piece of uncooked mutton left for me; for a long time I had only a piece about the size of a crown-piece. That was all the meat I had for the day. Sometimes, but rarely, I had a small piece of other meat with it. The other sisters had different meat when I had mutton. They often had other meat when I had mutton only.

To the LORD CHIEF JUSTICE: Each sister's portion was sent in. It was carved out of the room.

Examination continued: I believe Mrs. Star had charge of the meat. It sometimes happened that I was ill, and could not eat, and then the meat was kept for me for the next day.

The LORD CHIEF JUSTICE: Do you mean the same meat?—Plaintiff: I believed it to be the same. The sisters had bread and butter and tea for breakfast. The bread I had was stale. It was kept alone for me until it got dry. The other sisters helped themselves from the same bread. Mine was kept separate, and I recollect one piece being put on the table seven or eight days following for me to use from. My bread was kept in a damp cupboard in the refectory, and theirs was kept in the pantry. On one occasion the bread was mouldy, and I spoke to Mrs. Star about it, but it was still kept for my use, and I had to eat it the next meal. The sisters looked upon my leaving the bread as a fault against poverty and mortification, and I apologized for it.

To the LORD CHIEF JUSTICE: I never saw them eat any. (A laugh.)

Examination continued: On one occasion I had a few bones and some gravy for dinner. There was very little meat, if any. I complained, and then a very small portion more of meat was given to me. From June, 1864, to January, 1866, my food was not the same as that given to the other sisters. In May, when I was doing school-duty, I was placed under Sister Mary Bernard. Her name was Mrs. Meligan, and she was a messenger in Baggot-street when I was there. I was told to obey her in everything, and not to speak to any one who came to the school. The school was visited by Father Trappies, of Hull. When he came in I bowed to him and went away. I mentioned that fact to Mrs. Star, and said I was afraid he would consider me very rude in not speaking, but she said she did not care how rude and vulgar any one thought me. A visitor gave me a message for Mrs. Meligan, and I said I would give it to her. I had to acknowledge the fault on my knees that evening before the sisters. The Rev. Mr. Dwyer, of Huddersfield, came to the school with the Rev. Mr. Riddle. The latter spoke to Mrs. Meligan, and Father Dwyer came and asked me if I was ill. I said "No." Sister Mary Bernard came over to us. He asked me how long I had left Clifford, and I turned to Sister Mary Bernard and asked how long, and I then went into the school. Mrs. Star that evening told me, in the presence of all the sisters, I had broken the rules and vows because I spoke to Father Dwyer. I explained how it was, but she would not believe me, and I had to acknowledge my fault before the Chapter. Mrs. Star reproved me, and said I was only to look on myself as a pupil-teacher under Mrs. Meligan. Two sisters went to visit

the sick; but I was told to keep down my veil, and not to speak, but to do what the junior sister told me—reversing the usual practice. The day when I went to Hull a hair-mattrass was in my cell, but the following day a hard flock one was substituted. After I returned to Hull I never had a cell to myself. There was always one and sometimes two sisters with me. I had not sufficient bedclothes to keep me warm in winter, and had to put my day clothing on the bed. Mrs. Star reproved me for doing so, and she frequently came to my cell and threw them off the bed. The custom is two-and-a-half pairs of blankets in winter. I had two pairs of small old blankets. After this I had only one change of clothes, and I was left with only one coif and cape. I afterwards had some more things given to me. I saw Mrs. Kennedy wearing one of my coifs. My visitation clothes were old and discoloured. One night, whilst I was partially undressed and was washing myself, Mrs. Star came in and asked for my flannel skirt that my mother had knitted for me, and very rudely pulled it away from me. I afterwards saw another sister wearing it. I had an old worn flannel in place of it, nothing like so warm. She told me she had given that and other things of mine to other sisters to keep them warm, and that I should never get them again. In October, 1865, additional clothing was served out to the sisters preparatory to the winter. I had none. I complained of the cold, and Mrs. Star said I must bear it for my sins. She took away all my working materials, and said I was not to put a stitch in my clothes. She refused me cotton with which to mend my stockings. Mrs. Meligan told Mrs. Kennedy that no one could wear the tunic that was sent to be aired for me, and that she would have some one to repair it. My dress was remarked by the children in the school. On one occasion my summer clothes were given to me in April, while the other sisters did not get theirs until May. Sometimes I had to take off my coif, guimp, and stockings outside Mrs. Star's cell door, and was frequently kept standing there in that way in cold weather. When I applied for clothes once she said she did not think how I could stay in the house when I knew they all wished to get rid of me. There is a rule that when we go out we shall wear gloves. Mine were taken away and two odd ones substituted. One had to be turned to fit the other hand. My mother gave me two pairs of gloves when I last saw her. My hands were sore with the work I had to do. They were covered with chilblains and cuts. One of the sisters told me to put candle-grease on them, and I did so, but was rebuked by Mrs. Star for having done so without her permission. I believe I had some punishment for it.

The LORD CHIEF JUSTICE: Are you certain? —Witness: I am almost certain I had to acknowledge the fault. She made me take off some rags which were tied round the sores, and others she pulled off herself.

The LORD CHIEF JUSTICE: And did she say why?—No, my lord.

The LORD CHIEF JUSTICE: Were your rules so strict that you could not tie a rag round a cut finger without permission?—I never heard of such a rule, my lord. I did not know I was transgressing a rule by so doing. Mrs. Star compelled me, at the same time, to put my brass thimble on the sore finger. It pained me very much, and I said, "Oh, reverend mother, is this not cruel?" She was displeased with the remark, and I felt sorry for it immediately after I had made it, and I begged her pardon. She called Mrs. Kerr over, and made me repeat before her what I had said as to the thimble. I was not allowed to keep a needle or thread. A sister was appointed to give them to me when I was allowed to use them. This was not so in the case of any other sister. If I broke a needle I was obliged to bring the pieces to Mrs. Star. I am expert at needlework, but a lay sister and a novice were placed over me by Mrs. Star. I was not allowed to mend my own clothes. My boots were very much worn, and had holes through which the stockings could be seen. The stockings also had holes, and I had to black my foot to prevent the flesh being visible. My feet were often cold and wet.

To the LORD CHIEF JUSTICE : I had only the one pair of boots. The other sisters had two pairs, but one pair of mine was taken away by Mrs. Star. Each sister had three pairs of stockings, I had but two. I had a change of stockings once a fortnight. I was not allowed to mend them. About June, 1865, Mrs. Star went to Clifford, and Mrs. Kennedy remained at Hull in charge. I spoke to her about my boots and stockings, but she said she could not let me have others until Mrs. Star returned. She brought me a pair of over-shoes, but I could not get them on. She and Mrs. Meligan tried to put them on, but they would not stay on. When Mrs. Star returned she gave me a pair a little better for house use. I had frequently to tie a string across my foot and put paper soles inside my boot, as the soles were nearly worn out. Before my uncle came Mrs. Star gave me a better pair of shoes, but when he was gone she had them back. I was again allowed to have them shortly before the commission.

THIRD DAY.—*Friday, Feb.* 5.

THE examination in chief of the plaintiff, Miss Susan Saurin, was resumed.

In reply to Mr. DIGBY SEYMOUR, Q.C., she said : I had prayer and other books which I used at chapel. They were all removed ; also a MS. book of private devotion. A MS. book of devotion is generally left with a sister until her death. I saw mine in the hands of a lay sister. When I was allowed to see a letter from my friends it was only a few minutes before the bell rang. They were then torn up or kept. The greater part of some letters was obliterated.

To the LORD CHIEF JUSTICE : The lines were crossed over with ink.

Letters from whom ?—From my father.

Examination continued : Two of my sisters are Carmelite nuns. I had no letters from them for a long time. A few of their letters were given to me. I was allowed to read them, and they were taken away in my desk. After a time the correspondence ceased altogether.

To the LORD CHIEF JUSTICE : There was no rule limiting the number of letters the sisters might receive from their friends.

Examination continued : I remember about the 30th May, 1865, after coming from school at about four o'clock, being called up to Mr. Star's room. I had some tea and bread, and then went up and was called in by Mrs. Star. Mrs. Kennedy was there. The door was locked or bolted after I went in. Mrs. Star desired me to take off my clothes. I hesitated for a few moments, and then I remembered I was bound by the rule of obedience. I took off my veil and habit, and beads. She examined each article. She then unloosed my pocket and pulled it very roughly from me. The pocket she threw to Mrs. Kennedy. I asked her to let me take my handkerchief, as I was crying. She told Mrs. Kennedy to give it to me. She then told me to take off my skirt. I did so. She then ordered me to take off my stays. I did so. Each article I took off she pulled from me and examined. She undid my last skirt and examined my person.

The LORD CHIEF JUSTICE : Did she convey to you for what purpose ?—No, my lord.

Were you allowed to dress again ?—Before I was, my lord, she pulled the scapula and rosary off my neck.

What next?—Then she threw back some of my clothing.

Examination resumed : I dressed myself, and she then told me to leave the room. I never saw my pocket after. There was the first part of the rules in it in MS., also a pin-cushion, an "Examen" book with some writing, and a few blank leaves of paper sewn together to form a book. I had some memoranda for my confession written in the "Examen" book.

The LORD CHIEF JUSTICE : Do you say you never got your pocket again ?—I never did, my lord.

Mr. DIGBY SEYMOUR called for the production of the articles referred to, and certain articles were produced.

Witness : These are the things which were in my desk. The "Examen" book is not here.

Examination continued : I was sitting at work in the community room one Saturday morning afterwards. Mrs. Star came into the room. She told me to go into a small room which was off the community-room, and she called Mrs. Dawson (Mary Winifred), a community sister, to her. She told me then she wanted to see my stays, and ordered me then to take off my dress. I was standing opposite the open door. The sisters were constantly passing in and out of the community-room. I undressed. My clothing was reduced to one thin tunic. I was left thus undressed from shortly after ten o'clock until five minutes to twelve.

The LORD CHIEF JUSTICE : What was being done all that time ?—One of the sisters was directed to sew my staylace together.

To Mr. DIGBY SEYMOUR : It was January, and I was very cold. I threw my habit over my shoulders to keep me warm, and Mrs. Star took it off. She said she did not know how I could stay in the house; and, speaking to Mrs. Kerr, she said, "Was it not in July the bishop said there should be a quick despatch of me?" that the bishop had got a dispensation to absolve me from my vows, and that she was to be ready for a quick despatch, and to have a secular dress ready for me; and that she had one prepared for me for a long time. Soon after this the bell rung for dinner. On the following Saturday I asked her permission to write to my parents. She refused at first, but came to me a quarter of an hour before the time for going to chapel, before seven in the evening. She took a sheet of note paper out of her pocket and tore half of it off. She handed it to me, saying I might write a note to my mother, but not to attempt to ask them to come and see me, as she did not want to be annoyed by them. I took the paper, but I had neither pen nor ink. After some time pen and ink were given to me. I had then only ten minutes to write. I tried to write, and gave what I wrote to Mrs. Star. I do not know what became of it. On account of what had been said as to a dispensation from my vows, which greatly astonished me, I asked on the Sunday following to be allowed to write to the bishop. I got leave. Mrs. Kennedy sat opposite to me. She looked over me.

To the LORD CHIEF JUSTICE: She was facing me.

Examination continued: I asked Mrs. Star for an envelope. Mrs. Star said she knew her duty, and would send it herself. In the letter I expressed a wish to see the bishop.

Mr. DIGBY SEYMOUR called for the production of the letter.

Mr. CHARLES RUSSELL said they had not got it. The bishop had been subpœnaed by the plaintiff, and he could be asked for it.

Examination continued: I received an answer from the bishop, but not until just before the commission. I remember in the latter end of 1865—September, I think—having an illness like cholera. I was very weak—so weak that once in chapel I could not kneel. I had complained of being ill. I worshipped sitting. Mrs. Star on that occasion ordered me to a high seat or form. That was during mass. She knocked me with a book, as she had frequently done during mass.

The LORD CHIEF JUSTICE: What do you mean by knocking you with a book?—Struck me with a book on the head or shoulder.

Examination continued: I was comfortably seated on a low seat, but was removed to a high one. In the beginning of 1866 I noticed that there was a good deal of writing going on backwards and forwards in Mrs. Star's room.

Do you recollect anything having occurred previous to this time about a ring?—Yes.

What ring was it?—The ring I got from the bishop at profession.

Is that ring regarded with peculiar reverence, and as being peculiarly sacred?—Yes.

Is it a symbol of union with the Church?—It is.

Where did you wear it?—On the third finger of the left hand.

Examination continued: In August, 1865, Mrs. Star came into the community-room. She told me I had left some threads on the mat of the corridor. She then asked me for my ring. I was greatly surprised, and moved it a little on my finger. She pulled it off, and I never saw it after.

It was after that my brother, the Jesuit priest, visited me. I had not seen him for eight years previously. On the following day Mrs. Star told me in chapel that I was not to go to Holy Communion that day.

The LORD CHIEF JUSTICE: Did she give you any reason?—No, my lord; she gave me no reason.

Examination continued: She made a sign to me, when mass was over, to follow her, and I did so. When I got to the door she put a quarter-hour sandglass in my hand, as is usual when friends call, to signify the time allowed to see them. I never knew of any limitation being fixed in the case of relatives. Mrs. Star opened the visitors' door, and pushed me in, and there I found my brother. I remained with him half an hour. Mrs. Star next morning asked me why I did not acknowledge staying so long with my brother as a fault. I replied that I thought I had permission. She told me she had had a long interview with my brother. I did not see my brother after that. I did not see the bishop from that time. My reverend uncle, Father Mathews, came in November, 1865. As I have stated, just before the commission there was great writing going on between Mrs. Star, Mrs. Kennedy, and Mrs. Kerr, both in the library and in the community-room. On the second of January, Mrs. Kennedy gave me a note from the bishop, announcing that the commission would sit. I destroyed that note afterwards. It did not state the day on which the commission would sit. I wrote to ask what day it would meet, and I asked what were the charges against me. I added a wish that the bishop should be present, and said I should abide by his decision. I received a reply to the effect that I was charged with breaches of my vows, and that I should be furnished with the charges.

Mr. DIGBY SEYMOUR called for the letter addressed to the bishop.

Dr. Cornthwaite, Roman Catholic Bishop of Beverley, produced the letter.

Examination continued: I was never furnished with copies of the charges. No opportunity was given to me to prepare for the commission. Such opportunity was asked and refused.

What did you ask?—I asked that a private room should be allowed me, because I could not write in the community-room whilst the sisters were round me and talking. I was not permitted to go to my cell alone. A sister followed me whenever I went. I had a day when my uncle, Father Mathews, came. Mrs. Star went to Liverpool shortly before the commission. When she returned, she said to me that I little thought she should have heard what I told my Jesuit brother, but that she had heard every word I said. She said she had seen the Rev. Mr. Porter. She asked me had I told my brother that she had stripped me. I replied that I had, but that it was the first time I had mentioned it. Her reply was that if she had taken me from the top of the house to the bottom by the hair of the head I ought not to have mentioned it. I asked her, according to custom, whether I might not renew my vows on New Year's Day. She said she did not know how I could, as I had been absolved from them, but that perhaps I might, as I could not be absolved from my third vow without my own consent. She gave me a piece of soiled paper to copy the renewal, and took from me the printed renewal. It was after this my uncle called. He saw me twice alone. I had made memoranda before the commission, but they were taken away from me by Mrs. Star. She said as I told her they were for the bishop that she would send them to him. On the approach of the sitting of the commission I had better clothes given to me to attend it. Canon Walker was the president of the commission; Canon Chadwell, Father Feeney, Dr. O'Hanlan, and Father Porter were the other members. They sat two days. The bishop's secretary read a great file of charges against me.

Had you ever seen them before?—Never.

Was any evidence given against you?—No.

Was any sister or other witness called to support the charges?—No.

Mr. DIGBY SEYMOUR called for the files of paper referred to.

Papers were produced and handed to the witness.

Examination continued: These are not the papers I refer to. They were much larger than these. The names of several sisters were mentioned as having furnished papers to the commissioners.

The LORD CHIEF JUSTICE said that no doubt when the name of a particular sister was referred to the paper or charge she had supplied was placed before the commissioners.

[A summary of the charges was here read. They referred to breaches of rule, such as the Solicitor-General had referred to in the course of his opening statement.]

Examination continued: I was asked at the end of each charge whether it were true or false, and I said that it was untrue; but I explained so far as I could. The summary of the charges under the heads of disobedience, poverty, and chastity was read, and of the statements on which they were founded. My reverend uncle was present, and asked explanations of me, but I was not allowed to make statements of my treatment in the convent in reply. Father Porter, of Liverpool, one of the commissioners, took part against me. There was a difference between his manner towards me and that of the other commissioners. On the 12th of February, when the commission was over, Mrs. Star came to my cell about five o'clock in the morning. She advanced to my bed and said, "I want all your religious dress; you are to leave the convent to-day." Mrs. Kennedy, who was with her, took the greater part of it, and Mrs. Star secured my rosary and cincture. Part of a secular dress was left for me to wear. I refused to put it on. I had written, previously to this, to the bishop, who said in his reply that I was to leave the convent, and that I should be absolved from my vows. About nine o'clock the same day Mrs. Star came to my cell with Mrs. Kennedy and another of the sisters, and read to me, as if from a letter—to the effect that the bishop had absolved me from my vows, conditional on my hearing ten masses after I had received notice. She gave me the notice. I could not help receiving it. She said I was to be got rid of at the shortest possible notice, and she asked me would I go? I told her I would not; that I would rather die than leave the convent of my own free will. But I said it had pleased God to leave me

at her mercy, and she might do as she pleased. She said she could not put me out; and I said, "I will die in my cell." This took place in my cell. I was sitting up in bed. My sister's clothes had been taken away. Mrs. Kennedy threatened me with all kinds of vengeance from God and the bishop, upon which Mrs. Star checked her. They then left, but afterwards Mrs. Star returned with a secular dress. I refused to put it on. She took it away, but came in again with one of the sisters, and said she could not have me with the sisters, and that I must go to the bath-room. I went there. I had no fire allowed me. I lived there until the month of April. It was very cold. I was not allowed any religious books. A sister was with me day and night, but the sister had warm clothing and hot water bottles for her feet. Mrs. Star took away a piece of carpet I used for warmth. In April I was removed to the attic, by direction of Mrs. Kennedy. Mrs. Star was in it when I went there. It had been always used as a lumber-room, and was very dirty. I had to use sheets which had been used by me from the previous February. At night a sister slept in the corridor, and a rope was attached to the attic door and her bed. During the day a sister sat at the attic door. When I had been there a short time I was not permitted to leave it for any purpose. The window was darkened, and there was very little light. I had a rug and soiled blanket for my bed. The blanket was infested with vermin. I complained of this, but no change was made. There was a chair in the room, but it was put to a side to which I was told not to go, and I had to sit on the floor. When the weather became warm, the sisters were changed in my room; one day, eighteen times. The room was most offensive. On one occasion six sisters who had bad legs, and had to use liniments, were put there at one time. I was not allowed to leave the room once, for any purpose whatever, and at times I felt as if I was losing my senses. At one time I thought I was dying, and I wrote to my brother Patrick to come to me, and to let me know what my beloved parents would have me do. The greater part of the letter was dictated by Mrs. Star and Mrs. Kennedy. Mrs. Star told me the bishop would not let me leave the convent alone. My brother came over about the middle of March. He brought Sir Henry Cooper, an eminent physician, to see me. After that the conduct of the officials, and the food I was allowed became worse. I was not allowed to be alone with my physician. Everything that was said was overheard by Mrs. Kennedy or some other sister. My brother suggested that they should retire, as he did when the doctor saw me, but they refused to do so. The next day my brother came and took me away.

[It being now luncheon time, the court was about to be adjourned for a quarter of an hour, when a consultation took place between the learned counsel at either side. A paper was passed from one to the other, and finally sent up to the bench, whereupon his lordship retired to his private room, followed by the Solicitor-General and Mr. Hawkins, the leading counsel for the plaintiff and the defendant. It is supposed that a compromise was proposed, but that on one side or the other the terms were rejected.

When his Lordship again took his seat on the bench,

The cross-examination of the plaintiff by Mr. HAWKINS was proceeded with. She said in reply to the questions of the learned counsel : I was 21 years of age when I entered the convent at Baggot-street, Dublin. My two sisters were in a Carmelite convent in the county Dublin. I had a wish from an early age to become a sister, from a love of the poor and a liking for teaching. Two or three of the ladies in Baggot-street were known to my family. I had a conversation with the superioress, who explained the duties I would have to perform. I was acquainted with the rules of obedience, chastity, silence, and poverty. There are no austerities of obligation in the order. While a postulant I visited the sick. I was a postulant six months, and a novice two years. I was free from vows, but led the same life as the sisters during that time. There is more menial service performed by the postulants or novices than by the sisters. While a postulant I swept and dusted the cells, and did a little more dusting. I never saw a postulant or a novice wash a floor, or a professed sister. I never knew it to be enforced as a duty. The rules and constitution of the order were not given to us. They were read to us once a week or oftener. When we were postulants we were required to read from a book on the novitiate each day. I signed a document to the effect that I had made myself acquainted with the rules. I did so before I was professed. I had to do so, and I believe I did. My profession was made two years and a half after I knew what the rules were. By the vow of poverty, as explained, everything of every kind is renounced. I do not remember that by the rules I was to submit my correspondence entirely to the superioress. The book you are reading from seems to be an amplification of the rules and vows. [It was entitled "The Novitiate's Guide."] I do not remember to have seen it before. The book I refer to was not in print as this is, but in MS.

[It appeared that the book in question received the sanction of the Roman Catholic Bishop of York, in the year 1865, and was printed in the following year.]

The LORD CHIEF JUSTICE : The plaintiff cannot be bound by this book. She can only be bound by such rules as were brought to her knowledge before she was professed.

Cross-examination continued : I had access to the MS. book of instructions, and did read it. My friends were always treated as externs, but better than strangers were. I understood that the superioress had the power of forwarding or returning such letters as she thought proper. She always opens and reads all the letters that come. Letters to and from the bishop are excepted. It was explained to us that letters would be given to us except they contained expressions of love, or things of that kind, which it would not be proper for us to receive.

Mr. HAWKINS : Has not the superioress power under rule 4 to withhold a perfectly innocent letter if she deems it expedient to do so ?—We were told that perfectly innocent letters from our friends would not be withheld.

The SOLICITOR-GENERAL : A copy of these printed rules was not furnished to us, although we should have had them under the judge's order.

The LORD CHIEF JUSTICE : The witness admits that all correspondence should pass through the superioress.

The SOLICITOR-GENERAL said there was nothing in the rules as to the letters of friends being withheld, so far as he could see.

Cross-examination continued : I was taught, as part of my duty, to submit to the will of the mother in all correspondence, whether sent or received by me. I was on the most intimate terms with Mrs. Star down to the year 1860 or 1861. There were no complaints against me up to that time, except faults general to all the sisters. No unfriendly feeling existed that I know of. The first breach occurred between us about 1860 or 1861, when Mrs. Star asked me to tell her what my father confessor had said in my confession. She also wanted to know what the priest had said to me. I would not say that ; to reveal what is said in confession is contrary to the rule of the Catholic Church, because Mrs. Star told me that Sister Mary Alayois (Mrs. Ryan) had told her. I cannot say whether there was any one present when Mrs. Star asked me to tell her. It was in the convent, in Willow-street, Hull, she asked me. I had never before been asked to reveal my confessions. I did not think it a very extraordinary thing to be asked about what had passed in confession. I should say it would be a breach of honour to have revealed it. I do not know whether it would have been a breach of rule. She gave me time—quarter or half an hour—to remember what I had said, and came back to ask me. I do not know where Mrs. Ryan now is. Mrs. Star repeated the request several times. It was during one of the "manifestations of conscience" that she made the request the second time. I do not know how often she asked me. I mentioned the matter in confession, as I was in doubt whether I had been guilty of an act of disobedience.

To the Court : She might have complained to the bishop, or had advice of the ordinary confessor.

Mr. HAWKINS said that he had evidence to adduce to the direct contrary of this allegation.

Cross-examination continued : I may have brought counter-charges against the superioress before the commissioners. I do not remember having mentioned about the confession to them.

To the LORD CHIEF JUSTICE : There is a director and ordinary confessor to advise. Advice is given out of confession by the director during Retreat ; but I always consider it the same as confession. I do not know whether the sisters communicated the advice they received to the superioress. When I was advised to get up at three o'clock in the morning at Clifford it was to finish some shirts for a priest. Sewing for any length of time would be a breach of the Sabbath, but a little cutting out would not be. Cutting out for two or three hours would be. I do not remember that in March, 1862, a letter was found under the mattrass of my bed by Sister Mary Clare, and only know of my uncle's letter. I was going to send it without the knowledge of the superioress. I made no complaints in my letter of harsh treatment in the convent. Mrs. Star wrote me a letter of expostulation for the fault. She asked me whether I wished to return to Ireland, and I replied that I did. I did not consider it a fault to write to my uncle, who is a priest. I was unhappy, and wished to leave. When she charged me with keeping the calico and scissors, I felt it was a breach of the vow of poverty. I wished to get to another convent, and expressed my wish to that effect. She wrote to Baggot-street, and I knew it would prevent my being received there, as she magnified the fault. I did not complain that I had not sufficient mutton, but that I had not sufficient meat. The sisters then had beef, and I had a distaste for mutton. I had on one occasion a very bad piece, which disgusted me. The sisters had chops when I had cold mutton.

The LORD CHIEF JUSTICE observed that the learned counsel scarcely gave the witness time to answer the questions as to the cold mutton.

Mr. HAWKINS : Perhaps I have made a hash of it, my lord. (Laughter.)

Cross-examination continued : The sisters had sometimes stewed rabbit and ham when I had mutton. When I was refrectorian I never gave better pieces to the superioress than to the junior sisters. I first heard of it before the commission, as also of having been accused of eating in the pantry. I never did it. Neither did I ever take food from the children who brought their dinners to school ; but this, too, was made a charge against me. I never heard one of the children

crying, and saying I had taken part of her dinner. That was not charged against me. I had to scrape the paper off the crevices in the flooring on Easter Sunday with my nails. I was refused a knife to do so by Mrs. Star. It took me four or five hours to do it, and my knees were sore, but she refused me a piece of carpet. It was not a penance. I did not complain. It is not a rule at Hull that the professed sisters should take part in the menial work. I never saw them clean the grates or wash the stone steps. I never knew a sister anxious to do such work as being commendable. I have never had any communication with any of the sisters, professed or lay, since I left the convent. The sisters are allowed to keep watches, and mine was given up to me a year before I left. At profession everything becomes the property of the community, and my watch had been lent by Mrs. Star to several sisters and brothers. I do not know what the amount of the dowry is, whether it is £500 or £600. That matter is settled by my friends. Many sisters brought no dowry, and were better treated than I was. Up to the time I left I thought it a fault to complain, except to the superioress, however well-founded the complaint might be.

FOURTH DAY.—*Saturday, Feb. 6.*

THE signs of an increased curiosity were abundantly manifest round the precincts of the Court on Saturday, when scores of hopeless lingerers, who had long despaired of gaining admission, waited to witness the departure of the aggrieved Sister Scholastica, whose worldly designation is Miss Saurin, and whose complaints of long-suffering at the hands of Mrs. Star and Mrs. Kennedy, otherwise Sister Mary Joseph and Sister Mary Magdalen, are not unlikely to stir up anew certain slumbering questions relating to convents in England. Sister Scholastica's evidence, under the shrewd but considerate cross-examination of Mr. Hawkins, Q.C., and in re-examination by the Solicitor-General, principally occupied the time of the Court from ten o'clock on Saturday morning till the adjournment at twenty minutes past three. Persons wearied with the drone and the heat of the stuffed Court were eagerly interrogated, on their leaving, by other persons who pressed round the door. How was the case going? Did the plaintiff lose ground in cross-examination? Was it true that the Lord Chief Justice had snubbed the defendants' counsel? As three or four people came out, three or four were let in by the police inspector, who called aloud the number of those for whom space had been vacated. But it was a bootless privilege that many stayed so patiently and so long to gain. Of twenty permitted to enter not two could succeed in pushing their way far enough to see or hear. The attempt to get a really eligible place in Court was so plainly desperate that many who came prepared for a little squeezing and jostling remained but a few minutes, and then went away with apparent purpose of abandoning the endeavour. Few who thus left the spot were seen again ; but there were some who hovered there all the five or six hours during which the doors of

the Court were open. Artists, authors, actors—these last seem to make the law courts their study—were recognizable among the besieging crowd, as well as in the body of the chamber. Here, while some of the most interested parties to the case were walking to and fro in the great hall, anxiously conversing with barristers, gowned and wigged, indifferent hearers found themselves enlisted as partisans, and seized with eagerness upon every point. The plaintiff's replies to Mr. Hawkins, explaining as a reason for not informing the local superior of the convent at Clifford of certain delinquencies, that the local superior at Clifford was herself the delinquent, were so amusingly dramatic, and afforded so complete a surprise to all, judge and counsel included, tha the Court was for some seconds given up to the humour of the situation, till the more seriously-impressed began to demonstrate their feeling by hisses, and so get themselves and everybody else called to order. Symptoms of a temperate wish to stay this scandal were apparent now and then in the course of Saturday's proceedings. Immediately on the opening of the Court time for consultation was requested by the counsel and the Roman Catholic bishop who is prominently concerned in the action ; and they conferred together for half an hour or more ; but, in the absence of others who are interested, no arrangement could be definitely come to. On the adjournment of the case till Monday morning Miss Saurin left the court, protected against the too curious observation of the by-standers by a thick black veil, and departed in a cab, accompanied by her friends.

The LORD CHIEF JUSTICE took his seat on the bench at ten o'clock.

The Court and all the avenues leading to it were densely crowded, and intense interest was manifested in the proceedings.

A consultation took place with a view to the settlement of the case between the learned counsel of either side and Dr. Cornthwaite, Roman Catholic Bishop. When the conference had lasted about twenty minutes,

The LORD CHIEF JUSTICE said : Gentlemen, I fear I must call "time."

Mr. HAWKINS : I do not know whether your lordship will permit me to say so, but the fact is that matters have passed this morning between the Bishop of Beverley, my learned friend the Solicitor-General, and myself, which lead to a hope that your lordship and the jury may not be further troubled with the case. If you would allow us five minutes more, it is not improbable that much time may be saved.

The LORD CHIEF JUSTICE : If I thought there was a chance of a settlement I should not object.

Mr. HAWKINS : It really comes to this, my lord, whether we are to be occupied here another fortnight or to conclude the case at once.

The LORD CHIEF JUSTICE : What I fear is that we may be occupied the fortnight *plus* the time you may occupy in consultation.

The SOLICITOR-GENERAL : I may be permitted to say, my lord, that I made an offer to my learned friend yesterday, and that offer has been under consideration. Your lordship will, doubtless, have seen that interests other than those of the plaintiff and defendants are concerned.

The LORD CHIEF JUSTICE : That I see very plainly, and that is why I am afraid we may lose our time.

The SOLICITOR-GENERAL : An offer has been made, and the question is whether, under all the circumstances, it should be accepted.

The LORD CHIEF JUSTICE : Well, do not take more time than is necessary to consider the matter.

Mr. HAWKINS : I assure your lordship I will not.

The LORD CHIEF JUSTICE (to the jury) : Gentlemen, it is possible that we may save some days by the course suggested.

His Lordship then retired from the bench. The learned counsel for plaintiff and defendants, and the Bishop of Beverley, also left the court.

After the lapse of about a quarter of an hour the Solicitor-General returned into court, and, addressing his lordship, said : My learned friend Mr. Hawkins has requested me to inform your lordship that the time we have just occupied in consultation has not been wasted. In a case of this kind, perhaps people's feelings are rather sensitive. A short time since, thinking that it did not matter from which side the offer came, I said that I had made my learned friend an offer yesterday ; but the fact is that the offer really came from my learned friend, and he begged me to mention that circumstance to your lordship.

Mr. Hawkins shortly afterwards returned into court, and said : My lord, I am sorry to have trespassed so long on your lordship's time. I can only say that I have not wasted one single moment.

The LORD CHIEF JUSTICE : What is the result of your consultation?

Mr. HAWKINS : Well, my lord, I am afraid that until others, who cannot be communicated with this morning, have been consulted, no arrangement can be entered into.

The LORD CHIEF JUSTICE : That is exactly why I have been so reluctant to grant further time for consultation. I was convinced from the first that no terms could be agreed upon. At all events, we must go on for the present.

The plaintiff again entered the box, and her cross-examination by Mr. Hawkins was resumed : When I was kept standing at the schools at Clifford and Hull I was acting under the orders of Mrs. Star. She gave me the order before I went to Clifford. That was not when we were good friends ; it was after the August retreat in 1863. She told me Mrs. M'Keon would give me a distribution of time, and that I was to submit myself in all things to her.

To the LORD CHIEF JUSTICE : She did not tell me to stand personally. I was merely to obey Mrs. M'Keon.

Cross-examined : Mrs. M'Keon gave me the order to stand. She told me she had received the order from Mrs. Star. The rules directed that I was to obey the orders of my local superiors. Mrs. M'Keon was the local superior. I never knew before of a distribution of time being given to a professed community sister. I had not many times before that had a distribution of time given to me. Up to 1862 Mrs. M'Keon and myself were very good friends ; after that there was a coldness between us. She told me that if I were to see the letters from Mrs. Star I should not be surprised at her conduct. She told me I was not to speak to her, and she was not to speak to me, because I was a bad example. That was said when she was reproving me, and I dared not make any remark upon what she said. I asked Mrs. Star what I had done. She told me that she had given me too much liberty, and she was determined to pull me down. Mrs. M'Keon told me I was not to sit in the school. I don't know that she used the word "never." There were 100 children in the school, and I had to attend to the greater part of them. I had to teach needlework, reading, and writing, and give object-lessons. I never sat in the school after that. The same thing occurred at Hull. Mrs. Star herself gave me instructions about that. When I went from Clifford to Hull I was not aware that Mrs. Star was going to return to Hull. On that occasion I was sitting at work, and Mrs. Star snatched the work out of my hand, refused to allow me to tell the sister who was sitting by my side how the work was to be gone on with, and drove me out of the room. In five minutes after that we were out of the house on our way to the station. I put no extra clothing on. I had not one pair of stockings on, and I did not endeavour to put on a second pair over them. I was changing my stockings because it was the last day of the week, and I wanted to put on a clean pair. I changed one stocking, and then was interrupted by being told we should be too late for the train. We had to wait an hour for the train when we arrived at the station. It was my duty to carry the basket. I had to carry the umbrella over her ; when I held it equally between us she told me I was carrying it badly. (Laughter.) I got very wet. When she told me that we should miss the train, she dragged on my boot in a very rude manner, and I was pushed down the stairs ; so that I should have fallen down the stairs. I think I slipped down. I made no complaint when I arrived at Hull. My time was distributed thus : I had to sweep my cell out by six o'clock. The other sisters were allowed until ten to do so. I had to sweep the corridor and dust the pictures, and two altars. There were two flights of stairs and a second corridor. There was something written upon the tablets which were taken from me.

The LORD CHIEF JUSTICE: There is not a vestige of writing on them now, although there are traces of erasure.

Mr. HAWKINS: I am aware of that, my lord.

Cross-examination continued: When Mrs. Star took the tablets from me I asked her not to read what was in them. I had written there a few memoranda for confession.

To the LORD CHIEF JUSTICE: I told her it was for confession that I had made the entries.

Cross-examination continued: She read me out parts of the entries, and she said that they were about other sisters. They referred to one of the sisters staying on the tower for several hours with Mr. Collins. I was greatly disedified by such conduct, as it was against the rules. It was my duty to communicate such a circumstance to the superioress. There were other matters in the tablets. The entries were made two months before.

You say it was your duty to report such a thing to the superioress?—It was.

Why did you not?—Because she was at Hull.

In her absence, to whom was it your duty to report it?—To the local superioress.

And why did you not do so?—Because it was the local superioress herself who did it. (Much laughter and applause.)

Cross-examination continued: I intended to tell Mrs. Star of it. Mrs. M'Keon was the local superioress. I do not know who Mr. Collins is. I only know that he was a frequent visitor of Mrs. Star. (Laughter.) There is a Mrs. Collins, but I do not think that she was there upon the occasion. It would have made no difference to me if Mrs. Collins was there are not. I thought that the local superioress had no right to waste so much time. She was not accompanied by a sister, according to the rules. It was a very fine day. They had a telescope. It was contrary to the rule for a sister to be out of the enclosure alone. The tower does not belong to the convent; it belongs to Mrs. Grimston. I did not erase the entries from the tablet myself. I am quite certain that the tablet did not contain murmurings and grumblings. I don't remember making memoranda of occasions when I was put to improper work. This book (produced) contains entries such as "kept fasting after five o'clock," and other complaints. I made them after the commission. There is an entry of Mrs. Star saying of me before the sisters, "Your smooth way deceived them." This was the book taken out of my pocket when Mrs. Star stripped me, in May, 1865. I made the entries to ask Mrs. Star what they meant.

The LORD CHIEF JUSTICE: They are more than that, I think. Were these things what Mrs. Star had stated to you?—Yes, my lord; and I could not reply at the time because she was reproving me, and I was to keep silent.

Cross-examination continued: I made the entries for this purpose. When Mrs. Star reproved me so severely before the sisters it would have been contrary to the rules for me to have

replied at the time, and I took a note of what she said, in order to ask her about it afterwards. I believe I did speak to her on the subject subsequently, but I don't remember what she said, or if she said anything. During this time I was not at all in communication with my uncle, the Rev. Father Mathews. When I was reading my brother's letter she snatched it from my hand. She would have been much displeased had I asked for an explanation of her conduct. She had been so on many other occasions. She had on a previous occasion blotted out a part of one of my sister's letters. I am sure neither of my sisters would write anything which was unfit for me to read.

Mr. HAWKINS: You were, however, aware that the superioress had a right to make such erasures from letters received by the sisters.

The LORD CHIEF JUSTICE: There is a difference between right and power. But every such right must be exercised honestly, and must not be used for purposes of oppression. (Loud applause.) Pray let there be no more of those manifestations. The charge is that powers of this kind were abused for the purpose of driving the plaintiff out of the convent.

Mr. HAWKINS: We put it, my lord, that all these powers were honestly used for the good of the community generally.

Cross-examination continued: I saw a letter from my brother in answer to my writing— "Sister Scholastica is at Hull" yesterday for the first time. My uncle was at the head of an establishment at Drogheda. I did not make an application to him to take me in there. I wished to go back to Baggot-street. I have not made an application to go back to Baggot-street since my religious dress was taken from me. I love them and they love me. I have made no application to any religious establishment since to be re-admitted. On one occasion whilst I was with her Mrs. Star offered to send a sister with me to make a personal application to be re-admitted at Baggot-street. I refused her offer because I did not know where the sister might take me to.

Mr. HAWKINS: Do you really mean to say that you had any doubt that you would not be taken to Baggot-street?—I had. Mrs. Star was so severe with me at the time that I did not know where she would send me. I had sent a letter by her direction to my uncle asking him to take me into his establishment. When I was ordered to hold the dust-box it was a penance for some supposed fault, but I never saw any other sister compelled to perform such a penance. I am sure that I did not keep the duster on as a veil for a considerable time after I had been told to take it off. To the best of my recollection I took it off as soon as I got permission. When I was making the carpet Mrs. Star made me get up off a part of the carpet I was sitting upon and sit upon the bare floor. When I was stripped in 1865 I took off part of my clothes myself and part Mrs. Star dragged rudely off me. There were ten cells at Hull, and nine or ten inmates to occupy them. Some of the sisters objected to sleep alone, because they were afraid. It is an unusual thing for sisters to have a fire in their cells. I never asked for a fire until my clothes were taken from me. I had a mattrass, a bolster, a pillow, sheets, and two small blankets, which were soiled, and would scarcely cover the bed. I asked Mrs. Star for other blankets, and she told me to bear the cold for my sins. She came into the room on one occasion, and pulled off the blankets. I did not ask her what she did it for. I dared not ask such a question.

Mr. HAWKINS: Do you mean to say, if she had come into the room and pulled you out of bed, had kicked you, and had thrown you down, you would not have asked why she did so?— Witness: What she did was nearly as bad. (Laughter.) She came into my room when I was asleep, and pulled off the clothes roughly. I think between 1863 and 1864. I never asked the superioress why she did anything, neither did I ever remonstrate with her. My uncle was acting for me before the commission. On one occasion Mrs. Star came into the room with my tunic torn, and said it had been done on purpose. I never complained of my veil and asked for another. I never tore my veil in order to get a new one. Mine was taken from me, and another substituted for it. I never injured any of my clothes wilfully. I was never charged with having torn them. Before the commission I was charged with having sent too many clothes to wash, but the sister who superintended those matters told me that I had fewer clothes in the wash than any other sister, and wondered how I kept myself so clean. There is a rule that we are not to speak to "externs." We are always instructed to treat a priest as ladies would a gentleman. We were to acknowledge his presence, and to answer his questions, but not to stand and talk with him. I never remember to have spoken to a priest contrary to the rule. Mrs. Star might have said that I spoke to the priest unnecessarily. The rule imposes silence as far as circumstances will permit. Any deviation from the rules is deemed a fault, and at Baggot-street had to be acknowledged standing; but Mrs. Star made the regulation that the acknowledgment should be made kneeling. She obliged me to kneel before the novices and the lay sisters. This was done every morning. I do not recollect that Mrs. Star complained of my having unfairly distributed the plates at refectory. (Laughter.) In 1857 or 1858 the Cardinal visited the convent, and I had a pair of very old boots, and I took a loan of Mrs. Kennedy's boots for an hour or two, without asking her leave. It was the custom for us to borrow each other's things. I had not time to ask her leave. I thought no more about it until I heard of it again at the commission. My boots were too bad to appear before visitors in, and as I had to take refreshments to the Cardinal, and my dress was tucked up, I thought I was doing right to borrow the boots. Mrs. Kennedy had lent me the boots on a previous occasion. I told Mrs. Kennedy myself I had taken them. She gave me the boots herself immediately afterwards, and she had offered them to me before. After 1862 Mrs. Star gave me a verbal order not to send the school-children upon errands. I never sent the children upon errands contrary to the orders of Mrs. Star. It was their duty to put a little fuel on the fire when requested. It was a fault to be late for spiritual duties. Constant complaints were not made against me that I was late. It was a fault to be late for refection or for recreation. I never committed any such fault without making reparation by

acknowledging it as a fault. After that Mrs. Star introduced as a regulation that each sister was to kiss the floor when late for duty. (Laughter.) That was after 1862. I frequently kissed the floor. Mrs. Star and Mrs. Kennedy never kissed the floor, whether late or not. (Laughter.) They had no penance to perform. (Laughter.) I was frequently kept late at the school. There was no particular spot we had to kiss—we kissed where we liked. (Laughter.) I rang no bell in Hull after 1862, but I did at Clifford. I rang the bell late on some occasions. I had no watch, and the clock was in the convent. I never altered the clock for my own convenience, or to shield myself when I was late in ringing the bell, or late in performing my other duties. I was charged with doing so first before the commission. I was charged before the commission with having a light in my cell, but not with writing. It was against the rules to have a light in the cell after ten o'clock at night, except on one night a week, when we were allowed a quarter of an hour later. We had gas in our cells. I never had a candle in my cell. I never put a letter in a book so that one of the children might take it to the post. Mrs. M'Keon charged me wrongfully with having done so. I did not tell Mrs. M'Keon that the letter in question was one sent to me by a person in the village to read before it was posted. She did not afterwards tell me that she had made inquiries and found out that my statement was false, and I did not thereupon acknowledge that I had told an untruth about the matter. I heard for the first time, at the commission, that a prayer-book belonging to Mrs. M'Keon had been found in my cell. I never borrowed one of her prayer-books without leave. I made the tea when I was refectorian. I never poured out a good cup of tea first for myself, and put it aside with a piece of buttered toast. (Laughter.)

The LORD CHIEF JUSTICE: That would rather presuppose that she liked weak tea, because the latter cups would be stronger. (Laughter.)

MR. HAWKINS: But it was before the second water was put in, my lord. (Laughter.)

The LORD CHIEF JUSTICE: But, Mr. Hawkins, is this really a head of charge?

MR. HAWKINS: Not alone, my lord, but taken in conjunction with other matters, such as an unequal distribution of the plates at dinner; it shows an habitual infraction of the rule which requires that everything shall be shared equally.

The LORD CHIEF JUSTICE: Of course it might be important to show that she had been guilty of an habitual disregard of a very wholesome rule in a community like this, but surely the order in which she pours out the cups of tea can scarcely be material.

Cross-examination continued: Whenever I complained of illness, Mrs. Star, before 1860, when we were good friends, allowed me to eat between meals, but not after that date. She asked for a dispensation for me before 1859, but not afterwards.

Were you not frequently seen eating between meals?—I never heard such a thing until the commission sat.

You did not do it?—I did not.

Did you not take a pocket-handkerchief of Mrs. Milligan's?—Never.

Were you not charged with having done so?—
I never was.

Did not Mrs. Milligan, at Prince-street schools,
desire you not to send any one to answer knocks
at the door, as she would do so herself?—I never
heard of it before.

Did not a child who had answered a knock say,
"Sister Scholastica sent me"?—No.

And did not you say you did not ; whereupon
the child said, "Oh, you did, Sister Scholastica"?
—Such a thing never occurred.

Were you not forbidden to beat and slap the
children at school?—That is the rule.

Have you not beaten and slapped the children?
—Never.

Did not one child say, "Sister Scholastica beat
me because I told on her"?—I never heard of it
before.

Did not Mrs. Milligan look hard at you, and
did you not say, "I never touched her"?—No.
I never have touched a child except when it was
necessary to move it from one place to another.
I never hurt one.

You never touched one of them in temper?
—Never.

Did you ever take part of a child's dinner?—I
never did—not the smallest particle.

Do you mean to say that Mrs. Milligan did not
actually see you with part of a child's dinner?—I
never heard of such a thing until the commission.

Was it contrary to the rules to make accusations
against the rev. mother except to the bishop?—
Yes ; or to herself.

To herself, in the presence of others?—No ;
alone.

Did you not complain to Mrs. Star of herself
in the presence of others?—I do not remember to
have ever done so.

Will you say you never did so?—I never did.

Were you ever accused of having neglected
the schools?—Not till the commission sat.

Or of keeping a sick sister who was thirsty without drink for hours?—I am quite sure I never
neglected a sick sister.

Were you charged with having done so?—I
heard of it first before the commissioners.

Were you accused of having pinched the children?—No , and I never did.

Or of pulling their ears?—No.   Mrs. M'Keon
said I was rude to the children.

Did you not acknowledge as a fault in your
monthly letter to Mrs. Star that you had been
rude and unkind to the children?—I was obliged
to do so.   I had not been rude or unkind to
them.

Why were you obliged to write what was not
the fact?—Because everything the local superioress said was a fault, and said I had committed,
I was obliged to admit without making any comment upon it.   (Hisses.)

Suppose you had been told that you had
uttered an untruth, would you have admitted
that ?—No, that would have been a grave fault.

Well, if she had said you habitually neglected
your duty, would you have written that?—Yes.

Even though it were untrue?—Well, she would
understand what she meant by neglect of duty,
and I should take what she said.

The LORD CHIEF JUSTICE : It strikes me there
is an answer to be found in the nature of things.
The superioress might consider that to be a
neglect of duty or unkindness to a child as to

which the plaintiff might entertain a different
opinion, but she would consider herself bound by
the opinion of the superioress.   She may think
the judgment erroneous and severe, but she is
bound by it.   (Applause.)   I again say I trust
there will be no more of these unseemly interruptions.   So much for a small matter.   But if I am
accused of a serious and grave fault, I am not
bound to admit the correctness or the superiority
of anybody as to it.   The answer of the witness
is perfectly intelligible.   (Renewed applause.)

Mr. HAWKINS : I have to complain, my lord,
of having met with several interruptions—"applause in the gallery," as it is called—and disapprobation.   On behalf of my clients, I have to
represent the difficulty my learned friends and
myself feel in endeavouring to discharge our
duty.

The LORD CHIEF JUSTICE : There is nothing
so distressing to those who have to administer
justice as the slightest manifestation of approbation or disapprobation.   I trust there will be no
repetition of it.   Every one ought to wait until
both sides have been heard before forming an
opinion one way or the other.

Mr. HAWKINS : I assure your lordship I find
it almost impossible to discharge my duty.   I
know that your lordship and the jury are most
anxious to hear the case patiently to the end.

The LORD CHIEF JUSTICE : As I said before,
I do hope there may be no more of these unseemly
interruptions.

Mr. HAWKINS (to witness) : Suppose the local
superioress had said you stole a book, would you,
in writing to the mother superioress, say that you
had?—I would not.

Cross-examination continued : At the commission the summary of the charges was read to me.
In some instances I was informed which of the
sisters had given information respecting the
charges.   I was not allowed to give any explanation of the charges, except when my uncle put
questions to me.   When the charge was read to
me, I was asked whether I was guilty or not ,
and I said "Yes" or "No" according to circumstances.   I was two or three hours the first day,
and an hour on the second day, before the commission.   I understood that no charges would be
allowed to be made against the sisters or against
the superioress.   After the charges were made,
in a few instances statements of the sisters were
read in support of them.   I don't remember that
I made a series of charges against the mother
and the sisters.   I merely gave an explanation
when asked to do so.   I repeatedly asked for the
clothes I had been wearing to be produced, but
they were not produced.   Father Porter interrupted me frequently when I was giving explanations.   He said I held no office, which was not
true.   Dr. O'Hanlan was put upon the commission at the instance of my uncle.   My finger
became sore on account of the work I had to do.
I did not wear a rag on it because my thimble was
too large.   The superioress took away my silver
thimble, and made me put a brass one on my
sore finger.   She did not state that my own thimble
was too large for me.   I knew, after the bishop
wrote, that I was free to leave the convent whenever I liked, and that they were anxious to get
rid of me, but I would not leave voluntarily.   I
was not permitted to leave my cell after my dress
was taken.   I was confined within the four walls

of my room, and one of the sisters held the door. I wanted to leave the room, but they would not permit me to do so. Mrs. Star kept back a letter I wrote to my brother. I wrote a letter to Mrs. Star saying that I would never go of my own free will. I wrote that letter with my brother. My brother said my friends would take legal steps. My brother brought a physician (Sir Henry Cooper) to see me, and then took me away. From 1862 down to the year 1866 I never expressed a wish to go and was refused. I refused to leave because Mrs. Star had written to several convents, and I did not know where I should be sent. I never heard that my remaining there was disturbing the peace and quietness of the establishment.

Re-examined by the SOLICITOR-GENERAL: We had no access to the printed book of customs, which was kept by the superioress in her drawer. I never knew of any letters being withheld from the other sisters. In the case of the illness or the death of any of the relations of the sisters their letters were not withheld, but they were condoled with and kindly treated, and their friends were written to. It was open to the penitent to tell what had passed in confession, although it was not open to the priest to do. No person, however, has a right to make the penitent tell. Manifestations of conscience are quite different from confession.

Now, as to this very grave matter about having worn Mrs. Kennedy's boots for an hour or so. You say the Cardinal was coming to visit the convent?—Yes.

Cardinal Wiseman, I presume?—Yes.

And everything, I suppose, was put in order, and made to look as nice as possible for his reception?—That is so.

You thought your own boots were too old and too shabby to appear before him?—They were.

The SOLICITOR-GENERAL: You wished, in fact, to put your best foot foremost. (Laughter.) It is a very serious matter. (Renewed laughter.)

Re-examination continued: Those two letters (produced) are from my sister Jane. I did not see the first until some time after it was received. (The letters were read, and the second attributed her silence to illness.) Upon the receipt of the second of those letters they were both given to me.

The LORD CHIEF JUSTICE: I suppose there is nothing in any of those letters which was in any way objectionable?

The SOLICITOR-GENERAL: Not a word, my lord.

Re-examination continued: I was not allowed to bring any charge against the sisters or the superioress at the commission.

The LORD CHIEF JUSTICE: Do you mean to say that if you were charged with an offence before the commission you were not allowed to give an explanation of your conduct, if such an explanation involved a charge against either the sisters or the superioress?

Witness: That was the case, my lord.

The LORD CHIEF JUSTICE: I am not aware, Mr. Solicitor-General, whether your attention has been directed to the statements which were laid before the commission, and upon which Mr. Hawkins's cross-examination was founded. I think you should have a copy of them.

The SOLICITOR-GENERAL: We applied for a copy of them in May last, my lord, and were refused by the bishop, on the ground that they were privileged communications. They have been, however, furnished to the other side. I saw them for the first time when they were produced by the bishop on his subpœna.

The LORD CHIEF JUSTICE: I think you should have a copy of them before the witness finally leaves the box. You will then better understand the case to be set up against you. I look upon them as being in evidence.

Mr. MELLISH: They have never been put in evidence, my lord.

The LORD CHIEF JUSTICE: They have been in my custody all through the trial; but, if they are not in evidence, I can make no order respecting them.

The SOLICITOR-GENERAL: Perhaps my learned friend will give me a copy voluntarily.

Mr. MELLISH desired that his learned friend should put the papers in evidence.

The LORD CHIEF JUSTICE: Sentence was pronounced by the commissioners upon the plaintiff upon these statements. Other evidence there was none; and no person accustomed to the administration of law would call them evidence at all. Witnesses were not examined, and the plaintiff had not an opportunity of making a single statement in respect of them, and they were never submitted to her. As a matter of justice, the counsel for the plaintiff ought to be permitted to see what charges are to be made against her, and there is no other means of their knowing what they are, unless these papers are produced. Therefore, as a matter of fairness and justice, they ought to be produced, and copies of them given to the Solicitor-General. If they are not produced it will give room to the Solicitor-General to observe most strongly upon their absence.

The SOLICITOR-GENERAL here stated that in May, 1868, the plaintiff's solicitors wrote to the bishop, asking for inspection and copies of these statements, and his solicitor, after some delay, replied:—"His Lordship desires me to inform you that as these documents related to the discipline and good government of the convent, and were supplied for his own information as ecclesiastical judge and superior, he felt bound to regard them as privileged communications and cannot therefore furnish copies of them." His Lordship, however, furnished copies of them to the other side, so that it seemed they were only privileged as against one party. (A laugh.)

Mr. MELLISH: Well, my lord, what do you wish me to do in the matter?

The LORD CHIEF JUSTICE: Well, I think that in common fairness you ought to let the other side see them.

Mr. MELLISH: Why does not my learned friend put them in?

The LORD CHIEF JUSTICE: Why, you can hardly expect him to make evidence against his client of statements he has never seen, and which she never had even read to her.

Mr. MELLISH: Then, why are they wanted at all?

The LORD CHIEF JUSTICE: Because from the announcement of an intention to call the defendants, it may be inferred that these statements which they made before the Commissioners will form the basis of their present evidence against the plaintiff, and it is but reasonable that she should know what they were, especially as to this moment she had never heard their contents.

One of the jury stated that the statements were signed by the different sisters who made them.

Mr. MELLISH : If your lordship has read these statements, you will know that in Mrs. Star's there is one which puts us in this great difficulty—that to the minds of people generally it might convey a meaning quite different from what it would convey among the inmates of convents.

The LORD CHIEF JUSTICE : I must say that this statement was one which would be calculated to produce a strong impression on the minds of the Commissioners.

Mr. MELLISH said he thought not, and added

that no use of that part of the statement had been made in cross-examination.

The LORD CHIEF JUSTICE : Well, take your own course.

The SOLICITOR-GENERAL : All I can do, my lord, is to ask the other side for copies.

Mr. MELLISH : Rather than that my learned friend should make the refusal matter of observation, he shall have them.

The LORD CHIEF JUSTICE : Well, as the jury do not wish to sit late on Saturday, we will adjourn, and before our next meeting you will have seen copies.

The SOLICITOR-GENERAL expressed his obligations.

The Court then adjourned till Monday.

FIFTH DAY.—*Monday, Feb. 8.*

THE re-examination of the plaintiff, Miss Saurin, by the Solicitor-General was resumed :— I may have told my attorney that the mother-superioress pulled the clothes off my bed. He could only have heard it from me.

The SOLICITOR-GENERAL : I have no right to give evidence, my lord : but I certainly have the fact stated in my brief, and many other things which I did not think it necessary to open.

Re-examination continued : The sisters had "leaves" to borrow and lend boots to each other. I never recollect any one being told to wear less clothes except myself. I did not sew my clothes together so as to make them greater in substance though less in number. I was asked about it at the commission, and I explained that, according to the usual custom, I mended one old article with the best part of another old article. The watch that was taken from me had been given to me by my father. I told Mrs. Star as I had told the rev. mother at Baggot-street, that my father had lent me the watch. He wished me to keep it, but I told him that I should give it to the superioress, and that she might give it to whom she would. He said he had given me other things which were gone, such as silver crosses, and that he would not therefore give me the watch, but would lend it, so that being his it might not be given away. There was an inscription on it—my name, and "the gift of her loving father." I pointed that out to the rev. mother, with the necessary explanation.

Was there one of the priests at Hull with whom you had a conversation from time to time ?—Yes, but never an unnecessary conversation.

But did you converse with a priest ?—Never, except upon business.

Did you ever seek to attract his notice particularly ?—I never remember to have done so.

Well, did you do so frequently ?—I am quite sure I never did such a thing at all.

When he was in the convent, were you in a state of excitement ?—Oh, never.

Well, I must ask you. Did you particularly try to attract his attention ?—No.

Did you purposely and constantly put yourself in his way ?—I never did.

Never ?—I never did such a thing.

Well then, I take it that you never did so in the presence of Mrs. Star and Mrs. Kennedy ?—I never did it at all.

Do you know Miss Collingwood—Sister Mary? —Yes.

The LORD CHIEF JUSTICE : Sister Mary what? They are all Sister Marys.

The SOLICITOR-GENERAL : She was a lay sister, my lord. (To witness) : Was she at the schools with you ?—Yes.

Were you in her presence in company with any priest ?—I never was. A priest may have come into the school.

Do you remember going on your knees before the priest, pulling things out of his hand, and entreating him to go with you ?—I am certain I never did such a thing in my life.

In school ?—Never anywhere.

Do you recollect anything that could give a colour to such a charge ?—No, indeed I do not. I never had an idea of such a thing.

Do you remember one of the sisters having died, and having a medal attached to her scapular ?—I remember a sister dying, but nothing about the medal.

Had not sister Catherine a medal when she died ?—I never heard of it.

I am sorry to be obliged to ask you ; but did you take a medal from her dead body which she had expressed a wish to be buried with her ?— Oh, no, no ; I did not.

Of that you are certain ?—I am certain. She was greatly attached to me and I to her. I should be sorry indeed to have interfered with any wish she expressed.

Do you remember having heard another sister saying she had lost a medal ?—I never heard anything about the loss of a medal until to-day.

I am obliged to ask you. Did you take a medal belonging to any sister ?—Never in my life.

Now you have been asked about school-children's dinners. Did you take any food belonging to the children ?—Never. Sometimes children were left with me about a year old, and the mothers would leave some food for them—some bread or biscuit. I had charge of it, and gave it to the children. That is all I know.

You kept it merely to give it to them when they wanted it?—Yes.

But you never took any part of the children's dinners?—Never the smallest particle.

I must ask you the question in another form. If any of the children had a nice bit of pastry, have you ever taken any of it for yourself?—Never in my life. I did not hear of such a thing until something like it was spoken of at the commission about using the children's food; but it did not convey to my mind what the question you ask does.

Were you in the habit of not eating dinners and meals when the superioress was present, but of making a good dinner afterwards?—I never did such a thing.

I understand you to have told my friend that you never struck or pinched the children?—I never did.

Did you ever take note-paper or envelopes?—I presumed once to take a sheet of note-paper and an envelope, and I told of it myself.

Were you in the habit, behind the back of the superioress or local superioress, of making mischief with respect to them?—Not once in my life.

Have you told stories of them?—No; I am sure I never did.

This closed the examination of the plaintiff, which had lasted the greater part of four days.

The next witness was the plaintiff's mother, Mrs. Saurin, who stated that from her earliest years she took an interest in visiting the poor in her neighbourhood. She said,—Two other of my daughters are in a convent, and a son is a Jesuit priest. She was very desirous for a long time of becoming a nun, though I was not desirous of it. Finally we consented, and she passed her novitiate at Baggot-street. She appeared happy and contented there. On the occasions of my visits there I saw the mother superior and the sisters, and I had every reason to believe she lived happily among them. The proposal for her removal to England took me by surprise, and I went to expostulate against it. Her uncle, the Rev. Mr. Mathews, saw the Archbishop about it. The summer after she went, in September, 1856, I went over to Clifford to see her. She then seemed happy, and the mother superior seemed kind to her. Shortly after that (next year) Mrs. M'Keon and Mrs. Star came over to Dublin, and I went there to see them. My daughter had written to me that the mother superior wished to see me. I had an interview with Mrs. Star, who said my daughter was quite well, and very happy, and would write every month. That reconciled me to her remaining at Clifford. After that I had letters from her and Mrs. Star expressing the same feeling of satisfaction. At a later period, in 1861, I gave them to the Rev. Mr. Mathews to show how changed she was.

At this point the Rev. Mr. Mathews, the uncle of the plaintiff, was called upon to produce these letters, and said he had given them to the bishop.

Mr. MELLISH said the bishop was unfortunately unwell, but had left his papers, which would be searched in order to discover them.

They could not, however, be found.

The witness was cross-examined by Mr. MELLISH as to his having given them to the bishop, and he persisted in his statement. He further stated that in January, 1866, he wrote to the bishop for them in these terms:—

"I have only now, before closing this correspondence, to request you to enclose me the three letters of Mrs. Star to Mrs. Saurin, which I left with your lordship at York."

That letter was not answered to me, but there was a letter to Mr. Roberts, the plaintiff's solicitor, to the effect that he had a recollection of Mr. Mathews having shown him some letters, but he had no recollection of ever having had them in his possession.

The LORD CHIEF JUSTICE : No doubt they have been mislaid. It was some years ago.

The SOLICITOR-GENERAL : No doubt, my lord. All I want is to lay a foundation for secondary evidence of their contents.

The LORD CHIEF JUSTICE : We may now have the contents of the letters from the Rev. Mr. Mathews.

The rev. gentleman then stated that the general character of the letters was that they were highly commendatory of the plaintiff.

The LORD CHIEF JUSTICE : Was there any expression of dissatisfaction?

The Rev. Mr. MATHEWS : Not the slightest. On the contrary, the very opposite. They expressed the highest satisfaction.

The examination of Mrs. Saurin was then resumed : My recollection, she said, of the letters quite concurs with that which has just been stated. In the summer of 1861 I visited my daughter. I had visited her several times before and found everything going on satisfactorily. In the autumn of 1861 my husband was very ill, and I was anxious that my daughter should come over to see him. I wrote to the mother superior to express that wish. (Letter called for.)

A letter was produced in which was this passage :—

Mr. Saurin is much worse, and his illness may at any time prove fatal.

The LORD CHIEF JUSTICE observed that this showed there had been a previous letter.

Witness stated that she had no answer from Mrs. Star. Mr. Saurin got worse, and she wrote again in a more pressing manner. To this Mrs. Star sent this answer :—

My dear Mrs. Saurin,—I am sorry to refuse to comply with any wish of yours which may occasion pain to you. I assure you nothing would give me greater pleasure than to afford you any comfort and consolation in my power. So far from keeping her from being near you, I should be willing to allow her to return to Ireland altogether, if by so doing unhappiness could be prevented ; but, for the present, a visit is impossible, for reasons I cannot explain.

To this Mrs. Saurin said she replied in these terms :—

My dear Rev. Mother,—I cannot say how pained I am in being obliged to enter upon matters personal. You say at present a visit is impossible. I take it in a short time you will be able to let Mr. Saurin have the pleasure of seeing our daughter. How is it I never receive any answer to my letters? I always felt that in letting our child be a religious, she did not abandon what was always with her ; a duty, obedience to parental authority ; and I feel that I have still a right to hear from her frequently. Can it be that she has willingly given up this duty? Or have her letters been withheld, and has she become a slave? To neither of these conditions will I ever subscribe. You are the last person I should wish to break terms with, but I must insist upon our natural rights being respected.

And there was another letter from Mrs. Saurin, in which there were these expressions :—

The dear sister (her daughter) has made such an appeal to your generosity, I hope you will yield to it, &c.

Mrs. Saurin stated that at this time she had written several letters, which had not been answered. At last she wrote this:

Dear Mother Superior, — Your note afflicts me. Mr. Saurin wished to have taken a journey to see his daughter, but could not. He feels it a great privation to have a child beyond a reasonable reach of seeing her. His health and all our ages make it distressing. Perhaps it was wrong not to make an application to the bishop, but should these " peculiar circumstances " pass away it would save us all a great deal of trouble. I trust you will be able to give me a definite idea of the time when Mr. Saurin may expect to have the happiness of seeing his daughter.

Then, having no answer, Mrs. Saurin said she wrote again in October, 1862 :—

Dear Rev. Mother,—I am disappointed in not hearing from you. I am pained to intrude my private affairs, but the peculiar difficulties oblige me to do so. I am sorry to inform you that Mr. Saurin is worse, and that he is labouring under a disease which may at any time prove fatal. This is a state of things which I do not like to make known to our daughter, as it might overwhelm her. He is most anxious to see her when you think proper to permit her to visit Drogheda to see him. He wishes also to arrange his temporal affairs, and one of the conditions of our giving our consent to her going to England was that she should come to Ireland in circumstances such as these. Dr. Cullen sanctioned the arrangement, and you promised me that it should be so when I met you in Dublin. Hoping to hear from you, I remain, &c.

Then came an answer from the defendant, Mrs. Star, dated November 7, 1861 :—

Dear Mrs. Saurin,—I regret exceedingly to hear that Mr. Saurin's health is still declining. It would afford me the greatest pleasure to be able to allow your daughter to come over and see him if it were possible. I cannot explain the private affairs of the community, and can only repeat that she cannot go at present ; nor can I say when she can, nor if she ever can visit Ireland. It entirely depends on circumstances over which I have no control, and these obstacles may last for many years. I was no party to any arrangement for her to visit you. If once a sister leaves one diocese for another, the former superior has no control over her. The only promise I made I fulfilled, by taking her to Ireland on a former occasion. The only way in which I can meet your wishes is this. If you can arrange with any Irish community to take her permanently, I will endeavour to manage for her removal, but I should require to hear from the rev. mother that she is willing to receive her before I make the application to the

bishop. She told me last year that her father meant to leave property to the other children, in which case an arrangement might be made. The sum of £250 paid as dowry to the Baggot-street house was not transferred to us. Nor have we received the interest upon it. The custom is that the dowry belongs to the house where the profession takes place, &c.

To this the witness said she wrote this answer :—

Dear Rev. Mother,—I am in receipt of your letter, and I must say it is quite explicit; But either you or our daughter must be under a gross mistake about his intentions as to his disposition of his property. If he does anything, it will be of his own free will. You are mistaken as to the amount furnished to Baggot-street ; it was considerably above £300, and to that she has a right, by every law, human and divine. Her going to England to assist in working the mission there was on the condition I expressed at Dublin —that she should return when desired. And though the sum of £300 was small, you must know that many a good nun has not had a third part of that amount. I should be satisfied that she should remain wherever her superiors might decide ; but her rights I must maintain. I trust she is in good health. She does not answer our letters. It was promised that she should write to us every month.

[All this correspondence was in the autumn of 1861.]

The witness then continued her evidence.—In January, 1862, I saw the Rev. Mr. Mathews, and he made a communication to me. In consequence of that I went to Hull to see Mrs. Star. My daughter was at Clifford then. At Hull I saw first Mrs. Kennedy, and asked her what was the matter about my daughter. She said Mrs. Star, the mother superior, would tell me. Mrs. Star then saw me, and I asked what my daughter had had done. She said she had a light in her cell when she went to bed, and told untruths, &c. I said I would go to Clifford to see my daughter. She said if I went without a note from her I could not see her, and she gave me a note, with which I went to Clifford. At first I was refused access to my daughter. Then I said I had a note from the mother superior, and I was admitted. I saw my daughter from the door, but she did not come to me nor speak to me, and she seemed dull. Mrs. M'Keon then came in. At first she refused me leave to see her. At last she came to me. She was crying. I said, " My dear child, are you a prisoner?" I told her Mrs. Star's complaints, and asked her about them. She said she did her best, &c. I was there about two hours. I could not say how much of that time I was with my daughter alone. Mrs. M'Keon came in and out a good deal. My daughter made a complaint to me. I asked the cause of the great change I observed in her. On former occasions she seemed happy and comfortable, but now she appeared very much afflicted. The witness went on to state that in 1863 she lost a son, and wrote to her daughter (the plaintiff) about it, but it was some time before she heard she was aware of it. In September, 1863, she went to Clifford and saw her daughter. Both of us (said the witness) were much affected. She made statements to me. In consequence of that

I went to Hull to see Mrs. Star. She came into the room and stood looking at me for some moments without speaking to me. I asked her if she did not know me. She said yes. I asked after my daughter. She said she was at school. I afterwards saw her; she seemed very ill. She looked cold and badly clad. I communicated with the Rev. Mr. Mathews, and since then I have been guided by his advice.

Mrs. Saurin was then cross-examined by Mr. MELLISH, who asked her as to complaints made by Mrs. Star as to her daughter's disregard of the rules, &c., and also as to the circumstances of the interviews, with a view to show that she had seen her daughter alone as long as she pleased. She was further pressed as to whether Mrs. Star had not in 1861 suggested her daughter's removal.

Did she not ask you to remove her daughter, and say that if you didn't do so, she should be compelled to write to inform the bishop?—No; she never said anything about it.

Did she not recommend that your daughter should be removed to another community?—She said nothing about it.

Did you not suggest that she should be removed to Hull?—I said I thought that if she went to Hull, and they became reconciled, it would be better, and all this unpleasantness might pass away.

The witness was pressed a good deal with a view to show that this showed confidence in Mrs. Star, and a desire to bring her daughter more closely under her eye. (It should be explained here that the plaintiff was at Clifford and Mrs. Star at Hull.) The witness, however, said that what she meant was that if Mrs. Star had her with her and treated her with more kindness, they would be reconciled.

The LORD CHIEF JUSTICE: Perhaps the fair effect of the witness's evidence on this point is that she thought that if her daughter was taken to reside with Mrs. Star they would be reconciled and renew their old friendship.

The witness was then pressed a good deal as to the circumstances of the later interviews, and especially whether she had not been very violent, so that Mrs. M'Keon was afraid of her, all which she smilingly denied.

The next witness was the plaintiff's father. He said he had paid £300 as his daughter's dowry at Baggot-street—£50 first and £250 afterwards. The action, he said, was brought with his sanction.

Cross-examined.—He said he had received the following letter from Mrs. Star:—

Dear Mr. and Mrs. Saurin,—I am very sorry I should be obliged to write, but necessity compels me. I had hoped that the Rev. Mr. Mathews would have removed your daughter, Miss Susan Saurin; but, as no one has come to take her, I have to request you that you will remove her as speedily as possible. The bishop has absolved her from her vows, and required her to leave. While she remains here, though he does not wish to employ force, he will consider her and have her treated as a secular, and not as a religious. Also the bishop will remove the convent from Hull as a last resource. In conclusion, I have to entreat you not to force the bishop to use extreme measures, which can have no other effect than to add to your sufferings.

To this, on the 11th of February, the witness replied in these terms:—

Madam,—I have received your extraordinary letter. There is not much feeling mingled with its contents. I have had no authorized demand from the bishop, who, I am satisfied, would not sanction so cruel a course as is traced in your heartless letter. I am not in a position to comply with your last demand, and I am glad I have not the responsibility of giving an opinion upon your conduct.

To this Mrs. Star replied:—

Dear Mr. Saurin,—I am sorry you have felt hurt by the contents of my letter. I had no intention of giving you any pain that could be avoided; but the bishop is pressing for the withdrawal of your daughter, and I have to request you either to send for her, or, if you prefer it, can send her home at once on hearing that this course will meet your convenience. As the dowry paid upon her profession was received at Baggot-street, she has no claim upon our community, and in justice to their funds I am compelled to object to such a burden upon them. If you contend to refuse a home to your daughter, let me know, that I may take steps to find her one elsewhere.

To this there was no answer. The witness next received a letter from the bishop's secretary, dated February 20, 1866.

"Dear Sir,—The bishop desires me to say he has seen your letter to the superioress of the Hull convent, in which you state that you have received no authorized demand from him requiring the removal of your daughter from the convent, and he desires me to say that the demand was made by his direction and sanction; and that he saw the letter before it was sent to you."

To this the witness replied, in a letter dated February 22:

I am in receipt of your letter informing me that he has authorized Mrs. Star to write the letter I have already received. I am at a loss to understand what provision is contemplated for the future of my daughter. I cannot hold the authors of this proceeding blameless; and I am resolved, while anxious to discharge the duty I owe as a good Catholic to the Church—I am equally resolved to have some regard for the future position of my daughter.

The next witness was the Rev. T. Mathews, the Roman Catholic clergyman of St. Mary's, Drogheda, the uncle of the plaintiff. He was examined by the SOLICITOR-GENERAL, and stated as follows:—I am uncle of the plaintiff, and parish priest of Drogheda. I remember her speaking to me of her entering a convent. I recommended her parents to accede to her wishes, as she persisted. I was present in 1853 when she was professed. I heard that my niece was desired to join the new house of Clifford. Her parents applied to me, as they objected to her going to England.

By the JUDGE.—It is entirely at the discretion of the superior whether she should remain or not?—It is not entirely at the discretion of the superior. It was positively arranged with the Archbishop that she should return if she wished. I was in the habit of coming to England every

D

summer. I almost invariably saw my niece on those occasions. Down to 1861 I always saw her at Clifford. Until this year nothing could appear to be going better with my niece. I saw Mrs. Star once or twice, and was always received kindly both by my niece and her superior. Entire satisfaction was expressed by both. I was never asked her to correct any fault on the part of my niece. I almost always celebrated mass. It was the usage and custom to do so. Mrs. Star expressed herself pleased that I should do so. In September I again visited my niece at Clifford. I there celebrated mass. I think my niece expressed an opinion that she would like to go back to Ireland. She made no complaint, but I considered she said this as though the right to return still existed. In March, 1862, I received a letter from my niece—a scrap of paper, written in pencil, expressing her desire to leave. I am certain there was no complaint in it. Shortly before this I received a letter from Mrs. Star. This is one of the three letters I handed to the bishop on March 13, 1862.

The letter was then read. It was as follows :—

Rev. and dear Sir,—I am sorry to be obliged to write to you on a subject which I am sure will cause you pain. You are not ignorant of Sister Scholastica's wish to leave the community, and therefore I need only request you to obtain her admission into another community as soon as possible. She has committed the most grave offences, which call for severe punishment, and I must hope that in charity to her you will remove her as quickly as you can, otherwise I must appeal to the bishop to have her relieved from her vows, which are no longer an occasion of merit, but of sin. I will wait a week to hear from you before taking a decisive step. It will be necessary for me to hear directly from the superioress of the convent willing to receive her, as I could not let her leave in uncertainty," &c.

To this the rev. gentleman replied in a letter, dated March 24, 1862.

Dear Rev. Mother,—I am very much pained to think anything should occur in the relations of your sisterhood to render it desirable that my niece should go into another community. I cannot form a judgment on the merits of your statement, as I am in total ignorance of the causes of your displeasure with her. I own I am surprised at it, as she was always most exemplary, and I understood this to be one of the reasons you sought to have her removed with you to England. I should be glad if I could run over to England and see to the merits of this unpleasant affair, but this is a busy time with us; and as I hope all matters may yet run smooth I suppose it will be time enough after Easter. I do not wish to prejudge the case, but if I am to be concerned in it I shall endeavour to do justice to all parties. We are all under the wise and holy rule of God's Church, and we must abide by her decisions. I hope this arrangement will meet your views. I have not informed her mother of your letter, as she might think of something desperate. If you should not object, perhaps you will give me the address of the ordinary that I may communicate with him, and that all matters may be canonically determined.

To this the superior returned this answer, dated April 3, 1862 :

Dear and Rev. Sir,—I shall expect that by Easter you will have all arrangements complete for the removal of your niece. The address of the bishop (Dr. Cornthwaite) is at York. He is going to Rome. I must beg you to remove her as soon as possible. There is no use in applying to Baggot-street. The superiors there know her too well to receive her. The only course is to take her to Drogheda, where your influence may obtain her admission. Here she is, apparently, in a wretched state of mind, and it would be a kindness to her to settle the matter quickly.

The witness said he had received the following from his niece, the plaintiff—:

Convent, Clifford, March 1862.

Dear Uncle,—It seems a long time since I wrote, and I am going to trouble you with a few lines. I hope you are well. I do not see the least chance of my going to Ireland. The rev. mother has no idea of letting me leave for a long time. She does not know how I wish to go. I am sure she is afraid of our family. I could see that when we were in Hull. At one time she said that if any of us once took a thing in our heads we should keep to it. She complained of mamma's letter as "impertinent." She made a great mistake in some things she told me, which I can explain. I did not venture to say anything. You must not think me unhappy, and in health I never was better. The only thing is that I am unsettled, nor do I ever think I shall be here.

The witness went on to state that, in May 1862, he came over to England, and wrote to the mother superior this letter, from Liverpool :—

Dear Rev. Mother,—As soon as my Easter engagements would permit, I came to England to have this matter adjusted. Unfortunately, I came on the eve of the departure of the bishop for Rome, and I thought it not respectful to proceed to Hull and enter into the examination of a subject which belongs to him. You remember your second letter was of a very grave character, and I considered that only a responsible and competent authority should deal with it.

The witness stated that he saw the bishop on this occasion, who said that was the first he had heard of the matter. At this (said the witness) I was equally surprised, knowing the power belonged to him. The bishop said he would appoint a commission, and I said I should be satisfied if he would stay the action of Mrs. Star. The bishop (he said) gave me an order to see my niece. I took the order and proceeded to Clifford and saw my niece. I saw her alone, Mrs. M'Keon being present part of the time. I apprised her of the contents of Mrs. Star's letters. She appeared very much surprised. I told her that the bishop had given permission for her to write to him. This seemed greatly to surprise her, as she did not know that she had done anything to require it. Everything seemed to be going on well between her and Mrs. M'Keon. The witness went on to state :—In 1863 I was at Harrogate, and went to see my niece at Clifford. She appeared very much reserved ; she declined to walk into the garden. She refused, and I found that she was not permitted to do it. She made no complaints about herself. I experienced much reserve towards myself from the superior. I celebrated mass on this occasion. There was nothing absolutely unkind, but not that warmth displayed towards me as on other occasions. I understood that the bishop was shortly coming to the convent. I wrote to him on my return to Ireland, asking him to see Sister Scholastica. The witness went on to state :—In 1864 I went to Hull. It was about 6 p.m. when I got to the convent. After some time waiting a sister came in and asked, in an impetuous manner, if I had got an order from the bishop. I said that I did not require one last year. She said that things were changed ; that one was required now. In a very abrupt and impetuous manner she said that my niece "told lies." She shortly after went out and my niece came in. It was late. I did not wish to stay, and I asked my niece to go to the superior and inquire if she would like me to say mass in the morning, and at what time. She returned and said that the superior declined. I was much shocked at this, and called on the clergy there, and they were most horrified that I should have been refused permission to say mass. I was also refused to say the Benediction after service. After this, when I saw my niece, she came into the room with a quarter-hour glass in her hand—a most unusual thing ; it had never occurred before. The witness went on to state the following correspondence with the bishop. On the 28th of July, 1865, he wrote this letter to the bishop :—

My dear Lord,—Shortly before your visit to Rome I had an interview with you relative to the unpleasantness exhibited by the rev. mother towards my neice, at present at Clifford. Your Lordship kindly promised me to investigate the matter by investigation or otherwise. I hope by this time you are safely returned. I do not wish to say one word to influence your judgment, but in truth, I must say that from her childhood I never knew material for a better nun than there was in her. I feel that the rev. mother cannot have had much experience, as she has not been long in the Church, being a convert from Protestantism. Your lordship can judge better from the enclosed.

The witness received the following letter from the Bishop, dated September 15, 1865:

Dear Father Mathews,— I wished to have seen you, as I wished to speak to you as to your niece, to induce you to have her recalled home. I feel myself under the necessity of taking the initiative, and the visit of her brother is the most fitting occasion for a settlement. I have tried to follow out your wishes, but I have come to the conclusion that the best interests of the community require her removal. I will only add that her dowry will be repaid upon application to the mother-house. Your faithful servant in Christ,   R. ✠ CORNTHWAITE.

On the 20th of September the bishop wrote to the Rev. Mr. Mathews this further letter :—

I wrote you on the 15th to inform you that being under the necessity of requiring the removal of your niece, I intended to place her under the charge of her brother, and I then expected to hear from you in reply. Her brother, however, refused to take charge of her, and he wished to see me, but I was from home. Her brother wished the whole matter to be referred to you, and I wrote to ask you if you or any of your family intend to take steps for the removal of your niece. I hope so, for your sake and hers. If I have to take steps for the purpose I shall feel bound to do so. Her brother has raised two questions. He doubts the validity of the dispensation, and he speaks of his sister as a suffering saint, and makes a serious charge against the community. This representation has in no degree affected my first decision, and I have to request the removal of your niece. I feel I ought to endeavour to satisfy you, and therefore in this case I should appoint a commission to inquire into the whole matter, leaving you at liberty to attend. The rev. mother told me such a course would be painful, but she would be willing to agree to it if I desired it.

On the same day, the 20th of September, the Rev. Mr. Mathews wrote to the bishop in answer to his first letter :—

My dear Lord,—Your lordship's letter of the 15th has only just come to hand, and I cannot say how distressed and afflicted I am. I have always had the most unbounded confidence in your lordship's discernment and justice, and there must have been something surely fearful to necessitate this awful step. In the absence of all knowledge as to the cause I make no remark, as a little time must develope the whole matter. I will communicate with the parents, who must decide as to the future of poor Sister Scholastica. In the position of the case I am glad I have not that responsibility ; that responsibility rests upon the parents. I fear that their long pent-up feelings of exasperation may carry them too far. I will try to do my best as *amicus religionis* to have the matter satisfactorily adjusted.

On the 22nd of September the Rev. Mr. Mathews wrote thus in answer to the bishop's second letter :—

I am in receipt of your lordship's second letter. I have not been able to consult with the heads of the family. Your lordship's mode of dealing with the case appears extremely fair. If the parents desire an inquiry, an impartial tribunal such as that your lordship proposes must be satisfactory to them. It certainly would satisfy me. If the parents leave the case in my hands, as I think they will, I shall be happy to make all matters, as far as I can, and as far as justice to all parties concerned will allow, harmonize with your lordship's views. Though the course proposed will meet all the requirements of this painful case, though it is distressing to me, I trust I shall ever bow to the demands of justice, and concur in any course necessary to serve the interests of religion. If anything has been said that might annoy your lordship, you must make allowance for a natural feeling.

The witness was then examined with reference to some allusions in the bishop's letter, as to the authority to grant a nun's dispensation from her vows, and what dispensation really implied. He said that according to his view the bishop could not grant it, and that it must involve grave censure. He said—what I mean is that this dispensation must be obtained from Rome, upon a proper representation of well-ascertained guilt of a grave character.

The LORD CHIEF JUSTICE. — The bishop would have no power to give it?—No.

The LORD CHIEF JUSTICE.—And it can only be granted, you say, on the ground of misconduct?—Some misconduct of a grave character, well ascertained.

The LORD CHIEF JUSTICE.—Might it not be obtained on some special ground?—It might, possibly ; but as a general rule, and to the eyes of the world, it must involve some grave censure.

The LORD CHIEF JUSTICE.—Then "dispensation" hardly expresses the meaning of it?—It always appears to involve some grave degree of censure.

The witness went on to state that at this time his niece did not appear to have any idea that the bishop had been applied to with a view to discharge her from her vows. He went on to describe the interview he had with the bishop on the subject of the commission. The bishop, he said, read to me the charges ; they appeared trivial to me. I asked if they were the whole. He said they were the charges. They struck me as trivial—the ordinary faults that would occur in a human being.

By the JUDGE.—The bishop then said those were all the charges. He had a letter from Mrs. Star stating that she was going to Liverpool to see Father Porter, in order that he might be put on the commission, and that she would come over to Leeds to see the bishop. There was a discussion who should be put upon the commission. He said that he wished that persons truly impartial should be put upon it. The names of different persons were discussed by him. I assented to all, although I objected to Mr. Porter's name, as he was a partisan. I understood that he conducted the yearly retreats of the nuns at the convent, and as a delicate way of objecting I said that it was not right that Mr. Porter and Mr. Cunningham should be on the commission. To this he acceded, as I understood. As my niece was from Ireland I proposed that Dr. O'Hanlan should be on the commission, and the bishop considered him a very proper person. He said that if I chose I might be present ; meaning, as I suppose, that I should appear on my niece's behalf. I assented to that. I asked him that the parties making the accusations should be present that they might be cross-examined. I said that I would see to the attendance of Dr. O'Hanlan. Afterwards I wrote to the bishop to signify that Dr. O'Hanlan would act on the commission. The witness went on to state a correspondence which ensued between him and the bishop on the subject of the commission. On the 3rd of November, 1865, the bishop wrote to him :—

I accept Dr. O'Hanlan, and I have already appointed Mr. Porter. I have not settled as to appointing the Vicar-General. If I do I shall appoint five. If any of the family present themselves I will not allow the commission to act, and I require a written promise that in case the decision is adverse to your niece she shall be removed in 24 hours. If she is pronounced innocent, and, as a necessary consequence, if a case of conspiracy is proved against the other sisters, it will be for you to consider whether you will cave her in the community.

To this, said the witness, I returned no answer. I could not accept, and prudence would not allow me to dissent. The bishop wrote me again :—

Rev. and Dear Sir,—I wrote on the 3rd and you have sent me no reply and no promise. If it is not given I shall proceed on my own responsibility. I am aware that threats have been used, but they will not deter me, as I know the well-being of the whole community is at stake.

I (said the witness) had used no threats. I replied to the bishop in these terms :—

On the receipt of your Lordship's letter I saw the parents, and told them that your Lordship promised a fair and impartial constitution of the commission ; and they have authorized me to say that they are prepared to submit to the conditions imposed, that they will remove her (though it would be most painful to them) in the event of the commission finding her guilty. I should be happy if your lordship could be present at the commission, for I have every confidence in your justice.

On the 1st of January, 1866, the bishop (continued the witness) wrote to me stating that he had appointed a commission, consisting of Dr. O'Hanlan, Canon Walker, Canon Chadwick, and Mr. Pinel, with Mr. Porter, and that it would sit on the 10th of January ; and he added :—

To-day I send notice to the sister, as it would not be fair that it should come suddenly upon her. I have communicated nothing to the commissioners, that they may be quite unprejudiced and unfettered.

The witness then described what occurred on the occasion of the holding of the inquiry before the commission, at which he attended with his niece. He went to Hull to see her the day before. I arrived (he said) early in the morning at Hull, and saw my niece after a short time. She had a quarter-hour-glass in her hand. I was only a short time with her. Having travelled all night, I was too cold to stop, there being no fire in the room. My niece told me that she had had no information as to what were the charges against her. I told her generally as well as I could, from the summary of those the bishop had read over to me, but I could not enter into any particulars, as they spread over a period of seven years.

The LORD CHIEF JUSTICE : Was it conveyed to your mind that there was a charge of improper levity with a priest?

Witness : In a general way, but it was rather insinuated than distinctly stated. There was nothing definite. The witness went on to describe what occurred. He objected, he said, to Mr. Porter, as a member of the commission, as he was a partisan, and he showed himself to be so (the witness stated) all through the inquiry—most offensively so. The mere summary of the charges was read, but there were none of the nuns present to support them by testimony, and not even their statements were read over—that is, only portions of them, not the whole of them. He heard those portions for the first time. Moreover, he found the instructions (as they were read over to him) imported that if three-fourths of the commissioners thought the charges not disproved, they were to be considered proved.

The LORD CHIEF JUSTICE here suggested that as the instructions might have been misunderstood by the witness it would be better that they should be produced.

The SOLICITOR-GENERAL said the plaintiff had applied to the bishop for them, but in vain. He now asked the defendant's counsel for them.

They were not, however, produced, and the witness proceeded to describe what transpired. He said the commissioners refused to listen to any recriminatory charges against the nuns, even although they might in his view be really a part of her defence. He protested against this, but in vain. He, however, contrived to elicit from his niece a good deal of the hardships she had undergone, and the "enormities" which had been inflicted upon her, and of which he then heard for the first time; and the witness proceeded to say that he had again and again demanded that the witnesses should be produced, but in vain. The inquiry was held on the 10th and 11th of January. On the 12th he wrote to the bishop :—

I confess to a great disappointment. I hoped your Lordship would have been present. If you had been, common sense and decency would not have been outraged as they have been.

On the 13th of January the bishop wrote to the witness this letter :—

Rev. and dear Sir,—I have received the report of the commission in the case of your niece, and I claim the fulfilment of your promise to remove her. Had all gone in her favour I should have recommended this course, as it would have involved such a grave reproach upon the entire community as to require her removal. But the most important part having been proved against her, her removal becomes necessary. I will absolve her from her vows, but she must accept the dispensation before she leaves my diocese. I regret that I have no choice but to perform so painful a duty.

To this the witness replied in these terms :—

My dear Lord,—I never agreed to remove my niece under any circumstances. I merely stated that her parents authorized me to say that I, having assured them that your lordship had promised a full and impartial investigation, in the event of her being found guilty they would be prepared to remove her. I consider that the late investigation was not full nor impartial, nor such as your lordship promised. I remonstrated with the commissioners, but in vain. I was most anxious that your Lordship should be present. Had you been there you would have prevented an indecent exhibition, which made it worse than a cruel and offensive farce. I have only taken part in the affair as the friend of peace. But the parents feel most intensely the cruelty of the persecutions to which their daughter has been subjected. I am persuaded that if your lordship had been present and heard the details of the mouldy bread kept for her, and the duster put upon her head to wear even to chapel, and the ignominous strippings she had to endure before the reverend mother, and a silence never broken but by insult, your lordship would have assigned punishment in a very different quarter, where every principle of justice and religion had been so shamefully violated. All this, I presume, was without your lordship's knowledge, and I venture to say that such treatment never was dealt out to any "religious" before; and its exposure by any legal proceedings cannot fail to bring infamy upon the superioress, and discredit upon every convent in the three kingdoms. When the commissioners inspected, as well as they could, the clothes of my niece, they expressed their disgust. I presume your lordship will have heard of this. I must say I am sorry that your lordship could not discover any other mode of proceeding, except the removal of my unfortunate niece, whether guilty or not. I think it would be more in accordance with religion and justice to depose and expel the fabricators of false charges than to let all punishment fall on the persecuted sister, whose greatest fault was her patience and long endurance.

The witness said this letter closed his communications on the subject, and this closed his evidence.

SIXTH DAY.—*Tuesday, Feb. 9.*

"END of Act the First" was accomplished to-day, when the Court rose for hasty refreshment a little before two o'clock, and when there was a struggle at the doors between barristers who wanted to get out and all kinds of people who wanted to get in; while the fortunate holders of seats in the back-rows, and up in the gallery, kept their places, and applied themselves to flasks of sherry and packets of sandwiches. The bench, or that part of the Court which is supposed to partake the sacredness of the judgment-seat, was occupied all day—except during the brief interval we have mentioned—by persons whose rank and influence had procured them admission. All the front seats in the body of the Court were taken up by gentlemen in forensic costume, at least half as many wigs as heads being distinguishable between the clerk's table and the gallery at the back. In the crowd behind the last row of barristers many female faces were to be seen; and all the foremost spectators seated in the galleries were ladies, two or three wearing the garb of the convent. The plaintiff did not appear in Court during the proceedings yesterday; but her sister sat on the attorneys' bench directly in front of Mr. Hawkins, whose adverse comments on the case of Sister Scholastica were thus uttered right over the head of the other Miss Saurin. If possible, the court was more densely thronged to-day than it had been since the commencement of the trial; and it was much more orderly, the reproofs which the judge had felt himself called upon to deliver having, it would seem, had their effect. A little laughter was now and then audible; but, so long as judges will joke, and comedy is not denied to counsel, it can hardly be expected of the general public that they should preserve the silent solemnity of a Quakers' meeting. Besides, it would be something like tacit irreverence to disregard the sprightliness of the ermine—and advocates are not like ordinary mortals, if they would rigidly insist on the right of having their quips and cranks received in an awful stillness. That which was really censurable in the behaviour of persons who filled the public space of the Court of Queen's Bench on days prior to to-day, was the noisy demonstration of prejudice. It is by no means in accordance with the national boast which assumes fair-play to be an almost exclusively English institution that loud expressions of feeling should be heard in an English court of justice before half the cause has been set forth.

"Act the Second" was opened by Mr. HAWKINS, when the audience reassembled at two o'clock. In cross-examination of the plaintiff's witnesses, he had not materially shaken the case of the opposite party, nor cleared the way for the advance of his own. Such, at least, might have been the conviction of a perfectly unprejudiced and even indifferent observer—a conviction strengthened at every later stage of Father Mathew's evidence. Some tedious conversation, on the point whether or not another count should be added, delaying the commencement of Mr. HAWKINS' speech for the defence ; but when at last all hindrances were disposed of, and the whole Court had settled down to listen with profound attention, the line of persuasion marked out by the advocate was quickly made apparent. He first sought to impress upon the minds of the jury that strict nature of conventual obligations which would affect the whole question at issue. He read the rules, to show how implicit an obedience was prescribed, and he dwelt strongly on the circumstances under which the vow of a religious life is taken. It was the aim of Mr. HAWKINS to convince the jury that Miss Saurin had mistaken her vocation, and that she ought never to have vowed submission to the strict discipline of the convent. His able speech, for the most part temperate, though sometimes very severe upon the supposed levity and untruthfulness of the plaintiff, was chiefly effective in the elaboration of that main argument with which he started. Faults were detailed on the part of Miss Saurin—faults that would have been trivial but for the vows she had entered into, with a full knowledge of their obligation. On some matters of fact that had already been in evidence, Mr. Hawkins was so unfortunate as to trip. For instance, when he persisted in treating as a surreptitious communication the very letter which the plaintiff had sworn to as having been written at the dictation of Mrs. Star. It was by his fellow-counsel, Mr. MELLISH, that Mr. HAWKINS was at last set right on the subject, and had to give way on a point which he had laboured to invest with an importance really greater than it deserved. Witnesses for the defence were to have been called this afternoon ; but the speech of Mr. HAWKINS occupied the time of the Court till its adjournment ; nor can it be said that the three hours were unprofitably filled by his eloquent address.

The Rev. Thomas Mathews, parish priest of St. Mary's, Drogheda, uncle of Miss Saurin, cross-examined by Mr. HAWKINS : I did not say yesterday that a bishop had no authority over a sister without a faculty from the Pope.

The LORD CHIEF JUSTICE : The witness said, authority to expel.

Mr. HAWKINS : One of the rules is to the effect that the communities are subject to the authority of the diocesan.

Cross-examination continued : I consider that the bishop has no power to absolve a sister from her vows of obedience and poverty until a case is proved.

Has he not power to absolve a sister from all her vows, except the vow of chastity, without the authority of the See of Rome ?—I conceive not.

Mr. HAWKINS said he should contend, under the rules, that there was no necessity for any faculty directed to the bishop to expel a sister.

The LORD CHIEF JUSTICE said he did not think it was of very much importance in the case whether the witness's, or the learned counsel's views were correct.

Mr. MELLISH submitted that, if the bishop had power to expel, and exercised it, the plaintiff was a trespasser in the convent afterwards.

Cross-examination continued : I thought the bishop had read to me the entire of the charges made by the sister. I thought so. I also thought that those were the charges, the digest of which was read at the commission in the way I have explained.

Mr. HAWKINS read the instructions, one of which was that the accused should be called, and that the charges should be severally read to her ; that she should reply in part or detail, in any way that best suited her ; that no comment should be made, and she should then retire ; that, if it should be found that four-fifths of the commissioners agreed that the charges had been proved, each commissioner should give his opinion separately.

The charges were read over ?—So far as I have stated.

Were not the depositions or evidence of the sisters there ?—I believe they were.

Were they not read ?—The summary was, and, as I believe, most of the papers.

Was there anything you desired to read that was not read ?—I declare that it was an entire departure from the arrangement by the bishop with me.

In what respect ?—I asked for liberty to cross-examine the nuns, and I was told the bishop had instructed otherwise.

Was it not the Rev. Dr. O'Hanlan who made the objection to the other sisters being examined? —It was not.

Tell me any charge connected with breach of vows that involved a charge against others.—It was impossible to defend the plaintiff without going into the whole history of the matter. There was a conflict between the two, and it was impossible to defend the one without involving the other.

Tell me one charge.—The general charge of disobedience. How could I defend my niece without asking what had happened—what led to it—how it had been brought about? (Suppressed applause.) There was not either time or circumstance mentioned. The general charge spread over eight or nine years.

Tell me a charge on which she desired to give further information than she did.—I tell you the charges were general, and I found it impossible to defend her with the restrictions imposed.

Was the whole deposition of Mrs. Star read?—I suppose so. They were away from me, and what was read by the secretary he read with great speed.

The LORD CHIEF JUSTICE: It is a great pity these papers have not been produced.

Mr. HAWKINS: They are being copied for the other side.

The LORD CHIEF JUSTICE: Were they like the papers which were produced?—No, my lord. The papers produced were like the summary or digest.

Mr. HAWKINS: Did you ask to have them in your hand?—Not at all; I had no right.

Did you ask to read them when you had the interview with the bishop?—Not at all; it would have been an imputation on his lordship, who, I believe, read them correctly.

He did read them to you?—He did; and I said, when he had done, "My lord, it seems as if one mind had inspired them." (Laughter.)

Did you not, at the commission, make counter-charges against the sisters?—Not one.

Did not your niece complain in your presence that she was scantily clothed?—I made a difference as to charge. I did not conceive the tribunal, as directed by the bishop, had power to entertain any counter-charge.

But you examined your niece upon several matters which involved counter-charges?—I wished to get out all about the hardships she had endured.

Was there any one matter of evidence you desired to give that you had not an opportunity of eliciting?—Yes; several. I was checked, as I have stated.

There is a house for sisters of mercy in your parish?—Yes,

Did you make an application to have your niece received there?—No.

Why?—Because she had a right elsewhere, and that right I was determined to maintain.

Cross-examination continued: The sisters in Drogheda would have been glad to receive her. I do not think any application was made by her or on her behalf for admission into the establishment in Drogheda. The reverend mother there told me she wondered no application had been made. I said that where she had a right to remain she ought to remain.

Is she not desirous now of receiving your niece?—The fashion has not come up. (Laughter.)

The LORD CHIEF JUSTICE: Is your niece desirous of entering a convent again?—Oh, decidedly, my lord.

Mr. HAWKINS: Is not the establishment in Drogheda as small as that at Hull?—It is.

And why, she being desirous to go, and they being, no doubt, willing to receive her, do you not make an application on her behalf?—Because an injustice has been done her, and she would go there with the stigma of having been expelled. (Applause, which was quickly suppressed.)

Cross-examination continued: She is desirous of re-entering Baggot-street. The question as to Drogheda has not been considered.

Re-examined by the SOLICITOR-GENERAL: So far as I can recollect, these papers (produced) were before the commissioners. The charges made by the different sisters, relating to the same charge, were, as well as I recollect, in the same language.

To the Court: I brought the two letters of Mrs. Saurin to the bishop, with the letter of Mrs. Star to myself, to show how much and how recently she was changed, and how unfounded the charges must have been, from the tone of her former letters.

Mr. Patrick Matthew Vincent Saurin, examined by Mr. DIGBY SEYMOUR: I am a brother of plaintiff. I saw my sister at Hull and Clifford several times before 1861. She appeared to be perfectly happy and contented. I accompanied my mother to Clifford in the spring of 1862. Mrs. M'Keon told my mother she could not see her daughter. My mother said, "Oh, my goodness!" and Mrs. M'Keon said such were the rev. mother's orders. My mother asked the reason why, and she said she did not know. My mother then produced Mrs. Star's order, and Mrs. M'Keon asked why it had not been given to her at first. My mother said she felt very much hurt at being obliged to have an order to see her child. Mrs. M'Keon was then very civil to us, and got us refreshments. In January, 1866, I went to Hull alone. I went to the convent and asked to see my sister. After some time I saw her, but she was accompanied by a nun, who, during the greater part of the interview, seemed to be very busy dusting the chairs.

The LORD CHIEF JUSTICE: Did she stay all the time?—No, my lord; she came in and out.

Examination continued: I thought she wished to hear what passed between us, and, in consequence, I spoke very low. This was on the 17th of January, after the commission. On the 13th of March, 1866, I again went over to visit my sister, in consequence of having received the letter of the 25th of February. The same nun—Sister Dawson—came into the reception room before I saw my sister. There was a wardrobe in the room, which the sister locked. When my sister came in I was frightened at her appearance. I kissed her cheek. It was like kissing marble. I was so shocked I could not speak for several minutes. (Witness was here visibly affected.)

To the LORD CHIEF JUSTICE: She was hardly clothed at all, and she wore a rag on the top of her head.

To Mr. DIGBY SEYMOUR: I feared she would not live many days, and I asked her to write as I dictated to the reverend mother; stating that, if she consented, I would take her away at once. I had brought pen and ink with me. The letter stated that she would not leave of her free will, and that if they were determined to put her out, to do so at once, and that I would take her out. (Letter read.) I asked to see Mrs. Star; and she came in, and Mrs. Kennedy and another nun. A sister had brought Mrs. Star the plaintiff's letter.

The LORD CHIEF JUSTICE: It is suggested that you used harsh language to her. Is that so?—Oh, no, my lord.

Examination continued: When Mrs. Star came in—as she had known me before in Dublin—I wished to see whether she would acknowledge me. She did not. I then said, "You are Mrs. Star?" She said "Yes." I was very much affected at the condition of my sister; and I said to Mrs. Star, "Have you any womanly feeling?" or, "Have you any Christian feeling?" and added, "How can you, a religieuse, look on and see the condition to which you have reduced my poor sister?" She turned round to Mrs. Kennedy and smiled sarcastically. I made a motion to take off my top-coat to put it on my sister, and my sister said she would not have it on. Mrs. Star said I might take her. I took my sister by the hand, and said, "Here; do you give her to me, and I will take her and protect her." Mrs. Star said, "No; I will not implicate myself." Soon afterwards she retired. I remained some little time with my sister, who told me she felt very ill. When I went out there was a nun waiting in the hall, who took my sister up stairs.

She seemed to have charge of her?—Yes.

In April I received a letter, dated 18th April, 1866. She said:

My dearest Brother—You promised to come and see me. I would like very much to see you just once more. For weeks I have been ill. I think I will get my request to leave the convent in my coffin.

In consequence of that letter I went over and saw my sister. She appeared even more worn than before. Her clothing was, if not worse, not better. Her condition was such as to make me fearfully alarmed about her. In consequence I saw Sir Henry Cooper. I had seen Mrs. Star before I saw the physician, and asked for permission for him to see her. She said, "You may take her to him." I could not take her out into the town from her appearance and condition. Then I went and saw Sir Henry Cooper, and told him the state of things, and asked him to see her. He came the next morning with me. We were shown into the reception-room. After some time my sister came in, followed by two nuns. I had sent up word that Sir Henry Cooper was with me.

The LORD CHIEF JUSTICE: Did the two nuns come into the room?—They did, my lord.

Examination continued: When I introduced my sister I retired, asking the two nuns to retire also; saying that "This is a medical gentleman, and it is a matter of etiquette that he should see my sister alone." They took no notice of me.

The LORD CHIEF JUSTICE: Did they make any answer?—Not a word.

Examination continued: I remained in the hall for some time, and seeing that they did not co I out, I went in again and asked them to come ome but they would not. It was quite clear to me they wanted to hear what Sir Henry Cooper said to my sister. Sir Henry said, "Oh, do not mind, Mr. Saurin." I asked them again to retire with me, and they would not. I remained in the hall. Sir Henry Cooper came out after some time with my sister, and I asked her whether she had told him all. She said, "Oh, Patrick dear, I could not. They were listening to all I said." Sir Henry Cooper said, "You should have told me all." The two nuns came out into the hall, and remained close to us till Sir Henry went. I did not see Mrs. Star or Mrs. Kennedy on that occasion. Sir Henry told me his opinion afterwards, and in consequence of what he told me I deemed it necessary at once to remove my sister. I brought a cab to the convent next morning. I was brought into a small room, where there was a nice fire. (A laugh.) There I saw Mrs. Star and Mrs. Kennedy. They brought in Mr. Collins, and introduced him. He interfered in the matter, and I asked him what right he had to do

so. He said he was connected with a publication in Hull, and that he would expose the whole matter. I told him it was clear he had been brought there to insult me.

Well, to shorten the matter did you ultimately get your sister?—I did.

And you took her away?—I did.

Cross-examined by Mr. MELLISH: Mrs. Star did not say at the interview in January, she was most anxious that I should take her. I said, "Hand her to me, and I will take her away."

Did she say "All the doors are open"?—No.

And that the windows were open?—No.

Did you ask her to put her hand on her?—I took my sister's hand, and said, "Just give her to me, and I will take her."

Did Mrs. Star say "He wants me to use force —to commit an illegal act"?—She said I wanted her to use force. I wanted her to put her hand in mine and I would take her.

The LORD CHIEF JUSTICE: Why?—Because I knew she had a right there—that she was innocent, and I did not wish her to leave voluntarily.

The LORD CHIEF JUSTICE: It comes to this, you wanted it to be an act of expulsion?—Witness: Yes, my lord.

Mr. MELLISH: Did you not hear that there was a proper secular dress provided for her and that she refused to wear it?—No. I believed there was no other dress provided for her but that which she had on. That was my belief.

In May did you not hear from Mrs. Star that your sister was a secular and was at liberty to go?—No. She said I might take her to the doctor.

Mr. Michael Saurin, examined by Mr. WILLES: I am brother of the plaintiff. I saw her in Clifford in July, 1864, for about ten minutes. The bell rang, and my sister said, "That is for me; I must go." I said I would come again next morning, and she said, "Do so." I called in the morning, and was left in the hall about half an hour. A nun then came to me and said, "You cannot see Sister Scholastica to-day,"—that it was against the rule to see a sister more than once a month. I asked to see the reverend mother, and was told she was engaged. I said I was determined to see my sister, and that it was better I should be allowed. I resolved to get a magistrate's order to see her. I went to Father Trapper, the dean, and Father Motler, who was connected with the convent. Father Mofler went to the convent, but was refused permission for me to see my sister. I asked for a magistrate, but was persuaded to go to Leeds to the bishop. I went, but the bishop was not there. I had to return to Ireland without seeing my sister. I had come expressly to see her. I had not seen her for five years.

Letter from the bishop to Mrs. Star, dated July 17, 1864, read, stating it was a great error of judgment of her refusing permission to Mr. Saurin to see his sister, as he could have compelled her to grant the request; that she ought not to have run the risk of a refusal; and that she should at once write to Mr. Saurin to say she had permission from the bishop to allow plaintiff to be seen.

Reply of Mrs. Star read. She complained of Sister Scholastica as a bad example to the rest of the community, and added that submission was hard, but that she bowed with resignation to the will of the bishop. She added that she had allowed Mr. Saurin, as he had travelled all day, to see his sister for half-an-hour, and that when he called next morning, she "chose a most gentle sister to tell him it was contrary to the rule to allow him to see his sister a second time." (Laughter.)

The LORD CHIEF JUSTICE: Which is the gentle sister? (Renewed laughter.)

Mr. MELLISH: I am not instructed, my lord. (Laughter.)

Letter of the bishop to Mrs. Star read. It stated that his judgment had not turned on rule, but on prudence.

Sir Henry Cooper, examined by the SOLICITOR-GENERAL: I am a physician and magistrate. I saw Mr. Patrick Saurin on the 30th April, 1866. I went with him to the convent next morning, the 1st of May. A nun admitted us at a side-door, and took us into a large front room. We waited there for a quarter of an hour, when Miss Saurin was introduced by two nuns. Miss Saurin wore a secular dress—a very bad dress. I asked her to take a seat in a convenient position. The nuns placed themselves near—sufficiently near to overhear all that was said. Mr. Saurin said he would leave the room, and asked me, did I not wish the nuns to leave the room also? I said that they would not interfere with me, that they might remain. Mr. Saurin then left. He returned, and again suggested that the nuns should retire. Of that, or of anything else that occurred, they took no apparent notice whatever.

To the LORD CHIEF JUSTICE: They could overhear all that took place.

Examination continued: Miss Saurin was badly dressed. Her dress was quite insufficient. The season was particularly inclement for the time of year. The dress was insufficient in quantity. It was coarse.

Was she dressed like a lady?—Certainly not.

Examination continued: She complained of extreme weakness, nausea, want of appetite, great coldness, and that she was getting very thin.

Was she thin?—Yes, very thin. I had occasion to examine her chest. She was exceedingly thin—emaciated. I questioned her as to how it was she had got so thin. She told me she could not eat; and on pressing her on that subject she said that the quality of the food given her was bad.

The LORD CHIEF JUSTICE: That was on your pressing her?—Yes, my lord.

The SOLICITOR-GENERAL: She did not say so at first?—No.

Did you find she was cold?—Very cold, and the circulation very feeble. Her hands were almost blue.

Examination continued: I was there a quarter of an hour—perhaps more. She was in a very weak condition, without actual disease. I could not ascertain medically how she had been reduced to that condition.

But would insufficient and bad food and clothing, bad air, and want of exercise bring about the state of things you saw?—Yes.

Examination continued: It appeared to me she was under restraint. I had to repeat my questions.

Cross-examined by Mr. HAWKINS: Was there anything to prevent her giving you full information?—No.

The LORD CHIEF JUSTICE: Nothing physical, but there may be moral restraint exercised.

Cross-examination continued: I considered she was under restraint from the presence of the nuns. I saw and heard sufficient to form my opinion as to the necessity of removing her, and to give advice as to what should be done. I advised that she should be removed. I do not recollect whether I prescribed for her at that time. She was under my care for some weeks—till the middle of June—after she left the convent.

Was she not in a violent state of excitement at the time you saw her?—On the contrary, she was peculiarly quiet and calm.

The LORD CHIEF JUSTICE: Could you form an opinion whether her condition, languid circulation, cold, weakness, want of appetite, and so on, was the result of any disease?—I could not detect any ailment of any kind. She told me she had been stout and in good health, and I had no reason to doubt that fact.

Did she get better after she left the convent?—Yes; anyhow, when I last saw her, in June, 1866, she was in tolerable health.

Mr. Roberts examined by Mr. DIGBY SEYMOUR: I am attorney for the plaintiff. I was retained in April, 1866, and obtained the opinion of the Right Hon. Mr. Brewster. In May I went to Ireland to make inquiries, and saw Dr. O'Hanlan, amongst others. I spoke to him as to the commission.

Did you, in consequence of what he told you, consider his presence here as a witness for the plaintiff necessary?

Mr. HAWKINS objected.

The LORD CHIEF JUSTICE: It is a very subtle and ingenious way of obtaining his opinion. (Laughter.)

Mr. DIGBY SEYMOUR: The peculiar circumstances may excuse it, my lord.

Examination continued: I instructed Mr. Wills to apply to the Court for a subpœna to secure the attendance of Dr. O'Hanlan and the Rev. Mr. Saurin. He did so on Jan. 14. A paragraph appeared in the papers the next morning, giving a report of the application and the names of the witnesses. I took steps to secure the attendance of Dr. O'Hanlan and of the Rev. Mr. Saurin, but have not been able to do so.

Mr. Loftus Walsh, managing clerk to Messrs. Fanless, of Dublin, attorneys, deposed that on the 19th of January last, he was sent down to Maynooth to secure the attendance of Dr. O'Hanlan. He saw the hall-porter there. In consequence of what he heard he returned to Dublin, and called at Mr. and Mrs. Brennan's. Mrs. Brennan is Dr. O'Hanlan's sister.

Mr. HAWKINS: My lord, I am not going to make any observations on the absence of Dr. O'Hanlan.

The SOLICITOR-GENERAL: The candour of my learned friend is quite touching. (Laughter.)

The LORD CHIEF JUSTICE: I confess the gravity with which the remark was made almost made me smile. (Renewed laughter.)

The SOLICITOR-GENERAL: It is quite perfect, my lord.

Afterwards I called on other relatives of Dr.

O'Hanlan, but without result. I applied to the president of the college and to Cardinal Cullen, Archbishop M'Hale, and Lord Castlerosse, the trustee of the college. I took a great deal of trouble and went to various places to secure the attendance of Dr. O'Hanlan. On the 28th of January I went to the house of the Jesuits, in Gardiner-street, Dublin, with a view to secure the attendance of the Rev. Mr. Saurin. I could not find him. I was told he had left town. I saw the superior, but could not find out where he had gone to.

Cross-examined by Mr. HAWKINS : I do not know Dr. O'Hanlan's appearance. I know Father Saurin.

A number of letters were here put in. Eight letters—called confessional letters—written by the plaintiff by the orders of Mrs. Star to her as superior were put in. Then a number of letters which had passed between the superior, Mrs. Star, and the Bishop were put in. The first was the following, from the superior to the Bishop :—

Convent of Our Lady of Mercy, Hull, April 27th, 1865.

My Lord,—After many prayers for guidance, and after weighing well before God the whole matter in my mind, I have formed the resolution of resigning the office of superioress of this community, for which I beg your Lordship's consent. My reasons are simply these :—It is plain that either Sr. M. Scholastica or I must yield. She will not, consequently I must. It is not my intention to make any charge against her. I only wish to speak of myself and the community. I feel that I have not sufficient mental or physical strength to bear up against the anxiety she occasions me on account of the other sisters. I was obliged, as a matter of convenience, to remove her from Clifford last June. Since she has been here the whole spirit of the house has changed. We are not like the same happy community we were. Although peace is in the exterior, a settled gloom and constraint appear to have rested on us all. Recreation, which was once so joyous, is now a mere formality, and when the time of silence comes we feel relieved. There is not one of the professed sisters who does not bear an anxious and troubled look. If this tells on all as it tells on me the consequences may be serious, for I feel as one paralyzed, and without heart, mind, or spirit for anything. I do not shrink from trouble and anxiety so long as they do not go between my soul and God, for I am willing to sacrifice health, life, happiness, reputation —everything short of my salvation, for the happiness and welfare of this community, which is dearer and more precious to me than all in this world beside. I feel that my soul is in peril in my present position, and that I ought to resign for that reason and for the good of the community. I do not possess the virtue and talent to govern in trying circumstances. It is a fault of character in me which time has rather increased than lessened that I take things too much to heart, and I am too solicitious about those who are under my care. Another may govern and effect the good I had hoped to do with more ease and merit to herself and more fruit to others than I could in consequence of my natural disposition. The time prescribed by our rule for the resignation of

superiors is Saturday within the octave of the Ascension, when I hope and pray that your lordship will release me from my present dangerous responsibility. The election should take place on the following Thursday. In giving up my charge of the sisters, it makes me happy to give my testimony to their sterling goodness. They are, with that one exception, docile, simple, self-sacrificing, and laborious. They love God, love each other, love their rules, love the poor. I do not think your lordship need apprehend any unpleasantness in the community in consequence of that change. The sisters are quite prepared for it, and I expect that all will be tranquil. Hoping your lordship will accede to my request, and begging your blessing, I am, my lord, with much respect, your obedient servant in Jesus Christ,

SISTER MARY JOSEPH.

To this there was the following answer from the Bishop, dated the 30th of April, 1865 :—

Dear Rev. Mother,—Your letter has caused me great anxiety, and I have taken time to consider my reply. You say that either you or Sister Scholastica must yield. I cannot admit the alternative. If it be a question of one submitting to the other, the sister must yield to you. Where is your confidence in God? As He has placed you in your position He will support you.

Second letter from the Reverend Mother on the same subject, in answer to the Bishop's inquiries :—

Convent of Our Lady Mary, Hull, May 1, 1865.

My Lord,—I am sorry your Lordship has not granted my petition, but I still hope you will when you hear how things are. Sister Mary Scholastica need not know that she is the cause of the change. It is a most painful duty with me to enter into the subject of her failings—so much of the past must be brought to bear upon the present. The principal points in which she errs are poverty, obedience, and truth. If I close my eyes to her faults she perseveres in them with confidence. If admonished in all mildness and charity she denies them, and continues to transgress. If reproached with severity or her faults proved, she assumes a tone and manner of defiance. If given a penance, which is rarely done, she continues it longer than she was desired, to show how little she cares about it. If she seek to speak to me in private, it is merely to give vent to the bitterness she feels against me, and to reproach me with cruelty, tyranny, and persecution. Of late she has made the same accusations against me in the presence of the community. With regard to poverty I must refer to the past. We have long suspected her of stealing ; suspicions are not proofs, therefore I have been silent on that head. Within the last year I have discovered that my suspicions were well-grounded, and that her offences can be proved by different members of the community, who, through a mistaken charity, kept their knowledge to themselves, until by chance I made enquiries on the subject. I believe her late conduct has been occasioned by her vexation at the precautions which have been quietly taken to guard her against indulging this propensity in the convent ; but, like an incurable disease, if healed in one place it breaks out in another with greater malignity. We now fear she steals from the school-children. She is so artful, so dexterous, that it will be almost impossible for any one to detect her; but the eyes of the young are piercing, and their tongues ever ready to publish the weaknesses of others, and disgrace may come upon religion and upon us before we are aware of it. This last suspicion occurred to the minds of three of the sisters almost simultaneously about different things, and without communicating with each other on the subject. When at confession a few days ago, I mentioned my trouble about Sister M. Scholastica to N. N., for the first time, and told him of my fear of a coming scandal. He told me I was bound in conscience to make it known to your lordship, and very kindly offered to do so for me, if I would allow him. I thought it better to do so myself, as I feared it might come to the knowledge of the other priests if I gave him liberty to mention it out of confession. Sister M. Scholastica will never acknowledge these things. She speaks of herself as if she were a suffering saint and the victim of unjust persecution. What is more, she can draw one who does not know her thoroughly to the same belief. I feel that I cannot control her, and I shrink from the responsibility of governing a community of which she is a member. It grieves me more than I can express to occasion your lordship the least anxiety, and I would gladly have remained silent until the end of turn of office, but that I felt my spiritual danger, and had not sufficient strength to turn this occasion to the profit of my soul. Unless Almighty God gives me a great increase of grace, I feel that my position as that sister's superior will be a most dangerous one for me. With many regrets for troubling you with so much about myself and my feelings, and begging your lordship's blessing, I am, with much respect, my lord, your obedient servant in Jesus Christ.

SISTER MARY JOSEPH.

Then came a letter from the bishop to Mrs. Star, the superior:—

Be calm and patient, and put your trust in God. I am going to Ireland, and will do what I can to settle the difficulty. What convent did she come from in Ireland? Where did she spend her novitiate? Where was she professed?

Then there was a letter from the Rev. Mr. Saurin, the Jesuit priest, to the bishop, dated the 4th of August, 1865:—

My dear Lord,—I am soon to return to Dublin, and shall call at Hull to visit my dear sister, with whom I have had no communication for seven years. Will your lordship kindly send me an order that I may spend an hour, as often as I can, with her? Your charity will, I am sure, induce you to comply with this request. My brother was only allowed to see her once last year, and when he went again he had to return, poor fellow, without seeing her.

The bishop upon this sent to Mrs. Star, the superior, this letter:—

Let the good father have his own way, and perhaps you will do well to give him your confidence. I should like to see him.

On the 9th of August, 1865, the bishop wrote to Mrs. Star:—

I hope you are certain about the thefts, and that the facts are proveable. I was unable to move efficaciously in the matter before for want of faculties from the Holy See. I asked for them long ago, and have only received them to-day. State whether, in case of expulsion, the house at Baggot-street would do anything in the matter of the dowry.

On the 8th of August, 1865, Mrs. Star wrote this answer to the bishop:—

My dear Lord,—Your directions shall be obeyed. The rev. father shall see his sister as often as he pleases. I could not give him my confidence, as your lordship thinks might be well; but if I see him, I will urge him to obtain a change for his sister. But my reason for declining to speak frankly to any of the family is, that in 1862 Mrs. Saurin begged me, with the earnestness of a mother, to speak to her of her child's conduct. I did not suspect the snare; I felt for her, and I told her all. In consequence she expressed gratitude, and told me I had done right, and that her daughter would have no sympathy from her. And when she had heard all she could, she distorted the case against me, with the help of her brother the priest (the Rev. Mr. Mathews)—an able, clever man of the world, who fears disgrace to his family—and her representations have been submitted to your lordship. We know the sequel. Although her brother is a religious, yet at the beginning of his sister's career he helped to make her what she now is. He described her former superiors at Baggot-street as "tyrants" and "tormentors"; her letters breathed a spirit of sarcasm and contempt for the community, calculated to awaken a spirit of insubordination and uncharitableness. I cannot blame him for this; for her powers of misrepresentation would raise an edifice of falsehood on the least foundation of truth. They spoke to the Jesuit fathers, but they never spoke favourably of her, and told them not to meddle with her, but to guard her.

On the 21st of August there was this letter from the bishop to the superior, Mrs. Star:—

Dear Mother Superior,—Be good enough to receive this information I now give you. Give the enclosed to the Rev. Mr. Saurin. It is an order to remove his sister from the convent, Prepare clothes, I will send absolution from her vows.

P.S. You must still send me your papers, and let me have all the information you can.

The letter enclosed in the above to the Rev. Mr. Saurin was the following:—

Rev. and dear Father,—It is a fortunate circumstance that you should be making a visit to Hull, as it has become necessary to require the removal of your sister from the community. . . . I should prefer her being accompanied by you. Under the conviction that no other community will receive her, and that her religious obligations are a source of danger rather than of merit, I have thought it proper to commute them, and I will send the necessary documents. Upon application to the Mother-house your sister will receive her dower.

On the 15th of August, 1865, Mrs. Star wrote to the bishop :—

Upon receipt of your lordship's letter, I wrote to inquire what the community at Baggot-street would be willing to do as to dower. The superior replies that she will most willingly give it up. The thefts and other breaches of rules can be proved. I have directed each sister to make notes of their individual experiences of her conduct, which I can send you, and you will see the evidence. I feel grateful to your lordship for taking steps to relieve us from this painful trial—no doubt ordained by Heaven for some blessed end. Shall I ask the superior to find the dower, or shall I wait the result of the investigation ?

On the 24th of August the bishop wrote to Mrs. Star, enclosing a note for the Rev. Mr. Saurin, the Jesuit priest :—

Tell the father when you give him this note that I have told you the nature of the contents. If he refuses to remove his sister, tell him I will take care to have her removed, and that on no consideration will I permit her to remain.

On the 15th of September Mrs. Star wrote to the bishop :—

Father Saurin is still in Hull. Upon reading your letter to him he questioned the validity of the absolution without application from the person to be absolved. He was quiet, but steadily refused to take his sister, and said he would advise his uncle, the Rev. T. Mathews, and leave the matter to him to manage, as he had done hitherto. I do not think he would be induced to remove his sister. He said he did not wish to mix himself up with the quarrels. The family are clever, and I believe they will either try to gain time by temporizing, and in the meantime take measures to give trouble, or they will come over here and cause great scandal by publicity. I think the only way is to anticipate them by sending her home at once. They cannot complain of this, as her brother refused to take her.

Then the bishop wrote to Mrs. Star on the 17th of September, 1865 :—

Don't be in too great a hurry. Matters are fast tending towards a commission. They are taking such a course that a commission only will meet the case.

On the 17th of September Mrs. Star wrote to the bishop :—

Father Saurin came again to the convent. He spoke to me in a strange way. He said that his uncle (the Rev. T. Mathews) was a wicked man, who would go to any length to punish those who should displease him, and that on one occasion he had done so when the question was as to his sister's expulsion. He ascertained that a claim of damages would lie for £5,000, and that if it cost the family that sum they would not mind it. I said that if such a course was taken the sympathy would be with the community, but £20,000 would not compensate them for the public disgrace which would arise from the evidence given at the trial. I said, also, that there was no ground for a lawsuit, as his sister had not been decoyed. She had begged to be admitted, and she now

remained in the community against our will; that I had applied to her family to remove her, and urged her to go elsewhere. His object, I think, was to intimidate me ; and when he perceived he could not do so, he changed his tone. They might try to bring against us an action for defamation of character if they were informed of what had been stated against her. They will try and get the information, and then take proceedings against us. There is, therefore, every reason for our being prudent. The rev. father saw his sister a long time : I do not know what he told her.

Then came a note from the bishop to Mrs. Star, enclosing to her the letter written to him by the plaintiff, which has already been printed. The note from the bishop was short :—

I send the enclosed ; tell me how she acquired the information.

The enclosed letter from the plaintiff to the bishop was as follows :—

My dear Lord,—I hope you will forgive the liberty I take in writing to you in my deep sorrow. I did not know what sorrow was before. But the day and night I passed yesterday, I never shall forget. I did not know my position until then, when the rev. mother told me I was absolved from my vows ; that she was only waiting for the last orders to send me out at your lordship's desire ; that a secular dress was ready for me ; and that your lordship had said that I was to be ready for a " quick despatch." May I never live to see the day when I put such a dress on ! Never shall I seek shelter in my dear parents' home. I love them too dearly to let them see me in my sorrow. My lord, I can write no more. I can hardly see the letters while I write. I have been long in hope of seeing you. I also beg to be allowed a little longer time with my uncle. The last time he was here he was only ten minutes with me, and left abruptly, and I have never heard a word since. I have done my best since your lordship's visit to give satisfaction. I know I have many faults, but I never remember having wilfully broken my vows. I beg of your lordship, as the greatest act of charity to my poor sorrowful heart, tell me what I am condemned for. The rev. mother says I do not seem to feel anything ; but she does not know my poor heart. I hope they will not throw me on the world ; that is all I beg of God. With every possible respect, I remain your lordship's obedient child in Christ.

To the bishop's letter, enclosing this letter from the plaintiff, the superior, Mrs. Star, replied as follows :—

Dec. 10.

My dear Lord,—My reasons for mentioning the absolution were these : I believed she was fully aware of it, but depended upon her natural cleverness to conceal it. I thought she would be grateful if I could make her sensible of her position, and induce her to apply to her parents to make a provision for her ; and I thought if she received the advice it might help her to reconcile her friends to the change in her state of life, and avoid the publicity and pain which a commission must bring to all parties concerned. I had scarcely spoken when I saw my error, and repented of my indiscretion. I would not have entered on the subject, only I believed she had learnt the nature of your communication from her brother. Her letters to her friends contain allusions to something mutually understood, but which she wished to conceal from my knowledge, perhaps because she might suppose if I knew it she must cease her exacting ways, and assume a subdued and sorrowful exterior. This, however, is not the case, and her apparent unconcern and continual enjoyment of the gratifications within her reach make her an astonishment to us all, and make us think that the poor soul would be happier when freed from the restraints of conventual life.

On the 1st of January the bishop wrote to the superior, enclosing notice of the commission to the plaintiff :—

Give enclosed to Sister Scholastica. It is a notice of the commission. It is satisfactorily formed. Canon Walker is president ; Mr. Porter is a member. You will write to him, &c.

The bishop in a letter to Father Mathews mentioned the notice of the commission :—

I have sent a notice to your niece. I had a repugnance to keeping such a thing over her, but it would not be fair that it should come upon her suddenly when the commission meet.

In another letter to the superior the bishop wrote :—

I wish you to state to Sister Scholastica that she is at liberty to write anything she would wish to say to the commissioners. The charges are what she has over and over again been reproached with—breaches of the rules of her Order.

This was in consequence of a letter from the plaintiff to the bishop, begging to know what the charges were. That letter was as follows. It will be observed that it indicates she had had no answer to her former letter to the bishop, which he had sent to the superior :—

My dear Lord.—I did deserve an answer to my poor letter, but I am grateful that it is noticed even now. My cross is a heavy one. I hope they will not send me out of religion in which I have been for 16 years, nearly half my life. No one ever entered into it with a purer motive. Do not send me into a world I never loved. I did not know until lately that your lordship wished me to leave. Had I known it I would have gone anywhere at your wish. I now beg as the last favour that your lordship will be present at the commission. This also I beg of your lordship, to know when that awful day is to be. I also beg to be allowed a little time alone with pen and pencil to prepare for my trial.

It was in consequence of this the bishop wrote the note to the superior to allow the plaintiff those facilities. The commission sat on the 10th and 11th of January, and on the 17th the bishop wrote to Mrs. Star thus :—

I wish to tell you how matters stand. But do not do or say anything in consequence. Leave the matter to me. Let me know if anything happens which seems to require you to speak or not. I have given formal notice to the Rev. T. Mathews to remove her as soon as he can. I have not had any answer. What was called "the stripping" seems to have been satisfactorily cleared up. I am at a loss to know the meaning of wearing the duster about the house. Again, there is an accusation about you being shut up on New Year's Day in deliberation with the sisters, she being excluded.

The letters between the bishop and Mr. Mathews appear in yesterday's report, also those between the parents and the superior. Then there was the plaintiff's letter to the bishop after knowing the result of the commission :—

My dear Lord,—Forgive the liberty I take in writing to you—if you only knew my state of mind ! My uncle left without my knowing he was going. I am afraid I displeased him by being reluctant to say anything in my own justification. The little I did say was dragged from me. Let me remain in religion. I have been for years alone. My brother, who is here, called to see me last evening. He said he knew nothing of it. How I wish I could have written years ago to know what your Lordship wanted me to do ; I had not the least notion that you wanted me to leave. I could have got into another convent then, but now the rev. mother seems always displeased with me. I beg you to allow me to see you. I knew I had no chance if your lordship was absent. That was the reason I begged for your presence. Never shall I forget that day ! I fancy I can hear the awful words, "The accused is charged," still wringing in my ears ! Forgive my trespassing upon you, but I beg as a last favour that your lordship will allow me to see you.

To this the bishop replied :—

Dear Sister Scholastica, — Your letter has hastened a communication which would otherwise have been delayed until I heard from your uncle, to whom I have communicated my final decision. I have required, and hereby require, your removal from the convent. And I absolve you from your vows. You can refuse this ; but I shall in any case require you to leave the community, and that as speedily as possible. You are free to go, but not to stay. Under all the circumstances, as no advantage can come from seeing you, I must decline to see you.

This seems to have been mentioned in the following from the bishop to Mrs. Star :—

Give her the enclosed. Do nothing. Say nothing. Leave matters to take their course. I am satisfied with the explanation.

What this "explanation" was did not appear.

On the 9th of February the bishop wrote to Mrs. Star :—

In all you do have witnesses. Studiously avoid anything that can be construed into the use of force.

In a subsequent letter the bishop said :—

Your project of sending a priest with her is out of the question. She might do him great harm, whereas she can do you none. As to fear of inquiries in the case of Sister Ryan, such fears are groundless; for that was a case of removal out of the country. You can say that as she is absolved from her vows, she is not allowed to be treated as a religious. As a last resource I would remove the convent from Hull.

On the 14th of March, 1866, the bishop wrote again to the superior:—

Her determination to stay where she is is an answer to the brother's charge of imprisonment. My impression is, that she may feign to run away under the pretence of escaping; and I should like you to take steps to show your desire that she should go. I should prefer that this should be shown to some intelligent and influential Protestant in Hull.

The bishop enclosed an order signifying that "Miss Susan Saurin" was no longer a member of the community; that she had been totally absolved from her vows of poverty, chastity, and obedience; and that henceforth she had no right to continue an inmate of the convent, but was at liberty to claim her dower.

A paragraph from an affidavit of Mrs. Star, made in the course of the action, on an application for copies of the statements made to the commissioners against the plaintiff, was then read. It ran thus:—

I altogether deny the statement that either I or my co-defendant delivered any written charges or written statements of any of the members of the Order: and I say that neither I nor my co-defendant delivered to the commissioners any written charges or written statements of the members or sisters, nor were such represented before the commissioners.

Mr. MELLISH.—That is true.
The LORD CHIEF JUSTICE.—The latter part.
Mr. MELLISH.—And the former part.
The LORD CHIEF JUSTICE.—It may be literally true; that is, that the written statements of the defendants and the other sisters were not delivered by them to the commissioners. It has appeared that they were delivered to the bishop.

This closed the plaintiff's case.
After an adjournment,
Mr. HAWKINS opened the case for the defence. The first, however, took some points of law. The action, he said, was for several causes—conspiracy as well as slander or libel, and it was against two persons, Mrs. Star, the superior, and Mrs. Kennedy, one of the sisters. Now, there was no evidence of any of these alleged wrongs having been committed jointly by the two: and that being so, he said they had a right either to a nonsuit or to have one of their names discharged from the record, as the plaintiff could not in an action against both recover for some things done by one and for other things done by the other.

The LORD CHIEF JUSTICE, however, pointed out that there was evidence that things had been done by Mrs. Star—the stripping, for instance,— at which the other defendant had been present, aiding and assisting.

Mr. HAWKINS still urged that this was not so as to some of the causes of action, and that the plaintiff must elect upon which she would proceed; but

The LORD CHIEF JUSTICE said he should direct the jury on the close of the evidence as to what charges were proved or not, and he should decline to stop the case now.

Mr. HAWKINS then proceeded to address the jury with much earnestness on behalf of the defendants. He said,—You have listened, gentlemen, patiently for five days to this extraordinary history—a story which, as it was described in the glowing and eloquent language of my learned friend, Sir John Coleridge, and as it has been detailed to you in the evidence of the plaintiff, must have appeared to you a series of almost unparalleled persecutions. And it would be but natural if you were in some degree prejudiced against those ladies of whom these things have been detailed; but I hope, gentlemen, that you have endeavoured to keep your minds open, and I undertake on the part of the defendants—whom I shall call, with a body of witnesses for the defence—to remove from your minds those impressions which you may have formed from hearing the case for the plaintiff; and to show that it is untrue—if not in all its details, at all events in its main particulars, that it is untrue or grossly exaggerated, and that this is neither more nor less than a huge superstructure of falsehood or exaggeration, based upon a very slight and slender foundation of truth. Gentlemen, in the first place you must bear in mind that this is not a case arising between people in this outer world of ours, but among the members of a religious community, who have secluded themselves from the world—as you and I may think unwisely, but still sincerely and religiously, from the highest motives—to undertake works of charity and undergo penances and mortifications, and humiliations, and hardships, all undergone voluntarily, in the hope of thereby rising to a higher and purer state. Gentlemen, all this may appear to us perhaps visionary; but to them these are matters of high and solemn reality, and this is the nature of the life upon which they have voluntarily entered, and the obligations they have voluntarily undertaken. And you will agree with me, I am sure, that the considerations applicable to such a state of life are very different indeed from such as would arise, were similar matters to occur between ordinary persons in the world. And you can understand that as the essence of this religious life consists in the strict observance of its rules, many things which would appear under other circumstances perfectly trivial, may be deemed of great importance, and therefore this case must necessarily turn a great deal upon what were the obligations incurred by the plaintiff when she entered into this religious order, and what were the rules by which they were regulated. The learned counsel here read the following:—

Copy of the questions and answers signed by the plaintiff previous to her profession:—

1. Do you earnestly desire to become a good and fervent religious in this institute?—Yes.

2. Are you resolved to observe its rules and customs faithfully, as far as you have been made acquainted with them?—Yes.

3. Are you resolved to obey your superior in

all things, whether in matters of great or little moment, agreeable or disagreeable?—Yes.

4. Are you satisfied to spend your life in any office or employment assigned you, be it ever so disagreeable, laborious, or humiliating?—Yes.

5. Are you willing to receive and disposed to profit of *public* as well as of private reprehension and penance?—Yes.

6. Are you willing to have your faults made known to your superiors by whoever becomes acquainted with them, and are you ready to make the customary manifestation of conscience whenever you may be required to do so?—Yes.

SUSANNA M. SAURIN.

1. Do you find any serious difficulty in the practice of holy poverty or obedience, or in the observance of our holy rule?—No.

2. Are you firmly resolved to pass your life in the exact observance of our holy rule and customs without requiring or seeking for any dispensations or particularities in respect of food, clothing, lodging, or the like?—I am.

3. Do you esteem and love this institute, and do you find the exercise of its characteristic functions conducive to your own perfection?—I do.

4. Is there anything in its rule or constitutions, or in the approved customs of this congregation, to which you find a particular difficulty in submitting your judgment?—No.

5. Have you any doubts respecting your vocation of so strong a nature as to warrant a fear that you will be likely hereafter to abandon it?—No.

6. Are you willing to go to any of our branch houses, and to remain there as long as your superiors may deem expedient; and are you satisfied to be sent on a foundation to any part of the United Kingdom?—Yes.

Sister M. SCHOLASTICA JOSEPH SAURIN.

Act of Profession.

In the name of Our Lord and Saviour Jesus Christ, and under the protection of His Immaculate Mother Mary, ever Virgin, I, Susanna Mary Saurin, called in religion Sister Mary Scholastica Joseph, do vow and promise to God poverty, chastity, and obedience, and the service of the poor, sick, and ignorant, and to persevere until death in this institute of Our Lady of Mercy, according to its approved rule and constitutions, under the authority and in presence of you, my Lord and most reverend Father in God, Paul Cullen, archbishop of this diocese, and of our reverend Mother Ellen Whitty, called in religion Mary Vincent, mother superior of this Convent of Mercy, the third day of October, in the year of Our Lord one thousand eight hundred and fifty-three.

SUSANNA M. SAURIN,
(Called in religion Sister Mary Scholastica Joseph ✠).
Sister MARY JULIANA DELANY, Assistant.
Sister MARY VINCENT WHITTY, Superioress.
✠ PAUL CULLEN, Archbishop of Dublin.

After reading these documents, the learned counsel proceeded to read and comment upon the rules and instructions of the order:—

Of the Vow of Poverty.

1. As the sisters, in order to become more conformable to their heavenly spouse, Christ Jesus, have, in quitting the world, renounced all property in earthly things, they should frequently revolve in mind how tenderly He cherished holy poverty. He was born in a stable; He was laid in a manger; during the course of His mortal life He suffered from cold, hunger, and thirst; He had not whereon to lay His head; He died naked on the Cross. In his own person he consecrated this virtue, and bequeathed it as a most valuable patrimony to His followers.

2. The sisters shall therefore keep their hearts perfectly disengaged from every affection to the things of this world, content with the food and raiment allowed them, and willing at all times to give up whatever has been allotted for their use. They shall not give or receive any present without permission from the mother superior. When with her permission they receive any present from their relatives or other persons it must be considered as for the use of the community, and not for the particular use of the receiver.

3. Nothing shall appear in their dress but what is grave and modest, nor can they keep in their cells anything superfluous, nor any costly or rich furniture or decoration. All must be suitable to religious simplicity and poverty.

Of the Vow of Obedience.

1. The sisters are always to bear in mind that by the vow of obedience they have for ever renounced their own will, and resigned it to the direction of their superiors. They are to obey the mother superior as holding her authority from God, rather through love than servile fear. They shall love and respect her as their mother, and in order that she may be enabled to direct them in the way of the divine service, it is recommended to them to make known to her their penetential works and mortifications, with the advantages derived from them.

2. They shall, without hesitation, comply with all the directions of the Mother Superior, whether in matters of great or little moment, agreeable or disagreeable. They shall never murmur, but with humility and spiritual joy carry the sweet yoke of Jesus Christ. They shall not absent themselves from the common exercises without her leave, except in a case of pressing urgency; and if they cannot then have access to her they shall make known the reason of their absence at the earliest opportunity. They shall obey the call of the bell as the voice of God.

Of the Election of the Mother Superior.

1. The mother superior shall be elected from among those who have a voice in the chapter; she shall be distinguished for her virtue, prudence, and discretion; she shall be at least thirty years old, and of five years' profession, except in convents newly founded, and must have the majority of the votes for the validity of her election.

2. The mother superior, when duly elected, shall govern for three years; she may, with the approbation of the bishop, be re-elected for three years longer. In convents newly founded the

first mother superior shall govern for six years unless there be canonical reasons for her being removed from office during that time.

Such, said the learned counsel, were the rules by which, under the most sacred obligations, the plaintiff undertook to be bound when she entered this order. And he would undertake to satisfy the jury that these rules had been honestly and faithfully and sincerely carried out by the defendants, and that there was no foundation for the representation of the plaintiff that they had been perverted or abused. He urged that there was this strong presumption in favour of the mother superior (Mrs. Star), that she had been thrice elected superior by the voluntary votes of the community. Surely this of itself showed that she could not be naturally unkind or uncharitable. On the other hand, it was, he urged, quite plain that, from a very early period, there had been on the part of the plaintiff departures from the rules, which were regarded in the community as unfitting her for their order, and as requiring her departure. In February or March, 1862, this letter to her uncle was found in her cell :—

My ever and very dearest Uncle,—It seems a very long time since I wrote to you, so I am going to trouble you with a few lines before the holy season of Lent. I trust you continue quite well. I do not see the least chance of my going over. I mentioned there might be after Christmas, but, as I said in the beginning, rev. mother had no idea of letting me leave, at least for a long time. There were both postulants and novices dismissed from our community. I did not think it would be quite the thing to return with them, so I said nothing about it. Rev. mother does not know I wish to go. She is fearfully afraid of the family altogether. I could see that when I was in Hull last. One time she said anything any of you took into your heads you saw it done. Some one had been telling her. When she was over last she complained of mamma's impertinent letters, &c. ; she certainly made a great mistake in some things she told mamma. I said, "When I see mamma I shall explain all to her." Will you kindly tell her so? I do not know what to say, or only that I have long since placed the whole affair in the Sacred Hearts of Jesus and Mary, who I feel sure will assist you, my dearest uncle, to do what is best. You must not think I am unhappy. I am far from it, and my health has never been so good. The only thing I am not settled, nor do I think I ever can be again here ; the only thing, I regret poor mamma knowing anything about it, lest it might not be right ; also she may think I am not happy, which would be untrue. I must now say good-by. Believe me, dearest uncle, your ever grateful niece in Jesus Christ.

Sr. M. SCHOLASTICA JOSEPH.

(Envelope addressed to to the Rev. T. Mathews, P.P., St. Mary's, Drogheda, Ireland.)

It was upon this occasion the superior had written to her uncle the letter which had been read, requiring her removal. And in July the same year the plaintiff had herself written thus to her uncle :—

My dearest Uncle, — The community are determined I shall not remain. You know the archbishop and rev. mother at Baggot-street are determined I shall not return there. Unless you settle with your community to receive me, my dearest uncle, I know not what to do. The greatest act of charity you could do towards me is to settle it at once, if you can. If you write to say I can get to Drogheda, even for a while, rev. mother will send me, May I beg, as a great favour, you will not go to bishops or any one else about it? but do let me know by next post, as rev. mother says the community here will wait no longer, as they are determined to take measures without delay for my removal. If the community in Drogheda consent to my going there, rev. mother says they need never know why I leave here, only you wish it for the sake of my father and mother. You will be greatly surprised at this letter altogether—the horrid writing. For God's sake do not say a word to any of my friends, not even mamma—I know she would feel it so,—if you possibly can, I feel it is the will of God. He has some wise design in all. How can I ever forgive all the trouble, &c., I am giving you, and worse than the trouble? I again and again beg you will settle it for me, in charity, as soon as possible, and without any more fuss. Won't you write by next post?

Believe me your ever faithful niece in J. Ct.,

Sr. M. SCHOLASTICA.

These letters the learned counsel relied upon as showing that the plaintiff had, as early as 1862, been guilty of such infractions of the rules as were looked upon in so serious a light by the superior as to require her removal. Her great offence, he said, consisted in her clandestine letters to her uncle. The story she had told, he said, as to the origin of the quarrel—that the superior had required her to disclose her confessions —was absolutely false. There was not the least truth in it, and all probability was against it ; for such a demand would be looked upon by every Catholic as outrageous. Possibly the superior might have said to her that she hoped she confessed such and such faults to her confessor, or might have asked whether her director did not desire her to correct them ; but to represent this as a demand upon her to disclose her confessions was a most utter perversion of the truth. The true secret of her unhappiness was her unfitness for the life on which she had engaged, which led to constant breaches of its rules and obligations. Long before 1862 numerous violations of them had been discovered ; for instance, appropriations of articles to her own use, contrary to the vow of poverty—a book of devotion on one occasion, a pair of boots on another. These things might appear "trifles light as air," but they were repeated violations of religious rules of sacred obligation, and their repetition proved an utter unfitness for the religious life of the order. It was their duty to search for and find little articles believed to be secreted about her person ; that what was called the "stripping" had occurred— that is, her outer garments were removed, and her pockets searched, and several little articles taken away, her use of which was contrary to the rules—as writing utensils. It was found, on another occasion, that she had used these instruments of writing to make minutes and memoranda reflecting on the character of the sisters or her superior. Moreover, it was found that she beat the school children and took their dinners or their food. Upon these charges there had been a commission of inquiry, and he should call the secretary and several members of the commission to prove that it was conducted quite fairly. And he should call not only the defendants, but others of the inmates to prove these charges, and disprove the charges made by the plaintiff against the community. As to the alleged hardships, he should show that they were unfounded. No doubt after the plaintiff had been dispensed from her vows and required by the bishop to leave the house she had no right to remain there, and no doubt the community desired her departure. No doubt also they felt that she had no right to the unrestrained use of the house as before ; but to say that she had been imprisoned or ill-treated was entirely untrue. The statement that she had been debarred from resort to the necessary convenience was as gross a falsehood as had ever been uttered. There were six or seven of them in the house, and she had free access to one of them, though it was desired to prevent her from asserting the privileges of the members of the community by using such as were set apart to them. So of all her statements of ill-usage they were either utter untruths or gross exaggerations. In conclusion, the learned counsel asked the jury to consider what earthly motives these ladies could possibly have had to inflict all these persecutions upon the plaintiff ; and whether he had not suggested the more reasonable and probable solution of the case, viz., that the plaintiff was unfitted for the order, and yet would not leave the house, and by her constant breaches of the rules caused herself and all the other inmates constant inquietude and annoyance. The other members lived with the superior in peace and harmony. How was it that the plaintiff alone could not do so ? How was it that she alone for a series of years was found constantly accused of breaches of her vows and disregard of the rules of her order ? Was it not plain that she herself was the cause of all these unhappy dissensions, and that her removal was necessary to stop them, and to restore that state of peace and happiness in which these ladies had lived before, and in which, he hoped, they would continue to live after the verdict of the jury should have relieved them from these cruel aspersions on their characters ; for that was all they cared about. He believed the jury would not begrudge the time which would be necessary to fathom the case to the bottom. To the ladies he represented it was a matter of deep anxiety. So far as money was concerned, it was a matter immaterial to them whether the verdict should be for £5,000 or for a million ; and for this reason, that they had nothing to lose. (Laughter.)

The LORD CHIEF JUSTICE. And nothing to pay.

Mr. HAWKINS said he was assured by his learned friend Mr. Russell that such was the case. It was a matter of great anxiety to them, however, that their character, which had been wantonly and recklessly and untruly assailed, should be cleared, and he was mistaken if such would not be the result of the investigation. Of this he was sure, that, regardless of sympathy or prejudice out of doors, they would fairly and fearlessly arrive at a conclusion which they conscientiously believed to be founded in right, in truth, and in justice. (Applause and hisses, which were quickly repressed.)

SEVENTH DAY, *Wednesday, February* 10.

Mr. Hawkins' promise, or prediction, that th defence in the case of "Saurin against Star and Kennedy" will extnd over a week seems likely to be verified, and something to spare. Of the many witnesses who are to be called, that they may endeavour to rebut the charges brought by Miss Saurin against her spiritual superiors, one only has been put in the box, and her evidence lasted the whole of to-day, and left off with a prospect of reaching far into to-morrow. This witness was, it is true, the most important of all who are to be examined. She was the principal defendant, Mrs. Star, late mother superior—for, according to her evidence, she is so no longer—at Hull and Clifford. Before calling his first witness, Mr. Hawkins made complaint to the Lord Chief Justice, of the publication, in a morning paper, of a leading article, painful to the defendants, and prejudicial to their case. On glancing over the editorial comments in question, his lordship said they appeared to him to be a criticism on conventual and monastic institutions—on a system, that is to say, rather than on the interests and rights of persons who are bound by that system, and who are parties to the present trial. However, he thought it best that all expressions of opinion should be reserved till after the verdict.

There was the same crowded court to-day as yesterday, and other yesterdays before that. There were even more ladies present than there had hitherto been, the gallery being almost exclusively filled by them, at least in front; and the nun's garb was everywhere conspicuous. Mrs. Star gave her evidence with self-possession and dignity, her voice trembling only a little, at first from agitation, and at last from downright fatigue. She held before her a small crucifix, on which her eyes were sometimes bent, as though with a purpose to draw from it divine strength for her answers, when the questions from the Bench were a little more cogent than usual. Some of these answers, delivered after a pause of a few seconds, came with a scarcely disguised force of feeling; and no worldly dislike could have vented itself with greater intensity of feminine bitterness than was perceptible in Mrs. Star's manner of mentioning Miss Saurin. "I was acquainted with the plaintiff while at Dublin; not more with her than with the rest of the community; she was in the laundry, and I was in the school; in 1859 I went to Clifford, and soon afterwards applied to the Dublin Superioress for an additional sister; I named Miss Saurin, thinking she would be useful in the needlework and the laundry. She had not education sufficient for teaching." Such voluntary pieces of detraction uttered by anybody but a *religieuse* would, perhaps, have struck an indifferent hearer as being undoubtedly spiteful. They were curiously alternated with professions of Christian love and goodwill. "Did you order more laborious tasks to be given to Miss Saurin than to any one else?" Mr. Mellish asked his witness in reference to a particular occa-

sion. "No; but I ordered less." Hereupon the Lord Chief Justice, as with a shrewd and sudden thought that the lady did protest too much, asked "Why so?" The answer was prompt: "In order to avoid a breach of charity." Such is the terrible suspicious quality of that wicked worldliness which crowds the Court of Queen's Bench, that a cynical laugh ran through the auditory at the words of Mrs. Star. It will be seen that the judge put many questions to the witness, and her evidence was lengthened by statements and explanations which she herself volunteered, and asked to be permitted to make. One was something to this effect: "I wish to state that Miss Saurin's charge against me of having at such and such a date "— the witness specified the time with careful precision —"ordered her to take off her habit, and then of having caused the lining to be removed and searched, is entirely a misrepresentation." It had no basis in fact, she repeated, in answer to the Lord Chief Justice. "But," said her counsel, Mr. Mellish, "might not Miss Saurin, though incorrect in her date, have told the truth with respect to the same circumstances, which occurred perhaps at some other time?" The witness quietly assented, shifting her charge of inveracity to the mere mistake of a date. "And that," remarked the Solicitor-General, with calm severity, "'is entirely a misrepresentation.'" The small but not wholly select body of the public who filled the cabin which serves as the Court of Queen's Bench would seem to have had ears for all that passes there except for the mild expostulation of the judge on their noisy behaviour. They had shown some slight disposition yesterday to amend, but to-day they were as demonstrative as ever, laughing and applauding as freely as they would at a play. When the court broke up, and the witnesses departed in cabs, an outside mob gave a still stronger expression to their views of the case, and hooted Mrs. Star in the persons of at least half a dozen Sisters of Mercy, who were as "six Richmonds in the field," and bore the brunt of unpopularity instead of her.

The hearing of the case was resumed at the sitting of the court at ten o'clock this morning.

The Solicitor-General, Mr. Digby Seymour, Q.C., and Mr. Wills appeared for the plaintiff; Mr. Hawkins, Q.C., Mr. Mellish, Q.C., and Mr. Charles Russell were counsel for the defendants.

When the learned counsel had taken their places.

The Lord Chief Justice said: I think it right to correct an inaccuracy which appears in the report of these proceedings in one of the morning papers—namely, that if the bishop had dispensed with the plaintiff's vows she would have ceased to have any right in the convent. I said nothing of the kind, and intended nothing of the kind. [The paper referred to by his lordship was not *The Daily Telegraph.*]

Mr. Hawkins then called his lordship's attention to a leading article that appeared in the *Times* that morning, commenting on the case in a manner that was likely to greatly prejudice the defendant's case before they had an opportunity of being heard.

The Lord Chief Justice: I have not had time to read the *Times* this morning further than to glance over the report of yesterday's proceedings.

The foreman of the jury said he had just inquired of his brother juryman, and they informed him they had not seen the article.

Mr. Hawkins handed the paper to his lordship who looked over the article.

The Lord Chief Justice said, I confess I think it would have been better if the writer had waited until the case had ended, because observations made in the public press are likely to prejudice a case. At all events, it is likely to give annoyance to persons interested. From the cursory glance I have had of the article, however, I do not think the defendants have much to complain of.

Mr. Hawkins: I am not in the least making this application to your lordship because I believe that the jury will be prejudiced by it; but it is painful to the defendants to have these comments made before the case is ended. If your lordship will just read the end of the article I think you will be of a different opinion.

The Lord Chief Justice: It appears to me to be a comment or criticism on conventual and monastic institutions—on the system, rather than on the interests and rights of these parties.

Mr. Hawkins: I will not say more than ask your lordship to express an opinion upon the matter.

The Lord Chief Justice: Whilst I am ready to give the fullest latitude to the observations made by the writers of the public press on what passes in courts of justice, it is very desirable that nothing should be said before a case is ended.

Mr. Hawkins: I am quite satisfied with that expression of your lordship's opinion.

Mrs. Mary Ann Star was then sworn, and examined by Mr. Mellish, Q.C. She said: I am one of the defendants in this case. I was mother superior of the Sisters of Mercy at Hull and Clifford. I have ceased to be so now.

The Lord Chief Justice: Since when?—Since July, 1867.

To Mr. Mellish: I entered the convent of the Sisters of Mercy at Baggott-street, Dublin, as a postulant, July 12, 1850. I was professed as a sister on the 31st of January, 1853. In August 1855, I went to Clifford. I was appointed mother superior about a week after. It was a new foundation. Three went with me to remain on the foundation. I was appointed by the authority of Dr. Briggs, the late bishop, who delegated his authority to a priest, the Rev. Mr. Clifford. The appointment was for six years. Miss Saurin entered the convent in Baggot-street in November, 1850. There was a rule, and also a set of customs.

Mr. Digby Seymour said he would admit the rule, and customs handed in on behalf of the defendants.

Witness, to the Lord Chief Justice: The rules and customs were in force in Clifford. One alteration has been made in it with regard to visitors about four or five years ago. (Rules read.) The new rule is, in substance, the same as the old. The alteration was made by the community in Baggot-street, and in 1863 I got a copy of it at Hull. The rules are the same for all convents, but the "customs" differ. The convent in Baggot street had no authority over me after I left it. All postulants become by degrees acquainted with the rules and customs. They are read out to them while they are novices, and they are allowed to read them themselves before they are professed. There are also "instructions," with which they become acquainted. They are in MS. They are read for the novices. I was acquainted with Miss Saurin while we were both in Baggot-street — not more intimately than with others until after my profession. We met in some duties during our novitiate. She was principally engaged in the laundry, and I was in the school. She was sometimes in the industrial grounds. I was professed in January, and she in October of the same year. I got to know more about her after I was professed. She appeared to me to be very unhappy, and spoke to me of being unkindly treated by the superior. I always tried to reconcile her to her position. In 1855 I went to Clifford, leaving Miss Saurin in Baggot-street. Shortly afterwards I applied to Baggot-street for an additional sister. I named three or four; Miss Saurin was amongst the number. I applied for one only. I thought Miss Saurin would be useful at needlework and in household duties. We had a school at Clifford in which needlework was taught. I was not aware that her parents had objected to her coming until after she came, when she told me herself. I had only made one application for her. The duty I first gave her at Clifford was to teach needlework at school, and to teach the junior class the alphabet and words of one or two syllables, also the house duty, which was trifling, as there were only four or five sisters, and she had a lay sister under her. I went to Dublin in the year 1856. Miss Saurin did not accompany me on that occasion. I saw Mrs. Saurin while in Dublin. She expressed dissatisfaction at her daughter having been sent to England, and said that in consequence of the way Miss Saurin had been treated in Baggot-street and of having been sent away she would never put her foot in Baggot-street again. She said she had been badly treated in Baggot-street. I defended the superior at Baggot-street.

The Lord Chief Justice: I do not think we can go into that matter.

Examination continued: The Hull branch of the convent at Clifford was established in January, 1857. I was superior of the convent and the branch. The number of the inmates was advertised. Several postulants entered, and some of them became sisters. There were never less than four sisters at Hull, after the first month, including postulants.

The Lord Chief Justice: Do you call postulants "sisters?"—By courtesy, my lord—not by right.

Examination continued: Including novices and postulants, we have had as many as twenty-four sisters between the two houses. There were about fifteen of these professed sisters. In January, 1857, I went to Hull, and returned to Clifford in February. Miss Saurin went to Hull when I went to Clifford. I was at Clifford till April of that year. I was in weak health then. Mrs. Kennedy was left in charge at Hull when I was at Clifford. In August, 1857, Mrs. Kennedy was appointed by the bishop, Dr. Briggs, mother assistant.

Up to this time how, generally, had Miss Saurin behaved?—She had not been an observer of the rules. She particularly broke the rule of silence.

Did you observe that personally, or were you told by others?—Principally what I was told by others. I observed some of it myself. In April or May, 1867, Mrs. Kennedy told me she had a great deal of trouble with her.

What did she complain of?—Her intercourse with seculars, and principally with the young women who attended the night schools. Her irregularity as respected some of the duties of the community, such as coming in at irregular times.

Is this what Mrs. Kennedy said, or what you observed?—What Mrs. Kennedy said.

Explain what you mean by the duties of the community?—Spiritual duties in the choir, and attendance at meals.

She was not punctual?—She was not.

Did you speak to her in consequence of this communication from Mrs. Kennedy?—Yes, I did.

What did you say to her?—I told her what Mrs. Kennedy had told me, and asked her to be more reserved with seculars for the time to come, and to be more regular at her duty.

What answer did she give you?—She told me she would try.

Did she say anything more?—She denied the charge, and tried to excuse herself.

Examination continued: In July 1857, Miss Saurin came to Hull. I left Clifford either in April or May.

During the years 1858 and 1859 were you and Miss Saurin together at Hull or Clifford, or were you separate?—She was with me in Hull from the beginning of the year 1858 until October of the same year. In 1859 she was with me in Hull from July, and until April, 1860.

What were her duties in Hull at that time?—In 1858 she was housekeeper, and had needlework to teach at school, and she had a junior class to teach in the night school.

What was her behaviour during 1858 and 1859, from your own observation?—She was very irregular and unpunctual in coming to her duties.

What besides?—She did not observe the rule of silence.

Whom did she talk to?—To externs.

Did you see her?—Yes, I saw her talking to the school girls—the children of the school.

The Lord Chief Justice: Was she not allowed to speak to the children?—Yes, my lord; but she spoke unnecessarily.

To Mr. Mellish: It is not considered a breach of silence to say what is necessary to the children.

What else had you to complain of?—Disobedience to orders.

In what did this disobedience to orders consist?—I cannot remember all the circumstances.

What next?—Want of sincerity.

In what respect?—When accused of a fault she had commited, she would invariably deny it.

Mr. Mellish: Well, but she might be innocent of it?—She used equivocation at first, and afterwards would be obliged to admit the fault.

The Lord Chief Justice: She gave evasive answers?—Yes, my lord.

Mr. Mellish: Tell us what you mean by being obliged to admit it?—When she could no longer excuse herself, after I had proved to her that what I said was true, then she admitted it.

Had you a good deal of experience in speaking to all the sisters of their faults?—Yes.

And you expected that when a fault had been committed it would be owned to before it was proved?—Yes. She would throw her faults on the other sisters, saying they were the cause of them. For example: a novice came to me one day, and said Miss Saurin had been talking for a long time to a woman at the school; that she—the novice—had to wait for her, and that after a considerable time Miss Saurin said to her, "Now I have been waiting all this time for you, and I will be blamed for being late, whereas you kept me."

The Lord Chief Justice: This is what the novice told you?—Yes, my lord. I then spoke to Miss Saurin of it, and she admitted to me that she had said what was not true.

To Mr. Mellish: When I accused Miss Saurin of it she at first denied it, and said it was all a mistake—that she never meant it. I told her how she would lessen herself in the opinions of others by using those stratagems.

Can you give us any other instance of want of sincerity?—I cannot recall the incidents; but her general habit was to deny her faults when accused of them.

Had you any other grounds of complaint in 1858 and 1859? Did you speak to her on other matters?—Yes; I spoke to her continually of her faults—her want of truth especially. She admitted to me her want of truth, and also her disobedience.

The Lord Chief Justice: Disobedience in what particular?—Her non-observance of poverty.

Mr. Mellish: In what did that consist?—In 1858 and 1859 she had a great deal of things which she ought not to have had, and which I could not account for her having.

Things of what sort?—Working materials, such as pieces of calico. She told me it was what remained after making some ceremony work.

Had it been supplied by you?—Yes, and she did not return it to me when the work was done.

What use did she make of it?—I believe she applied it to her own private use.

The Lord Chief Justice: What became of the calico?—I desired her to give it up to me, and she did so.

I thought you said she applied it to her own private use?—She might have so applied it, my lord.

The Lord Chief Justice: Pray be more cautious.

Witness (to Mr. Mellish): One of the sisters missed a book, "Devotion to Jesus," and I found it amongst Miss Saurin's clothes in a cabinet. asked her about it, and why she had taken it, and she knew I had given it to another sister, and she said she had found it. She added that she was keeping it for me. I told her that that could scarcely be the case, as she knew I had given it to another. She then admitted she had taken it and said she had done wrong. I had given it to Mrs. M'Keon in her presence. Also in that year she took a pair of boots of Mrs. M'Keon's.

Was that on the occasion of Cardinal Wise

man's visit?—It was. She had not my leave to take them.

To the Lord Chief Justice: She could not borrow them without my permission. That is the rule, and it applied to all the sisters.

To Mr. Mellish: There are certain things which can be lent or borrowed on leave; but beyond that, to lend or borrow is a breach of poverty.

Are boots included?—No.

The Lord Chief Justice: Would it be a very heavy fault to borrow a pair of boots without leave?—I would not consider it the very gravest fault. But I do not know whether she did not intend to keep them.

Examination continued: I have known her to take food between meals without permission. That is against rule.

Did you see her doing so?—Yes.

Under what circumstances?—On going into the pantry one day I saw her before a ham. (A laugh.) I asked her a question and she could not answer me, her mouth was so full—(much laughter)—and the lower part of her face was besmeared with grease. (Renewed laughter.)

Did you speak to her?—When she saw me she turned pale. (Laughter.)

The Lord Chief Justice: She turned pale?—Yes, my lord, she was almost fainting for a few moments. I saw she was conscious of her fault. I looked at her seriously, but thought that the confusion she had suffered was a sufficient punishment for her.

Examination continued: I remarked that she scarcely ate anything at meals when I was present, and what she did eat was eaten with disgust and disrelish, as if it made her ill. She was housekeeper, and excused herself from being at the table. She had not to cook—a lay sister or a servant did that. The lay sister carried in the dinner after it had been carved. In consequence of her indisposition to eat I desired a sister to prepare food for her—broiled meat, eggs, or custard-pudding—between meals. I thought it necessary for her health, and her partaking of that food was not a fault. I observed also that she used partiality in the distribution of the food. The juniors were given small helps and of the worst parts. The plates were covered with tins, and ought to have been impartially distributed with equal helps. I had to re-arrange the plates, so that the seniors should not get all the best bits.

Did you get a bad help yourself?—Yes; and very little. (A laugh.)

Did you send for more?—No.

Examination continued: She denied the charge of partiality most obstinately, and said she had treated all alike.

To the Lord Chief Justice: It was Miss Saurin who carved. She did not bring in the plates; but hey were distributed under her direction.

Do you know that, or do you assume it?—I assume it.

Mr. Mellish: Did you speak to her about it?—Yes. She denied it. I said that Mrs. M'Keon had told me that she (Miss Saurin) neglected the juniors, and gave the seniors the best bits. Miss Saurin replied: "She has no reason to complain, for I always give her a good dinner to keep her tongue quiet." (Much laughter.)

Examination resumed: In April, 1860, I sent Miss Saurin to Clifford. I did not send her, as she said, to get up the school again, but because she had set such a bad example to the junior sisters at Hull, and especially to keep her from unauthorized intercourse with seculars. She was more exposed to that at Hull than at Clifford. She had more opportunity for gossiping.

With whom?—With school-girls and visitors. There are more visitors at Hull than at Clifford. Different sisters reported this to me. They are here to give their own evidence. I took Miss Saurin to Dublin with me in September, 1860. I think I had promised her mother that I would take her over sometimes. We stayed partly at Baggot-street, and partly at one of the branch houses. She did not go home, but remained in one of the convents. Her relatives came to see her as often, and for as long as they wished. I saw Mrs. Saurin. Nothing passed more than ordinary conversation. I returned to Clifford from Dublin in the beginning of November, 1860. Miss Saurin accompanied me. I went to Hull for a few days.

Either in the year 1860, or at any other time, did you request Miss Saurin to tell you her confession to the priest?—No; I did not.

Did anything ever pass between you and her on that subject at all, that you can recollect?—She once told me herself the advice the priest had given to her.

The Lord Chief Justice: Of her own accord?—Yes. When she told me of it, she accused herself for not obeying him.

When was this?—I cannot tell the precise time, but I recollect the circumstance.

To Mr. Mellish: I spoke to her of her writing letters to her relations. I said they were not like those which sisters usually write; that they were tender and affectionate in their expressions.

The Lord Chief Justice: Do you speak of letters to her father and mother?—Yes, my lord, and to other relations. She said she had asked the advice of her confessor, and that he said she might or ought to write affectionately. Sisters are allowed to write affectionately to their friends, but not in the excessive manner she did. She was in the habit of volunteering information about her confession until I stopped it.

The Lord Chief Justice: Are we to understand that she might write to her parents affectionately, but not tenderly?—Not excessively—not using expressions of tenderness.

The Lord Chief Justice: Do you recollect any of her tender expressions?—No, I do not; but the whole tone was more excessively affectionate than that of any other sister.

Mr. Mellish: "My ever and very dearest uncle." Is that too strong an expression towards an uncle?

The Lord Chief Justice: The uncle was a priest. It might be towards a secular uncle. (Laughter.)

Mr. Mellish: Do you expect a general reserve?—Yes; that is part of the instructions.

These natural affections are to be repressed?—Yes, within reasonable bounds.

The Lord Chief Justice: Do you understand that a nun is not to love her father and mother as much as a secular should?—She may, and perhaps more.

But not to express it?—They may express love to their parents, but they are not to be excessive in their demonstrations of affection. They are told that everything should be moderated by religious reserve.

Mr. Mellish : Have you ever required her to tell what she told the priest or the priest her in confession?—Never once. Never.

Did she say to you she could not remember what he said?—No such conversation occurred.

And did you give her time to remember, and then ask her again?—No.

Did you say that no other sister in the community would refuse you?—No.

Had you ever asked any other sister?—No. Miss Saurin named one sister the other day here, but she went to Australia in 1859.

The Lord Chief Justice : I did not understand the plaintiff. o fix a date.

Mr. Mellish : The fact of her being away is only mentioned to show why she cannot be called to contradict the plaintiff.

Examination continued : I was absent from recreation in 1857, for several days, owing to my engagement at the out schools ; but not in any subsequent year, except, perhaps, once or twice when business required. I never absented myself with Mrs. Kennedy for the purpose of leaving Miss Saurin no one to talk to.

Did you ever desire that she should be alone with the novices and postulants?—No ; on the contrary, Miss Saurin remained at Clifford from 1860 until 1864, with the exception of an occasional visit to Hull for a few days. She came to a retreat nearly every year. When I went to Clifford I received statements from Mrs. M'Keon. I received them from time to time. She did not enter much into detail. The reports have been destroyed. I generally destroyed such letters. The letters of Mrs. M'Keon to which I refer have been destroyed within the last two years. They were very unfavourable to Miss Saurin. They complained of Miss Saurin's disobedience, and said she would do just as she liked.

The Lord Chief Justice : You say the letters have been destroyed within two years. When were they destroyed!—Defendant : Yes, about two years—since the action commenced. My reason for doing so is this : They contained matters of conscience, and I would rather suffer any penalty than allow the letters to be produced, as they contained private matters relating to Mrs. M'Keon. They would have been useful to us in other respects. The action commenced on the 10th of November, 1866.

The Lord Chief Justice : I should have taken care, and so would any judge, that those parts were not read. I doubted the expression, "within two years," and that is why I asked the question. —Defendant : The letters were destroyed early in 1867.

The Lord Chief Justice : Were you aware that a summons had been taken out for an inspection of the documents before the letters were destroyed? —Defendant : I do not think so. In 1861 plaintiff did not treat the sisters properly at Clifford. She gave them bad salt butter, whilst she provided me and herself with good She was irregular in her duties—talked to seculars—the young women of the village, who came on Sunday evening for instruction. She meddled with the laundry work, by washing her own things when another had been appointed for that duty. She gathered unripe fruit from the garden when forbidden, and I saw it concealed in the pantry.

The Lord Chief Justice : What fruit?—Defendant : Gooseberries. (Laughter.)

The Lord Chief Justice : About how many?— Defendant : About half a pint or a pint. In July we do not burn lights, but go to bed without candles. She used candles. I found one in the refectory half burnt. She said the plumber had been using it. I found he had wanted it, but only for a few minutes, and he could not have burnt so much of it the time he required it. (Laughter.) I spoke to her again about using the candle, and she did not then deny that she had used it for her private purpose. I often have found three half-burnt candles broken behind some plates or saucers in the pantry. That was not the place to keep them. She had the sole charge of the candles, and no one else had used them. I told her, in 1861, no community washing should be done on a certain day. I went to the kitchen, and met one of the sisters, who told me that Miss Saurin had washed her clothes against my orders ; and when I spoke to her she said she had done it because her clothes were so badly washed the previous week by Sister Bridget, the lay sister. I spoke to plaintiff, and she replied she would do nothing to be drummed at. I afterwards spoke to her of her spiritual danger, when she admitted her faults, and doubted if she knew her obligations, but she would try to be better for the future. She spoke to strangers when she was forbidden, and she came into the room where I was with a visitor unsolicited, and spoke to the stranger—that is against the rules. She was acquainted with the stranger, the Rev. Mr. Collimore, the chaplain of the convent. The rule is not to speak to the chaplain without permission.

The Lord Chief Justice : Is that the reverend gentleman to whom you refer in your statement of charges against the plaintiff?—Defendant : In which of the statements? I refer to two.

The Lord Chief Justice : In whose presence she was in a state of excitement?—Defendant : No ; that is another. There was a statement made to me about this time that she prevented the bells being rung at the proper time for the community exercises. I reproved her in the presence of the sisters for not allowing the sister bellringer to ring the bell at the proper time for dinner. The clock at Clifford was frequently altered. Miss Saurin denied that she had ever done it. One Sunday the bell rang for church, and all were ready to go to church except Miss Saurin. I sent the other sisters to church, and remained to accompany Miss Saurin. I begged her to hasten, lest we should be late for mass, which is considered a grievous sin on Sunday. She did not appear to me to hasten, but to be very slow in her movements. As the clock struck ten we left the house, and when we arrived at the church it was ten minutes before the mass bell had rung. The clock must have been put forward, and no one could have known it but herself. She must have done it for her private purpose, and she seemed to be aware of the clock being fast.

The Lord Chief Justice : I can understand a late person putting it back, but not forward. —Defendant : She appeared to be fond of getting up early, and, by putting the clock on a quarter of an hour, she got that additional time. Others can better testify to that than myself. They are forbidden to rise before the appointed time, whether they can sleep or not. Plaintiff acted as infirmarian. One of the sisters had the mumps. (Laughter.) Miss Saurin, I found, had given her thick, hard bread, with very little butter, and a small complement of tea. This sister told me she could not eat the bread, but she had drunk the tea. I spoke to Miss Saurin about it. At this time another sister was ill, and very feverish, and I discovered that she had not had a drink from early morning, although she was suffering from extreme thirst. I went to the school, and directed Miss Saurin to prepare a drink, and spoke to her of her uncharitableness. Miss Saurin left the school, but did not give the sister the drink until late in the afternoon. I gave her the order about half-past one or two o'clock.

Mr. Mellish: Do you remember about this time giving her some shirts to cut out?—I do.

Did you tell her to cut them out on a Sunday? —I do not know; but I do know that she spent two or three week-days cutting them out. This was at Hull.

Did she ever cut out shirts on a Sunday in Clifford?—I do not know.

How many shirts were there to be cut out?— Fourteen. She was not to make them all. Several sisters made them. One made seven of them, and school children helped.

Did you order her to get up at three o'clock in the morning to do work?—No. If she got up at three o'clock, it was her own act, and in perfect contradiction to my strict orders. The sisters desired to get up early, and obtained leave from me to rise at a quarter before five.

The Lord Chief Justice: Who were the shirts to be made for?—One of the priests at Hull. He sent them for the school children to make. They could not make them, and the community did. On one or two occasions, at her request, they were allowed to rise at four o'clock, but leave was only granted by entreaty.

Did you ever say to her, "I have allowed you too much liberty, and I am determined to put you down?"—I never did.

Did you ever do anything of that kind?—No. I put her under restraint in her intercourse with seculars; but the rule was not more strict in her case than in that of others.

Examination continued: In May, 1861, I found a piece of calico and a pair of scissors in her lap; also a needle. I asked her where she got them.

Did she show you your own name written on the calico in pencil?—I do not know; but I know I was satisfied with her explanations—quite satisfied. I found a veil in her cell. I questioned her as to it, and she said she had taken it. She had no need to have taken it, even for convenience, as she had two of her own. In August, 1861, Miss Saurin was at the retreat at Hull. A chapter of the sisters was held on the 24th. I reproved Miss Saurin in chapter for her insincerity, disobedience, irregularity at duties, and murmuring. Only community sisters are present at chapters. She said nothing at the chapter, but after she came to me, kissed me, fell on her knees, and said she was most grateful to me for the reproof I had given to her. She said that, in gratitude, she would pray for me every day so long as she lived, and that, if her former superior had acted towards her as I had that day done, she would have been a very different person.

She promised to begin from that moment a life of edification and reparation, and she seemed to consider it one of the greatest benefits I could have conferred on her. She seemed sincere, and I was thankful she was in such a good disposition as she appeared to be. She returned to Clifford. I received a letter from Mrs. Saurin in 1861, after the retreat, enclosing £5, and requesting me to send her daughter to Dublin on account of her father being in a precarious state of health, and his wishing to see his daughter before settling his temporal affairs. I replied, on the 4th of October, 1861, that circumstances prevented my allowing the plaintiff to leave, and suggested that he might as well come over, the weather being mild, and the voyage so rapid and easy between Kingston and Holyhead; that he might take the voyage with benefit to his health. I also returned the £5. I refused to let her go because, since her visit to Dublin in 1860, her conduct had become worse with regard to obedience and the observance of rule—which includes nearly everything. I thought a visit to her family would unsettle her. I observed that after every time she saw her relatives she became more disobedient, troublesome, and exacting.

The Lord Chief Justice: In what respect?— With regard to food and clothing; and she was demanding as of right, and making her wants known in an exacting manner.

By Mr. Mellish: I was willing to let her return to the convent at Dublin altogether, and most desirous she should do so. In 1862, the letters were intercepted at Clifford. I was not there at the time, but an intercepted letter was sent to me at Hull. I considered writing that letter without leave an offence which incurred dismissal. That was always taught us—no matter to whom the letter was written. It was on account of that I wrote to Mr. Matthews, having previously written a letter of expostulation to Miss Saurin herself. I never saw that letter after I sent it to her.

By the Solicitor-General: I did not take it from her myself.

By Mr. Mellish: I wrote to her previously one letter of expostulation, telling her how much I regretted her committing such a fault, and I told her that if she had informed me of her wish I would have given her every facility for leaving our community, and so have prevented her committing such an offence. She wrote me a letter in reply, which I destroyed shortly after receiving it. (The letter of the witness, dated the 13th of March, 1862, which has been already published, in which she said she was not in ignorance of Sister Mary's wish to leave the community, was put in and read.) Those were the true sentiments I felt at that time. Miss Saurin came over to Hull after this letter was sent—about 25th July, 1862. I spoke to her about it, and she was told that, if she insisted on remaining in the community, it would oblige us to make her faults known which we had previously concealed. I was not present then. Mrs. Kennedy will say what her reply was. On the 27th of July I pressed her about having sent a letter. She denied she had ever sent a letter without permission since she had come to England. I told her I knew she had sent one without permission, and she again denied it most positively and repeatedly: but, after some time, she admitted sending two to her uncle, the Rev. Thos. Matthews. The intercepted letter would have made a third. She said she had never sent one except to him, though I had received one or more letters in reply to one or more which she had written to other people. I think I received one from one of the Carmelite sisters beginning something like this: "I received your letter of the 10th of April," showing that Miss Saurin had sent letters which had never come either under my observation or that of the local superior. So far as I remember at the present time, no one was present at the interview with Miss Saurin. I do not remember anything more that she said. That was not the time she signed the written acknowledgment. Soon after that she spoke to me, and denied again having sent a letter without permission. I can only give the substance of what she said—I don't remember the words. She said, "When I acknowledged to have sent two, I did not know what I was saying; it was all a mistake. I was sick, and did not know what I was about." I told her I knew she had sent the letters, and she still persisted in saying she had never sent them without permission. I next conversed with her on the subject when she came and voluntarily acknowledged her faults a few days afterwards. She knelt down of her own accord, and said, "Oh, reverend mother, the lies I have told! I did send the two letters to my uncle, and wish to acknowledge having denied doing so. All my previous denials to Mrs. M'Keon were false, and the admissions I made to you in July were true; and my subsequent denials were false." She spoke of Mrs. M'Keon as having been almost a complete dupe of hers. She said, "Poor Sister Mary Agnes! I gave her so much trouble," and asked me if she might kneel down and beg her pardon. She led me to suppose that she had deceived Mrs. M'Keon very much by the lies she had told her. I asked how it was she then made all those admissions? She said it was one of the instructions that had been given on the previous day, at the retreat, on the apostacy of Judas, which she thought so applicable to herself, that had induced her to come. I then asked her if she would have any objection to sign an acknowledgment of deceiving Mrs. Kennedy and Mrs. M'Keon. She made no difficulty, and expressed her willingness to do so. Subsequently she made the acknowledgment, in the presence of Mrs. Kennedy and Mrs. M'Keon, that she had written and sent the two letters to her uncle—all that she had acknowledged to me—and asked their forgiveness. One acknowledgment, I think, was written on August 4th, and one on the 6th. (Documents handed to witness.) These are the two acknowledgments. One is in her handwriting, written at my request. The second I wrote, for I thought the first was not sufficiently explicit, because it did not explain the purport of the letters.

By the Court: I told her the purpose of getting this acknowledgment was in order that the bishop might see it.

By Mr. Mellish: By my suggestion she also wrote resolutions for the future. That is the ordinary practice in retreats. She gave me a copy, but it was destroyed. I am not sure whether it was a copy or the original that I got. Mrs. Saurin came to me about the 9th of April, 1862; it was during Easter-week. She told me she had met her brother a few days before, and he had asked her if she had heard from Hull, and from what he said she supposed there must be something wrong; and, in her anxiety, she came over to me first, not to her daughter. She begged to know what her daughter's conduct had been. I told her in general terms of her disobedience, breaches of rule, particularly of the rule of silence, and of the clandestine correspondence which had been discovered. I particularized a few of her faults. Mrs. Saurin agreed with me in every particular, and said I was right in the manner in which I was acting towards her. I asked her to obtain admission for her daughter into another community, and said I had not applied to the bishop in regard to her daughter's misconduct, as I hoped it might be unnecessary to expose her faults to his lordship if her friends would arrange for her removal at once. Mrs. Saurin seemed very indignant, and frequently exclaimed, "Oh, the rule, the rule," as if she considered the observance of rule of the first importance in a "religious." I told her it was likely, if I applied to the bishop, that her daughter would be dismissed from the community. Mrs. Saurin said, if she was dismissed she should never enter her parents' home again, and should have no sympathy from her. She also said what she had heard from Father Matthews was the first intimation she had had of any unpleasantness between her daughter and the community.

The Lord Chief Justice: It is unfortunate none of this was put to Mrs. Saurin herself.

Mr. Mellish: I did, my lord. I asked her if she had said, "Oh, the rule, the rule."

The Solicitor-General and his learned juniors dissented.

The Lord Chief Justice: I never heard anything about "Oh, the rule, the rule."

Mr. Mellish: I can assure your lordship I put it to her, but after she had denied the whole conversation, I may not have put the whole of the questions which I have down on my brief. I may have stopped at two-thirds, because she distinctly denied the whole conversation. She did not speak out, if your lordship will recollect.

The Lord Chief Justice referred to his notes, but, finding no record of such examination, said the two versions of the conversation were very different indeed.

Examination continued: I had given orders to the local superior at Clifford not to allow Miss Saurin to see her friends, but I gave Mrs. Saurin an order to permit her to see her daughter when she went. Mrs. Saurin asked me to take her daughter to Hull, to be under my own eye, and then all would be right. I said I could not, as her example was bad. I told her it was strange that she should only have heard from her father about the intercepted letters, and I quoted one to her, at which she seemed much confused, and muttered something which I could not catch. She said she was going then to her daughter at Clifford. I said I was glad she had come to me first, as she could not see her without the order which I gave her. The bishop came from Hull on the 25th July, 1862. I communicated with him on the subject.

By the Court: I gave the order not to allow any of her friends to see Miss Saurin after I discovered the clandestine correspondence, and I revoked it after seeing Mrs. Saurin. Her friends saw her after that without hindrance.

By Mr. Mellish : The 25th of July was the first time I saw the bishop, and I spoke to him in general terms of Miss Saurin's misconduct, but I am not aware that I spoke of anything in particular.

By the Court : I can't say whether I referred to the clandestine correspondence. I applied to him for re-admission for her into Baggot-street, which, if not granted, would oblige me to apply for her being suspended altogether.

A letter to the bishop from the witness was then read, in which she stated that she had consulted her councils in regard to the dismissal of the plaintiff, and asking him to have her dismissed from the community.

Witness : The council I consulted was the assistant-mother, the bursar, and the mistress of novices. They were Mrs. Kennedy and Mrs. M'Keon. There was then no mistress of the novices. Mrs. M'Keon was then mother-assistant. I had had a correspondence with Baggot-street, but the letters were destroyed.

By the Court : That was at the end of July or beginning of August of that year.

By Mr. Mellish : I generally destroyed letters the day after receiving them. I got no answer to my letter to the bishop. Miss Saurin went back to Clifford in August, 1862 ; but previously to that she had written to her uncle, the Rev. Thomas Matthews. I had advised Miss Saurin to gain admission to the convent in Drogheda, because I thought her uncle's influence might tend to assist her. She refused to do so, and said she would never go to Drogheda. On the 27th of July I told her I was about to write to Baggot-street to ask the community to receive her, and that I had the bishop's permission for doing so ; but I felt sure my request would be denied. She then was told it was likely she would be dismissed from our community ; that we were determined to do all in our power to obtain her removal. I advised her to write to Drogheda ; but said, "You always told me you would never go to St. Mary's, Drogheda ; therefore you are quite at liberty to do as you please. It is your affair and not mine, and it is quite optional with you. I just tell you how things are." She replied, "I wish to go to Drogheda, now I see how things are," and said she would write to her uncle to try and obtain admission for her into the convent. She then wrote the letter herself. I did not write it for her on her slate, nor did I dictate it to her, except one passage. This is the letter :—

"My dearest Uncle—The community are determined I shall not remain. You know the archbishop and the rev. mother at Baggot-street are determined I shall not return there. Unless you settle with your community to receive me, my dearest uncle, I know not what to do. The greatest act of charity you could do towards me is to settle it at once, if you can. If you write to say I can get to Drogheda, even for a while, rev. mother will send me. May I beg, as a great favour, you will not go to bishops or any one else about it ? But do let me know by next post, as rev. mother says the community here will wait no longer, as they are determined to take measures without delay for my removal. If the community in Drogheda consent to my going

there, rev. mother says they need never know why I leave here, only you wish it for the sake of my father and mother. You will be greatly surprised at this letter altogether—the horrid writing. For God's sake do not say a word to any of my friends, not even mamma—I know she would feel it so—if you possibly can. I feel it is the will of God. He has some wise design in all. How can I ever forgive all the trouble, &c., I am giving you, and worse than the trouble. I again and again beg you will settle it for me in charity, as soon as possible, and without any more fuss. Won't you write by next post?—Believe me your ever-faithful niece in J. Ct.

"SR. M. SCHOLASTICA."

What I dictated was this, except that they are not my exact words :—"The reverend mother says the community here will wait no longer, as they are determined to take measures without delay for my removal." I was writing to Baggot-street at the same time.

The Lord Chief Justice : If you only knew in reply to your letter that the plaintiff could not return to Baggot-street, how is it such an answer is given here?

Witness : I will explain that. When the clandestine correspondence was discovered, I wrote to Father Matthews to apply to the Baggot-street community, and to Mr. M'Naghten, the President of the Irish College, to obtain the plaintiff's admission into the community, but the applications were refused, and I told Miss Saurin so.

The Lord Chief Justice : If you knew the President and the mother at Baggot-street were determined she should not return there, what was the motive of your writing again in July to ask them to take her?

Witness : I did so in order to give her another chance, because I had not made a personal application.

The Lord Chief Justice : I presume you did not propose to give her a character ?—No. I did not tell them at Baggot-street all the faults she had ; but I told them in a general way that she was imperfect.

The Lord Chief Justice : That was a very imperfect way of telling them if you intended to give a candid representation.—Witness : I think I told them about the clandestine correspondence.

Examination continued : I had told Miss Saurin, I think, the result of the application made to Baggot-street by Mr. M'Namara and Mr. Matthews. The bishop held a visitation in the winter of 1862. Miss Saurin was then at Clifford, and she came to Hull. She saw the bishop at the visitation. The result was, nothing was done in regard to my application to remove her at that time. She afterwards went back to Clifford. It is not true that in July, 1862, I ordered her to take off her habit, and took out the lining. Some such transaction may have taken place, but it was in June, 1864. In 1858 or 1859, or previously, I told her I had received letters from her Jesuit brother which I had not given her. I think there were two which I did not give her until subsequently ; because he had spoken so disrespectfully and contemptuously of her former superiors in Baggot-street. I was afterwards informed that she had read them to the servants. The letters spoke of her having been put in the laundry in Baggot-street as an indignity. He called her former superiors, Madame Pity and Madame Maguire, and hoped they had given her her fortune on leaving. I said it was a pity that he had chosen to write such letters as he had done to her. She then acknowledged that her brother was wrong in having written as he had done. I don't know if she ever went to a drawer and saw her brother's letters. I gave her her brother's letters afterwards of my own accord. I never heard about the drawer until I heard it on the trial. I never said to her that she was to consider herself a novice to the rest of the community. What I did say to her was this. I was advising her to leave our community, and I said if she did not, perhaps she would get, as a penance, put the lowest in the community, and not be employed in the schools, but be employed in menial work.

The Lord Chief Justice: From that, I presume she had not been employed up to that time in menial work?—All the sisters are more or less employed in menial work.

What did you mean by imposing the penance of being put lowest in the community, and being employed in menial work?—I meant being entirely employed in menial work, instead of being partly employed in the schools.

By Mr. Mellish: I told her I did not think she could bring her spirit to submit to that, and I advised her to do all in her power to join another community. When I told her of the penance which might be imposed, to try the sincerity of her resolutions and the probability of her amendment, she told me she would be willing to be employed in any work—no matter how menial or laborious—provided she was allowed to remain in the community. She never got any penitence. I may have told Mrs. M'Keon to give her a distribution of time; that is common to all sisters. I impose one on myself. (Laughter.) Its object is to occupy the different parts of the day. I don't remember what the distribution was, if she had one.

By the Court: We have a horarium, which is approved by the bishop, and which determines the spiritual exercises of the community. The hours intervening are employed in such other manual or spiritual work as the superior may appoint. The distribution comes on during those times which are not marked in the general horarium.

Re-examination continued: The general horarium applies to the whole community. All the sisters, more or less, perform menial work. I ordered that less should be imposed on the plaintiff than on others.

By the Court: That was in order to prevent any breaches of charity or any want of peace and quietness. I heard she wanted to assist in the washing, and I wrote to the local superior not to allow her to do such labour.

The Lord Chief Justice: But if it gave her satisfaction, why not?—She would have had to get up earlier in the morning, and that I did not wish. I think the local superior imposed it upon her, but when I heard of it I was not pleased, because I did not wish her to have anything which might be considered the work of a servant.

Examination continued: Mrs. Feron presided in the school at that time. She was not a novice.

Miss Saurin was put under her in the school; but that was not the least indignity. I did it because Mrs. Feron was better qualified in point of education to conduct the school than Miss Saurin. She was not ordered to be put junior to the other sisters, including the lay sisters. She had the charge of getting the schools clean; but the pupils performed the work of sweeping. In May, 1863, I went over to Clifford, and it was then I took away Miss Saurin's watch. Up to a certain time the sisters were allowed to have watches; but I introduced a rule that, as the watches became out of order, they should be given up to me. I was going to provide clocks, as being more generally useful. I got clocks for general use. The watches I have still. I did not have the watches repaired on account of the expense. I thought it more economical to have clocks. The present mother superior has eight or nine of the watches. Miss Saurin's watch has been given back to her. I asked for her watch when I went over, because I understood it was out of order. She went to her cell and brought me the watch. I think I went with her. In handing it to me, she said, "It is not my watch: it belongs to my brother." I said, "That can scarcely be," and I opened the watch and showed her the words engraved on the cover, "The gift of her loving father, M. Saurin." She then said when her father gave it to her she had told him perhaps she would not be allowed to keep it, and that he said then, "I only lend it to you; it shall be Tom's watch." But I think at that time her brother was not living. She had leave to have that watch as her own, and as the property of the community; but it was a breach of our rules to have a watch as a loan from an extern, and to have retained it she ought first to have obtained permission. Nothing was said about disposing of the watch in a lottery.

The Lord Chief Justice: Did you take away the watches of other sisters at the same time? —I took away some previously and some subsequently.

By Mr. Mellish: The watch was out of repair when I took it. I next saw Miss Saurin in 1863. She came over to the annual retreat in August, 1863. She spoke then, in general terms, of her own disobedience, which, she said, gave her a great deal of trouble. I said to her that it was customary with the sisters to particularize. She said she could not particularize, because her friends were so much mixed up with her that, if she told her faults to me, it would compromise her friends. I ordered her then to write a monthly statement of her faults to me, as all the other absent sisters were to do, from that time. They were only the external faults and violation of rules. I did not tell her that when she returned to Clifford she would have to endure great penance and suffering. She said she was very sorry for the faults she had committed. She wished me, in her name, to beg pardon of the Clifford community, and to tell them she was resolved to do better for the future. I told the community, and asked them in her presence to help her in every way that they could. I never told her she would have to wear cast-off clothes of lay sisters if she remained in the convent, or anything to that effect. I never said in August, 1863, she would never be able to endure the punishment which would be put upon her. I told her she was to have no unnecessary communication with externs, and I ordered the local superior to be more vigilant. She then went to Clifford and remained until the June of next year. I don't remember that I ordered any additional duties to be put upon her; but at the end of every retreat the duties are changed, and Miss Saurin may have had more or less to do, but I don't remember any special directions. I did not order that work should be specially done by her. Brushing and polishing floors and cleaning cells are done by all the sisters. I do not do so myself at present, but I have done so. No order was given by me that Miss Saurin should be put to more than ordinary domestic work, or that she was to have any different food to the other sisters. I received the monthly letters which have been read.

The Court then adjourned to Thursday morning.

EIGHTH DAY, *Thursday*, *February* 11*th:*

Mrs. Star's examination-in-chief was prolonged this day from the sitting of the Court to the breaking up thereof, a wearisome iteration of statements, and a painfully slow reading of papers, so inaccurately copied from their originals that corrections were called for in every sentence, dragging out this mere beginning of the beginning, or first stage in the prologue, to the evidence for the defence. The plaintiff, Miss Susan Saurin, in a secular black dress and a close black bonnet with the thickest of veils, sat on the bench below the leading counsel, accompanied by her sister and uncle, Father Matthew; Mr. and Mrs. Saurin, the parents of the young lady, watching the case from the gallery. Nuns and lay sisters, waiting to be called as witnesses, were seated in different parts of the court; and there were even more ladies present than have yet been seen since the trial began, sitting in rows of five and six together, instead of being sprinkled among the throng. A few prominent members of the aristocracy had places on the bench or near it. A good deal of the evidence was embarrassed by the difficulties of separating the tunic, stocking, and thimble-cases, and fixing them to their proper periods. Miss Saurin was told by her superior that she ought to have asked for "proper remedies," and that her unauthorised use of the convent tallow showed a "spirit of appropriation," defined by the witness in her evidence to-day as an apparent disposition in Miss Saurin to regard many things as her own which were merely intended for her benefit in common with the sisterhood, and in this manner to violate the vow of poverty. The mutton question, and the bread question, and other questions which had previously been much handled, were again brought into prominence. The stripping case was gone into somewhat minutely, the "taking off each article, one after another," being described in a string of questions and replies, till the matter of the "large pocket," and its "heterogeneous contents" was reached and made the most of. It did not, however, affect very materially the imputed "spirit of appropriation," Miss Saurin's worst offence with regard to the pocket having been her secretion of a pencil and tablets with notes unpleasing to the eye of the lady who detected their presence. Certain words used by Mrs. Star, in preceding conversations with Miss Saurin, had been jotted down in these tablets. "A smooth way that deceives" was one of the phrases; and there were others so abbreviated and reduced to simple signs and figures that they were impossible of interpretation. Little was adduced in the way of fact to support the charges of appropriation, or to bear out the more specific assertions in Mrs. Star's letter to her bishop, that Sister Scholastica was much given to pilfering. There had been losses of gloves among the sisters, the witness said. "Did *you* ever lose a glove?" asked the Lord Chief Justice. "Yes," was the answer; and "So have I; a good many," was the rejoinder. The rules, the customs, the very phraseology and nomenclature of convent-life puzzled the legal gentlemen not a little; and the clearing-up of several trifling mystifications caused occasional laughter. There was, for instance, a good deal of talk about "silence days," and a string of questions depended from the assumption that the rebellious sister had committed a peculiarly grave fault in violating one of these same "silence days;" till any special significance that there might have seemed to be in the answers of the witness to Mr. Russell was suddenly and amusingly destroyed by her informing him that *all* days are "silence days" except Sundays. It had been no "silence day" for Mrs. Star, this second day of her examination; and the judge, commiserating the fatigue which now and again weakened her voice, rendering it at times scarcely audible, closed the sitting at half-past four o'clock.

The hearing of the case was resumed at the sitting of the Court this morning.

The examination in chief of the defendant, Mrs. Star was resumed. She said, in reply to Mr. Chas. Russell; Between the time of the retreat, in August, 1863, and the following June, I received monthly letters from the plaintiff, and reports from Mrs. M'Keon, the local superior at Clifford. Things were not going well. There were continuous complaints. In June, 1864, it became necessary to make a change in the staff at Hull and Clifford, in consequence of the health of some of the sisters. In consequence of the representations made to me, I had resolved to remove Miss Saurin from Clifford to Hull in August, 1864. In the June of that year I went from Hull to Clifford with Mrs. Kennedy and two novices. I removed Miss Saurin in June, instead of in August, as I had intended, at the request of Mrs. Kennedy, who was to remain at Clifford as local superior. I told the plaintiff to get ready to accompany me. I did not see her until about three-quarters of an hour before I left. I then told her she was to go with me to Hull, and was only to take a change of clothing with her. The rest of her clothing was to be sent after her in a week. She brought more than I desired her to take. Part of the things were put into a basket. She brought the other things without my knowledge.

The Lord Chief Justice: How did she convey

them?—They were tied under her habit and skirt, and fastened in a bag under her cincture.

Examination resumed : I went into her room. Mrs. Kennedy may have been with me ; I do not remember. She had on a pair of stockings, and she was putting another pair over the pair she had on, although she had left another pair to be sent after her. As far as I can remember, I think I told her she was not to do so, as one pair would suffice.

Now plaintiff had said that she had put on one stocking and was not allowed to put on the other, and that she went to Hull with one stocking on. Is that correct ?—Certainly not.

The Lord Chief Justice : What she said was that she had one stocking on, and was putting on the other, and that they told her not to do so, but that she put it on.

Examination resumed : She had on a pair of stockings on going to Hull. I do not remember Mrs. Kennedy pushing on her boots roughly. I saw no such thing. Mrs. Kennedy saw us to the door. She did not push Miss Saurin down the steps. I do not believe any such rudeness occurred. Miss Saurin made no complaint whatever of such a thing. It would not have been wrong for the plaintiff to have made a complaint of a sister if it were well founded. When we set out for the railway station the weather was fair. The rain came on shortly afterwards. Miss Saurin held the umbrella because she walked on the left hand of me and her right hand was in the middle. She carried a very small wicker basket. I carried a similar basket, and was also carrying other things.

She said you wanted more than your fair share of the umbrella. Is that so ?—No; it is not. I once told her to hold it straight.

Was she more wet than you ?—No ; it was not very wet—merely a shower.

Examination resumed : When I went to Clifford with Mrs. Kennedy and the two novices, I gave no direction as to taking bedding from Miss Saurin. The sisters were left to arrange the matter among themselves, and they thought that, as some were leaving next day, they would not trouble Mrs. Grimstone on the subject. I never heard a complaint on the subject until I heard it from her at this trial. After we got to Hull I gave her a distribution of time on paper, and asked her to copy it on to her tablet. She commenced to do so very slowly on blank pages. She had not to efface anything from the tablet in order to write the distribution of time. I took the tablet out of her hand to write the distribution of time myself, she was doing it so slowly ; and I perceived that she had made notes on the tablets respecting the sisters and different incidents that had occurred in the convent. I turned over the leaves of the tablet ; I found also remarks on the meals.

Did she say anything ?—Yes ; she said, " Do not read my confession."

What did you say?—I replied I would not read her confession for any consideration ; but I said, " What I see written here are the words and actions of others, and nothing about yourself." She then said she had written those notes at the retreat. I replied, " Is it possible you have occupied the time of the retreat in noting down what had occurred in the community?" She said, " Oh, no, it was not for the retreat ; it was for you, reverend mother, I wrote them." I said "That can scarcely

be ; for I see here a notice of a direction of my own, and you would scarcely report me to myself." The words were " Not allowed to speak to Mrs. Grimstone." The only sister whose name, or rather initials, appeared written on the tablet was Mrs. M'Keon. I spoke to her about writing such notes, and told her not to write similar ones any more, and not to have a tablet or pencil without permission—that when she required writing materials I would supply them. She appeared very much confused and ashamed, and I allowed her to efface from the tablet what she had written.

The Lord Chief Justice : Did you allow her or direct her?—I cannot recall the words I used. They were to the effect that she might rub out what she had written, as I did not wish to keep it as an evidence against her.

Did she efface the writing?—She did, eagerly.

Examination continued : I think it was on that occasion I asked her to empty her pockets.

Why?—That I might see she had no more writing materials.

How many pockets had she on that occasion ? —I think six ; but at least five. (Laughter.)

The Lord Chief Justice : What is the usual allowance? (Renewed laughter.)—It is usual for a sister to have one large pocket and a watch pocket.

Examination continued : One of her pockets was an independent or loose pocket ; the rest were in her clothes.

What were the contents of the pockets ?— Well ; they contained a heterogeneous mass of odds and ends. (Laughter.)

Of what kind ?—Bags filled with bits of calico, thread, bits of silk—a variety of things of that sort.

The Lord Chief Justice : Can you name anything else ?—Bits of calico.

The Lord Chief Justice : I have got the calico. (Laughter.) Were these things forbidden ?— No ; she might have had permission for them.

Had she ?—She had permission for working materials ; but whether for these particular ones I do not know.

Mr. Russell : Was there anything unusual in the quantity?—Yes. It was very strange to see such a mass of things with one individual, and concealed in her pockets.

Examination continued : The things themselves were trifling things. She had also a penknife ; she told me the blades were broken. She told me she wished to get new blades put into the knife. From the manner in which she spoke, I judged that the knife was her own. She did not say it was, but I was led to infer it. I afterwards found that it was not her knife.

When ?—After her separation from the community I desired that everything she could claim should be put together, in order to be sent to her. This knife was amongst the things ; and one of the sisters claimed it, saying, " This is my knife, reverend mother. It was taken from me in 1859."

To the Solicitor-general : I have got the knife yet, but it is not in town. It can be sent for.

Examination continued : Amongst other things in her pocket she had a small paper of starch. She had no right to it, nor had any other sister. Starch is not specifically forbidden, but it is not a usual thing to have. She said she had asked Sister Mary Evangelista (Mrs. Fearon) about it, I said I would inquire about it, as Mrs. Fearon was at Clifford. On a subsequent day she came to me, and said that the starch had not been given to her by Mrs. Fearon, but by a lay sister. I did not act roughly with her on the occasion of the emptying her pockets. I endeavoured to put my hand in one pocket, and she held it. I advised her to sew up all her pockets except one. The lining of her habit was double the usual width. I told her I wished her to lessen the width. She measured it with me along with mine, and it was found to be double. I put a small cut in her lining to mark the place. She cut the lining out herself, and settled it in a different room to the room in which I was, and she did not take off her habit to do so. On that occasion I spoke to her about her clothing. The sisters in Clifford were allowed more clothing than those in Hull. They did not wash so frequently, as there were fewer persons to do the work, and the community was smaller. I told her to leave with me the superfluous things over and above what the sisters had in Hull. She had more of some articles, but her other clothing had not been sent from Clifford up to the time the order for her dismissal was made. Her clothing was as good as that of the other sisters, and, in some respects, it was better; but, taking it generally, it was as good.

Did you ever direct any exceptional treatment as to her dress up to the time of her dismissal?—No. She was treated on an equality with the other sisters up to her dismissal. I mean by that, the time of her separation from the community. I spoke to her in June, 1864, about Baggot-street, and told her she might make an application for her removal there. I had heard that there had been a change of superiors there since 1862, when the last application was made there; and I told her so; and, that she might have a chance of being re-admitted, that I would send some one to accompany her, and that, if the superior at Baggot-street refused to receive her, she might return to our community, but not as a member of it.

The Lord Chief Justice: In what capacity, then?—As a visitor. What I meant, and she understood, was that she was not to have the privileges of a sister.

The Lord Chief Justice: One consequence of which would be that she would be liable to be turned out whenever you wished?—She would be liable, my lord; but I did not say so at the time. (A laugh.) I did not admit it to my own mind.

Mr. Russell: Was it your intention at the time to get her out by false pretences?—Oh, no.

The Lord Chief Justice: I do not think she had such an intention.

Mr. Russell: What did she say?—I think what she said was that she would consult with her uncle.

Cross-examined: In July, 1864, a question arose as to a knitted petticoat. It is usual in the summer to change the character of a sister's clothing. I went to her room. I had waited for the very hot weather. I bought her a thinner petticoat than she was wearing, and took away the heavier one. There was no rudeness used by me on that occasion. She did not complain to me of any rudeness.

The Lord Chief Justice: But would not complaining to you, the mother superior, be a breach of the rule?—It would all depend on the manner in which it would be done. The sisters are bound to make known all their wants.

The Lord Chief Justice: That is a very different thing to complaining to the reverend mother of herself.

Mr. Russell: Would it have been wrong of her to have said, "Reverend mother, I would rather keep it on?"—No.

Did she make any complaint about your taking away the skirt?—No; she made no objection to it.

Examination resumed: The skirt I left her was as good as the other sisters wore. It was exactly similar. In winter there is a redistribution of heavy clothing to those who have not their winter clothing by them.

The Lord Chief Justice: Then you did not take winter clothing away from all the sisters?—No, my Lord. There was an exception made in her case.

Why an exception?—Because I found when she came from Clifford she spent a great deal of time in re-modelling and re-fixing her clothes. I told her not to do so; that I would have her clothes repaired instead.

Well; did the skirt want repairing?—I took charge of it, my lord.

Making that difference between her and the rest?—Yes.

To Mr. Russell: She had sent more clothes to the wash every week than was usual. That was one reason I made the exception in her case. I remonstrated with her about it, and told her the lay sisters who did the washing were not strong, and were overworked.

To the Court: I cannot say how much more she sent to the wash than others. I had received information on the subject.

To Mr. Russell: A general regulation had been made in 1862 or 1863, limiting the sisters to such articles of dress as might be needful. In place of giving up her superfluous clothing she joined them together, or sewed parts of one on another, so as to increase the bulk without decreasing the number. It was not done with a view to repairing one article with part of another. She did not tell me she was doing so.

To the Lord Chief Justice: It was after her return to Hull in 1864, when all her clothes were brought from Clifford, I made the discovery.

Mr. Russell: The plaintiff states that after you took her skirts you wore them yourself?—No; I did not.

What did you do with them?—There were two knitted skirts taken, and I gave them to two sisters, Mrs. Fearon and Mrs. Rafter.

To the Court: I took one skirt in July, and the other as soon as her clothes came from Clifford.

To Mr. Russell: It was in the winter of 1864 I gave the skirts to the two sisters. I thought they required additional clothing.

The Lord Chief Justice: What did the plaintiff get instead?—She had a warmer habit.

But did she get a skirt?—No, my lord; but she had a warm winter habit, which the others had not.

To Mr. Russell: The habit is the outer garment —the skirt is the petticoat. There are light summer habits and heavy winter ones.

The Lord Chief Justice: Had the two sisters you speak of winter as well as summer habits?—One had and one had not; but the one that had was delicate.

Examination continued : By the rules all the property is in common. Clothes may be changed from one to another. It is quite usual, and frequently done. Her clothing in the winter of 1864 was sufficient. No complaint was made in that year that her clothing was insufficient. If she had made a representation on the subject I should have inquired for myself, and given her more if I found she required more. At the end of 1864, or the beginning of 1865, she asked for another veil, different from that she wore. I said I thought the one she had was good enough. She had brought it with her to England.

The Lord Chief Justice : In 1857?—Yes.

It was seven years old ?—Yes ; but I have been wearing the veil I have on me now for ten years.

Examination continued : Her veil was good. On the following day I saw her veil on her, and it was torn in two places. There were no tears in it on the previous day—certainly not in the places in which I saw it torn on the next day. On the day following that it was torn in five additional places. I then gave her another veil. I gave the torn one to another sister to mend for herself, and she wore it nearly daily for three years. I thought the plaintiff had destroyed the first veil wantonly, and therefore I gave her a better one.

The Lord Chief Justice : Did you reprove her. —No, my lord ; I thought it was useless.

Examination continued : She always kept her stockings before that time in good repair. I found in 1864 that when they came from the wash they were torn in many places, and that repairs were done in parts not usually worn away—in the legs of the stockings, and not in the feet. Once or twice on giving her clean stockings I asked her for the soiled ones, and I found they had not tears in them, and had not tears in them when they came back from the wash. I once gave her a fine toilet towel, without any hole in it, and she sent it to the wash so torn that it never could be used after. Her tunics, or under garments, were given to her in good repair. They were of the same quality as I wore myself ; when they were sent to the wash they could scarcely be repaired.

The Lord Chief Justice : Did this happen every week ?—For several weeks.

To Mr. Russell : These tears could not have been the result of accident, as the articles were of the same quality and age as my own. This was in 1864, and as to the tunics, in the winter of 1865. In March, 1865, I saw that Miss Saurin had either a piece of calico or a piece of paper round the finger on which the thimble was worn. I asked her why she had it on, and she said that the thimble was too large for her, and that that was the reason she wore the rag. I said, "You had better have a smaller one," and I gave her a bag of thimbles to choose from. I think she tried on one or two, and then said that the one she had been wearing would do. I may have taken out two or three, but I made no selection. She afterwards said her finger was sore. I looked, and the finger on which she wore her thimble was not sore at all.

It is suggested that you selected a brass thimble, and put it on her sore finger to make it hurt her ?—She said so.

Had you any such intention ?—No.

Did you do any such thing ?—No. The finger she wore the rag on and on which she wore a thimble was not sore at all. There was a sore on the top of the first finger, but at the side which could not be touched by the thimble.

You are quite certain about that ?—Quite.

The plaintiff says that you made her wash some tallow off her finger which she had put on to soothe a chilblain. Did you ever do so ?—I remember her taking tallow, but not that she put it on her finger. I never desired her to wash tallow off her finger either on that or any other occasion. Nothing of the kind happened. Of that I am quite positive. Some time in the year 1864 or 1865 I found in her room, and in other parts of the house, small pieces of tallow—not very much. One had fallen on the floor, and had been trodden on. Finding tallow in her cell and in the community room where she was, I asked her about it, and she told me then or later that she had taken it for her chilblains. I told her she should not have taken it, and that if she had applied to me for a remedy for her chilblains she should have had it. The sisters might take a little tallow, certainly, without breach of rule. The fault I found was the letting of it fall about the house. I never ordered her to wash tallow off her hands. I may have told her to wash her hands, but the washing had no reference to tallow.

Did you ever tell her to wash her hands in order to inflict pain on her ?—No, never to inflict pain.

Did she acknowledge having taken the tallow as a fault ?—No ; I reproved her, that is all.

Examination continued : The next morning after the matter of the thimble, in the community room, in the presence of the sisters, she knelt down to beg pardon for her conduct of the previous day. She had been very violent about the thimble, after she took the brass one.

The Lord Chief Justice : Then she did take another thimble ?—She did.

I understood you to say she told you the one she had would do ?—So she did, my lord ; but I said I thought it better she should have one that would fit. I required her to take it, and she did.

Examination continued : She begged pardon of the sisters for the bad example she had set them. What she had done was this : After she got a thimble from the bag which fitted her, and was required to take it, she said, "I am a persecuted poor creature."

Did she allege that the finger on which she was to put it was sore ?—Yes.

And you examined it, and found it was not ?— I did. It was not sore.

To the Lord Chief Justice : It was then she said she was a poor persecuted creature.

What sort of a thimble had she been wearing—silver or brass ?—I think it was a steel one.

What was the one she was required to ake ? —A brass one. All that were in the bag t brass.

Mr. Russell : What kind of thimbles do the sisters wear ?—Silver, brass, ivory, or steel.

The Lord Chief Justice : Did you take her silver thimble from her ?—That was in June, 1864.

Why did you do so ?—It had been given to her by an extern.

By whom ?—By Mrs. Grimston.

One of the supporters of the convent and school?—Yes; a benefactress.

Mr. Russell: Should she not have asked leave before she received it?—Yes.

Did she do so?—Not from me. She might have asked leave of the local superior.

The Lord Chief Justice: Did you ascertain whether she had or not?—I did not.

Was it not right that you should have done so?—It was not necessary. I did not wish her to retain it.

Mr. Russell: Why?—Because I saw in her a spirit of appropriation. (A laugh.)

In what way?—She appeared to regard all things which were given to her as her own, contrary to the spirit of the rule of poverty. Everything should be regarded as belonging to and for the use of the community.

To the Court: When a sister receives a present she must give it to the superior, who can retain it or give it back as she judges best. I have taken things from other sisters in a similar manner. It was a constant practice with me as an exercise of poverty.

To Mr. Russell: That practice is not carried out so strictly in Baggot-street, but it is in other communities.

Examination continued: Next day, as I have stated, the plaintiff begged pardon on her knees for having lost her temper, as she appeared to have done. She then made an indirect charge against me.

The Lord Chief Justice: While she was kneeling?—Yes.

What did she say?—She spoke about her food.

Still kneeling?—Yes, my lord. She spoke very incoherently.

To Mr. Russell: I cannot give her words, but there is another witness here who can who heard her more distinctly. She complained of sisters turning their backs upon her at recreation. She spoke of the bread to the effect that she got bad bread. She said it was either black or mouldy. She also spoke of persecution and tyranny. She added that she could get into another convent if she chose, but that she would not go. She was very excited. I was not conscious of having done anything to persecute her. What I did was to make her good, quiet, and happy. I told the sisters that the self-accusation of faults was not intended to give an opportunity to the imperfect to give vent to their bitter feelings—that I had allowed Sister Scholastica to speak as she had done without interruption that they might know her, and judge for themselves of the manner in which she had spoken to me in private for many months. I then addressed Miss Saurin, and said, "I excused you yesterday because I saw you were in a passion; but to-day you coolly and deliberately give vent to your bitter feelings, and accuse me of tyranny and persecution. You have just now said that you could get into a convent if you liked, but that you would not go." I then pressed her to go. I said, "Do go;" and spoke to the effect that we would all be very thankful. I was then in very delicate health, brought about by the anxiety I experienced on account of Miss Saurin.

The Lord Chief Justice: Anxiety of what sort?—The danger the community were in and herself; and also on account of the reports I had heard about her.

What reports?—About the children's dinners.

Do you mean to say those reports affected your health?—The anxiety I felt did.

To Mr. Russell: The reports were made to me by three sisters. They were to the effect that they had reason to believe that Miss Saurin took part of the children's dinners. I felt unequal to correct her. I feared it might become public and and bring disgrace upon us. I spoke to her on two occasions about it in presence of the community. The complaints continued after that. I did not censure her when speaking to her, nor did I tell her of the reports.

You were worried and anxious about Miss Saurin?—I was.

Examination continued: In April, 1865, I wrote to the bishop, in consequence of this anxiety, offering my resignation. (Letter, already published, read.) I had spoken to the bishop about Miss Saurin in 1862. Between that and 1865 I made no complaint to him about her. When I wrote there were postulants and novices at Hull. There had been and was no difference with any one of the sisters except the plaintiff. The letter stated the facts truly. I was anxious to be relieved of my responsibility. I received a reply from the bishop, asking what where the points of difference between us, and I wrote the letter of the 1st of May, stating honestly the facts. The passage in reference to stealing from the school children was written in consequence of the reports I had received. The bishop, in his reply, asked where she passed her novitiate, and I informed him. In May, 1865, Mrs. Saurin came over to Hull. Miss Saurin was out when her mother came. She was at the out-school, where the sisters taught the poor children. When Miss Saurin returned she had dinner before she saw her mother. I then sent her to Mrs. Saurin. That was about a quarter or twenty minutes past four. Her mother came at three. The next religious exercise the sisters have to attend is at five o'clock. She was with her mother until the warning bell rang. She then asked me might she remain from lecture, and I said "Yes," but that she should attend vespers at twenty-five minutes after five. They are part of the daily office which the sisters have to say. When we had commenced vespers, Miss Saurin came to the chapel and asked me if her mother might come on the following morning early for a few minutes to say good-bye. I made a sign for her to go to her place in the chapel. It is against usage to speak while vespers are going on. She went to her place; and when vespers were concluded, in about twenty minutes, without waiting for the additional prayers, which are usually said after vespers, I told Miss Saurin she might return to her mother and remain until matins, at 7.20 p.m.

The Lord Chief Justice: Matins in the evening?

Mr. Russell: They are said over night. (A laugh.)

Examination continued: The long visit in the evening was in place of the short visit in the morning, when she was required to go to the school.

Mr. Russell: She states you caught her by the shoulder and drove her into a place in the chapel?—Nothing of the kind. I motioned to her. My hand may have touched her arm, but there was nothing whatever like rudeness. It all took place in the presence of the other sisters in the choir.

Examination continued : Soon after her mother's visit Miss Saurin expressed a desire to go to some other convent. In consequence of the reports I had heard as to the children's dinners, I changed her from the infant school, where she had no sister with her, to the Prince-street School, where she had Sister Mary Bernard—Mrs. Nelligan—with her.

To the Lord Chief Justice : There were reports afterwards of children's dinners being taken at Prince-street also.

To Mr. Russell : I did not tell Sister Mary Bernard my suspicions or the reason I was sending her. Mrs. Nelligan made a report of what occurred at Prince-street. I sent an articled pupil-teacher to the school. The sisters who attended the out-schools took a luncheon with them each day. I said to all the sisters that the children should not be asked for their dinners for any purpose whatever, even for another poor child.

To the Lord Chief Justice : The children brought their own dinners with them.

To Mr. Russell : They used to be put in a cupboard in the morning. The sisters had access to it. I directed that if the children did not finish their dinners at once they were to take away what remained. I told Miss Saurin in particular not to meddle with the children's dinners on any pretence whatever. She said she would not. This occurred in chapter in the presence of the community. I asked her to repeat my directions, to see that she understood them, and she did so.

To the Lord Chief Justice : This was soon after she went to the Prince-street school.

To Mr. Russell : I was at Clifford for two months soon after that time. On my return I found that the complaints as to the sisters' dinners still continued. About May, 1865, she asked for a lace for her stays, and I gave her one. In four days afterwards she said it had gone to pieces. It had not been perfectly new. When she asked me for another, I asked her into my private room. Mrs. Kennedy, who was then mother assistant, was present. I told Miss Saurin to take off her veil and part of her under-clothing. After she had taken off her habit I think I put my hand upon her petticoat, and said, "Take this off." She did so. According as she took off her clothes I put out my hand to take the articles. I found she had three small bags round her neck, in two of which she had scapulars and some bonnet ribbon.

The Lord Chief Justice : What part of the dress is the scapular ?—It is no part of the dress. It is a devotional ornament.

Examination continued : I took off the bags. She said, "Do not take my scapular," and I therefore replaced them on her neck. She then took off her pocket by my direction. Her tunic or inner garment fastened round the neck and extended nearly to the feet and to the wrists. That part of her dress was not disturbed by me or by my direction, nor was it by Mrs. Kennedy or by her direction. Miss Saurin made a movement to open it herself, and I said, "Do not do that ; you must not do that." I held my hand out for her pocket, and she gave it to me. I examined it and found a pocket-handkerchief, which I handed to her. I did not examine the pocket until she had taken off her skirts. It was a very large pocket. I found a collection of small things, such as I had found before in her five or six pockets. There were two roughly-made tablets. She had no leave to have the like. There are words and marks on them. (Produced.)

Mr. Russell : Please to read as well as you can what is on them.

Witness : I see the words, "The smooth way which deceived you."

The Solicitor-General : Were all these things on the leaves when you took them from her?—I do not know that all were. I know that this was. I am not sure the rest was not.

The Solicitor-General : Only read what you are sure was.

Witness (reading) : "The smooth way which deceived you." "Spoke to Anne privately. Clifford."

Mr. Russell : Who was Anne ?—A lay postulant. She had no permission to speak to her. Then there are letters which I do not understand : "wen . . tho . . me."

Anything more ?—Yes ; the words, "Not to see mamma mor." I understand that to refer to her not being allowed to see her mother the morning I have referred to.

The Lord Chief Justice : What did you understand by "The smoothed way that deceived you?"—That was a remark I made to her.

Oh, you had told her that of herself ?—Yes, I told her she had a smooth way which deceived me for a long time.

Examination continued : I did not give the pocket back. I kept part of the contents. She had written on other leaves found in the pocket. The whole of this matter lasted from about twenty or twenty-five minutes past four till five, when we had to attend a spiritual exercise. The time exceeded half-an-hour, but not much, and Miss Saurin dressed in the time. I had bolted the door on the inside to prevent any one intruding. Except Mrs. Kennedy, no one knew of what had occurred. It was not mentioned amongst the community. During the month of May the reports made to me by the sisters as to the children's dinners had increased, and I wished to find out for myself whether there was foundation for them. I examined the pocket to see whether there was any portion of a dinner there. There was not. I did not tell her what my object was. I allowed her to suppose that I wished to see the condition of her stay-lace. I did not like to accuse her about the taking of the dinners.

The Lord Chief Justice : Surely it was not necessary to search her pocket to see the condition of her stay-lace ?—Oh, no.

And the moment she saw you searching her pocket, she must have known that that was not your object ?—I did not tell her what my object was.

Mr. Russell : She says that you and Mrs. Kennedy tore off her clothes. Is that so ?—Mrs. Kennedy did not touch her at all. I touched one of her petticoats and took off the boots, but I did not pull off anything, or act rudely towards her. I treated her as gently as possible.

She says that each article, as it was taken off, was thrown rudely away. Did that occur ?—No.

Was there any violence used?—There was not.

The Lord Chief Justice : Was there anything done to expedite the proceedings—that, I think, was the suggestion—anything to make her quicker in her movements ?—Nothing, my lord.

After adjourning for a short time for refreshment, the examination of the witness was resumed by

Mr. Charles Russell: In the earlier years of your being superior did you understand that the plaintiff was delicate in the matter of appetite?—Yes, I had understood that, and I had ordered her to have exceptional things; that continued up perhaps to 1859. From then to 1866, she appeared to be in good ordinary health. I had not ordered her to be treated differently to the other sisters, except in one respect. I had been told at Clifford that she had not eaten the meat which had been given to her for her dinner, so I told the refectorian to give her less than the other sisters of meat, because she did not eat it, but if she did eat it it was to be increased to the same as the others. What is not consumed at one meal by the community is served up the next, indiscriminately. If a sister does consume habitually what is given to her, the allotment is always diminished in that way until they could eat more. That was the only exceptional treatment of the plaintiff; but it was an exception generally applied. A few days after coming to Hull, she came and said, "Rev. mother, I am ashamed of my large appetite." I said, "Do not be ashamed, but always eat plenty; you know very well I am always contented when I see the sisters eat well, because it is a sign of good health." She was then getting the small portion of meat. After she said that, either in September or October, she came and said that a priest who had been speaking to her, told her to tell me she could not eat mutton, and to give her something else. I replied that he had given me quite a different direction, and told me she was to have the same as the rest of the community. She then said, "It is only mutton I cannot eat, and of everything else I only get the same quantity." Upon that I told Miss Saurin I would settle the difficulty for her, and I told the refectorian, in her presence, that she did not give plaintiff enough for dinner, and that for the future she should give her the same as the rest of the community in quantity as well as in quality. That was then always done until she was dismissed. After that she left portions unconsumed of mutton; nearly all. I have known her to reject a portion of beef also. At Clifford it is a fact that they often had mutton. It is not true that she had to eat mutton when the others had something else.

By the Court: She never had mutton brought back to her which she had left when the others had other meat. She never was treated exceptionally as regards the sort of food.

By Mr. C. Russell: She complained to me of want of food on two occasions. In 1864 she came to me and asked to have more bread. I said, "Certainly." She went back to her place in the refectory, but did not take any more bread. I followed, and asked why she had not; and she said, "How could I take it, when I could not get it?" The bread was on a table near. I then said, "There was an abundance of bread on the table. There is no regular server at collation, and you could serve yourself, as I and others do; but go back now, and take whatever you require." She refused, and did not. The second occasion of complaint was at another collation, soon after. She pushed an empty plate towards me, and asked for more bread. I pointed to a plate on the table below her. She rose, and took what she wanted. Except on those two instances she never complained of wanting more food. Once during her last residence in Hull, in 1864 or 1865, one baking of bread moulded a little. We baked our own bread; but we all partook of it until it was consumed. We did not have it more than one or two days. I knew Miss Saurin pared off the mouldy part much more than the rest of the community. She was, in respect to that bread, in the same condition as the rest of the community. No other moulded bread was ever given to her. The statement by her in the community-room was after that. In August or September, 1865, I remember she complained of being unwell. She rose as usual, and at mass I saw her sat down on the kneeling-cushion. I directed her to sit on the stall—a higher seat. Later on she came and told me she was ill, and asked for a drink of tea. I told her to go to bed, and I would send the tea to her. She went to her cell, and I sent the tea to her. On visiting her afterwards, in about half-an-hour, I found she was lying down in her clothes. Sister Mary Elizabeth was with me. She described symptoms like diarrhœa. I told her to undress and go to bed. I proposed to give her remedies, but she declined to take them. I paid her a second visit later, and found her in bed covered with clothes. Her face was very red. On that I said she appeared very hot, and I removed the counterpane. She made no objection when I did so. She remained in bed the whole of that day. I told the sister who remained with her to attend on her to take all her clothing to repair. I removed the counterpane from a motive of kindness entirely. She suggested no complaint. Next day she was up to dinner, and, seeing her about to take apples, I told her not to do so, in consequence of the illness she had described. After dinner she told me it was only a pain in her leg she had, and not diarrhœa. About this time she told me she was suffering from internal pains, so I told the servant not to give her cucumber, for fear it might be injurious to her. She did not have it that day, but she did next, when she was well. Seniority does not regulate promotion, and it is no indignity for a senior to be placed under a junior. The community urged me in the autumn to go to Clifford for my health. I left Mrs. Kennedy in charge at Hull while I was away. I recollect Mr. Saurin's letter to the bishop about the 8th of August. In August, 1866, I became aware some of the sisters in the house were communicating with the bishop on the subject of myself. Every letter should be sent through the assistant-superior in cases where the sisters wish to communicate with the bishop. Mrs. Kennedy told me several of the sisters had written about me, and read extracts from two of the letters that had been sent. It was asking that something might be done about the plaintiff. I did not suggest their doing so, and did not know of it until afterwards. I got the bishop's letter about seeing Mr. Saurin at Hull on the 9th, and replied on the 15th. Before that I had received a letter asking if the charges could be proved. It was in answer to that I directed the sisters to make notes of their individual experiences. At that time Mrs. M'Keon was at Clifford. Two sisters at Clifford and ten at Hull made statements. I told them to write their individual experience of Miss Saurin from the first time they knew her ; but no other suggestions at that time. They brought me rough copies of their statements. I read them over. I believe they were destroyed there and then. As they came to me, I asked them about every circumstance, "Could they really be positive ?" If they did not satisfy me that they could be positive, and there was any doubt, I told them they might mention it as a doubtful matter, but not to speak of it as positive. If they had not mentioned facts that I knew of, I asked them about those circumstances, repeating the same advice about positiveness. If they remembered them, I suggested to them that they might write them in their statements. I told them to write with great moderation, and not to use strong language. One sister did not join, and that was a lay sister, Miss Mary Collingwood. My report was not the first report sent to the bishop. The lay sisters' depositions were not written by themselves, but by Mrs. Kennedy, and I think by Mrs. Kerr. The lay sisters were not in the habit of composition. I recollect receiving a letter from the bishop, enclosing one from Father Saurin. It was received on the 22nd of August. My report was not at that time sent to the bishop. I am almost sure it was not ; but there is a postscript to that letter, saying, "You must still send me your report." So that it is clear I had not sent it at that time. According to the bishop's direction I prepared clothes for the plaintiff's leaving, and handed the letter of dismissal to Mr. Saurin.

By the Solicitor-General : A document was handed to the witness which she identified as a letter written by herself which she had copied from a rough draft, and she was of opinion she had consulted Mrs. Kennedy. It was the letter sent by her to the bishop, dated August 22, 1865, and sent the same day. This document was put in and read. It contained the original charges against the plaintiff, which have been given over and over again in evidence, about her want of true religious feeling, her falsehood, and her breaches of the rules of poverty and community.

On this the witness said that a summer cloak, which had been given to her in perfect order, became in a few weeks torn and damaged. She made excuses about losing a pocket handkerchief in the street, a neckerchief in the school, and a pair of gloves. Those three were all in 1865.

By the Lord Chief Justice : Did you ever lose a glove yourself?—I daresay I have.

So have I ; a good many. (Laughter.)

By Mr. C. Russell : She ought to have dined at the first table in former years, but she had absented herself when she was refectorian.

Mr. C. Russell : Tell us now about the forwardness of the plaintiff with a clergyman.

Witness : The sisters are not allowed to converse with a chaplain without permission. I saw Miss Saurin frequently offend in that respect. The paragraph I wrote in my report to the bishop in that respect is quite correct.

By the Court : I heard of it first in 1857, and I saw it myself in 1858, '59, and '60.

By Mr. Russell : She went to the parlour or hall to meet the priest ; that was forbidden. I saw that at Clifford in 1860.

By the Court : It was in 1861 that she came back, after half going upstairs, and interrupted my conversation with the priest.

By Mr. Russell : She told me she felt herself so uneducated and useless, as her principal duty was school, that she wished to return to Ireland. It was reported to me that when she knew one of the letters had been discovered, she went to the local superior, expressed great sorrow for what she had done, and wished to see Father Harding. That same night she afterwards confessed that she had a light in her cell, and wrote another letter, which she sent off next day.

By the Court : My statement to the bishop was a general statement, including what had been written by the other sisters.

By Mr. C. Russell : I wrote that deposition according to the best of my belief. I recollect the Rev. Mr. Saurin coming, in September. I gave him the bishop's letter, and requested him to remove his sister. No scandal about this matter had got out through me at that time. Father Saurin refused repeatedly and decidedly to take his sister away. He said he would leave it all to his uncle. After that I suggested to the plaintiff, in December, 1865, to board in some continental convent. I advised her at her own request. They receive ladies who like a religious life without taking vows. Father Matthews had been about the 24th of October, and I made a similar request to him about removing her. In December, 1865, Miss Saurin asked to have the lace of her stays mended. I asked her for it, and she said it was in her stays. I thought a few moments, and saw she might make a grievance about it, so I asked her to go in an adjoining room, and said that one of the sisters would do what she required. Beside the plaintiff there were present Mrs. Dawson and Mrs. Kerr, and I asked Miss Saurin to take off her clothing. She did so, one of her petticoats, her stays, and tunic remaining on. The door was closed, but while the lace was being mended the portress came with a message to me. I saw while she was undressed that some of her other clothing required mending, just a few stitches, and I directed a sister to do what was necessary. That was done, and the plaintiff was dressed again in about a quarter of an hour.

Mr. Russell : The plaintiff has said you ordered her into a room, and that she was left standing in it opposite the door while the sisters and lay sisters were passing and repassing in the passage ?

Witness : No ; that is not true. It was a room off the community room. It is not true that the door was left standing open, and no one came in but the portress. She said to me, reproachfully, "This is the fifth time you have stripped me." I asked her to repeat the five times, when she repeated the 31st of May, and when I took the counterpane off, but I don't remember any other, though she may have named another. I thought at the time I was doing a kindness to her. I believe while the lace was being mended I put something about her shoulders. At the end of December she came and said she wished to speak to me. I took her into the reception parlour, and she told me she saw the sisters so unhappy at she had resolved to leave the convent. They were at that time, as I have described them in my letter, not as happy as they had been. She asked me to advise her what to do, and I declined to give her advice, and said she never followed advice that I gave her. She again asked me, and

I said, "The only advice I can give you is never to enter another convent as a 'religious,'" because I did not consider she had any religious vocation. I said what appeared to make others happy made her miserable—that is, observance of poverty and obedience. She then said she would enter another convent, and I told her not to enter an active order, as she would have temptations in it which she had not power enough to withstand. I got the bishop's letter on the 2nd January giving her notice about the commission. I suggested that Brother Porter should be on the commission, because he knew the case and knew the community.

The Lord Chief Justice: That is a reason why he should not have been on it. Did you state those reasons to the bishop?—I do not remember what I stated.

By Mr. Russell: Brother Porter knew the community and the case by giving retreats and by having received letters from me on the subject. I wrote to him at the time of the discovery of the clandestine correspondence, in March, 1862, and asked him for advice. After suggesting his name for the commission, I think I wrote to him. My letter to him was never returned. I went to Liverpool in December previously to accompany a sister who was about to pass her examination for a certificate at a training school, I called then on Mr. Porter. A few days after I learned Dr. O'Hanlon had been put on the commission. After reading the letter about the commission to the plaintiff, I offered her writing materials, which she declined then, but the next Sunday she asked for some paper to write down her feelings for the commissioners. I at once gave her a sheet of note paper, and told her if that was not sufficient I would give her as much more as she required. I sent a message to her in the afternoon to say if she wished she might remain in from church to write. I believe, however, she did attend church. She asked for a private room to write, but there was no private room except the superior's. I told her she could write in the community room with the other sisters, who were writing further notes of what they could remember, to be used at the commission.

The Lord Chief Justice: This is the case of a person writing a defence which ranges over years; that I take to be a very different one from the case of the other sisters, who were only writing notes. Could she not have written in her own cell?—Witness: There was no fire in her own cell.

By Mr. Russell: She had not asked me for permission to write in her own cell.

By the Court: There is only one cell with a fire-place. Cells are sleeping rooms. Except in not giving her a private room, I did not put the slightest restriction on her, or prevent her writing whenever she wished. On Monday, the 8th, I sent a message, and told her that would be silence day, and she might remain at home from school all day to write; for no one would disturb her, I heard she declined that offer, and said she should have quite time enough the next day. Silence day is when no conversation is allowed. If she had remained at home from school, no one would have prevented her from writing in the community room. There would have been but one sister in the room with her. She went to the school on the Monday. On the Tuesday she did remain at home, and that also was a silence day.

On the same afternoon I saw her uncle. He came to the convent. and she went to see him. I cannot say whether I gave her the quarter glass or whether she took it; but she went without any remark, and in a quarter of an hour returned and asked for more time.

By the Lord Chief Justice: The use of the quarter-hour glass is always insisted on, except with parents, unless by permission of the superior.

Examination continued: At the end of the quarter she came and asked for more time with her uncle. I asked how long she required. She said a quarter of an hour would be sufficient. She went accordingly. At the end of that quarter she came again and told me her uncle wished to see me. I went, and he told me he wished to see his niece longer, in order to prepare for the commission. I said it would not be just not to allow, and told him he might see her as often and for as long as he wished. He came in the afternoon. We keep a fire in one of the reception parlours and in the library on alternate days. I had the fire in the library that day, and was writing in it; so Father Matthew had to go into the reception room, where there was no fire. He made no complaint about that, and it did not occur to me to suggest one. I thought it likely he might come that day, but I had no notice of it. He came back about six o'clock that same evening, and remained till nine o'clock. There was no fire there then. He came next morning again, and stayed as long as he wished. He had a fire then. If he had suggested a fire on the first day, I should have been willing to get him one.

By the Court: There was not a frost at that time—not until the 10th.

By Mr. Russell: I recollect, after the commission, Mr. Patrick Saurin came to the convent. There was no restriction of time in his case. He stated one of the sisters stayed in the room dusting. I know nothing of that; nor do I believe it. When I got the bishop's answer I gave it to her. I asked her if she understood the letter, and she said she did. On the 12th February, 1866, I and Mrs. Kennedy went into her cell, and her religious dress was taken away by my directions. I had provided her a black woollen secular dress, which was taken to her cell before ten o'clock in the morning. It might have been eight o'clock. The dress was warm and respectable. At that time she was excited. I told her, when I went in, that she was not to rise till she was told, and that she was to leave the convent that day. On the 9th of February I had received the absolute dispensation. In my subsequent dealings with the plaintiff I avoided anything which could be construed into force. I read that letter to her between nine and ten. She had been sitting up in bed in the cold all that time, and I brought a shawl and wrapped it round her shoulders, but she shook it off. She was then sitting up in bed.

The Lord Chief Justice: In a state of excitement?—Yes. (Laughter.)

Examination continued: I requested her afterwards to put on the clothing and leave the convent. She said she would not. I told her after that I wished her to move into another cell where there was a fireplace. She was still in bed. I told one of the lay sisters to light a fire for her in that room. That was done, and I directed her bedclothing to be moved in after her. That was not a bath-room. The bath-room was next to it. This was a dressing-room attached to the bath-room ; but we used it as an infirmary or as a cell. The plaintiff would not dress that day, so far as I am aware. I saw the fire lit in that room. On the 13th of February, I saw she did not intend to leave the convent. She moved from one room to the other with her petticoats on, and I think, a shawl ; but she would not put on the secular dress. I sent a message to her on the 13th that she might come every day to the library, where there was a fire, excepting while the chaplain was at breakfast, in the morning, before nine o'clock. I heard of her going there only once. I sent sisters, and went myself, to reason with her, up to the 15th, about going away, but she always refused ; so on the 15th I wrote to Mr. and Mrs. Saurin requesting them to remove her as soon as possible. I then received Mr. Michael Saurin's note, in which he stated that he had received no authorised demand from the Bishop of Beverley. In reply to that note the bishop's secretary on the 20th sent the demand, and I again wrote requesting that she should be removed. I provided her with a secular dress, and afterwards with a cap, which was offered to her some time in March, because she was then continuing to wear a shawl over her head. She assumed the secular dress on Sunday, 12th of February. It was on the 13th of March that her brother came. She then wrote a letter to me to say she would never leave the convent of her own free will. Her brother requested to see me, and

I sent for him to the library ; but understanding that he refused to come, I went to him. When I saw him, he said to me, "Have you no pity, no compassion?" I said I thought her family were treating her badly in not taking her away. He replied, "You have her imprisoned here." I said, "No, we wish and desire her to go, and all the doors are open to allow her egress." He then said, "Just put your hand upon my sister and put her outside the door, and that will be sufficient." He did not say, "Just put my sister's hand in mine, and that will be sufficient." I refused to do as he requested. I said it would be actionable ; that I could use no force beyond words ; but that I would ask his sister to go. I then turned to Miss Saurin and said, "I wish and desire you to go." She replied, "I will not go."

The Lord Chief Justice : Had she any fire in her room between the period of her dismissal and the visit of her brother?—No, not after the first day. She had not come to the room where she was invited with the fire in it. As I saw she intended to remain, I did not have a fire in the cell after the day when she moved into it, as I did not wish to give extra work to the lay sisters. The fire was continued from day to day in the library, and I sent messages to her afterwards to come down to me there at any time. It was open to her if she had chosen to come.

By Mr. Russell : Except in the case of a sister being sick, fires are not lit at all in the cells or bed-rooms.

The Court then adjourned to Friday morning.

Ninth Day, *Friday, Feb.* 12.

The considerately ordered adjournment of the great Convent case at a somewhat earlier period of the afternoon than is usual, left the proceedings to-day in the middle of the chief defendant's cross-examination, a convenient point for breaking off having been reached. Unless by long protraction of this extraordinary trial the public should begin to tire of the mouldy bread and other unsavoury repetitions, a great culmination of interest is yet in store for those who are waiting to hear or to read the summing-up of the Lord Chief Justice. To-day the principal sensation was caused by the production of the worn-out stockings and other clothing brought by the plaintiff from the convent in Yorkshire, and of various articles mentioned in the evidence, such as the scapulars and a relic believed by Sister Scholastica, from whom it was taken by her superior, Mrs. Star, to be a piece of the True Cross. On the occurrence of this spectacular incident there was very noticeable excitement in court, the barristers, as well as the general public rising *en masse* to get a sight of everything brought out of the large bundle. Realism seldom fails to heighten the effect of language, even when those to whom the double argument is addressed are men of intellect and culture. Parliament, it is true, laughed at Burke and his dagger "business ;" and it was but the semi-educated audience of Exeter Hall that groaned and shuddered and waxed pale when a noted emancipationist rattled before them the real identical rusty chain which had bound some wretched negro to the whipping-post. But if proof were needed that ocular illus-

tration commands a readier and a more attentive notice, than the clearest statement or most forcible appeal that words will carry, such proof was this day given in the Court of Queen's Bench. Of the clothes which were exposed for general view, it may fairly be said that their mean and sordid quality, their age, and their approximation to that state which is past mending, might satisfy the most rigidly interpreted vow of poverty. Mrs. Star's cross-examination is expected to conclude in time for Mrs. Kennedy to begin her evidence to-day.

The hearing of the case was resumed at the sitting of the Court at ten o'clock.

The examination in chief of Mrs. Star, one of the defendants, was resumed. She said, in reply to Mr. Russell : A mistake was made on the 26th of March as to Miss Saurin's food. She did not get any until half-past twelve o'clock, in consequence of the sister who had charge of supplying her with food forgetting to bring it. I reproved the sister for neglect when the fact had been brought to my knowledge.

How was Miss Saurin treated, in regard to food, after she had ceased to be a member of the convent?—She had breakfast the same as the rest of bread, butter, and tea ; for dinner, meat and vegetables to eat, and water to drink.

Did she dine at the same hour as the sisters —Perhaps a little later.

Examination continued : Lent commenced on the 14th of February, and during Lent she had the food which was allowed by the Church to seculars who were fasting. The rules of the Church with regard to that season were observed.

Did the rules to which you refer differ as to sisters and seculars?—No; except in the case of those who were ill.

Examination resumed: Miss Saurin was not confined to her room from February. There is a garden attached to the house at Hull, and she was at liberty to go into the garden. I never refused her permission to do so. I sent her a change of clothes at the end of the first week after her separation from the community. I ascertained that she had only two articles, and I then went to her and inquired why she had not put on all I had sent to her. She said she did not know they were for her. I replied, "If that were so, why did you take two articles?" I can't remember what she said. I pressed her to take them, but she said she would do very well with what she had. At this time the bed linen was changed in rotation—two beds each week. I think there were thirteen or fourteen sisters in the community about this time; that was, a rotation of about seven weeks. No complaint was made to me of vermin being in the blanket, but I heard she complained to a sister that she had had a blanket given to her that had been used in the children's dormitory. It was not so. She had not used the blanket since the summer before. It is not true that she had sheets given to her that had been used as covers for the lottery tables. I can't say positively of my own knowledge. I heard she complained of it. She was not guarded and prevented from leaving her room for any purpose. The directions I gave were that her movements were not to be controlled in the least, but that she should be allowed to do just as she liked. I gave directions, however, that she should not be left alone. On the 30th of April, about noon, I ordered that a particular door should be kept locked, because Miss Saurin was in the habit of going to the room and remaining so long that she inconvenienced the community. There were other rooms of the same description to which she had unlimited access.

By the Lord Chief Justice: A rope was attached to her door and the sister's bed in the corridor, but it did not fasten the door.

Defendant: She was afterwards moved to a room higher up—one of a range of cells, because she was not a member of the community. It was a larger room than she had previously occupied, and it was lighted by a window. The same room has been, and is now, occupied by a sister. Miss Saurin was in the habit at night, or early in the morning, of getting up and going over the house alone, and I understood she had been seen in the corridor at five o'clock in the morning in her tunic and without stockings. I have learnt that since, but I feared she might. I gave directions that a sister should sleep in the corridor, and that a string should be attached to her bed and Miss Saurin's door—that if Miss Saurin should come out it should awaken the sister, and she should accompany her about the house. The sisters are forbidden to rise before the call. The rope did not fasten the door. There was nothing to prevent Miss Saurin's going out. The ordinary furniture of a sister's cell consists of one chair or one stool for each occupant, and when I went to her I found her sitting on the floor, although there was a stool in the cell. I then ordered two chairs to

be taken to the room, but I don't know if she used them. I did not desire Miss Saurin not to use a particular chair, but not to go and sit near the sister who was attending her. She might have put the chair in any part of the room. In 1864 or 1865 there was a general cleaning of the house at Hull, and Miss Saurin asked to be allowed to take part in it, but I declined to let her. I did not give directions for extra menial work to be imposed on the plaintiff at Clifford. I never gave directions for her to stand in school hours at Clifford. It is usual for sisters to stand in school when teaching, but I always told them to sit when possible. The faults in her monthly reports would be trifling, except in the manner in which she mentions them and as to the taking of the paper. An alteration was made in the rules by Mrs. Kennedy in Hull with reference to sewing and other material, etc. My impression is that the alteration extended the leaves instead of restricting them. A chapter was held at Hull in May, 1864, for the election of a superior, my first term of office—six years—having expired; after the first the re-election is only for three years. The first is an appointment for six years by the bishop or by election. At the end of that time she can be re-elected for three years, and again for three years. After that period she becomes a sister and is subject to the superior appointed or elected to that office. Plaintiff was entitled to send to the chapter for my resignation. It only lasts a few minutes. There was nothing to prevent her being present. None of the Clifford sisters were present. There is a particular form of resignation. The re-election took place on the octave of the association. I don't know if I was unanimously re-elected. The votes are taken in secret.

Mr. C. Russell: The votes are taken by a kind of ballot. The rules prescribe that the billets should be of the same form, and folded in the same manner, and distributed to the sisters the day before the election. Each sister has to write the name of the sister she votes for. She must not intimate for whom she voted, nor be curious to know how others voted.

The Lord Chief Justice: Do you suggest this as a mode by which vote by ballot might be practically carried out? else I dont see what use it is. —Mr. C. Russell: Then I will not pursue it, my lord.

Examination continued: Plaintiff's statement about the dust-box is incorrect, and I know nothing of my forbidding a sister to help her about the matting. All she had to do was to roll up the matting and let it fall down the steps. I did not, on going to Clifford, say to her, "I will show you what I can do." In October, 1865, Miss Saurin came to me and complained of cold. She asked me for a petticoat, and I gave her the warmest of the two that had originally been hers. I had previously directed that those who had not woollen jackets should apply for them. Miss Saurin did, and I gave her one the next day. She complained of her stockings in 1864 or 1865, but they were as good as the other sisters', and I paid no attention to it. I think I had kept them in repair for her. She also complained unnecessarily of her tunic, but a week after I got her a nearly new one. The condition of her boots—that of being in holes—must have happened in 1865, when I was at Clifford, if it ever occurred, but it is not within my knowledge. Mrs. Kennedy was the assistant superior at Hull, and in consequence of what she said I left a pair of boots for Miss Saurin. When Miss Saurin came from Clifford to Hull, in June, 1864, she had two pairs of boots—they were allowed to the sisters at Clifford because they went out every day. The sisters at Hull usually had only one pair.

The Lord Chief Justice : What if they got wet ?

Defendant : Then they had shoes to change. Each sister has light shoes, strong shoes, and boots.

Mr. Russell : Plaintiff in her evidence said Mrs. Star gave her a pair of house shoes, but they were so old that she had to tie them on with string across her feet, and put paper inside because the soles were worn out.

Defendant : I gave her a pair of boots, and not shoes—the pair I had taken from her the year before. She was then on an equality with the rest of the sisters at Hull. I found Miss Saurin had allowed the furniture to be thick with dust. She said she had not sufficient time allowed her for properly dusting it. I knew she had, and I waited before speaking to her again to see if she would make use of the few minutes she would have at free time to dust it. She did not apply it, and I said to her that if I found the community room in the same state I saw it in that morning, I should require her to wear the duster on her head as a penance. I went upstairs and took the dust off with my finger. She said she had dusted the room twice that morning. I then got the duster for the purpose of putting it on her head. She objected to wear it, because she said it was wet or damp. I gave it to one of the sisters to take it to the fire and dry it. She did so. Miss Saurin then objected to wear it because it was dirty. It had been used, but it was not dirty.

The Solicitor-General : An intermediate state (A laugh).

The Lord Chief Justice : According to your view it had not been used enough.

Defendant : I said it was not dirty. She stooped down as if she wished to wear it, and I put it over her veil. This was about one o'clock. It was her duty then to remain in the community room, but at 3.35 I went upstairs and saw her walking in the corridor with the duster still on. When she came near me I said, "Sister, you may take the duster off now." She bowed to me, but said nothing. I have no doubt she heard me. She, however, still continued walking up and down wearing the duster. Five minutes afterwards she went to the choir to an exercise, still wearing the duster. She continued to wear it during vespers and matins, and other religious duties. We then went to the refectory, and she wore the duster during the meal there, and also during another visit to the chapel. I did not tell her again to take it off, because I wished to see whether she really had understood and heard what I had said. We then went to recreation at about a quarter past five, and then when I got into the room I found she had taken the duster off of her own accord. If she had not heard my order at 3.35 she would not have been at liberty to take it off without my leave. These penances are very usual in our convent for faults.

The Lord Chief Justice : Have you ever put a duster on before ?—Defendant : a towel or clothes are worn on the head for sending clothes to the wash unmarked. The sisters ask for penances sometimes. Miss Saurin had fewer penances than the others.

Do you remember a sister having been ordered to wear a pair of boots about her neck by way of penance ?—I do not.

You say that some of the sisters asked to have penances imposed on them ?—Yes ; and Miss Saurin herself has asked for penance. The penance I gave her, for example, for receiving a visitor without my permission, was to read aloud on her knees the chapter of the rules on obedience until she knew it perfectly, and then to repeat it from memory on mornings.

Mr. Russell : A good deal has been said about Miss Saurin having kissed the floor. Now, have you performed that penance yourself ?—Yes ; often.

And others ?—Yes. Mrs. Kennedy, the present superior, has frequently done so.

Was there anything exceptional in the treatment of Miss Saurin in that respect ?—Nothing whatever.

I believe the only exceptional penance in her case was the taking off her ring ?—The only exception I can remember.

The Lord Chief Justice ?—The ring was not restored to her ?—No, my lord.

Examination continued : On another occasion, for remaining with a visitor, the punishment imposed on Miss Saurin was to acknowledge the fault every day for a week.

The Lord Chief Justice : Who was the visitor? —Her brother. She had my permission to remain with him an hour, but she remained with him half an hour longer. The extra half hour would have been readily granted to her if she had applied for it.

Examination continued : Miss Saurin did not feign kissing the floor, but remained on the boards of the room when it was done. When the commission was sitting she asked permission to perform public penance. I gave her no permission, but she did it of her own accord. I do not recollect penance being imposed on other sisters with regard to visitors. They had penance for other things.

Did they submit to it without reluctance?— Yes ; and with pleasure. Our novices consider it a bad sign if they do not get penance ; they fear they are going to be dismissed.

Examination continued : I kept back some letters from Miss Saurin because they contained something which she ought not to see.

How many did you keep back ?—At least five, and perhaps seven.

Examination continued : I have kept back letters from Mrs. Kennedy, but I do not know for what reason. There was nothing exceptional in my treatment of the plaintiff upon that head. It is understood that the superior can give or withhold letters when she thinks fit. It is not usual for the sisters to preserve even the letters of their friends. They are desired not to keep them unless they contain something for their spiritual good. There is a sister in the community whose brother—a monk—writes her most beautiful letters on her spiritual state. These might be preserved, as may also business letters in reference to property.

The Lord Chief Justice : Is a sister allowed to keep a letter from her father or her mother containing expressions of affection?—Ordinary letters are destroyed.

Then such a letter as I have alluded to might not be kept?—No.

It would be thought too worldly to be preserved?—It would be destroyed, lest it should prove a distraction to the sister receiving it.

Examination continued: During my government of the convent no difficulty occurred with respect to any other sister but Miss Saurin. Since May, 1866, when she left, there has been no disturbance in the community. The duty of a sister consists in visiting the sick and teaching in the schools, in addition to her own religious duties. Her time is fully taken up with those things. Only one letter to Miss Saurin was obliterated. It was a letter from her father, and I obliterated six or seven lines.

Why did you do so?—Because they made a reflection on the community. The writer spoke of those who, he said, were making his child unhappy. I thought that he intended to refer to me and the sisters.

Examination continued: The same thing would be done in the case of other sisters if it were necessary.

The Lord Chief Justice: Can you remember any other instance in which it was done?—I kept back a letter that came to a sister from her sister.

Why did you do so in that case?—Because the letter contained expressions which were too complimentary to one member of the community. (A laugh.)

Examination continued: I did not punish the plaintiff by keeping back any letter which I thought she ought to see.

The letter to Mrs. Star from the bishop, inquiring why plaintiff had worn a duster on her head in the choir, and Mrs. Star's reply were then put in evidence.

Mrs. Star, cross-examined by the Solicitor-General: I was born in the city of Dublin. I am a Catholic. I have been a Catholic all my life. I joined the order of Mercy as a postulant in 1849. I had a dangerous illness then, and my friends would not consent to my remaining. I left the Glasgow convent on the 11th of July, 1850, and came direct to the Baggot-street convent in Dublin. Miss Saurin had not yet entered the convent. I left Baggot-street in 1855 to establish a community in Yorkshire. Mrs. Delaney, Mrs. M'Keon, and a lay sister accompanied me. Mrs. Kennedy came in about a week, and Miss Saurin in about nine months after.

Is one of the most binding rules of the order absolute obedience to the will of the superior?—Not absolute.

Well, how is it qualified?—The sisters are bound to obey the superior in all that is without sin, as far as her authority extends. For example, if a superior thought that a sister, for a certain fault, ought to be placed last in the community and deprived of her vote in the chapter, she could not impose that penance without the permission of the bishop. I might propose it, but I could not put it into execution.

You might hold that punishment over her.—Yes.

Is it part of the virtue, excellence, or goodness of the nun to think according to the thoughts of those above her, and to submit herself, her mind, and thoughts to them?—Yes.

Is it a desirable thing in a nun to submit her judgment as far as possible to that of her superior?—Yes.

She would feel that to be an obligation if she could do it without sin?—Not as an obligation. She would feel it right to do so.

Is it the duty of a novice to obey the mother superior as if she held her authority from God rather than through servile fear?—That is one of our rules.

And if that be so of a novice it would be still more the duty of a nun?—Yes; having taken the vows.

That portion of the instructions which speaks of regarding the voice of the superior as if it was the voice of an angel, is influential on the consciences of the nuns?—Yes.

Is it the duty of the superior to lovingly correct and sweetly admonish sisters when they are wrong, without lessening the gravity of their faults?—It is.

Cross-examination continued: I consulted Mrs. Kennedy and Mrs. M'Keon about the treatment of Miss Saurin, and no one else. There is nothing in our written customs or printed rules about expulsion for writing letters without leave. The authority of the superior to withhold letters is traditional. According to custom the mother superior is to open all letters to sisters, whatever position they may occupy in the community. I withheld a letter from Miss Saurin's Jesuit brother for some weeks.

Why was it better to deliver the letter to her after some weeks than when it was received?—I spoke to her about the letter, and she condemned her brother for having written it. I either read the letter to her or told her what was in it.

Did you condemn her brother also?—I did.

And like a good nun she agreed with you?—Not if I was wrong.

But was it not her duty to submit her judgment to yours if she possibly could?—Yes, if she considered my judgment did not err.

I believe you expressed your opinion about her Jesuit brother rather strongly?—I expressed my opinion, but not very strongly, as far as I recollect.

Cross-examination continued: Miss Saurin said her brother was wrong either before or after I said so. I cannot now tell which. When she had expressed disapprobation of him I gave her the letters. I thought they would do her no harm then, as she knew their nature. I knew nothing about a letter which came to Clifford, announcing the death of her brother, Thomas Saurin, being withheld from her; but a report was made to me that on the very day the letter was received a notice was put upon the chapel-door begging the prayers of the sisters for the repose of his soul. Miss Saurin must have either read the letter herself, or been informed of his death. I do not believe the letter was withheld. I never saw it. In Lent, Miss Saurin sent me a letter which she had written to her uncle, and in it she referred to the death of her brother. I forwarded the letter to her uncle. I do not remember the time when I first entertained doubts as to the vocation of Miss Saurin. I never asked her to tell me her confession to the priest. I may have asked her what advice was given to her with regard to ordinary matters, but not as to her sins. In 1862 I had a clear opinion that her vocation was not for the life of a religious. In saying that the superior of Baggot-street Convent knew her too well to take her back, I alluded to a conversation I had with the superior when she accompanied Miss Saurin to England. She told me that Miss Saurin would not be an advantage to our community, as she was given to being "underhand." The letter which Miss Saurin wrote to her uncle, asking him to get her into the convent at Drogheda, was partly the same as my conversation with her. I did not like the letter, because it repeated the conversations, and I should have preferred her expressing her own sentiments.

There is this passage in the letter: "The reverend mother says they need never know why I leave here, only that you wish it, for the sake of my father and mother." Did you say so?—That is not exactly the truth. What I suggested was that she might go to Drogheda for a while, and then there would be no necessity for telling. She could not stay there without the leave of the community.

Would not the community approve if the superior approved?—In a case of that kind they would be free to judge for themselves.

Would they not probably have approved?—It does not follow as a consequence.

Cross-examination continued : I addressed Miss Saurin's letter to her uncle, and had it posted.

Was there anything in it of which you disapproved?—I did not like the letter throughout. I did not ask her to rewrite it, as I did not wish to enter into any differences with her. At the time she was writing to Father Matthews I was writing to the mother superior at Baggot-street. We were sitting at the same table. The result ultimately was that Sister Scholastica had to stay in our community.

The Solicitor-General : Now, I think I understood that from the latter end of 1862 until 1864 Miss Saurin remained at Clifford?—Yes, she remained there until 1864, excepting for occasional visitations.

Now, with reference to these penitential letters of acknowledgment, were they written by your desire?—Yes.

Did you keep all these letters?—I think I kept them all. I thought it a matter of prudence. I did not tell her I should keep them. I don't think the letters were altogether true as representing her state of mind, nor as statements of fact. I don't remember that I ever told her so. I formed no settled judgment, however, on that point. The impression made on my mind was that they were not true. Some were true, some false. I don't think I ever told her that she would not be able to bear all she would have to go through, though it appears in one of the letters from her as if I had. I did not say anything to her about that, because I wished to act cautiously. I believe it to be a pure invention ; but I did not tell her so. I had spoken about Miss Saurin to Father Lands, not favourably. She mentions confessing to him in a letter in August, 1863, and about the bad opinion he had of her. I had told him very little about her, and that little, I believe, was entirely my own knowledge of her. I had been with her two months in 1861, except that time she had been at Clifford and I at Hull, therefore, in some degree, what I told him must have been what I heard from others. Others

may have spoken to him about her besides myself. I believe they did. I think Mrs. M'Keon and Mrs. Kerr saw Father Lands. They, however, can speak for themselves. All the other sisters who were away made monthly acknowledgments. I kept those of Mrs. M'Keon because they had reference to Miss Saurin. I have no reason to think that the letter conveying the news of her brother Tom's death was kept from her. A letter from her implies that she only got the account from her own mother ; but I only understand that to mean that she had only got the details from her mother. On the death being announced to her she sent me a letter to send to her uncle. Miss Saurin was engaged with the lending library at Clifford, where the village people get books changed on a Sunday. Two sisters attended to it —the plaintiff and Mrs. M'Keon. Only one sister has to speak, and the plaintiff represented that it was difficult not to speak to the people. That was a special direction from me, at the time Miss Saurin was second sister, that only the local superior should speak. Her speaking would be a breach of the rule of silence, and she used to speak more than she should have done, so I made the rule to keep her to her duty. I heard of it from report, and I knew her propensity for it, so I said she was not to speak at all. I told her that the acknowledgments in her letters were very trifling compared with what they should be.

The Lord Chief Justice : Did you not say there was nothing in her acknowledgments which a saint might not have written?—I may have said that.

By the Solicitor-General : The letters expressed sorrow. I hoped she would confess more. From what I knew of her characteristic faults, and from reports of the other sister, Mrs. M'Keon, I assumed that she was not telling me the whole truth. I also saw letters on the subject from Mrs. Fearon to Mrs. Kennedy, which I read and returned to Mrs. M'Keon, who destroyed them. It was Mrs. Kennedy's duty to report about the plaintiff so far as concerned what took place with her. It was in January, 1864, that Miss Saurin wrote to ask me whether she might have her little leaves again. All the other sisters did the same, asking for a renewal of their permission. I think I wrote to Mrs. M'Keon, the local superior, that all the sisters should have their leave renewed. At that time I think the plaintiff had a pen, but no paper; for after the intercepted letter she wished herself not to have writing materials, for she said the sight of a pen and ink made her shudder. To the best of my belief, she had a pen and a blotting-book.

The Solicitor-General: From 1862 down to 1865 or 1866 you did not write to the bishop, making complaints against Miss Saurin?—I wrote to the bishop in 1862, but not again until July 26th, 1864, when I wrote to him about the visit of the plaintiff's brother. The letter is highly unfavourable to Miss Saurin. That was after the bishop had rebuked me for not letting her see her brother a second time. The bishop held a visitation in 1862, and the result was, he said we were to go on with the plaintiff, and she was not dismissed. He did not make any decision.

The Lord Chief Justice : He took no action? —Witness: Decisions were announced on other matters, but not on that.

The Solicitor-General : You say in your letter

to the bishop of the decision, that "it gave her and her supporters an immense triumph over us, of which they showed full appreciation whenever they had an opportunity." She had supporters then?—I meant by that her family, her relations. I believe Father Matthews, I think from what I heard, showed having triumphed over us whenever he had an opportunity, and her other relations did the same. Her mother, I should say, also did so. Her brother Michael had shown it in his visit. I don't mean by supporters any one in the convent. Her father might have been one, because he once wrote a very strange letter, part of which I obliterated. I had not seen the Jesuit brother at that time. Two letters from her sister, one dated the 4th and the other the 16th of August, I think I gave her together. I kept the first until after the retreat, which terminated on the 15th. I kept one of these letters, because it contained an untruth. I let Miss Saurin read it, and required it to be given back to me. My reason was, that I believe her family exaggerated very much, and this was an instance of it. That same year, in June, 1864, I examined her pockets. She had five or six. (Some things handed to witness.) I don't think these were in her pockets. These (books and papers) were in her desk. They were taken and not returned. (They all appeared to be devotional notes, written by the plaintiff, of the most orthodox character.)

The Solicitor-General: Look at these written pages, and tell me if there is anything in them for which, either as regards breach of rule, or their moral character, or anything else, you should take them away?—Witness (after examining the writing and identifying it as the plaintiff's) said: In one case she had documents belonging to other sisters in her book, and this had been written by another sister, it would have been wrong to keep it. My reason for taking away these papers was, that when I saw she made notes to the disadvantage of the community, I took from her every facility for doing so.

The Solicitor-General: I see there is something secular amongst them, for here is a specific for the tooth-ache. I suppose they have tooth-ache even in convents. (Laughter.) Then, here again I see "New Testament Notes of different chapters," is there any harm in that?—I took away those papers altogether.

Did you take the trouble to look what she had got in her papers or desk?—No; I did not.

Did you return them, when you found them so innocent? Here is "St. Cecilia," of which the subject is much better than the poetry.

The Lord Chief Justice: It is not Dryden's, I suppose.

The Solicitor-General: No, my lord; that is better known as "Alexander's Feast." Here is "Things Difficult to be Done: bearing the cross and suffering with patience," which is so solemn, that I do not like to read it. Here is "A Prayer for a Sister." What was the use of taking that from her?

The Lord Chief Justice: She has given you a general answer in regard to her reasons?

The Solicitor-General: Would it not have been common fairness to see what they were before taking them away, or when you found out what they were, to have given them back? Here, I see, is "Twelve Degrees of Humility, communicated by St. Thomas Aquinas." Here is,

"With downcast eyes and pallid cheeks, with virgin hands," and so on. Here is "Prayers for the Present Wants of Holy Church." That is pretty orthodox surely. Will you point out a single one of these papers which you took away, or a single word in them which, according to your notions of morality, or Christianity, or anything else, is discreditable?—The reason why they were taken away was, not that there was anything in them wrong, so far as I saw, for I did not examine them, but I took them from her that she might not make notes upon them to the disadvantage of the community.

Did you look to see whether there was a single scrap or note to the disadvantage of the community?—No ; I did not.

Did you see whether on many there was room to write a scrap?—On some there was, on others there was not. They were to be returned to her when she left the convent.

The Lord Chief Justice: At the time that you took them away. Did you intend to return them, or did you only form that intention when she was about to leave?—When I took them away I had no intention of returning them, for I then had no hope of her leaving the community. But I kept them, and then, when I had the hope of her being dismissed, I intended to return these things and everything else belonging to her when she left.

The Solicitor-General: Here is a parcel of papers, taken from her desk, produced by you in this case. Can you point out a single word or letter to the disadvantage of the community? (Parcel handed to the witness.)—I don't know that there is anything; but they were all taken from the same motives.

Don't you know that there is not?—No; I don't know that. I don't think I ever looked at them.

You took them away because you profess to have discovered on something else which you took away things to the disadvantage of the community?—Yes.

That being your reason for taking them away, why on earth did you not see whether they confirmed your view, and whether they did not contain something?—Because I did not think it likely she would leave in her desk or in her books anything of that kind.

Then why not return what was of no harm?—I can give you no reason, except that it never entered my mind.

Did you not think she set some value on them?—I did not advert to it.

But she adverted to it, and begged you not to take them?—I don't remember that.

But did she not manifest her dislike of the proceeding?—She was not present when I took away her desk. When she removed to Hull, in 1864, her desk and books remained at Clifford, and when they were brought to Hull I took these things out before giving the desk to her.

Look at these leaves, from a MS. book of devotion. They were taken away, were they not?—Yes.

Where is the rest of the book?—I think it must be among her other books. These, I am told, come out of her "examen" book.

Pray what is an examen book?—It is a small book for noting down either the acts or omissions of any certain virtue.

For the purpose of examining the conscience?—Yes. Every nun has them.

Then why did you take hers away?—Because she made no use of it ; but this is not her examen book, but an examen, which is quite a different thing.

What is an examen, then?—An examen is an explanation of the virtues to be practised and the different degrees of a virtue.

Is that a thing a nun has a right to keep?—Yes.

Then why take it away?—For the same reason I have already given.

The Lord Chief Justice : You say you took all these papers because you thought she might use them for the purpose of writing notes on them unfavourable and disparaging to the community—to the other sisters ?—Yes, my lord.

Had you no other motive such as this, that it occurred to you she might use the paper for communicating with her relatives without your knowledge?—No, my lord, I am sure that never occurred to me.

The Solicitor-General : Now here is a book that belonged to the deceased sister, whose medal, to use plain English words, you imputed to the plaintiff that she stole ?—That is implied.

Has there been an inscription in that book ?—At present there is not.

That is not an answer to my question. I said, " Has there been an inscription in that book ?"—Yes, there was.

When was it rubbed out ?—About the 20th of January, 1865.

That is a book which was given to her by a deceased sister, and which she had by your permission?—Yes, until 1865, when all the sisters' devotional books were given up, by my instructions, as an exercise of poverty. There was then a redistribution of them. That was the way it was taken from Miss Saurin, and it was then the inscriptions were rubbed out by orders.

The Lord Chief Justice : When had there been a similar exercise of poverty before?—I don't remember that there had been one before of the whole community, but of individuals there had been.

Were the books redistributed to the same sisters again ?—I don't think so.

The Solicitor-General : Will you undertake to say that?—They were, so far as I know of, distributed indiscriminately ; but a sister may have had again one or two of the same books.

Was there any other book containing an inscription from a dying sister to another sister, except that of the plaintiff's ?—Not that I remember.

At that time was the accusation known to you about Miss Saurin having stolen a medal from the same sister?—No ; I did not know of the medal at that time ; it was not until August, 1865.

When was the inscription erased?—I think it was in 1865, on the 1st of January. Yes, I am sure it was in 1865, and not in 1866.

The Lord Chief Justice : Do you know whose handwriting is in that book ?—Some of it is in the handwriting of Mrs. Delaney ; the rest I do not recognize.

The Solicitor-General : Now look at these tablets ; were they covered with writing when you took them away?—No ; when I first saw them some of the pages were partly written on. I gave her a distribution of time to copy into that book. The distribution of time would not fill two sides

of note paper. It is more than a " horarium." Here is an example of one—(handing paper to counsel). There are several on that paper. I found other things written on the tablets, and I took them from her. I read part of what was written on three or four sides of the tablet. I took them away because I found other entries on them than what related to herself. They were not her own faults that were recorded, but what perhaps she may have considered faults in others. She did not ask me to return them.

The Lord Chief Justice : Did she not say, " Pray don't read my confession?"—Yes ; I said, I won't read your confession on any consideration, but there are other things. I let her erase from the tablets what she had written.

By the Solicitor-General : When was the rest of the writing rubbed off?—Either just before she left the convent or just after. She effaced the writing, with a pocket-handkerchief and her mouth. The tablet has not since been in her possession. It has been since washed, either just before Miss Saurin left the convent, or just after, by a sister whom I directed to do so. I will undertake to say that the washing did not take place after November, 1866.

By the Lord Chief Justice : Mrs. Rafter was the sister who wished it. She is at Hull, and of such constitutional delicacy that she cannot come. (Laughter.)

By the Solicitor-General : It never occurred to me that she might require to make notes in her own defence. When I proved to her that her writings were not confessions, she did not want to repeat them.

The Lord Chief Justice : You say there was matter affecting other sisters beside'Mrs. M'Keon. Do you remember any other matter?—She remarked about a visitor which another sister had. She did not name the sisters themselves, but circumstances connected with the sisters. I recollect, too, that she remarked on what was said to her, but at this length of time I cannot remember whether the tablets contained anything else.

By the Solicitor-General : You recollected what they contained at the time when you made your deposition for the bishop ?—I drew out my statements from notes. My memory, a year after, was fresher than it is now. I have tried to remember.

Now here are things said to have been found in her pockets. That, I am told, is a scapular ?—Yes.

A sort of devotional emblem which you wear round your neck. It is commonly put into a bag ?—Yes, it may be, there is no harm in putting it into a bag.

Did the scapular bags make up two of the five or six pockets which Miss Saurin carried about her?—No ; she had three small bags for devotional objects besides five or six pockets.

When you took the scapular bags did you also take a relic case ?—Yes.

Was it in that piece of paper? (Paper handed to witness.)—I don't think it was. It may have been. It was something like that.

Was it or did it profess to be a piece of true cross ?—I could not say that it was. It had no such authentication. I don't know with what belief the plaintiff wore it.

Does that piece of paper say it was a piece of wood of the true cross?—Yes. She had not a relic case with the piece of true cross. I think what she meant by a relic of the true cross was a piece of wood that was in the paper. I don't know whether it was taken from her. I don't recollect. I can give no reason for taking such things from her if they were taken. I admit taking a relic case from her. It is now in Hull.

Here is a card with our Lord kneeling with a cross on the world ; on the back is a prayer, and beneath it, " Pray for your fond sister Mary Theresa Magdalen." Why was that taken away? —I think that was taken from her for the same reason as I told you before, to prevent her making notes on it to the disadvantage of the community.

The Lord Chief Justice : You did not suppose she could write on that picture?—I did not know; but she might. I thought she might.

The Solicitor-General : You know that she has a Carmelite sister, and that this is from her ? —It may have been from her sister. I do not wish to dispute about that. I have seen that sister's handwriting, but I don't remember it so as to say that the writing on this card is hers.

Do you mean to tell the jury you thought she might make notes on that to the disadvantage of the community ?—I have told you before that all these things were taken from her at the same time, and that I did not observe them or advert to them.

Very good. Now, then, let us turn to the matter of mending the stay-lace, and making her undress. What was that done for ?—My object was to see if she had taken any of the children's dinners.

What ! Did you look for the dinner in those scapular bags ?—Yes.

Did you find it ?—No.

Did you expect to find it in the relic case ?— No.

Then why did you take that ?—I can give no reason.

Give me any other reason than that of wishing to inflict an indignity on her ?—It was not for that purpose. I told her I would return it to her when her conduct became better.

I thought you undid her things and undressed her for the purpose of finding the children's dinner ?—I did not undress her.

Well, then, you touched her dress nominally to look at her stay-lace, but really to find a dinner, which you did not find. What justified you in taking her relic case ?—My reason was that I would take it away until she grew better.

What had she done ?—I had found notes with her, to the disadvantage of the community.

You never gave it to her back ?—No ; but it was ready for her on leaving the convent, if she had let me know.

I understand, then, that you never made any degrading difference in your treatment of Miss Saurin as compared with any other sister, such as putting her to menial occupations, reducing the quantity of her dress, or anything else ; and that there were none of those indignities put upon her, but when she did wrong she had penance like any other sister, neither more nor less ?—Yes.

Is it true that her under-linen was not allowed to be changed more than once in a fortnight ?— That happened once or twice at the very outside ; but others did the same. It could not be more than twice. I think it was only once, if once. It was not habitual that I know of. I think I must have had knowledge of it if it was.

By the Lord Chief Justice : It was caused by a hard frost in the winter, when the lay sisters found it very hard to dry the clothes.

By the Solicitor-General : I am speaking now of 1864 and 1865. It may have happened at Clifford, but I don't remember that it was by my orders, and I did not give any special order with regard to Miss Saurin. It may have happened at Clifford, because they only washed there once in three weeks ; but if it did, all the sisters were equally affected. I recollect taking some stout skirts from Miss Saurin, and giving one to Mrs. Fearon and one to Mrs. Rafter. I believe they were given to the plaintiff by a relative. She got one back in October, 1864, and the other, I think, in February or March, 1866, and took them from the convent with her. I think I should know them again if I saw them.

The Solicitor-General : I think I understood you to say that she never had any stockings worse than other sisters ; that bad stockings were not peculiar to her ?—No. I know, at the present time, of sisters having stockings just as bad.

What stockings did she go away with ?—Not a very old pair.

How long had she worn them ?—I think for several weeks. I don't think I could recognize them again. The dress she had was a brown, decent dress. It was old, but she had a new one.

Are these the skirts, stays, and stockings? Look particularly at the stockings, they are very interesting. (Some very dilapidated articles of feminine attire were here handed to the witness, who, after examination, said)—Yes ; I believe they are the stockings.

Is that the underclothing ?—It has been washed, I am told, and somewhat improved. (A brownish-yellow-looking garment, which had been referred to in the case, in convent language, as a tunic, but which, in less saintly parlance, would be called a chemise, was here handed to witness.) After examination she said : Miss Saurin got her under-clothing clean a short time before she left us. That underclothing she wished to have, although I offered her better.

You say, on one occasion, after showing a spirit of appropriation, she made an indirect charge against you, talked incoherently, and appeared very much excited ?—Yes.

That she talked about mouldy bread, persecution, and tyranny?—Yes.

Now was not what she said that she had not relished the mouldy bread sufficiently, and that she had not been sufficiently self-abased ?—No ; what I said yesterday I say again to-day, and I believe it. Your version is not correct.

She did not seem much overcome?—I don't think she cried or that she abased herself much. When she commenced to speak she was cool, and there was no cause on that morning to excite her when she gave vent to her feelings against me. There is a form of self-accusation with us. She did not make use of any form. The form is only used in chapter ; this was in community. In 1865 my dissatisfaction had reached such a head that I determined to get rid of her. In April, 1865, I tendered my resignation, not on the ground that either she or I would have to go, but bona fide. I hoped the bishop would accept it. There were several other sisters qualified to fill my place—nine or ten, including Miss Saurin, Mrs. Kennedy, and Mrs. M'Keon.

By the Court: Qualification for being superior is being above thirty years of age and five years of profession, except in the case of convents newly founded.

By the Solicitor-General: I knew the bishop intended to dismiss her if the charges could be proved. Mrs. Kennedy also knew that when she made her depositions, but I don't know whether the other sisters did. I did not correct the depositions that were made. I read them over, and told the sisters to change anything that was too confident, if they were not perfectly sure of it; and I reminded them of other things which they seemed to have forgotten. All were supervised by me except two written at Clifford. I believe what the sisters wrote they believed to be true. What I wrote I believed to be true, and I spoke of it as my own knowledge.

The Court then adjourned till Saturday morning.

Tenth Day, *Saturday, February 13th:*

The cross-examination of Mrs. Star by the Solicitor-General, one of the most notable and most eagerly looked-for episodes of the Great Convent Case, was continued to-day, and was brought to a conclusion in the middle of the day's sitting. That it was a severe cross-examination may well be supposed: but the keenest and the best-aimed shafts might have been designed to show how a great lawyer can afford to dispense with what is significantly called the "license of counsel." Having elicited from the witness a few such admissions as that changes of dress were denied Miss Saurin, during her fortnight's confinement in the upper room, and that, when she asked for clean sheets, they were not given her, Mr. Coleridge said, interrogatively, "You wished to make her uncomfortable to induce her to go?" To this the witness replied, "You may draw what inference you please;" and her antagonist rejoined, "Then I shall draw it." The taking of the ring, which is worn as a sign of union with the Redeemer, was another point of the cross-examination. Whence, the Solicitor-General asked, did the Superior derive authority for the act of deprivation? Was there any rule, any custom or tradition? The answer was in the negative; but the witness declined to admit any knowledge of its being a great indignity to take away the ring from a nun's finger. Mr. Mellish re-examined the defendant, and succeeded in removing at least an impression which, had it remained, would certainly have affected her case unfairly. She had said that, in sorting papers and destroying a great many of them, her selection of certain papers for preservation was governed by the belief that they would be "useful." This ambiguous phrase was explained satisfactorily, the witness declaring that she had not meant to exclude evidence that might have served the plaintiff. It was as being useful to the case, and not solely to the defence, that the letter had been preserved by her.

Mrs. Kennedy, the second defendant, now took the place of Mrs. Star in the witness-box, and gave evidence of much the same character as that which the first witness had given in the early stages of her examination. The Court rose before Mrs. Kennedy's evidence was concluded; but the early adjournment did not greatly conduce to an abatement of the demonstration outside Westminster Hall when the parties to the action were leaving.

The hearing of this case was resumed at the sitting of the Court this morning.

The cross-examination of Mrs. Star by the Solicitor-General was resumed: We got yesterday to the preparation of the depositions, as they are called, for the bishop. You say you told the sisters to use moderate language, and to confine themselves to their own knowledge?—I told them not to write anything about which they were doubtful.

And to use moderate language?—Yes.

The rules you prescribed for the sisters you prescribed for yourself?—I should do so.

Now I see that the first thing is the general charge as to Miss Saurin's want of moral courage, and so on; and that between 1856 and 1860 she took a book and hid it in her cell—that she either hid it or kept it concealed from observation. Is that so?—One of the sisters asked me for a small book belonging to her, namely, "Devotion to Jesus," of which I have already spoken.

Is there a lock upon anything in the cell?—No, there is not.

Then a person might go to a cell and take anything out of it?—Yes.

And that was a right you availed yourself of on fitting occasions?—Yes.

What do you mean by keeping it hid or concealed from observation?—The cell was not the place for it.

Is that what you mean by having it hid or concealed from observation?—No; I found it in the cell concealed beneath her clothes.

Was the cell the right place for her clothes?—Yes.

Whereabouts was the book?—Amongst her clothes.

In a drawer?—No.

Where then?—In the lower part of the wardrobe.

And amongst the clothes was the book?—Yes.

Did you go purposely for it?—Yes; because one of the sisters told me it had been taken.

The Lord Chief Justice: I think we should have more accurate description of the precise position of the book. The jury must understand what you mean by concealing it. I suppose the clothes were on the shelf?—Yes.

The Lord Chief Justice: And was the book on the top, under, or in the middle of the clothes?—It was not on the top, but it may have been in the middle or underneath.

Cross-examination continued: Have you got the book?—I could send for it; it is in Hull.

Had each sister a copy of the book?—Well, some may have had and some not. It may have been the only one in the house.

I know it may have been. I want you to tell me whether it was or not?—I cannot say.

Whose was it?—I had given it to Mrs. M'Keon.

I told her in Miss Saurin's presence that she might have it. I think this occurred in the community room.

But you are sure that Miss Saurin was present?—Yes; she was present when Mrs. M'Keon asked for the book. It was thus as far as I remember: I told Mrs. M'Keon she might have the book. Whether I handed it to her or told her she might take it I do not recollect.

How long was this before you found it in Miss Saurin's cell?—My impression is that it was a week or ten days.

Had Mrs. M'Keon taken the book or not?—I believe she had.

Do you know, one way or the other?—Not from my own knowledge, but from other circumstances.

Did she ask it from you?—Yes.

Who, up to that time, had had the use of the book?—I had had it myself.

And in about a week or ten days Mrs. M'Keon asked you for it?—She said, "I miss the book you gave me, and I cannot help thinking that Sister Scholastica has taken it."

No doubt she could not help thinking it. And you found it?—Yes.

And that is what you meant by stating in your deposition that between 1856 and 1860 she had a book and concealed it from observation in her cell?—Yes; and Miss Saurin acknowledged it.

What account did she give of it?—When I asked her had she taken it, she evaded the question.

I know what your opinion of evasion is. Tell me, what did she say? and then I can judge for myself.—I do not remember.

Give me the substance of what she said. Did you ask her whether she had got it?—I think so.

What did she say?—My impression is that she said she had not.

That would have been a lie, would it not?—I cannot tell what she said. It was either a denial or an evasion.

What did you go on to say?—I cannot tell, but I conveyed to her that I knew she had taken the book.

Then you knew she had?—I had found the book at the time. (Laughter.)

Oh, then, you were putting her through a sort of cross-examination. When you told her you knew she had taken it, what did she say to that?—She said she had found it.

Found it where?—She did not say.

Did you ask her?—I do not remember.

Did anything more pass?—She told me she was keeping it for me.

Was your own name in it?—I think so.

And she told you she was keeping it for you. That, of course, was a highly suspicious circumstance. Tell me this, was Miss Saurin's own name in it too?—I think it was.

That, of course, was pregnant with suspicion. Had you given the book to her?—No.

How, then, came her name in it?—When we were in Ireland she gave the book to me.

Oh, then this very book about which you wrote in your deposition that she had concealed it in her cell she had herself given to you?—Yes; her name was in it as presenting it to me.

Well, when the discovery was made, what did you say to her?—I said, "You were present when I gave the book to Sister Mary Agnes, and you

knew it was no longer one of the books to be used by you."

That was a home thrust. What did she reply?—She acknowledged that she had committed a fault against poverty, and promised to be better in future.

The Solicitor-General: I should like to see the book. Can you send for it?—I do not know whether it can be found.

The Solicitor-General: We will pay the expense.

Mrs. Star: Oh, the expense does not matter.

But that is what you mean by taking a book from a sister between 1856 and 1860, and keeping it concealed in her cell?—Yes.

Very well. You made a rule as to clothes. Had that rule special reference to her, or was it for the observance of the whole house?—It was a general rule.

You say in your deposition, "I knew she had more clothes than any of the sisters. I do not know how she managed to have such an unaccountable accumulation of materials of every description." And you add, "To remedy this defect I made a rule." Do you still say that the rule was general, and not special?—It was not made with the intention of being limited to her.

What was the "unaccountable accumulation of materials of every description" to which you referred—what you told us yesterday?—Yes, those trifling things.

Now, did you think that the bishop would understand that by "an unaccountable accumulation of materials of every description" you meant ribbons and bobbins, and hooks and eyes? Would "accumulation of materials" have conveyed the notion of bobbins to the episcopal mind? (Laughter.)—I do not know.

Well, a bishop is, of course, above us all. But do you think it would have conveyed that idea to an ordinary mind?—I do not know.

Now, in candour, don't you think there is a little touch of exaggeration about it?—I do not think there is.

Oh, very well. You think it moderate language, considering the facts?—I do. (Laughter.)

You go on to say, in your deposition, that she cut up some clothes and joined them together, so as to lessen the number without materially lessening the substance. Did she not lessen the quantity?

Mr. Mellish: Not the quantity that was worn.

The Solicitor-General: Was not this what she did—cut out the bad parts of some and substitute pieces cut from others?—I do not think so.

She says so. Do you mean to contradict her?—What I believe she did was, where she had three articles, to cut up one and add it to the other two.

Was the result of what she did the production of a decent petticoat?—I do not know.

You do not mean to say it was doubled?—It was not only doubled, but there were six thicknesses and parts. (Laughter.)

That is, there were six petticoats, and there ought to have been but one?—No; I do not mean to say so.

What, then, do you mean? Have you got them?—No; they were taken to pieces long since; and then it was found out there were six coverings.

Do you mean to say it was as good as six?—No;, but I mean to say that the materials would have made two.

Well, but ought there not to be two thicknesses on each?—Yes.

And is there not a hem?—Yes.

With two thicknesses more?—No; there is not a double on the hem I cannot speak of these things myself.

Then you do not know it of your own knowledge, although you make the charge?—I knew it by feeling the weight.

Do you not know that she cut out the bad parts and put in their place parts of other garments?—I do not.

The Lord Chief Justice: I understand you to say that these things happened before you made your regulations to diminish the number?—Yes.

The Lord Chief Justice: And her object was after the regulation was made to evade it by multiplying thicknesses, so as to have equal weight?—Yes.

The Solicitor-General: This was about the time you took away the clothes and gave them to Sister Fearon and Sister Rafter. You say in you deposition, "I then took care of her clothes myself." What you meant by taking care of them was giving them away?—That is not what I meant.

But that is what you did?—I did, but that was not taking care of them.

You go on to say that since this regulation the destruction of her wearing apparel has been most unaccountable. Did you allude to the veil and the tunic?—Yes; and to the stockings.

Meaning that she tore them up and made holes in them, although you had not seen any portion of them?

The Lord Chief Justice: The witness says she saw the veil one day without a rent, and another day with several.

The Solicitor-General: Will you undertake to say that on the day you saw the veil there were no rents in it?—There may have been, but I did not see them. The rents of which I speak were not on it. If they were on I must have seen them.

But even in convents do not some people wear out their clothes faster than others?—Yes.

Some are more or less careful?—Yes.

Did it not occur to you that that might have been Miss Saurin's case? She had to go amongst children and others, and to do work in which it might have been that things would tear.—My impression was that it was done designedly.

You go on to say, "She was so clever, she always had an excuse which satisfied me."—It satisfied me for the time.

But afterwards there came a time when it did not satisfy you?—Yes.

When did you make inquiries?—I do not remember.

How came it that, being satisfied, you became dissatisfied if you did not make inquiries?—On reflecting upon the excuses given, they did not satisfy me.

Did you ever take the trouble to find as a fact whether what she said was true or not?—I do not know that inquiry was necessary. If it was, I certainly should have made it.

For example, you say that she used to be late, and made excuses which satisfied you, and afterwards you were not satisfied. Did you ascertain whether the excuses were true or untrue?—I found it out either from observation of my own or from inquiry, or perhaps both.

Then you did inquire?—I may have done so.

Why did you inquire?—I do not know whether I did inquire.

Then, for all you know, what she said was true?

To the Lord Chief Justice: How often did it happen that she absented herself from table?—She was habitually absent, my lord, but I do not know how many times I asked how it happened.

The Solicitor-General: But this was only while she was refectorian, and she ceased to be so in 1861?—I do not know.

She says so. Do you mean to contradict her?—I think she was refectorian in 1861.

Then right or wrong, true or false, the conduct you brought up against her, in 1866, had ended with the cause of it in 1861?—I do not know what you allude to.

I have been reading your deposition as to her absenting herself from table, and as to her being so clever that she gave you answers which satisfied you. Now, whether she was right or wrong, did not that cease in 1861?—She was not under my personal observation.

Mr. Mellish: My learned friend is asking whether, after she ceased to be refectorian, she ceased to misbehave as refectorian, and it is so obvious that witness cannot understand it. (A laugh.)

The Solicitor-General: Very well. Then you charge her with forwardness in her conduct in reference to one of the priests in Hull, as to which you say: "I observed that she constantly put herself in his way, and sought to attract his notice by certain little arts. She constantly talked to him whenever she had an opportunity; and although I could not say positively there was anything wrong beyond disobedience, yet an indefinable feeling pervaded my mind that all was not right on her side. I felt very uncomfortable, and sent her to Clifford. I believe the priest was really deceived as to her real character, and saw nothing but friendly amiability and good-natured kindness in her attentions to him." Now, what do you mean by that. Did you mean to make a charge of improper behaviour against her?—By no means.

By no means?—No charge whatever against her moral character.

What did you mean by saying that when the priest referred to was present she became in a state of excitement?—That she was not in her ordinary state.

And this made you feel uncomfortable?—It made me feel uneasy.

You saw the other depositions before they were sent to the bishop?—Yes.

Now attend to what is said in other depositions on the subject of this priest: "When I was at school I noticed that Miss Saurin's manner was very familiar with one of the priests. I once saw her on her knees beside him, pulling the things out of his hand and entreating him to go with her." What did you mean by sending that to the bishop? Did you mean to impute any impropriety?—No; it entirely turned upon a rule.

The Lord Chief Justice: What rule?—15th chapter, page 37, in which sisters are directed never to be seen running giddily about the convent, and "at all times and places to observe in her deportment gravity becoming a religieuse."

The Solicitor-General : And all you meant to convey to the bishop was that she had broken that rule?—Yes.

Would it not have been better to have said so?—It did not occur to me at the time.

Do you mean to say that when you wrote of her excitement when the priest came, of her using arts to attract his attention, of her speaking constantly to him, of her putting herself in his way, and of your uneasiness of mind on the subject ; and when you added to that the sister's deposition about pulling things out of his hand and begging of him to go with her—do you mean to say you believed that all that would not have been regarded as a charge against her moral character?—I felt confident that neither the bishop nor the sister who wrote it would think it was a charge against her moral character.

You thought it would be regarded as a breach of the rule as to gravity of deportment. Is that what you mean?—Yes.

You speak in one of your letters of her family being wily people, who might appear to be quiet, but yet be preparing for much scandal. What scandal did you allude to?—No scandal having reference to anything immoral.

The Lord Chief Justice : She referred to possible legal proceedings.

The Solicitor-General : I intended to have referred to another letter, in which she speaks of being alarmed about a grave scandal.—I have no copy of the letter.

The Lord Chief Justice : I suppose you refer to the letter to the bishop of the 1st of May, 1865, in which she says she mentioned her troubles about Sister Scholastica to her confessor, and told him her fear of a coming scandal.

The Solicitor-General (to witness) : Had the scandal referred to in that letter anything to do with her conduct towards the priest?—No : it had reference entirely and solely to her pilfering.

Pilfering what—the things you took out of her pocket?—Yes.

You say again in your deposition that she " told innumerable falsehoods." Of course, strictly speaking, that is incorrect. Did you mean to convey that it was her habit to tell falsehoods— that falsehood was the colour of her life?—I believed her to be very insincere.

Well, that is a very mild form of putting it. (A laugh.) Did you not mean by innumerable falsehoods perpetual lie-telling?—No ; I would understand by perpetual, never ceasing. (Laughter.)

True ; but your own word is innumerable. Now, about this unripe fruit. Was not the place to keep it the pantry?—Yes.

And that was where you found it?—Yes, it was hidden on the top shelf. I went to look for something else that was required.

And there you found the gooseberries?—Yes.

Well, a gooseberry-picker is always said to be at a distance—that is to say, gooseberry-pickers remain at a distance while young men and young women are making love. (Laughter.)

The Lord Chief Justice : May not the unripe gooseberries have been placed in the pantry for tarts?—I desired that they should not be picked, but allowed to ripen.

The Solicitor-General : Do they make such things as gooseberry-fool in a convent?—They may.

Have you ever made gooseberry-fool yourself? —I may have done so.

You sometimes took it yourself in a morning, I am told?—(Laughter.)—Yes.

Did you never kiss her and tell her all would be right when she made the written acknowledgment of her faults?—Never. I had made up my mind to apply to the bishop for her removal, and I never changed the intention.

There was, then, no forgiveness for her—not even if she acknowledged her faults, and sought forgiveness with tears?—I did not believe in her promises of amendment.

You tell the bishop you had taken the best advice you could obtain upon the case. Whose advice did you take?—That of Mr. Porter, Mrs. Kennedy, and Mrs. M'Keon. I made her sign the second acknowledgment, because I did not think that the first one was sufficiently explicit. The mere writing the letters to her uncle, if it had been done with my permission, would not have been a fault. The gist of her offence was her having done it without my permission.

The Lord Chief Justice : Is it an offence for a sister to desire to change her convent without the sanction of her superior?—It would depend upon her reasons.

The Lord Chief Justice : What reason would justify her in desiring such a change?—If she found any hindrance to her in the way of her salvation, she would be perfectly justified in desiring the change.

The Lord Chief Justice : But suppose that the reason was that she did not like her superior, and wished to change for what she might think a more suitable government for herself; would there be anything wrong there?—I think she ought to apprise her superior of it.

The Solicitor-General : But supposing, rightly or wrongly, she felt she had not justice done her by you ; would she be wrong to try to get rid of the temptation caused by your injustice to her by changing to another convent?—She ought to have apprised me of her desire, and no objection would have been thrown in her way.

Now, you charge her with having told the bishop falsehoods in 1862. Just give me one.— That she had never given anything away in her religious life without permission, except a small picture. She gave a book to a girl. I believe it was originally provided for her by her family.

Did you know that at the time you wrote this statement?—No.

Then you could not have referred to that when you wrote it. Tell me something to which you did refer when you said she had told falsehoods to the bishop?—I cannot recollect further than about the book she took from Sister Agnes Mary, the boots she took from Mrs. Kennedy, and the food I myself saw her take.

You say, "I never knew the depth of her malice until then." To what did that refer?—To her notes about the tower.

But was it not a breach of the rules to go up the tower?—No ; a sister superior can always dispense with the rule for herself or for anybody else. It would have been wrong for Sister Scholastica to have gone up the tower without permission. It would be the duty of a sister, when she sees a fault, to mention it to her director. If Sister Scholastica had really considered that it was a fault, it would not have shown her great depth of malice if she had noted it. It was the way the entry was made that showed her malice. It was, "Sister Mary Agnes on the tower for two hours alone with Mr. C." That implied a good deal. Directly I saw the entry, I inquired about it. Sister Mary Agnes said she had taken Mr. and Mrs. Collins up the tower for a short time to see the country. The entry was more than exaggeration ; it was an imputation.

You made inquiry of Mrs. M'Keon ?—Yes.

And you also made inquiry of Mr. Collins ?—I did.

The Lord Chief Justice : Forming a judgment how far she was right, you must take into consideration not only what she saw written on the tablet, but what she afterwards ascertained as to the facts.

Cross-examination continued : Mrs. M'Keon told me that they went to the tower, it being a fine summer's day, to take a view of the country round. Mr. Collins gave me the same account of the matter, and added that they were not more than twenty minutes there.

Cross-examination continued : There was an entry about mutton-chops having been provided for a clergyman who came to visit us. There were entries relating to different articles of food, and other matters, showing malice. She acknowledged to me that she had taken part of the dinners of two children, and had eaten it. Mr. Cullamore was the confessor at Hull. She took him in. He is a very kind-hearted man, and he took her part. She also deceived Mrs. Grimston. She withdrew her assistance from the convent in consequence. Mr. Grimston said he wished to give his support to the boys' school, and therefore he could not afford to give us any further support. I saw Father Porter twice at Liverpool on this subject. I thought it likely he would be one of the commissioners. It did not occur to me to ask Father Matthews and his niece into a room with a fire. Father Porter was with me in the library at the time.

Was Father Porter at the fire in the library, while Father Matthews was out in the cold with his niece ?—Father Porter was in the library, and there was a fire in it. (A laugh.)

And was he talking over the affairs of the next day with you ?—Very little of them.

The subject was not entirely excluded ?—No.

Had he dinner there ?—No.

Well, did he take refection ?—No.

Tea ?—No.

Nothing at all ?—Nothing ; (after a pause) he may have taken tea, but I quite forget.

Come, I think he must have taken tea. (Laughter.) Any chops ? (Laughter.) Was it a meat tea ?—No.

Cross-examination continued : I think there was a place for plaintiff to sit down in the bathroom. There were two chairs in the room. They were placed in a part of the room where she was forbidden to go. I am not aware that she had permission to remove them. When I saw the plaintiff she was sitting on the floor. I did not ask her why she was sitting on the floor when there was a chair in the room. There was a stool in the room also. She made use of the

stool and the chair for other purposes, and I was told she actually did sit on the chair. I am convinced that the chair was not taken from her. We did not wish to make her uncomfortable. I did not consider one way or the other about it. The only thing that I ever did to induce her to leave was not giving her a change of clothes. I asked her to go—dearly. When she asked for clean sheets, they were not given to her. I referred her to her friends, and told her that they must provide things for her.

You wished to make her uncomfortable to induce her to go ?—You may draw what inference you please.

Then I shall draw it. (Laughter.)

Witness : I never knew that she had been prevented going into the library. The room to which she was removed was not a lumber-room. We had purchased a good deal of furniture, which was put into the unoccupied rooms, but that was removed before she was put into the room. The room was a small one, and a second bed occupied a great part of it. There was no extra furniture except the second bed. She could not walk conveniently from one end of the room to the other, but she could walk in parts of it. I never heard that the sister who slept with her was obliged to dress outside because there was not room to dress inside the room. There was a second sister outside the room. A sister who had sprained her knee was put into the bath-room with her. That sister did not use liniment, as was stated.

Do you really mean to say that Miss Saurin had liberty to go out of the room when she chose, and for requisite purposes ?—Yes.

She was ill, was she not ?—I don't know.

You did not ask ?—No.

The Lord Chief Justice : No representation was made to you of her being ill ?—No, my lord.

Witness : She was in the upper room for a fortnight. We acted in her case as we always do in cases of dismissal of postulants and novices. Not one of the professed sisters was ever dismissed, except the plaintiff, in our community. When she left the house I did not see her, but, I said, " I am sorry she has left in that way, because I should have wished to give her the kiss of peace."

The Solicitor-General : There are many more things I might ask you about, but I confine myself to one subject. Why did you take the ring off her finger, she being a professed sister at that time ?—I knew that she must leave the convent.

How did you know it ?—I knew that the bishop had sent the absolution to me.

When was this ?—August or September.

Then you had got it in hand ?—Yes, I thought she would not have been willing to give me the ring ; but she did give it to me.

Did she not beg that it might not be taken from her ?—No.

But she did not like it to be taken ?—No.

Then how did she show her dislike ?—I do not remember.

Did she not cry ?—No.

Nor remonstrate ?—Not that I remember.

It never was restored to her, of course ?—No.

Well, I will just ask you had you authority to take the ring from a professed nun ?—I think so.

It was a sign of union with her Lord, was it not?—Yes.

I suppose you had no right to dissolve that union?—No.

Well, where did you get the power to take away the symbol?—I did not consider I exceeded my right in doing so.

But where did you get it from, was it from rule?—No.

From custom?—No.

From tradition?—No.

Well, if you did not obtain your right from rule, custom, or tradition, where did you obtain it from?—I do not know that it is mentioned anywhere.

It was an indignity, was it not?—Witness: I do not know.

The Solicitor-General: Will you have the goodness, without my again asking the question, to repeat that answer to the jury.

Witness: I do not know that it was an indignity.

The Solicitor-General: Do you really mean to say so?—Witness: I do.

The Solicitor-General: Very well. I have no more to ask you.

This concluded the cross-examination.

Re-examined by Mr. Mellish: I cannot recall to mind an instance of a ring being taken from professed nuns. There is no rule about expulsion at all—it is left to the bishop. The bishop has the absolute power of expelling. I have heard of professed nuns being dismissed, but I never knew of any case personally except that of Miss Saurin. When I kept back the death of her brother, I was at Hull and she was at Clifford. I had made an order that letters for all sisters should be forwarded to me. I did not keep back the intelligence of her brother's death; on the contrary, she knew it, I believe, on the very day the news was received. It was posted on the chapel door.

The Solicitor-General begged permission to put a question to the witness as to the letters and papers which she destroyed.—The witness, in reply, said: In the summer of 1866, thinking I was dying, I destroyed a number of papers, including many relating to Miss Saurin, as I was desirous of arranging the papers relating to the community. When the action commenced I collected all the papers connected with Miss Saurin, and I picked out of them such as I thought would be useful to her, and such as I thought would not be useful generally I destroyed.

After a brief adjournment for lunch, the witness was re-examined by Mr. Mellish: You were asked as to when you first communicated to Baggot-street the facts unfavourable to Miss Saurin—was there not constant communication between you and the superior in Baggot-street?—Independently of everything else, we corresponded, and so do other members of the community occasionally. When I was superior I wrote perhaps once a month; or two or three might pass, and then there would be an interval of a month.

Did you generally report anything which happened in the community?—No, not at all—not anything unfavourable. As a rule, I should not report anything unpleasant which occurred.

I think there is an expression in your letter to Father Matthews of the 3rd of April to the effect that the superior at Baggot-street knew Miss Saurin too well to receive her again. Did that relate to anything you had communicated by letter to her?—No; it related to Mrs. Norris's own knowledge of her, which I knew from statements made verbally to me. I wrote to Mrs. Norris on the 27th of July, the same day that Miss Saurin was writing to her uncle, and at the same table. That was the first communication I had with the superior at Baggot-street with respect to the clandestine correspondence. It is not true that I ever said to Miss Saurin that she would never be able to bear all she would have to undergo. What I did say to her on that occasion was to this effect. I proposed to her that it was no matter whether or not the community thought as I did, time would not make things better, and, though my superiority might end, my successor would have the same opinion of her as I, and that if I were her I would go to another convent, and not remain where every one mistrusted her. The two letters I kept back were sent by a sister of Miss Saurin's, who is not a nun. I kept them back because it is not usual to give them during a retreat. I took those two letters away afterwards. She was allowed to fully read them. I remember once giving her a letter just before an exercise, and I waited while she had full time to read it; but she continued reading it apparently, so I asked her for it, and said I would read it for her. That was the only case in which I took a letter away before she had read it. The things that have been produced were part from her desk and part from her books. I did not read what was taken; I only took away everything like paper to prevent her making notes. I did not tell her why I did it. All of the things were not taken at the same time, nor were they all taken by me. The little pictures and prayers I did not take from her. I cannot point them out. Some were found in her books when the books were changed in January. In April, 1866, I was in Clifford, and I left word that if Miss Saurin left the convent while I was away to give them all to her. On looking over them one of the sisters recognized there one picture or more belonging to her, and which she had missed for some time; consequently, Mrs. Kennedy took all the pictures out of the books, in order that any belonging to the other sisters might be taken from them, and the remainder then given back to Miss Saurin. I believe they were all in her possession; but whether they belonged to her rightfully I cannot say. When that distribution of books was made, it was with the intention of taking away everything from Miss Saurin.

The Lord Chief Justice: I understood you distinctly to state that the order which you gave had no special reference to her?—No, my lord. It is done as an exercise of poverty, so that we may be disengaged from all things connected with this world.

Mr. Mellish: The more a professed sister is attached to any particular thing, the greater is the reason for taking it from her?—Yes. (Laughter.)

The Lord Chief Justice: The whole thing is perfectly logical. If you desire the extinction of the notion of property, the best way is not to allow these things to remain long in the possession of individuals. If the end is right, the means seem perfectly reasonable; and we must look at it from the point of view they do.

G

Mr. Coleridge: We don't complain of an equal distribution, my lord.

The Lord Chief Justice: If a person submits herself voluntarily, and this is honestly done, no one can complain of it.

Mr. Mellish: You said Mrs. Rafter was the sister who erased the tablets, and that she is not in a condition to come here. What is her condition?—Our fear is that she would get an attack of congestion of the brain. From anxiety in connection with the commission, she did get such an attack. There was another sister present who is here. When I took away her religious dress I provided a new black dress, which she wore from the middle of February until within a fortnight of the time she left. She then pinned it down the back, because she said it was too large, and then, in putting it on, it was reported to me that she would have torn it to pieces in the strain of putting it on. I then had another, which was not new, given to her, and the new one was taken away to be kept respectable. On her leaving she should have had it, and other clothing, if she had only applied to me. I had offered her a mantle and a bonnet, which she refused to take. The things she went away in were the inferior clothing. I had everything very nice and ladylike for her if she had only given me notice. I had no notion she was going away until I saw her walking up the hall with her brother, with a black woollen shawl over her head. The book of hers I found in the cabinet between the clothes was not in its right place ; the chapel was the proper place for all devotional books.

The Lord Chief Justice: It would be no great harm having a devotional book in her cell?—No; but sisters are not allowed to remain in their cells for any length of time in the day. The sisters also have books for study, which are kept in a general library.

Mr. Mellish: Tell us, if you please, what this refers to in Sister Mary's deposition : " I once saw her kneeling by the side of a priest, pulling things out of his hands, and entreating him to go with her."—So far as I can understand, it was this : The things which the priest was using were tools. I think he was fastening a desk down in the school, and that Miss Saurin went into the school, knelt down beside him, and asked him to go away with her, I believe to take some lunch. That was considered to be too familiar. There was no moral imputation against her, but her manner was too forward.

Under what circumstances is a professed nun allowed to write without submitting the letter to her superior ?—When a nun desires to be removed, and does not wish to give her reasons to her superior, she may write to the bishop—indeed, it is her duty. That letter is sent without even being sealed. She should give it to the assistant superior, who should not read it, but seal it and send it to the bishop. The bishop's reply to her, if any, should be given to her unopened. The bishop has power to give her leave to change her convent. Under the Pope he is the next superior.

The Lord Chief Justice: A sister cannot change her convent without the permission of the bishop? She cannot go beyond the precincts of his diocese without permission.

Mr. Mellish: Did not Miss Saurin acknowledge to you that she took part of the dinner of two of the school children and eat it ?—Yes. She told

me who the children were. They were a brother and sister of the name of Swain. She told me she had eaten part of the pastry they had brought. Mrs. Grimston had no news of what took place inside the convent except what Miss Saurin told. Anything she told would be a violation of the rule not to tell an extern anything which passes in a convent. I took off her ring in August or September, 1865, after receiving a letter from the bishop, saying that he had got the absolution. I thought Miss Saurin would then leave without a commission. If it had been decided that she was to remain, the ring would have been restored. I asked her for it, and she gave it to me. I did not take it off. No one was present. I should consider that an indignity if it had been done in public or in chapter ; but as it was done in private, and with no one present, I do not think it was. I have learned since answering this morning that the ring was taken away from two other sisters for a time, as a penance.

The Lord Chief Justice : The ring is never permanently taken away, I presume, except where it is intended to deprive a sister altogether of the character of a nun ?—Yes, my lord, and then it is taken away like the religious dress, and as part of the dress.

Mr. Mellish : You said that shortly after the commencement of the action you collected the papers together, destroying some and reserving others. I wish you to tell us again what you preserved and what you destroyed ?—I preserved those which I thought would be useful—that would instruct our solicitor.

Do you mean your solicitor ?—Yes.

Or her solicitor ?—I did not advert to her solicitor. (As this was diametrically opposite to what the witness had stated in reply to the last question of the Solicitor-General before adjourning for lunch, there was considerable sensation excited in Court, and some laughter.)

The Lord Chief Justice : Did you destroy any papers which, in your judgment, were of importance to either ?—No, my lord.

The phrase useful or not useful is ambiguous, and we are anxious to know what it is you meant by the papers you destroyed.——Papers which I did not consider evidence, or that would not convey information on the subject. I thought it would not be useful to have a great quantity of papers.

Mr. Mellish : Now I will put the question plainly to you. Did you destroy anything which you thought would be useful to the plaintiff against you ?—No, not one.

The Lord Chief Justice : I thought she could not mean to use the terms she employed in their full sense.

By Mr. Mellish : In the bed-room the one bed was opposite to the door, and in the middle of the floor there was a camp bed. Miss Saurin occupied the best. The chairs were against the wall. Assuming the door to be at the south, the chairs were on the west, and nearer the bed than the door, at first ; but afterwards a chair was put near the door. Miss Saurin sat on the floor, but I have heard she sat on chairs sometimes.

Mrs. Julia Kennedy was then called and sworn. In reply to Mr. Mellish, she said : I was one of the sisters of mercy in the convent at Hull. I previously had been in the convent at Baggot-street. I am now superior at Hull. In August, 1855, I went with Mrs. Star, when the convent at

Clifford was founded. I filled different offices. In 1857 I was mother-assistant at the convent at Hull. Since that time I have held all the principal offices in turn. I was mother-assistant up to the year 1861, when that office was changed to that of bursar. I held that till January, 1863, when I was appointed mistress of novices, which I held till May, 1864, when I was again appointed mother-assistant, but kept in charge of the novices as well. That continued till Miss Saurin left the convent. I was always one of the "discreets," by virtue of my office. I was slightly acquainted with her in Baggot-street, but I had scarcely spoken to her—our duties were different. Miss Saurin joined before I did, in August, 1851. I became a full sister in April, 1854. I was principally employed in the schools in Baggot-street, and Miss Saurin in the laundry and work-room. She always struck me, from the beginning, as being very unhappy, judging from seeing her crying, and from not being with the other sisters. I seldom saw her with the others. The thought often occurred to me that I wondered she was so silly as to stay in the convent if she were not happy. In August, 1855, I went to Clifford, and Miss Saurin came in May, 1856. In July, 1856, I left Clifford and went to a convent in Liverpool. I returned when the convent was founded in Hull, in January, 1857. In February, March, and April, 1857, Mrs. Star was at Clifford, and left me in charge in Hull. Miss Saurin was left under my care, with the other sisters, in Hull. I did not see much of her, for I was employed daily for ten hours teaching school. She was housekeeper, but during that short time I noticed her extremely irregular at her duty, especially at meals in the refectory; so that I was obliged to stand in the hall and insist on her going into the refectory in time for grace. I had frequently to reprove her for breaches of the rule of silence, especially with regard to the young women attending the night-school.

The Lord Chief Justice: How is that rule enforced, first as regards conversation between sisters themselves, and secondly as regards conversation with externs?—The rule is simply this: sisters are not to speak unnecessarily to each other, except at the time appointed for daily recreation. At other times, when they want to speak necessarily, they are told to do so in a low voice, and as briefly as possible. That rule is enforced with regard to externs more pointedly than with regard to those in the convent. No sister has permission to speak to an extern without permission of the superior, except she is in such an office that she is obliged in the discharge of her duty to do it, and then she is only allowed to speak so far as duty obliges her. Sometimes in large schools there may be ten or a dozen sisters employed, but it is only the sister in charge of the school who has permission to speak with visitors. Any other who is spoken to should refer the visitor, as briefly as possible, to the sister in charge.

The Lord Chief Justice: That is merely the rule in theory, but what is the rule in practice?— It is a rule in which we are very strict. Miss Saurin infringed that rule by staying with young women beyond the time for schooling, talking idly in the room, and I could not succeed in making her obedient on that point, though I spoke frequently to her. I also observed a want of

principle and uprightness in her general conduct. For instance, I was obliged to send her one or two days in each week to an out-school at some distance from the convent, and after a time I saw that she returned home generally about half an hour before the appointed time. When I reproved her for it, and called her to account, she put the blame upon the clock; but I afterwards learned from the pupil-teachers that she had got them to put on the clock. As an example of this, one of the managers of the school complained that he had met the children in a street, at a distance from the school, at half-past two, when they should not have left school until half-past three o'clock. Miss Saurin had presided there on that day. I complained to her of that. I felt quite ashamed before the priest, who was the manager, though for her sake I did not explain to him. She always had an excuse, and it was nearly always something the matter with the clock. At the end of April Mrs. Star desired me to take her to Clifford. I did so, and I was obliged to report her conduct to Mrs. Star, as I have told the Court. I went back to Hull, and Miss Saurin stayed at Clifford, so I saw her no more till the end of the year. In January, 1858, she came to Hull. Mrs. Star was there then. Miss Saurin was then made housekeeper and refectorian. She was only the superintendent of the storekeeping department; her duties were rather less than more than other sisters. I remarked all 1858, '59, and '60, while she was refectorian, from December, 1857, to October, 1858, and from July, 1859, to April, 1860, while she was in Hull, that she kept all the places under her charge in a most disorderly state; pantries and kitchens I scarcely ever saw orderly while she was in charge. I noticed constantly breaches of all the rules— silence, obedience, poverty, etc. As regards silence, she seemed to me never to observe it, as it was customary for the other sisters to do, so far as my observations went. I constantly heard her voice in the kitchen. I noticed her putting herself in the way of all externs. For example, I had charge of teaching a large class of young women on Sunday afternoons, and on going to that class at three o'clock I have sometimes met her running away from it when she saw me coming. She ought not to have been there, but she had been talking to them, which no other sister would have done. That school was held in the convent. With regard to poverty, she did not seem to have the slightest regard for her vow. She had a habit of taking the clothes and other things allowed for the sisters' use, and making use of them. Sometimes they were returned, when no longer fit for use. Under this head I may class the boots which she took out of my cabinet. Some time in 1858 I made inquiries, and on passing through the refectory some time after, I recognized them on her. I made her take them off and give them to me. She said she had mistaken them for her own, or made some such excuse. I had never given her permission to use them.

By the Lord Chief Justice: I certainly never lent them to her. If I had been willing to do so I should have been obliged to ask the superior's permission. You must do so, either to borrow or to lend.

By Mr. Mellish: Some month's later I felt so sorry anything I had should be a temptation to her that I asked and got permission to give them to her, because I saw she had coveted. I noticed her unfair partiality in the distribution of food, which is against the vow of poverty. The rule is that any sister in charge of temporalities cannot alter, give either better or worse, less or more, than the superior allows. All is equally distributed, unless there is a special direction given by the superior for a legitimate reason. What I observed was that she took far more care of the senior sisters than of the young sisters. One of the seniors mentioned this to Mrs. Star, who reproved Miss Saurin, and did all she could to break off that habit ; but without effect, so that Mrs. Star, as a means of preventing this partiality, used sometimes to change the plates in the refectory, where each sister has an appointed place. On one occasion she changed my plate from the head of the table to the foot, and when the one which I got was uncovered I found it contained nothing more than a bare bone. (Loud laughter.) If it had not been changed I should have had what Miss Saurin always gave me—a very good dinner. I said nothing about it then, and I merely mention it now to illustrate what I remarked of her partiality. The plaintiff during those times seemed to live in a way little short of miraculous. Her health seemed almost miraculous, judging by the little I saw her eat. I do not exaggerate, I'm sure, when I say I have seen her eat not more than an ounce for breakfast, the same for dinner, and again for supper. She was on this account a constant source of anxiety to Mrs. Star and me. We thought she must have some extraordinary internal complaint, because she looked so well and seemed to eat so little.

The Lord Chief Justice: Was the mystery ever cleared up?—Yes, my lord. Afterwards we found out that she was all this time eating plentifully. We did not then suspect her, because we had never heard of such a thing. So far from having any such suspicion, Mrs. Star took her to a physician, and explained the case to him. That was in 1858 or 1859, and the physician's name was Dr. Davey. For the same reason Mrs. Star used to make her keep her bed until ten o'clock in the morning, because she thought she must be very weak ; and she also gave directions to one of the sisters, to give her broiled meat four times a day, with other things between. The doctor knew at once there was nothing the matter with her, and he said, the second day, that she was imposing on him. He gave her no medicine. Mrs. Star was always, getting her a dispensation from the Church law on fasting, because she believed Miss Saurin could not support nature without it. She "disimproved" daily all those years in regard to her duties. Another fault, and perhaps the worst, was her want of truth. As a rule, we could scarcely believe a word she said. Mrs. Star was the last to see and believe it; so that she corrected me on two or three occasions for want of charity when I cross-questioned Miss Saurin. I can give particular instances of want of truth at a later period up to the time of her leaving the convent. The effect of that habit of untruth on me was that I made a resolution that I would turn my eyes as much as I could from her faults, so that I should not see them, and I kept to that all the time she was in the convent. For that reason I think there are few professed members of the community who know so little of her faults as I do. (Laughter.) In 1860 Miss Saurin was re-

moved to Clifford, partly by my advice, on account of the bad example she set the junior sisters. Of her conduct there I only know by report. She came over to the annual retreat in 1861. At a chapter during that retreat, Mrs. Star gave her a serious reproof for those faults which I have mentioned, disobedience, and breaches of poverty and silence. She took it remarkably well at the time, and expressed great thankfulness, and we were all very much pleased to see her in such good disposition. The next instance of my coming in contact with her was at Hull, in July, 1862. I had then heard of the clandestine letters. Writing letters against the will of the superior is against canon law, so it is not set down in our rules, or in those of any other order. It is considered such a grievous fault that we were instructed that the commission of it would entail expulsion, or at least would deserve it. The superior has full permission either to give or withhold letters from a sister, to send or to keep back. That is the practice and tradition of our order. The only exception to that is the case which has just been mentioned. A sister may, without permission, write to the bishop, or send a letter through the bishop, if she wishes it, and if she don't wish the superior to see it. There is no exception to that rule, and it would make no difference that the letter was to her uncle, who was a priest, except the bishop gave her special permission to send it.

The Lord Chief Justice: The bishop's is an authority to which you must all bow ?—Yes, my lord, except that he could not oblige us to break our rule.

By Mr. Mellish : She came over to Hull, in July, 1862, and on that occasion she wished to stay away from the community and not to join it. Mrs. Star sent me to try and coax her to come down and join the community. The only way I could succeed was telling her that her fault had not been made known unnecessarily—that was sending the clandestine letters. Miss Saurin said she looked upon it as such a great fault that she was ashamed the sisters should know she had committed it. No one knew of it then, but Mrs. Star, myself, and the two sisters who had discovered one of the letters. After much expostulation I induced her to come down and join the community. She acknowledged to me, on that occasion, that she had written and sent the letters. She, of her own accord, went down on her knees some days later in the rev. mother's room, Mrs. Star, Mrs. M'Keon, and myself being present, and acknowledged that she had written and sent two letters to her uncle, independently of the one which had been intercepted ; also that she had deceived Sister Mary Agnes very much in the matter, and that she had told innumerable lies. I can't swear to the words exactly. I don't think I was present when the second acknowledgment was written by Miss Saurin. On the occasion of the visitation in September I asked his lordship to dismiss her on the ground of the clandestine correspondence. I also added, in a general way, that she was a very imperfect "religious." I did so from conscientious motives—as a duty to the community, to have a bad member separated from them. She then went back to Clifford, and I remained at Hull, till I went in June, 1864, to Clifford. I know that four of us went down, and Miss Saurin pressed very much to give up part of her bed to us. I went to her cell one day to hasten her dressing, to catch the train, as Mrs. Star was waiting for her, and assisted her to dress, but I deny that I was in the least degree rude to her. I did it to oblige her, and I never touched her going down stairs. I have no recollection of putting her boot on. I saw her and Mrs. Star start. She was taken away suddenly, because Mrs. Star feared that if she was left she would have all the villagers there to see her start. She was to have remained at Clifford till August, but I begged as a favour that she might be taken then to Hull. I was going to stay at Clifford. My motive was that I had brought two novices to instruct for their profession and I feared she would disedify them. I returned from Clifford in August, and remained at Hull afterwards until after the plaintiff went away. Her manner towards Mrs. Star, when I saw her, was most disrespectful. As an example: on one occasion a general direction had been given to all the sisters to lessen their bed covering, as the weather was growing warm ; it was April or May. A single blanket was to be put on each bed, instead of a double one—the usual allowance in winter is two pairs. All the sisters complied with the direction, except Miss Saurin. The cell-sister saw she had not complied ; but she feared to speak to her herself, and came and told Mrs. Star. Mrs. Star went to Miss Saurin's room, and told her to take it off. She came back with the blanket in her hand to the room where I was. Miss Saurin followed her, and made quite a disturbance, though

it was an hour of strict silence. She spoke in a loud excited tone of voice, and altogether in such a manner that any one who did not know the circumstances would think that Mrs. Star had been very much ill-treating her. I remember that one of the expressions she made use of was, " My very bed clothes are dragged off." At all events her behaviour was such that Mrs. Star gave her back her blanket, and let her have her own way. That was a shocking example in a religious community. (Laughter.) I know that for years Mrs. Star was very kind and considerate to her, until her conduct obliged the superior to be strict. No doubt the vigilance exercised over her would be very hard—tyranny indeed—to another who did not deserve it. But if you take her whole career into consideration, it was simply what she deserved, and what was necessary. I never heard Mrs. Star speak unkindly to her all the time she was in the convent. The only time I heard her speak severely was in the case of the reproof, in chapter, in 1861. Mrs. Star was never unkind to any one. She was remarkably kind and considerate to every one, especially to the sick. I never heard of a kinder superior, of one who exceeded or even equalled her in attention to the sick and dying sisters. She never had any difficulty with any other sister. While Miss Saurin was away, the convent was most peaceful and happy ; nothing could be more so.

The Court then adjourned to Monday morning.

ELEVENTH DAY, *Monday, February* 15*th.*

Again was the Court of Queen's Bench crowded to excess this day, by a tithe of the public seeking admission. The body of this incommodious hall of justice will seat just sixty persons in the four rows of benches that fill that space of the ground area behind the barristers. Of the sixty who sat there to-day twenty-two were women ; while in other parts of the court, or at least in the galleries, the proportion of female auditors was even larger, forming indeed the clear majority. This fact considered, it may seem very impolite to observe that the general conduct of the strangers present was indecorous beyond the degree which has been so deplorably reached on former days. The "inane laughter" of this assembly was reproved by the Lord Chief Justice in a tone of unmistakeable contempt and disgust ; but whether the offenders were unconscious of having made themselves despicable, or whether they are of the class that avowedly "likes to be despised," it is certain that the scornful rebuke from the Bench had not the smallest effect on them. The witness Mrs. Kennedy gave her evidence with remarkable firmness ; and when, yielding at one period of her cross-examination to an unusual warmth, she retorted on some smart words of the Solicitor-General's, the Lord Chief Justice took occasion to compliment her on the general tone of her answers, and expressed a hope that she would not detract from the favourable impression she had made. Notwithstanding the obvious truth which the judge found it necessary to enforce while Mrs. Star was under examination on Saturday, that

there are two points of view, from one of which there is nothing absurd in the propositions that startle and puzzle folks who can only comprehend, as a possibility, their own way of looking at the monastic or any other question, the "inane laughter" still rushes in, taking the gravest topics for rich jokes, and the most severely logical deductions for wild topsy-turvyisms of moral philosophy. A calm and rational, though earnest, Protestant, whose convictions are the faithful fruit of cultivated judgment, and a habit of "proving all things," might groan in spirit to see and hear how the Reformed Church is represented in the public seats and corners of the Court of Queen's Bench : and a Protestant of another sort, a hot sectarian, though a well-educated and naturally shrewd observer, would find at least as much to deplore in watching the injuries which those "inane laughers" are inflicting upon the credit of their country's established religion.

The hearing of this case was resumed at the sitting of the Court this morning.

Examination of Mrs. Kennedy continued : In June, 1864, Miss Saurin came from Clifford to Hull. The schools were reopened in August. I had principal charge of them, and Miss Saurin was employed under me. It seemed as if I could not trust her.

The Lord Chief Justice : Just explain why ?— She disobeyed my directions.

In what respect ?—She neglected the duty imposed upon her.

Mr. Mellish : Explain in what respect ? I

had given her charge of a class to teach the reading of monosyllables. I examined that class, as it was my custom to examine all classes, six weeks after she had charge of it. I found that the children, instead of having made any progress, had forgotten even their letters. I speak of most of them, as a rule. Our schools being under Government, it is our duty to make the children progress steadily. I was obliged to take the class from her, and give her one of infants. In the same manner, she did not keep proper time there. She shortened the children's time. She dismissed them too soon. The reason I considered this a serious matter was, that our schools being under Government, we should, to obtain the grant, have the lesson she shortened to last at least two hours. I gave a different sister charge of the fires, and all the other sisters, Miss Saurin amongst them, orders not to interfere about the fire. She transgressed that order.

The Lord Chief Justice : In what respect?— By sending for fuel ; and on one occasion she had so much put on that the stove became red, and the lives of the infants were consequently endangered.

Examination continued : I spoke to her frequently as to her breach of this order. With respect to the dinners of the children, I observed nothing myself ; but two or three of the sisters reported to me that Miss Saurin took the dinners, and that they had very good reason to think that she did. I reported the matter to Mrs. Star. Most of the children are poor, but many are very comfortable, and their parents gave them nice things. They were the children of tradespeople. When this was reported to me first, I gave another sister charge of those children's dinners. I believe I told Miss Saurin not to touch the children's dinners ; but I know that I told the other sister to take special charge of them, to see that they got them, and also what was left. But still the suspicion continued, and Miss Saurin was removed to another school.

The Lord Chief Justice : Where was she removed to?—To a school at a distance—an infant school—in which another sister should be always in the school with her, which was not the case in the convent school.

Examination continued : I recollect that on the 31st of May, 1865, Miss Saurin had her clothes off. I advised the mother superior, Mrs. Star, to ask Miss Saurin for her pocket as she came in from school, in order to see if she brought the children's dinners home with her to the convent. The mother superior said that Miss Saurin would give her one pocket and perhaps have three or four others that she would not give. It was that decided her to make her take off some of her clothing, to see whether she had more pockets than one. On that day, after supper, as we call tea, at about twenty-five minutes past four, the mother superior called her into her own room. No one was there but the mother superior, Miss Saurin, and myself. The mother superior bolted the door inside, to prevent any one coming in ; but Miss Saurin could have unbolted it if she wished. I then sat down at a table to write, I was writing all the time. The mother superior told her to take off some of her clothing, her veil, habit, and so on. I could not tell what she took off, or what she did not, for I only glanced at her once ; but I know that the mother superior's manner was ex-

tremely gentle. I could not tell all that was said ; I was not listening. We were out of the room at five o'clock, for we had to go to spiritual lecture. I saw what was taken out of her pockets, and I heard the notes which were taken from her read by the mother superior. (Notes produced.) I think these are the notes, but I scarcely looked at the book.

The Lord Chief Justice : Are other notes in the book now ?—Yes, my lord.

Mr. Mellish : I cannot understand them.

Mrs. Kennedy : We understood them very well.

The Lord Chief Justice (reading the notes), " A. Smith was which deceived me." That I should say refers to something which had been said to her. " Spoke to Anne." That was one of the servants." " Not to see mamma more ;" " Every day adds to your guilt ; " Not having " something " done at ten o'clock ;" " Scolded for sending a sister of my message ; I had not done so ;" " These novices I have never been with." That is the sort of memoranda.

Mrs. Kennedy : It is difficult to make out the meaning now, but then we understood them very well.

The Lord Chief Justice : The spelling is not very good.

Mrs. Kennedy : Oh, she can't spell at all. (A laugh.)

The Lord Chief Justice : Yet she was sent to bring up the schools at Clifford after they had fallen off.

Mr. Mellish : I intend, my lord, to ask some questions as to that.

Mrs. Kennedy : She mentions " hard bread." I asked her as to that, and she acknowledged she had not got it.

To Mr. Mellish : I saw the food she got, as I sat near her. I never saw the least difference made with her except that at times she did not eat all she got for some months after her return to Hull in 1864. I do not think she ever finished her meat for four or five months—at all events when it was mutton, and it was generally mutton. It was the custom when a sister could not eat as much as the others that less should be given her. There were at least two others at the same time in whose regard the same order was given. The very day she complained of it, the mother superior that very evening in my presence directed the sister refectorian to help Miss Saurin as plentifully as the rest of the community, no matter whether she finished it or not. Her food was not different in the least in kind or quality from that of the other sisters. I never saw any difference made.

The Lord Chief Justice : Is it true that when the other sisters had other meat she was given mutton ?—That is quite untrue. I speak as a mother of the community and I speak for myself.

Examination continued : She also said that I rang for a plate of crusts for her. That is quite untrue. There is not the least foundation for what she said as to that.

The Lord Chief Justice : Do you remember any such circumstance as the bread failing and your going for more?—No, my lord. Another remark she made in her evidence was that one day when she complained to me that she had not had enough, and when I sent the Sister Lewin for more, I took the plate and sent the Sister Lewin back with the plate to take off some. The reverse of her representation is the fact. I sent the Sister Lewin back for more—as much as the plate could hold. (Laughter.)

Examination continued : I never saw any difference in her dress to that of the other sisters. I know that she destroyed her clothes. I do not mean to say she did not wear old clothes. We all wear our clothes as long as we can keep them together, as a practice of poverty. For instance, this is the fourteenth year I have been wearing this habit, and I have never had one since. It is also the habit to take off old clothes from one sister and give them to another.

State what you know as to her destroying her veil?—I noticed a veil torn, which she must have torn. It was a better veil than the one I was wearing. I believe it was newer. Then I observed day after day additional rents, until the mother superior had to give her another veil.

What became of the old one?—Oh, another sister wore it, and if I am not mistaken is wearing it still. Her name is Mrs. Hewetson. In the absence of the mother superior I had charge of Miss Saurin's clothing, and I gave her an article which I had examined myself—a tunic.

What is that?—It is a linen article, like a lady's night dress. I examined it the first time she sent it to the wash, and there might have been a pin-hole in it. The next week it was handed to me by the laundress a mass of rags. I questioned the two laundresses, and they both assured me it had been sent to them by Miss Saurin in that state.

The Lord Chief Justice : Was there any other evidence which came to your knowledge of her destroying her clothes?—I believe there was, my lord, but these were those of friends.

Examination continued : During the summer, some part of 1865, the mother superior was absent. The morning after she left Miss Saurin came to me to complain of her boots. I asked her why she had not complained to the mother superior before she went away, because I had not authority to give her new articles of dress. I said I would do what I could for her. I examined the boots and saw that the soles were cracked, but there was no holes in them. And these are the boots as to which she said she had to blacken her foot owing to holes in her boots and stockings. I gave her a pair of my own goloshes to wear over the boots. When Mrs. Star came back I reported what had occurred, and Mrs. Star gave her boots immediately.

The Lord Chief Justice : She says that she got a pair of shoes which she had to tie on. Was that so?—She got a pair of boots, and also a pair of shoes,

Examination continued : I do not know of my own knowledge that Miss Saurin complained of having her feet wet owing to bad boots. I heard a sister say she had heard her say so.

The Lord Chief Justice : How many pairs of stockings had she?—I do not know, I myself had two ; others had three pair.

The Lord Chief Justice : If she only had two pair, and one got wet and the second pair were in the wash, how would she manage?—If she were short of stockings, she could easily have got the loan of a pair.

Examination continued : Mrs. Star consulted me as to sending in her resignation before she did so. She was very delicate. I know she was really desirous of resigning. I did all I could to dissuade her from resigning, as I knew the community would be very sorry if she resigned. In August, 1865, before I made my deposition, I wrote to the bishop.

The Lord Chief Justice . This was about the time the sisters wrote the depositions?—Yes. It happened in this way. We were all anxious lest Miss Saurin should take the children's dinners, and thus bring disgrace on the convent, and one of the sisters who is now dead—Mrs. Dawson—came to beg of me to write to the bishop. Mrs. Star did not see the letters before they were sent. She knew I was writing. This is the letter. (Produced.)

The letter which was dated the 18th of August, was put in and read. The writer said she wrote as a matter of conscience ; that since Christmas the reverend mother's health had been failing, owing to her anxiety as to Sister Scholastica ; that the community had almost obliged her to go to Clifford for the benefit of her health, and that she had come back improved ; but that, since her return, renewed anxiety on the same subject had again affected her health ; that grace and nature combined to make them all desirous of saving the reverend mother from sorrow, which, if left unremoved, must bring them all to grief. The charge as to the suspected taking of the children's dinners was then referred to.

Examination continued : After that I wrote out what is called my deposition. The rev. superior told me the bishop wished us to make notes of our experiences of Sister Scholastica. I received no answer to my letter to the bishop. I wrote out my notes to the best of my recollection.

The " deposition " referred to was then read. It commenced thus : " I have known Sister Mary Scholastica for fourteen years, and judging of her by the facts which have come to light within the last few years, I consider her religious career has been one of the grossest falsehood, deceit, and treachery. I cannot think she had a vocation, and her only aim in religion seems to have been to gratify vanity by excessive care of dress and personal appearance, and her endeavour to attract the attention and affections of externs, to sow discord between the superioress and her subjects, and to satisfy her appetite by yielding to a love of eating and great particularity in her food. She has always shown a want of the spirit of poverty and obedience." The deposition then went on to state in detail many of the circumstances mentioned in the course of the witness's evidence.

Mr. Mellish : Did you believe all that you wrote in that deposition?—I did. I may add that I did not know then, although I know now, that there is a great deal in that is not legal evidence.

You were not called upon in a communication of that kind to confine yourself to strictly legal evidence.

Mr. Mellish : What was the " positive falsehood " of which you spoke, and which you say she persevered in violently?—She came to me to say her summer cloak wanted to be repaired. I had heard the mother superior directing a sister to repair it a couple of weeks before, and I told Miss Saurin I was sure she had done so, but she asserted positively the sister had not. I felt she was telling an untruth, and in the evening I called her and the sister to me at the same time, and asked the sister in her presence whether she had not repaired the cloak. She assured me she had done so particularly well. Miss Saurin denied it again and again, and was very noisy in her manner.

The Lord Chief Justice : Is that a breach of propriety ?— Yes, my lord. She denied it repeatedly, and made use of the expression, "As sure as my hand is on my body," which was not ladylike.

What noise did she make ?—She shouted out.

Mr. Mellish : And that is against the rule ?— Oh, very much.

Examination continued : Did Mrs. Star to your knowledge, ever require a sister to tell her confession ?—Never.

The Lord Chief Justice : Or what the priest said to her ?—Never, to my knowledge.

At all events, she never asked you ?—Never, my lord.

To Mr. Mellish : It never occurred except in 1857, that Mrs. Star and I were absent from recreation, and left Miss Saurin alone with the novices. When I say it never occurred, I mean when sisters were not dying; for when a sister was dying we always remained with her. In 1857 it occurred because the rev. mother attended an out school, and I had to do so also. A great deal of business had to be done, and we were obliged to devote the usual time for recreation, or the greater part of it, to the business for about a fortnight. Nothing of the sort occurred in 1859.

To the Lord Chief Justice : I am positive as to that. The mother superior of Baggot-street came over to Hull for the last time in 1859. She was there also in 1857.

To Mr. Mellish : My watch was taken from me before Miss Saurin's was taken.

The Lord Chief Justice : What was the object of taking them ?—It was too expensive to keep the watches in repair, and clocks were found to be cheaper.

The Lord Chief Justice : The plaintiff said it was intended to dispose of the watch in a lottery. Was that so ?—There was no truth in it.

Was there ever a lottery of watches ?—No, my lord. There was a lottery with watches in it, but not sisters' watches, but inferior watches. It is customary in all convents for sisters to offer watches and other things for the benefit of the poor. I have eight or nine watches now in my possession as superior.

Mr. Mellish : Was a letter ever taken from you ?—Yes : one I remember very well.

Was it kept for a time or entirely ?—Entirely. The rev. mother burned it.

And you were mother assistant then ?—Yes.

Have you kept any of Mrs. Star's letters since you became mother superior ?—I think not. I kept a letter from one of the sisters in which a member of the community was very much praised, and I feared it would make her vain. (Laughter.)

Do you remember Mrs. Star giving a letter to Miss Saurin from her brother Patrick, and then snatching it away ? It was said by her that you were present.—I do not. I have rather a bad memory. (Laughter.)

The Lord Chief Justice : Setting up a noise of that kind is very objectionable.

Examination continued : All the nuns in the convent do household work. For instance, I often swept the school at Clifford, about which she made a complaint ; and as it is I sweep the room in which I sleep, and another, which is called the mother superior's room. It is quite the spirit of our order. Hard labour is one of our characteristics.

To the Lord Chief Justice : The work of cleaning the corridors, passages, and rooms is distributed amongst the sisters by turns. There was no exception made in her case. I produce the distribution for January, 1868. Changes are made sometimes in three months, sometimes in six months, sometimes not for a year. If a sister becomes ill it necessitates a change.

The Lord Chief Justice : It would appear from this document that all, without exception, had, a portion of the work.

Examination continued : I remember what the plaintiff stated as to the mat. It is a heavy one ; but other sisters have had to clean it as she had.

Examination continued : On the 8th of Jan., 1866, the mother superior sent me to Miss Saurin to say she might remain all day from school to write to the commission. She would not stay away. She told me she would have plenty of time the next day. She said in her evidence I watched her writing. I did not. I was sitting at another table. I was not in court, but I am told she said so. There is one thing I would like to remark. The evening before the commission I was present while Father Porter was with the mother superior. After the bishop had written the letter of the 10th of February, and she was removed from the community, each of the professed sisters took it in turn to stay with her, and I took my share. I asked to do so, because it was a very disagreeable duty.

Had she liberty to leave the room ?—She had. Generally when I was there she left her room. I never prevented her.

Could she go down to the corridor ?—Yes, as much as she pleased. One day I met her on the corridor, saying her prayers, and I said to her, "You know no secular is allowed to walk about in that way, and you ought to have some regard for the regulation."

The Lord Chief Justice : What did she say to that ?—I do not know, my lord.

Did she continue in the corridor ?—I am not sure. I did not stop.

Mr. Mellish : Was she prevented from going to certain places ?—No ; certainly not.

Who cleaned her room ?—I do not know whether it was the sister who slept with her.

You did not sleep in the room ?—I did not.

Did she go to the chapel ?—Yes, on Sundays, and, for a time, on week days.

The Lord Chief Justice : While she was in the bath dressing-room ?—Yes, for a time, and she could have gone afterwards if she had wished.

Examination continued : I took part of her religious dress away. That was on the morning she was to leave for home to her family. On that morning we rose earlier than usual. I saw the secular dress which was provided for her. It was a good, new, ladylike dress. I saw the bonnet and other articles. They were all good and ladylike.

Examination continued : After her brother's

visit on the 13th of March she seemed to try by all means to make herself ill.

What did she do?—She abstained from food. She could not possibly be supported by the quantity she took.

Was proper food provided for her?—Yes; the same as the community got.

What else did she do?—She would sit up in her bed without clothing for a long time; then she would get out of bed and put her feet into a basin of cold water, and so on. When I say got up without clothes, I mean no bed covering. She had her tunic on.

Examination continued: I knew that the library was open to her.

To the Lord Chief Justice: She was not sent to Clifford to get the schools up. She was sent there for a particular reason—to be out of the way of the novices at Hull.

To the Lord Chief Justice: She had only charge of the lower class in school. She could not teach any other. She could not even read or spell well.

To Mr. Mellish: Industrial work is taught in the night-school. There was not much else done there.

The Solicitor-General rose to cross-examine, when

Mrs. Kennedy said: I beg your pardon. There is one thing I wish to add. Mention has been made of Mr. Collins. He is between sixty and seventy years of age, and is well known in the Catholic world as the editor of the English Catholic paper, the *Tablet*. He was editor of the *Hull Advertiser* when we went to Hull, and the then bishop (Dr. Briggs) gave him a particular charge of the convent in all matters in which we might require his services. When we wanted business transacted with the bishop he went to York and transacted it for us. The present bishop also said we should consult Mr. Collins in all things as to which we might require his assistance. That was the reason we sent for Mr. Collins the morning Miss Saurin left, as her brother had disturbed the convent, and behaved very rudely indeed.

The Lord Chief Justice: You mention in your deposition that the effect of these dissensions and difficulties was such that Mrs. Star showed a certain degree of tremor when Miss Saurin approached her. Did you witness that yourself?—I did, my lord.

In what way was she affected?—She seemed to be agitated, and wished to avoid her; and, as I mentioned, she asked me to stay with her when Miss Saurin was present.

Cross-examined by the Solicitor-General: You say she could not spell or read well. Have you read those letters she wrote?—Yes.

You know that in one of them she apologises for untidy spelling and asks for a dictionary?—I do not remember.

But you are anxious we should know the fact. Now, what is done in the night school? You say there is very little.—The girls are classified according to their abilities.

Do they read and write?—Yes; but in comparison to the day school the teaching is nothing.

Are the girls older or younger than in the day school?—Older, as a rule.

Then she superintended the night school, but was not fit for the day-school?—She had only a lower class in the day school.

But superintended the night school?—I have no knowledge of it. The night school you refer to was at Clifford. She did not at Hull.

You told us she superintended the laundry at Baggot-street?—Yes.

Do you not know that a sister of Lord Mostyn succeeded her in that duty?—A sister of Sir Pierce Mostyn.

You know she succeeded Miss Saurin?—I know she did harder work than any in the convent.

Perhaps so. But did she succeed Miss Saurin at the laundry?—I do not know. I was not in Baggot-street all the time.

But you were there after Miss Saurin left the laundry. Now you wished to convey a certain impression as to Miss Saurin in connection with the laundry. I wish to know whether you wish to convey the same impression in regard to Miss Mostyn?—I don't know anything of the matter of my own knowledge.

Who succeeded Miss Saurin?—I do not know.

Was it not Miss Mostyn?—I do not know.

Do you not know it was?—Witness (sharply): I do not know. (A laugh.)

Will you undertake to say it was not?—I undertake to say I do not know. (Laughter.)

You say that in Baggot-street Miss Saurin was always crying?—I did not say "always."

The Solicitor-General: Well, "often."

The Lord Chief Justice: That is not "always."

The Solicitor-General: I did not think that you meant every minute of every hour of every day. Was she habitually crying?—I said "often."

I know you did, and I wish to ascertain what you meant. Was she habitually crying?—I simply said "often," and that is what I meant.

What do you mean by "often"?—I cannot tell. I was thinking when it struck me.

Was it on most days?—Not on most days.

Once or twice a week?—I cannot tell.

But so as to be different from others?—Yes.

What did you mean by saying on Saturday she did not mingle with the other witnesses?—I did not say so.

Do you mean to say that?—You have a note taken of what I said; you will know by that.

The Solicitor-General: I know; I have a note of it.

Mrs. Kennedy: Then, excuse me, you have a wrong note of it. (Laughter.)

You say that when you were sister superior at Hull she used to stand in the hall, and you were obliged to insist on her coming in to grace?—Yes.

Was that habitual with her?—Yes; at least it happened often during the three or four months I was in that position.

How often?—I cannot tell the number of times.

About?—I cannot tell.

Once a week?—I cannot go beyond what I have said with truth.

The Lord Chief Justice: Without tying yourself down to any precise number, state how often you think it was.—Mrs. Kennedy: It occurred about half a dozen times.

The Solicitor-General: In four months?—Three months.

The Solicitor-General: I said four months.

Mrs. Kennedy: And I said three months. (Laughter.)

The Solicitor-General: You said three or four. I fear we shall not get on.

Mrs. Kennedy: No; I fear we never shall. (Renewed laughter.)

Now about her coming from school early. Was that habitual?—I noticed it several times.

How often during those four months?—I cannot tell.

Please to remember, Mrs. Kennedy, Miss Saurin has been expelled from the order and almost destroyed in Catholic society, and I must ask you to think about how often?

The Lord Chief Justice: Was it once, or twice, or thrice?

Mrs. Kennedy: It was oftener than three or four times, but I cannot tell how often.

The Solicitor-General: Was it so often as to become a habit with her?—Yes; I think so.

And she laid the blame to the clock?—I heard so from the pupil-teachers.

Did you tell her you would inquire of them?— I am not certain whether I did or not.

Who were the pupil-teachers?—I heard it from Bridget Conolly, and I think from another.

Who was the priest that told you he met the children out of school early?—The Rev. Canon Motler.

You say that her kitchen, pantry, and other places she had charge of were kept in a disorderly state. Was that habitual?—Yes.

You saw that?—Yes; from December, 1857, to October, 1858, and from July, 1859, to April, 1860.

While she was refectorian?—Yes.

Was it the business of the housekeeper or of the refectorian to clean the pantry, kitchen, and so forth?—In a small community like ours, the refectorian.

She had to do both duties, then?—Yes. She had a lay sister or a choir sister under her.

And she had, I suppose, also to cater for the convent—to see the tradespeople and buy what was necessary?—Yes.

And to pay the accounts?—The small accounts; the large accounts I paid.

While she was refectorian what were you?—I had charge of the schools.

How did you know about the pantry and kitchen?—I saw them.

You went in to look?—A mother assistant had a right to do so.

You say she never observed silence. When does that apply to?—All the time I had her.

That is, while she was refectorian?—Yes.

Had she not necessity to speak to those who prepared the dinner?—Yes; but I allude to loud and unnecessary speaking, and speaking at a distance.

You may have a bad memory, but you have a keen mind. You anticipated my next question. You do not say she was not to speak to the maids? —Not more than was necessary. I assure you every word I state is truth. She spoke a great deal without the least necessity. She seemed to me almost to reside in the pantry. (Laughter.)

Did you ever speak in a loud tone of voice?— I do not say I did not, but I did not break the vow of silence.

The Solicitor-General: I am not saying anything to your discredit.

Mrs. Kennedy: Oh, I have nothing to hide.

Well, you may have spoken in a loud tone?— I may have done so, but her breaches of silence were habitual. I could say nothing less with truth.

Hers habitual and inexcusable?—Most remarkable.

Yours occasional and justifiable?—Yes.

You say you have seen her speaking to the young women in the Sunday-school, and running from the school?—Yes; she had no business to be there. The class was under my charge solely.

How often has that occurred?—Up to the time she left Hull. I have given you the date.

How long did it happen?—You have the date. If you just calculate you will see.

The Solicitor-General: I fear I shall not succeed in getting it. Please to remember, Mrs. Kennedy, that it is important to my client, whose whole life is at stake.

The Lord Chief Justice: I really cannot allow that observation to be repeated, Mr. Solicitor. You said so once or twice before. That is matter of observation for the jury.

The Solicitor-General: I shall not repeat it after that intimation from your lordship.

Mrs. Kennedy: I judge from the manner in which Mrs. Star was cross-examined that I must be cautious.

The Lord Chief Justice: I must say that thus far I have never seen a witness who gave her evidence better. Do not let me have occasion to depart from that view by your not fully answering the questions.

The Solicitor-General: I must ask you how often you saw her running from the schools?—If you look to your notes, I think you will see I said it might have been two or three times. But I say more about talking to the girls and to externs who came to the convent, and to whom she had no necessity to speak.

Now as to taking clothes, you say she was in the habit of doing so?—Yes.

And she took your boots?—She did.

Were not her own boots bad?—She had, I think, the best boots in the convent, and the best supply.

Cardinal Wiseman was coming to visit the convent?—Yes.

And she took a worse pair of boots than her own to go before this great dignitary?—It was not necessary that she should go in boots.

The Solicitor-General: When was it, about, that the effect of the plaintiff's untruth on you was such that you determined to turn your eyes away from her faults, and continued to do so as long as she remained in the convent?—I think about 1859. I did do so, and for that reason I think there were few who knew as little of them as I do. I really did my best to see as little of them as possible.

I observed you to say that you had cross-questioned her on several occasions; will you give us an instance of what you mean?—Well, for instance, I heard her once saying something which I knew was not true, to my own knowledge; and I cross-questioned her as to the why, the where, the how, and so on, and the mother superior found fault with me for doing so. I wished to show her how untruthful Miss Saurin was, by convicting her, as it were, out of her own mouth. I committed a fault in so doing. I did so two or three times, I think, successfully; but, being a fault, the rev. mother stopped me.

The Solicitor-General: I think you said she used to eat so wonderfully little that it was almost miraculous?—Yes; she ate wonderfully little, so that it was quite a wonder. That was the case when mutton was being eaten as well as when other meat was served.

I believe at the time of Dr. Davey's attention to the plaintiff in this respect, he was attending another sister in the convent?—Yes; Dr. Davey was attending another sister when he was called to the plaintiff. On the second day Miss Saurin was the portress, and he said to the mother superior, "The sister you were trying to impose upon me opened the door." Her little eating was a matter that I could not turn my eyes from.

I think that you mentioned writing letters without permission was an offence against the canon law; will you tell from what writer on canon law you get that?—St. Basil says that is a case for excommunication. If I had known you were going to ask me that, I would have brought the book and shown you. I was reading it last night in a book, the title of which I forget, in which the case is quoted from St. Basil. The book was in French, as I do not understand Latin.

Do you think it was within the canon law for the superior of the convent to impose those penances upon a sister—such as kissing the floor and so on?—Certainly, well within the canon law.

And taking off the ring?—Certainly. In the second part of our rules you will see that it is a duty imposed upon the superior to impose penance, the nature of which is left entirely to her discretion.

The bishop would not have to be referred to?—No.

Is that where it says "She is sweetly to admonish and impose such penance as she shall judge expedient?—Yes, it is in Part II., section 3; it is also repeated in another place. I may add that those penances of which the plaintiff complained so much—kissing the floor and acknowledging her faults—are what we all do from time to time.

Have you always understood it to be a matter of conventual life and death to write a letter without permission?—I always understood it to be a very grievous fault, punishable by expulsion; that was what I was taught during my noviceship. I never knew any one to write without permission except Miss Saurin; with permission they may write to any one and about anything, I was present when she admitted her fault, and apparently she did so from her heart, and expressed great sorrow, Mrs. Star received her confession kindly. I don't know whether I made any communication to Father Porter previously to Miss Saurin's acknowledgment, but I did subsequently. The mother superior, I should say, also made a communication; but I am not aware that any of the other sisters did. Perhaps the sister who found the letter did, but I am not sure. I don't think I mentioned anything to him about Miss Saurin. It was a trouble to me whether I should mention it to him or not. In preparing for confession, it is the duty of every one to examine her conscience, to see what faults she had committed, and to me it was a great trouble to be obliged to condemn for so great a fault as untruthfulness. I felt puzzled, because I could not behave otherwise than that she was untruthful. I would not think of telling the priest who the person was, and what she did. I would only tell my own fault, and

accuse myself of want of charity. It was a scruple which I could not help. It was not part of my duty to make note of what I was going to say, and I never did until I made the deposition for the bishop. I may perhaps, two or three times in my life, have made notes for confessional purposes. I never made notes in my examen book to help my recollection in confession. I don't think it is the custom, and certainly I never did so; but if a sister wished to do so for the purpose of helping her conscience, I see no objection to doing so. I don't know whether I was present when the books and pictures were taken from Miss Saurin, but I wish to explain a part of that transaction for which Mrs. Star was unjustly and severely blamed. It really was I who took part of those papers and pictures, and it happened in this way. A great many of these papers and pictures remained in Miss Saurin's books after the distribution, and some of the sisters came and said they thought she had some of their pictures and prayers in her books, so I brought all of them into the kitchen and spread out the contents upon the table, and told them at their leisure to look if there were any belonging to them. I then totally forgot all about them, so, instead of returning the remainder to Miss Saurin, they were left, and put away with her other things to be given to her when she left the convent. To that extent I took away the prayers and pictures, and not Mrs. Star. I said that Miss Saurin was removed rather suddenly from Clifford because the rev. mother was afraid of a good many of the villagers coming up to bid her good-bye if they knew she was going. That fuss was made if it was known that any sister was going away, and we would rather avoid anything of that kind.

The Solicitor-General: Now about that school stove; you say Saurin kept up such a fire as to endanger the lives of the children?—Yes, if one of the infants had fallen against it, there is no doubt she would have been severely burned.

By the Lord Chief-Justice: It was a stove standing out in the room, just at the bottom of the gallery, where the infants sat, with nothing round it. It had a door which you could put up or down. When that was closed the stove became red hot and dangerous to any of the children who were passing. I gave strict orders to Miss Saurin, who was bound to obey me, not only as mother assistant, but as chief in the school, to keep the door of the stove down, but she habitually disobeyed my orders. It was by my advice that on the 31st of May her pocket was taken off and searched. She had only one on then, and no dinner belonging to the children was then found, I paid no attention to what was in the pocket except the note-book and a packet of needles. The needles struck me, because an evening or two before she had come to me, and told me she had no needles to finish her work, which was untrue. I mean to repeat now, that Miss Saurin had the same sort of food, both in quality and amount, as any other sister in the same situation. She was at the Prince-street School from April, 1865, until she was separated from the community. She dined at that time at four o'clock, after coming home; that is the custom. I was present when she used to dine, and I say then she had the same food in quantity and quality as any other sister in the same situation. A sister went with her every day, who shared her luncheon and took dinner with her after she came back. Her portion was increased on one occasion, in June or July, 1865. It happened in this way. One day on sitting down to table, Miss Saurin came to me and said "May I have some meat for dinner?" in a loud, exacting way. I was greatly surprised, and said, "Have you no meat?" She said, "Only a scrap." I looked over to her plate in the distance, and there seemed to me as much as on the rest; however, I did not hesitate, but sent a servant who got a good deal more on her plate. Miss Saurin said in her evidence that I sent it back with the meat taken off it. In that June or July I noticed that, during the absence of the reverend mother, she ate mutton every day as if she liked it. She was sitting at the head of the table very near me, and came from her place to me. I said her tunic might have had a pin-hole. I meant a very small hole, as it had begun to wear out a little. There were not a good many. I am only sure of one hole. I said she was noisy when she denied that her cloak had been mended. She then said it had been torn, as sure as her head was on her body. That I consider an example of the unladylike conduct to which I have referred. I have seen such a thing as a sister's watch being sold by lottery to raise money to relieve the poor. I have eight or nine watches now in my possession, for which I have an idea of obtaining some sacred plate for the service of the altar. As a rule, we make up fancy work for sale at these lotteries. I think Miss Saurin's watch was taken from her in October, 1863. There was no question about a lottery at that time, nor was there one before December, 1865, which at that time we did not at all foresee. I consider I have rather a bad memory. I had not made any notes in reference to this matter until I wrote out my deposition for the bishop, and that I have lengthened a little for the purpose of this trial. I don't think I should have remembered less if I had not written that deposition, and I am sure I have remembered very little compared with what I might have done if I had had a better memory. The paper the Lord Chief Justice had was the one which I actually wrote. I wrote that out, I think, from a few rough notes, which I destroyed immediately. I also wrote the deposition for one of the lay sisters, Mrs. Hewitson. I took down what she dictated. I don't remember her giving me any notes. I did not supply any materials. The lay sisters are not accustomed to composition. The notes I made for the commission I believe were destroyed. I gave them to the mother superior, and I did not see them after. They were destroyed when we found they were not required. I made them for my own examination. I discussed this matter with the lay sister Hewitson, but not generally with the other sisters. I think I went over the matter with Mrs. Nelligan, and by my advice she admitted part of her deposition. It was perfectly well known these depositions would be required, but we did not talk on the subject when all the community were together. I think I was alone with Mrs. Nelligan when we talked the thing over. Most of the sisters wrote together in the community room, and I think in silence, except a necessary question or so. I wrote in my own room. I lengthened the deposition for this trial. I said as much as I could, as I remembered so little. Mrs. Star gave a di-

rection to all of us to confine ourselves to what we knew, and to be moderate. My first sentence is, "I consider her religious career to be one of the grossest falsehood, deceit, and trickery." I don't say much for the moderation of that, but I think it is true. (Laughter.) I saw some of the depositions—perhaps most of them—but not all. I don't know anything about her distribution of time. I don't think there is such a thing in existence. I found her walking up and down the corridor, saying her prayers. I saw her kneeling —she may have been in front of a "station." I cannot remember her exact positions. The "stations" are pious objects about the convent. I thought she might as well have said them in her room. She was acting contrary to the rule then; no secular has a right to go about the convent. My objection to her praying in the corridor was that the novices knew nothing about her. They were under the impression that she was ill, and I did not wish her to be seen kneeling there in the state she was in. I mean to say the novices did not know at that time she had been expelled, and it might have happened they would not have known it at all. The novices have not access to the library. I saw the dress she went away in that was old. She got that because she was pinning the new one in such a way as to strain and tear it. That dress was lady-like, but the other was an old one. I did not see the stockings. I would have wished her good-bye before she went if we had known she was going. The moment she had gone the mother superior turned to me, and said she was extremely sorry she did not know she was going, as she would have liked to have given her the kiss of peace. I would also have been very glad to give her the kiss of peace. I never had any ill-feeling towards her of any description, and I would have given her the kiss of peace with the greatest pleasure ; but I had not the slightest idea she was going. I knew Sir Henry Cooper had been there the day before, but I did not know what advice he had given her. While she was in the bath-room and in the attic she was mistress of her own actions, and could have gone where she pleased. It was true that a sister was with her, who may have said, "You cannot go out just now." The reason of that was that there were at that moment novices passing in the corridor, and we wished to conceal her from them. She was only stopped verbally, but I don't know whether she was told she might go when the novices had passed. With regard to the closets, there was no prevention. She would not be allowed to go to the community-room ; but that was the only exception that I know of. It is not true that she was confined to her room for all purposes. She left her room on an average ten times a-day ; no one ever prevented her. A sister would have accompanied her wherever she went. On one occasion she tried to force herself into a room where I was with the mother superior, and we had to bolt the door to prevent her coming in. We kept a sister with her because we feared that, if left alone, she would have written on slips of paper to say that she was imprisoned, and that we should have had a disturbance about the convent. It was to prevent that she was watched. There was nothing to prevent her leaving the convent at any moment she had chosen. We should have been only too glad for her to go. Indeed, we asked her to do so several times. She would not have been allowed to go alone. The bishop gave orders to that effect.

The Lord Chief Justice : You would have told some one to follow her?—We should have gone with her.

By the Solicitor-General : If she had gone, it would have been as a secular, and one of us would have gone with her in our religious dress. That is always done when a sister ceases to be a "religious." I should not consider that an indignity if a person deserves it. You don't say, in the case of legal punishments, that people are treated with indignity when they are treated as they deserve.

The Lord Chief Justice : Quite right.

Re-examined by Mr. Mellish : I took the papers out of the books because Mrs. Star was then absent. It was because some of the sisters told me that there were pictures missing that I looked over the books which Miss Saurin had given up. I think I examined Miss Saurin's mantle, and saw myself that it was mended, when she denied that it was.

This concluded Mrs. Kennedy's ordeal in the witness-box. As she left, she gracefully thanked the Lord Chief Justice for his patience, and his lordship, in return, paid her a well-merited compliment for the admirable manner in which she had given her evidence.

Sister Mary M'Keon was then sworn, and examined by Mr. Charles Russell : My name in religion is Sister Mary Agnes. I first entered the Baggot-street Convent, and was there while Miss Saurin was a novice. I thought she was rather discontented. I was engaged in the schools, and I very seldom met her. She was in the industrial schools and the laundry. In November, 1860, I was appointed sister superior at Clifford. She went there, and I was her immediate superior. I had to report her for being disobedient to my directions and to the reverend mother's. There had been reason to complain, before 1860, for breaches of silence and obedience. She was often about at morning meditation. I have known her take the sisters' things and wear them without their permission. From 1860 to 1864 she was very much with me. I reported to Mrs. Star how she was going on. It was also my duty to speak to her about her faults. I did so frequently, but she told me the rev. mother knew of her faults, and passed them over. In the August retreat of 1861 Mrs. Star reproved her in chapter for her disobedience, insincerity, and other faults. That was not the first public reproof. She took it well. She and I returned to Clifford, and she murmured very much at the reproof which had been given to her. That is against our rule of obedience, and against the rule of not mentioning anything which takes place in chapter, which is a formal assembly of all the sisters in the community. From August, 1861, to February or March, 1862, I saw no change in her conduct. I think she had charge of seeing the schools were cleaned. She had the children of the day-school and the young women of the night-school to do the work. I still kept reporting to Mrs. Star when I went to Hull. In February, 1862, Mrs. King had charge of the cells, and I recollect her reporting to me that she had discovered a letter under the mattress of Miss Saurin's bed, and an ink-bottle belonging to the school between the

pillow and the bed. It was not proper for any sister to take it to her cell. I had missed that ink-bottle, and had inquired about it of the children, but not of the plaintiff. We were taught in Baggot-street to look upon secret letter-writing as a very grave fault, entailing expulsion. I at once wrote to Mrs. Star, and sent the letter which had been found. She sent back a very kind letter of expostulation and remonstrance to give to the plaintiff, which I read myself first. I told her I had felt it necessary to write to Mrs. Star, and the plaintiff said, "How did you know I was going to send the letter?" I talked to her, and advised her, and she acknowledged how wrong she had been in writing the letter, and how thankful she was to have been preserved from the greater sin of having sent it. The next day, Ash Wednesday, she came and said she would find great difficulty in confessing her fault to the ordinary confessor, and begged me to send for the extraordinary confessor, Father Arnux. I wrote to the reverend father to come over, and he came the next day (Thursday), and saw Miss Saurin. It is not right for sisters to have lights in their cells without permission. They always go to bed without lights, except on one night in the week, when they are allowed for washing. On one evening she may have a light in her cell till a quarter past ten o'clock. Saturday evening was the night with us. That was for the purpose of washing. That rule had been acted on from the beginning at Clifford. She had not asked me for permission ; but on Ash Wednesday night I saw a light under her door. I knocked, and the light was at once extinguished. I asked why she had the light. She made some excuse. The Friday following I spoke to one of the school children, who took our letters to the post, Mary Murphy. She told me she had taken a letter to the post on the previous day, and that the plaintiff had given it to her. I asked to whom it was addressed, but she said she did not know, because the sister had put it into a book, and told her not to take it out till she got to the post office. The child was eleven or twelve years old. I wrote that evening to Mrs. Star, telling her about that fact. Mrs. Star replied, and then I spoke to the plaintiff about it. She first denied what I charged her with. I then told her what the child had told me. She then said that it was a letter which had been sent her by a person in the village to read before being posted to a friend at Leeds—the person was said to be Mary Murphy's mother, and the person it was sent to was Mrs. Watson, of Leeds. If that had been true it would not have been proper for Miss Saurin to do so without permission. She denied most solemnly having written and sent another letter to a relative. She some days after again denied it, and said she had made a promise not to speak any more about the letters. Some months after she said the promise was before the blessed sacrament. She had been to communion on the Friday after first denying sending the letter. I recollect after Mrs. King inquired of Mary Murphy's father, a joiner, who said they had not written to Mrs. Watson. I communicated this to Mrs. Star. I wrote to the mother superior explaining my difficulty, but all my letters were destroyed by her. I remember Mrs Saurin and Mr. Patrick Saurin coming to see the plaintiff. At that time an order was necessary, and I begged the plaintiff to go to her room. I told Mrs. Saurin I was very sorry she could not see her daughter, but she handed me a note containing an order, saying very rudely, "Do not say another word, but send me my child." I went and asked Miss Saurin to go down and see her mother. She refused, and said she did not like to see her mother in the same room with her brother. I sent for Mrs. Saurin up to the community room, and the interview took place there. She then sent Miss Saurin for me. I went up, and she spoke very rudely to me, asking me if I had been so mean as to search her daughter's bag, and ask a child if her daughter had sent letters to the post. I advised Mrs. Saurin to take her daughter away from our convent, and suggested Baggot-street. I said I did not think she could be happy after all that had passed. Mrs. Saurin asked her daughter if she thought she could be happy, and Miss Saurin said she thought she could. I promised to let Miss Saurin, at her mother's suggestion, write to the rev. mother for forgiveness. Mrs. Saurin asked her daughter if she had not written to the rev. mother for money and permission to go to Dublin with one of the Sickling Hall fathers. Miss Saurin evaded the reply, and Mrs. Saurin said, "You did, I know you did." Then Mrs. Saurin proposed that the plaintiff should write another letter, begging forgiveness, and asked me to help her. I did so, and corrected the letter she wrote. In July, 1862, the plaintiff and I went to Hull to the annual retreat. She would not join the community at dinner ; and she told me while going in the railway carriage that she thought she was going to Hull to be dismissed for the clandestine letter-writing. At that time the community knew nothing of this letter having been written. I was present when she signed the written acknowledgment about sending the letters. I remember a letter coming to her which acknowledged from one of her sisters the receipt of one from the plaintiff. The letter came from Fern House Convent, near Dublin. I was not aware of the letter which the plaintiff had sent to which that was an answer. It ought to have passed through my hands. I think that was about May, 1863. The affair of the letters did not seem to trouble the plaintiff's mind. She told me in 1863 that her uncle had told her that if it had not been for the discovery of the letters they would have been obliged to take her back at Baggot-street. During 1862 and 1863 she was very disobedient as to silence. She only kept silence when there was no one to speak to.

The case was then adjourned.

It was announced that the evidence for the defence could not close before Thursday night. It will probably run into Friday, and the Lord Chief Justice said after both parties had consented to sit to have the case tried out, this being the last sitting in term at Westminster, that he should take a day after the evidence to digest the enormous mass, so as to be able to present the case clearly to the jury.

Twelfth Day, *Tuesday, February* 16th:

With the end of this case in sight, the pettiness of its details now begin to weary those who, comprehending the true magnitude of the issues involved, are to any extent interested in the decision. But though the evidence, after the two defendants had passed the ordeal of examination, became of necessity rather insipid, there has been no decrease in the number of applicants for admission to the fag-end of the feast. To-day the crowd at the door was as persistent and importunate as ever ; and the crowd in the court scarcely less appreciative of such comedy as could be extracted from the questions of counsel and the replies of the witness. Some wonderful people, not content with bringing disgrace on the London public by their behaviour in the hearing of the Bench, have taken to writing their offensive comments, and sending them anonymously to the Lord Chief Justice. By way of refinement, or rather let us say aggravation, of such despicable conduct, one of these unintelligible beings chose the Solicitor-General as a medium of communication, and actually sent the precious letter under cover to him for delivery to the judge. It is a pity that the culprits will, in all likelihood escape detection ; but meanwhile the indecorum —certainly not so scandalous—of laughing, applauding, and hissing in open court might be effectually checked by picking out the most prominent offenders and either committing them into custody or ordering them to be expelled. As for those lads and hobbledehoys who hover as near as they can get to the door of exit, to hoot the witnesses and to cover the operations of pickpockets, there is the double excuse that boys will be boys and blackguards will be blackguards. But a tolerably efficient police regulation prevents any large collection of persons close to the spot whence the cabs take their departure; and, on the whole, the persons giving evidence in this case— mostly women, be it observed, whose seclusion from the world might serve in some measure as a plea for gentle and considerate forbearance—are enabled to escape the persecution of that pervasive class of our fellow-citizens who would mob anybody at the bidding of anybody else, or in obedience to a cry which they don't understand.

The hearing of the case was resumed at the sitting of the court this morning.

The examination of Mrs. M'Keon by Mr. Charles Russell was resumed. She said: Towards the end of 1862 I had reason several times to speak to Miss Saurin about faults. In Nov. of that year the bishop made a canonical visitation at Hull. After that visitation the plaintiff continued under my care at Clifford, to which we immediately returned. Her conduct did not improve, and I frequently reproved her.

Did you scold her, or speak to her kindly?—I think I spoke to her kindly. She always had some excuse to make.

Examination continued : Her manner was very disrespectful to me, and that in the presence of the other sisters. Once she told me in their presence that it was my business to see had hot tea. She was complaining of her food. I had told the refectorian to take particular care of Miss Saurin.

The Lord Chief Justice: Did the plaintiff know that?—I do not think she did, my lord.

Examination continued: The reason I gave the direction was that she was constantly in the habit of complaining of her food. Up to our going to Hull for the August retreat her conduct did not improve. She had charge of dusting the parlour and hall, and of seeing that the schools were clean; she had charge also of teaching needlework in the poor school in the morning, and in the afternoon in the better school. She also taught the infants in the gallery their letters.

Did the plaintiff go to Clifford in 1860 to get up the schools?—No.

Was she equal to that task in point of literary education?—She was not.

Was she equal to teaching anything beyond the alphabet?—The alphabet and monosyllables.

Examination continued: Some of the young women in the night school were taught their letters by her.

(A letter was here handed up to the Lord Chief Justice.)

The Lord Chief Justice: This is one of a series of offensive letters which I have been constantly receiving since this case commenced, and in reference to it.

The Solicitor-General: It came to me for your lordship without a word of explanation.

The Lord Chief Justice: I find myself the object of slanders and all sorts of charges and attacks with regard to this case.

The Solicitor-General: I regret that the writer should have made me the unwitting channel of conveying the letter.

The Lord Chief Justice: The writers may save themselves the trouble they give themselves. I take no heed of their charges.

Witness: I wish to mention that in February, 1863, the plaintiff said she had not received a letter announcing the death of her brother.

Mr. Russell said that he should come to that matter in its proper order.

Examination continued: At the August retreat Mrs. Star, at the request of the plaintiff, asked me and the other sisters to pray for her (plaintiff), and to help her. I did not hear the request given, but Mrs. Star said it in her presence. The request was well received by the sisters.

Did you ever perceive anything like personal illwill towards the plaintiff on the part of the sisters?—Never.

Examination continued: We returned to Clifford after the retreat. Between August, 1863, and June, 1864, Miss Saurin was as troublesome as ever. I wrote to Mrs. Star on the subject. On one occasion I wrote, saying I would rather beg my bread from door to door than be superior over Miss Saurin.

You were thinking of going to Dublin again? Yes; I should have done so rather than remain with her.

Why?—I found it so hard to manage and control her.

Examination continued: After Miss Saurin left Clifford in the summer of 1864 we were exceedingly happy. Except those occasioned by her, we had had no unpleasantnesses of any kind. She frequently broke the rule of silence with externs in school, with the school-children, and particularly with the lady, Mrs. Grimstone, after she had been forbidden to speak to her. I have sometimes been obliged to call away the children from her. It was not a fault to speak to them in the course of teaching. I speak of unnecessary talking. It was reported to me by Mrs. Fearon that plaintiff lost time by unnecessary talking in the night-school. I do not remember reproving her for it. It was part of her duty to visit the sick. She remained beyond her prescribed time. The sister who was with her—Mrs. Fearon—will speak as to her conduct. She also visited a person—Mrs. Greenwood—to whom she had not been sent.

The Lord Chief Justice: Is that a fault?—Yes, my lord. Those who are to be visited are marked down on a card.

Mr. Russell: You visit only when invited?—Yes.

And that without regard to creed or sect?—That is so.

And, in the case of the poor, material assistance is given?—We bring them what we can.

The Lord Chief Justice: How long did she remain with Mrs. Greenwood?—An hour.

Was anyone with her?—Yes, Mrs. Rafty; but Miss Saurin was senior, and the other was obliged to do as she directed.

To Mr. Russell: The sisters never go alone visiting the sick; two always go.

Examination continued: I have myself seen Miss Saurin out of the school at least a dozen times when she ought to have been there. She made excuses which I did not believe. If she had any occasion to leave the school she ought to have obtained permission from me or from another sister. I have known the clock to be put back to suit Miss Saurin's convenience. I did not see her putting back the clock. She was in the reception room, seeing a visitor, and she stayed longer than she ought. A sister had rung the warning bell for dinner at five minutes to twelve, and when she went to ring the second bell she found it ten minutes to twelve. She will be here to speak of the matter. She reported the circumstance to me.

The Lord Chief Justice: Did you report the circumstance to Mrs. Star?—Not at the time, but subsequently I did.

To Mr. C. Russell: It was my duty to report to Mrs. Star everything serious that occurred. The putting back of the clock caused great confusion. The clock went all right after Miss Saurin left. In consequence of her irregularity in attending evening meditation on Sunday, I had to change the hour in order that she might be there.

To the Lord Chief Justice: She had a class on Sunday evening to instruct young women, and she remained there longer than she ought.

To Mr. Russell: Everyone had to kiss the floor for being late as well as Miss Saurin, if they were late. I had not so long as I was superior, but after I ceased to be superior, in January, 1867, I had to do so if I was late. It is a part of the duty of the sisters to recite the daily office in the choir, which is part of our own chapel. It was my duty to recite at one side of the choir, and Miss Saurin's at the other, but she did it so irreverently I had to take her to my side and get another sister to recite in her place. I have known her to send the school children of errands, contrary to my directions.

The Lord Chief Justice: Sending them out of

school?—Yes, my lord. That was contrary to custom, as well as express direction.

Examination continued: She continued to do so after I reproved her for it. On one occasion she sent a child to another village about a mile distant.

The Lord Chief Justice: Let me understand, did she send the child during school hours, or was the child asked to do so and so as she passed?—I do not know, my lord.

Mr. Russell: You do not know whether the child lived in the village or not?—I do not, but she ought not to have given any message to the child.

Examination continued: She countermanded orders of mine to the refectorian, and she remained longer with visitors than she ought. They were not her own relations, but people of the village. She had not asked permission to stay longer than the prescribed time. There was no restriction to her seeing her relations. On the day I stopped some time with Mrs. Saurin, I did so at her request. There was no restriction put upon Father Matthews as to staying. On one occasion he remained from ten in the morning until four in the evening, with the exception of an hour, and that was of his own free will. I only saw him when he requested. I never asked a sister to watch the plaintiff when she was with her relations. I remember once ringing the call-bell when plaintiff was with a visitor—Miss Heppenstal. She had long exceeded the prescribed time. She came out when I rang the bell, and said she could not come. Her manner was disrespectful.

The Lord Chief Justice: Was it her duty to come on hearing the call-bell?—It was, my lord.

To Mr. Russell: My admonitions to her were generally very useless. There are stated hours for rising and going to bed. I have known her to rise before the prescribed time and remain up beyond the bed hour. She had no leave, and I often remonstrated with her for doing so. Miss Saurin remained in her cell when she had no right to be except during sleeping hours. On one occasion I wished to get into her cell and she prevented me doing so, although I told her that the mother superior had given me direction to visit the sisters' cells from time to time. On another occasion we were making some dresses for orphans in the village, and I asked her to help us, and she said she would do no such thing, and that she would have nothing to do with them. I repeated my directions three or four times. The other sisters were present. This was in June, 1864, immediately before her removal. At last she did the work, but so badly I was obliged to have it all undone. They were black stuff dresses. The dress she made did not fit the child. She was clever at needlework. The dress had to be made over again.

Was it the plaintiff who cut it out?—I do not think it was.

Well, it might not be her fault as she did not cut it out?—She ought to have managed to make it fit.

Were the children there to have them tried on?—Yes.

And did the other sisters try the dresses on the children?—I think they did.

Who cut out the dresses?—Mrs. Fearon.

Did she cut out all the dresses?—Yes; there were only two.

Examination continued: I remember the Inspector of schools one day examining the lowest class. I told Miss Saurin to examine the class for him. I had prepared her for it. I repeated the direction in the presence of the inspector, and she refused to do so, and persisted in the refusal in his presence. I was obliged to examine the class myself. I remember when at Hull, in 1857 or 1858, missing a book which had been given to me by Mrs. Star. The books of devotion were kept in the choir. I made inquiry for the book, and told Mrs. Star I thought Miss Saurin had taken it.

Why did you think she took it?—Because I thought she would like to have it.

Was that all that was in your mind?—That is all I remember now. There were other things in my mind then.

Examination continued: Mrs. Star told me she found the book amongst Miss Saurin's clothes. I once gave her a habit to repair, and when it was returned a piece—about three quaters of a yard—was cut out. It ought not to have been cut out, and was not used to repair the habit. I saw it afterwards in Miss Saurin's own habit, and I made her restore part of it. She brought it from her cell. In consequence of reports made to me by Mrs. Fearon, and of what I witnessed myself, I wrote to Mrs. Star to the effect I have stated, that I would rather beg than continue superior over Miss Saurin. In 1863, a regulation was made as to keeping the pantry door locked. I believe the regulation was made on account of Miss Saurin. She was very particular about her dinners, and said she had a dislike to mutton. Her mother had told me in 1862 that she never knew her to object to mutton. I told the refectorian to give her bacon, which she liked, whenever it was in the house. Her food was never worse than that of the other sisters. She seemed to me to be very happy while she was at Clifford.

Were you happy while she was there?—No.

Examination continued: Some of the children at Clifford brought their dinners to school. I remarked that Miss Saurin took charge of the dinners, but I did not know that she took any part of them.

Did she take charge of all the dinners?—No; only of the dinners of the more comfortable children. I did not prevent her doing so.

Examination continued: The mother superior directed that the excess of clothing should be sent to Hull. Miss Saurin joined on some of hers so as to retain them. Some of the sisters had a good deal to send. I saw two pocket handkerchiefs of Miss Saurin's sewn together. They were a yard and a quarter long. (Laughter.)

The Lord Chief Justice: Then the number of things was diminished without diminishing the quantity?—Yes, my lord.

Examination continued: She patched one skirt upon another. They were quite good, and did not need repair. If they required repair she ought to have asked permission to cut up an article, and she did not ask leave. She was fond of altering her dresses. We saw the alterations when made. She had had no permission from me, as superior, for doing so. She used to interfere with the laundry work, by ironing her own clothes, and I reproved her for doing so. When she was refectorian at Hull, I remember seeing myself that she favoured some people at the expense of others. It is a rule in the community that as to food and clothing all the sisters should be on a perfect equality. I remember Mrs. Star changing the plates. Miss Saurin spoke sometimes very unkindly of the sisters to me, pointing out any defect she could see. That she has done frequently. I had reason to doubt the truth of her statements. I remember finding the guard of the stove in the school broken. A child told me in her absence that she had broken it. When she came in she denied it, and the children said, "Oh, you did, sister." It is not true, as she stated, that after August, 1862, I gave plaintiff a distribution of time. I never did so.

The Lord Chief Justice : You are quite certain as to that ?—I am, my lord.

Examination continued : It is the duty of the mother superior to give distributions of time? —It is not unusual for her to do so.

Were further duties put on her, as she stated, in August, 1863 ?—No. She had no more to do at Clifford than any of the other sisters.

The Lord Chief Justice : You allude to household duties ?—Yes, my lord.

Examination continued : She never was directed to clean the stone steps. She had to see to its being done. It was the duty of a servant, or lay sister, and, in their absence, of a village girl. I never saw the plaintiff do the steps, and I never heard of its being done by her. The community house at Clifford is very small. The household work was equally distributed amongst the sisters. I had the first floor to do myself, swept and dusted it, and waxed the floor when it was required. I put no extra work on Miss Saurin. I had no orders from Mrs. Star to do so, and I did not. Once Miss Saurin asked to be allowed to preside over the laundry, and I gave her permission. I was blamed by Mrs. Star for doing so, as she (plaintiff) was obliged to get up earlier to give directions. I never told plaintiff to stand at school while teaching. I never remember her having made such a charge against me before she gave her evidence. During part of the teaching she had necessarily to stand; while teaching counting on the ball frame, for instance.

The Lord Chief Justice : Was there any direction given by you or Mrs. Star that she should stand while it was necessary to do so for the purpose of teaching ?—Never, my lord.

Examination continued : There was no exceptional order given in her case. She was free to sit when it was not necessary to stand. With respect to the letter announcing her brother's death, I gave it to her on the afternoon of the day I received it, The custom was to send the letters to the mother superior. I did not do so on this occasion, as the death of a relative was an exceptional case. It was not sent to Mrs. Star at all I should have given the letter to Miss Saurin in the morning, but it was Lent, and I did not like to give it to her before dinner.

Why ?—That she might be able to take her dinner.

From motives of kindness ?—Yes, altogether.

The Lord Chief Justice : You are quite sure you gave it to her on the day it arrived?—Quite sure.

Examination continued : I requested the sisters to pray for the repose of the soul of Miss Saurin's brother, and put up a notice on the chapel door to that effect.

You are quite certain this occurred on the day the letter was received ?—I am quite sure.

Mr. Russell : She says she was sent to the school after getting the letter. Is that so ?—It is not. She remained in her cell from dinner hour till supper. If she went to the night school she did so of her own accord.

Examination continued : I did not know of bedding being taken from Miss Saurin when Mrs. Star and Mrs. Kennedy came with some sisters and novices. The sisters vied with each other which should give the visitors accommodation. I gave up either a mattress or palliass. It was not worth while applying to Mrs. Grimston, as the additional accommodation was only required for one night, and it was summer. I remember Miss Saurin writing the monthly letters to Mrs. Star. I do not think I gave her any directions as to what she was to say. She may have asked me something about it.

Did you, unasked by Miss Saurin, ever suggest what she should say in her letter ?—I never remember having done so.

Can a sub-superior control a sister in what she is to write to the superior ?—No, she should not see the letters, and Miss Saurin's letters were fastened up before being given to me to forward.

The Lord Chief Justice : Then you never saw them ?—Never, my lord.

Now, as to the visit to the tower, when did it take place ?—In June, 1865, Mr. and Mrs. Collins paid a visit to the convent. They were stopping for a time at the village of Clifford, where they had lodgings.

Mr. Russell : And you took them to the top of the tower ?—I took them over the schools and the gardens, and Mrs. Grimston's place, and then to the tower, a small ornamental building at one corner of the garden, separated from our garden by a hedge.

Had you, as superior, discretion to go there ?— Yes, and we passed through the schools, and, as we did, Miss Saurin saw Mrs. Collins.

How long did you remain on the tower ?— Twenty minutes or half an hour.

You are sure you were not there two hours, as she states you were ?—Quite sure. And if Miss Saurin saw me on the tower she must have seen Mrs. Collins also. The whole visit only lasted about an hour.

Examination continued : Mrs. Star has never asked me to tell my confession or any part of it. It would be a very grave fault. She has not, to my knowledge, asked any of the sisters to do so. I never heard it suggested until this case was at trial. I sent in a "deposition" to the bishop.

[The "deposition" was read, and set forth the circumstances detailed in Mrs. M'Keon's evidence. It added that Miss Saurin was very fond of speaking to the priests, and of putting herself in their way for the purpose.]

The Lord Chief Justice : What was the conduct of the mother superior towards the sisters? —Exceedingly kind.

Was there ever any difficulty between any other members of the community and the mother superior ?—Not that I know of.

So far as your knowledge goes this was the only instance of difficulty ?—Yes, my lord.

Were you present on the occasion of the plaintiff making the acknowledgment as to the clandestine letters ?—Yes.

H

Was she called upon by the mother superior to acknowledge the fault, or did she do so spontaneously?— Spontaneously. The mother superior called in Mrs. Kennedy and myself. We went in, and the plaintiff knelt down and begged pardon, and said that what I had stated previously about the letters was true; that she had deceived me.

Did she receive any orders to kneel down?— No, my lord.

To Mr. Russell: I believed the statements in the deposition to be true. I was never conscious of any feeling of ill-will to the plaintiff.

Cross-examined by the Solicitor-General: Mrs. Star wrote to me to write out the deposition. She said it was the wish of the bishop I should do so. I destroyed the letter after reading it. Mrs. King, another sister, also wrote a deposition. We wrote them in the same room, and spoke of them.

Did you see each other's depositions?—She did not see mine, but I saw hers.

Did you write this?—No; I made some alterations in it, but not in its matter. I corrected some grammatical errors, and that is all.

Cross-examination continued: She is a professed sister. The regulation as to candles in the cell was not made after Miss Saurin wrote the letter. The choice of day was taken away before Miss Saurin came. On a Saturday evening the sisters had a quarter of an hour extra. The gas was laid on for a quarter of an hour extra. The name of the school-girl who wrote the letter was Mary Anne Murphy. Miss Saurin told me it was a letter that one of Mary Anne Murphy's parents had written to a person in Leeds, and that she had been asked to read it. I did not go to the Murphys to inquire as to the truth of the matter, lest there might be a scandal. The letter from Miss Saurin's sister, from which I inferred that other letters had been written by the plaintiff, came from one of her religious sisters.

Must not Miss Saurin have known that all her letters should come to her through you?—Yes.

And that if there was any allusions in them to letters she had written, you must needs see these allusions?—Yes.

Examination continued: She had no leave from me to write. I was away from Clifford for a day or so. Miss Saurin had no permission to write then.

Was she not senior sister in your absence?— Yes.

The Lord Chief Justice: Could she give herself permission to write?—No, my lord.

The Solicitor-General: Could you give yourself permission?—I always sent my letters to the mother superior.

But you gave yourself leave to go up the tower at the other side of the hedge. Would it at all mitigate the offence that she was senior sister when she wrote?—I think not.

Or that it was to her sister, a Carmelite nun, she wrote?—No.

Must not she have known that the letter to her Carmelite sister would be opened and read before being given to her?—Yes.

And that the answer must go through you?— Yes.

Cross-examination continued: I called away children from Miss Saurin as she broke the vow of silence. They were sewing, and could not

sow and talk. I saw that there was disorder. I did not hear what was said.

Might it have been a religious conversation?— No; I saw that there was disorder.

May she not have been expounding the difference between a hem and other work?—No.

How do you know that, when you did not hear what was said?—The children looked too pleasant for that. (Laughter.)

How often did you see her talking unnecessarily to the children during the four years she was at Clifford?—Frequently. I cannot say how often.

How often did you call the children away?— Once.

Did not the schools get on flourishingly for all that?—Not the sewing.

That was what she was clever at?—Yes.

The children looked too pleasant to learn to sew. (A laugh.) Tell me how often did Mrs. Fearon report about Miss Saurin?—Very frequently.

Cross-examination continued: Plaintiff was late on Sunday. She told me the women in the class kept her. She could have come away if she wished.

Did you think she was doing any great harm? —Yes.

Why!—Because she was late for meditation.

But you changed the time of that?—Yes; but she was late for community exercise.

You put that in place of the meditation?— Yes.

And she lost it?—She was late for it.

What is community exercise?— Supper. (Laughter.)

It is my ignorance not to have known it. It would be convenient if you called supper supper. Did she lose her supper?—No. She was late for it. Once she said she would fast, but she came down afterwards and had her supper.

Well, now, Mrs. M'Keon, tell me in candour, do not women out of convents talk?—They do.

And these women talked to Sister Scholastica? —She said so

Sometimes it is a little difficult to prevent it. Tell me, was it not her duty to lock the door after the women were gone?—Yes.

Then, if she went before they were gone, she must have locked them in?—She need not have done so. Other sisters found no difficulty in not being late.

Now, as to the clock; was it a good one?— No, not very.

And as to visiting Mrs. Greenwood when on sick duty; was Mrs. Greenwood ill?—I believe she was ill; but her name was not on Miss Saurin's card, and that makes all the difference.

Cross-examination continued: On the occasion that I found Miss Saurin out of the school, and the children running about, she made an excuse that she had to go. I did not believe her.

Might it not be possible that she told the truth?—Once perhaps it was; but this occurred several times, and she was away for five or ten minutes.

Cross-examination continued: On the occasion that the clock was put back ten minutes, Miss Saurin was not too long with the visitor, but she was late in getting the dinner. She acknowledged that she put back the clock. She said she did so to suit her own convenience, and I told her it was a very wrong thing to do. The convent at Clifford has ceased to exist.

How came that?—It is not necessary to state.

Did the bishop know of it?

Witness: Has this anything to do with the examination?

The Solicitor-General: Very well. Now, about irreverent reading; what do you mean?—She said the words imperfectly. She had a difficulty in reading the Latin.

Is that what you call irreverent?—She read it hurriedly. She might have read it slowly like the other sisters. She read it hurriedly.

Was she nervous?—Not at all.

Did she say anything about being removed to the other side?—No.

Cross-examination continued: I had given Miss Saurin special directions not to send the school children of messages. That was in 1859. She did not send them so often after that.

To the Lord Chief Justice: Before I gave her special direction she had a rosary and beads, and she used often to lose them and send the children to look for them.

Cross-examination continued: When she sent the child to the next village it was with a piece of glass to be cut for a devotional picture for the school children. I do not know whether the child lived in the village. It involved expense. I do not know how much. It was against rule, and I told her it was very wrong of her to have done so. She wished to make presents of the devotional pictures to the school children.

What was the harm of doing as she did besides being a breach of rule?—That is all. It was a breach of obedience.

If she had asked permission, then, there would have been no harm in it?—No.

You are sure you did not give her permission?—I am; and she acknowledged she had done wrong.

Did you report the matter to Mrs. Star?—I told her of it.

Cross-examination continued: On one occasion I had ordered vegetables, and she sent a child after the man and ordered some apples. She had no right to do so. That is what I meant by saying she "countermanded" my orders.

Who were the visitors with whom she remained too long?—Young women who came from the village for instruction.

To her?—Yes.

Oh, then, there was no harm in what took place?—She ought to have dismissed them.

The Lord Chief Justice: Do you know what she was talking about?—I do not, my lord.

The Solicitor-General: I should not have understood by "visitors" villagers who came to her for instruction.

Witness: That only occurred once. There were other visitors also to whom occasionally she has gone and remained beyond the prescribed time without leave. I have named Miss Hepenstal. She was delicate. I am sure she did not require instruction. I allowed Miss Saurin to see her, but she exceeded her time. The call-bell was rung several times before she came out. The rule as to "obeying the call of the bell as the voice of God" applies to bells rung for tea as well as to bells rung for service.

Do you mean to say that disobeying the call

of the bell is the same kind of thing as disobeying a command of God?—Yes.

Do you really say that?—Yes.

Examination continued: When I rang the call-bell she answered me in an insolent manner —that she had heard the bell, and would not come, or rather could not come.

"Would not" was your gloss. Did she say why?—No; I did not ask her. I thought it unnecessary.

What was her insolence?—The manner in which she said she had heard the bell and could not come; her manner of saying it.

You say she got up before the prescribed time?—She did.

Tell me any occasion on which she did so.—Once when I was sleeping in the room with her, she got up and answered a bell. She had no right to do so.

Any other?—Another time she was out before the time she ought to be, and she told me she was looking for birds'-nests. (Laughter.)

Are birds under the term of externs? (Renewed laughter.)—Witness: that is not the question. The question is as to her getting up and going out before the prescribed time.

Well, now, as to the dress for the child. She did not cut it out; but it was her duty to make it fit, and fit it didn't?—It was her disobedience in not making the dress at first I spoke of.

But she did make it after?—Yes.

Well; we have heard of a man who said he would not go, but afterwards went. You think she might have made the dress fit if she liked?—I think so.

Cross-examination continued: I thought she did not like me to have the book that Mrs. Star gave me, and which was afterwards found among the clothes.

In consequence of her dislike to mutton, had she for twelve months very little more than bread and water?—She had a full portion of meat.

I know; but when she could not eat it, had she little more than bread and water? She had whatever else was going. She told me once that mutton made her sick for two hours, but she then got suddenly well, and had a very good tea. (Laughter.)

Did she say that in joke?—No.

You say that you never read her monthly confession?—Never until this action commenced.

In one of them she says to the rev. mother, "I know Sister Mary Agnes; yourself would feel my want of confidence in closing my note." What does that mean?—I know it would lead one to believe that I used to read her letters, but I never did so.

Did you ever give her a distribution of time from the mother superior?—I do not remember.

You did not give her a distribution of time to copy from a slate?—I do not remember; but if I did, it would be no harm.

You state positively you never gave her directions to stand while teaching at any part of the lessons, when she might sit?—I did not. I may have said that one could teach better standing than sitting, but that had no special reference to Miss Saurin.

Cross-examination continued: The course was to send on letters received at Clifford to the mother superior at Hull. They were read and then sent on. I had the right to read them.

To the Court: The mother superior decided whether they should be given.

The Solicitor-General: The "custom" says that the local superior can open any letters she thinks to be on business, but that other letters are to be forwarded to the mother superior unopened.

Witness: The mother superior gave me express direction to open all the letters. She had power to alter the custom. I think she had the power from tradition, but I know I got the direction owing to the distance between Clifford and Hull. The letter about Miss Saurin's brother was never sent to the mother superior at all. Miss Saurin never complained to my knowledge of the letter being kept back from her. I heard her mention it for the first time in this court. Miss Saurin and Mrs. Grimstone appeared to be very friendly—more intimate than I approved of. Mrs. Grimstone was a benefactress of the institution.

Did she not withdraw her support soon after Miss Saurin left?—No.

Did she withdraw her support?—I will not go into the affairs of the convent.

The convent is shut up?—Yes.

Do you know that Mrs. Grimstone has withdrawn her support?—You must consult the superior as to that.

But do you know it?—It is not connected with the case.

Well, now about the tower. Were you on it?—Yes.

And you had a pretty view of the country?—We had.

And the time passed pleasantly?—It did.

And quickly. May you not have been there more than twenty or thirty minutes?—That is the time we were there.

Are you and Mrs. Collins externs?—Yes.

Now the things you have detailed were those which led you to write that you would rather beg your bread from door to door than continue to have charge of Miss Saurin?—Yes.

Re-examined by Mr. Mellish: I wrote what were really my feelings at the time. Mrs. Greenwood who was visited without leave by Miss Saurin, was not very ill. Although the fault may appear to be a slight one to us, it appears a grave offence, because if a sister could go wherever she liked, all order and regularity would be destroyed. When she made the excuse for being in the garden that she went to look for birds'-nests, I did not believe her. I gathered from her manner that she was not telling the truth. I never took away her "leaves" from her. I had no power to do so. She applied to me for her leaves, and Mrs. Star at once told me to let her have them. I delivered them to her on the permission to have them. The superior has power to dispense with a custom, if doing so in the particular case be not contrary to the rules.

This ended the witness's examination.

The Foreman of the Jury expressed a hope that in the evidence yet to be given minute details might be avoided, with a view to the saving of time.

Several jurors said that they desired to hear all the evidence.

The Lord Chief Justice said that, in one point of view, the details might be of great importance. On the one hand it was alleged that they were exceptionally imposed upon the plaintiff with a view to degrade and punish her; on the other hand, it was contended that, in the eye of a member of the community, they assumed a very different shape, and were besides necessary for discipline, and only such as all members of the community experienced and voluntarily subjected themselves to.

Mrs. King (sister Mary Clare), examined by Mr. Mellish: I was a novice in the convent in Baggot-street in 1855. In 1857 I went to Hull, and there became a professed sister in 1859. I was there with Miss Saurin from the end of December, 1857, till October, 1858, and from July till September, 1859. After I was professed I was with her from 3rd April, 1860, till November, 1862, at Clifford. After that I very seldom saw her. In 1857 and 1858 Miss Saurin was housekeeper. I had charge of the laundry. It was my impression that she rarely observed the rule of silence. She appeared to me to make friends of the servants and externs—the girls and people coming to the convent. I several times heard her reading to the servants letters she had received from her relatives. One of them was a letter from her Jesuit brother. Some passages related to treatment that she had received at Baggot-street in being employed in the laundry. In one of these her brother designated the superioress and assistant-superioress at Baggot-street as tormentors, torturers, and tyrants. There were a servant and myself present when Miss Saurin read the letter. She had charge of the pantry, and I frequently saw there food which was not prepared for the sisters. I suspected that Miss Saurin made use of it herself, and I reported the matter to Mrs. Star. She reproved me for saying so, and said she was sure Miss Saurin would not be guilty of such a grave fault. In 1858 or 1859 the rev. mother gave me directions to give Miss Saurin broiled meat, beef tea, custard pudding, or anything else she could take, between meals. I gave her the extra food, and I often found great difficulty in making her take it.

Do you remember anything about the chaplain's breakfast?—Yes, I frequently saw tea prepared for the chaplain, poured out in the pantry, and I used to see Miss Saurin bringing hot toast under a tea towel into the pantry. Soon after it was gone. It was after the chaplain's breakfast I saw the things.

The Lord Chief Justice: Oh, then, it was toast he had had but did not use?—Yes, my lord. It was heated first in the kitchen, and then brought by her into the pantry.

Examination continued: This was the time she complained of bad appetite. I know very well that Mrs. Star and Mrs. Kennedy were deceived about her appetite. I remarked that she told lies about the number of things she sent to the wash. I was a novice at that time and under her. There was nothing remarkable in her manner towards me at that time. I often heard her reprimand the sisters, I suppose for faults she saw in them. The kitchen and pantry, of which she had charge, were very disorderly. She frequently disobeyed the orders of the rev. mother.

To the Court: This very often happened, but I cannot call any instance to mind just now.

Examination continued: In September, 1852, when I became a sister, I went to Clifford, and was there when Miss Saurin came. I had charge of the housekeeping, the second class in the school, and other duties, such as sweeping and dusting in the convent. I missed some cakes, and found a part of one of them under Miss Saurin's bed. On another occasion I saw a cup of tea poured out in the pantry, and I found the cup soon afterwards empty in the school where Miss Saurin was. In January, 1861, I missed a small piece of bacon and some bread, and sometime afterwards I found them in her cell cabinet. I once saw her altering the clock. I saw her hand on it. On another occasion she put the clock back ten minutes. I did not see her do it; but she acknowledged it to me, and said she was in the reception-room with a visitor, and feared she would not be in time for dinner. In February, 1852, I found a letter under the mattrass of her bed, directed to the Rev. Mr. Matthews.

To the Lord Chief Justice: I had charge of all the cells to see that they were in order.

To Mr. Mellish: Each sister made up her own cell. I found the letter in a book, "St. Liguori on the Commandments."

Did you find anything else?—Yes. I first found the ink-bottle under the pillow, and that led me to look further. It was a school ink-bottle. I brought Sister Mary Agnes (Mrs. M'Keon) up after some time, and showed her the letter. I never spoke to Miss Saurin about it. I did not see Mrs. Star till the following August, and then I think I told her. I am almost sure I told her all about it. Sister Mary Agnes spoke to Mary Anne Murphy about the posting of a letter, and I saw Mr. Murphy, and asked him whether it was true he had written to Mrs. Watson, of Leeds, and he said he had not, as he saw her occasionally. I told Mrs. Star that also. At Clifford Miss Saurin had the same food as the rest of the sisters. I carved the meat. I may have given her less mutton, as she did not like it: but I gave her as much of everything else as we all got. She did not do any more menial work than the other sisters. She had charge of the stone steps, but she did not do them herself. Her clothes were equal to the other sisters. She was treated at recreation like the rest. I never saw anything different in the conduct of Mrs. Star or Mrs. M'Keon towards Miss Saurin and towards the other sisters. I wrote a "deposition" for the bishop. It was not dictated to me, or any part of it. (The deposition which mentioned the foregoing incidents was read.)

Examination continued: The statements made in that deposition are all correct.

Cross-examined by Mr. Digby Seymour: I wrote out the deposition at Clifford. Mrs. M'Keon was writing at the same time. I first wrote a rough copy, and then I wrote it again. Mrs. M'Keon corrected the last copy. She did not change the substance. I wrote altogether from memory. I distinctly remember the words being read from Miss Saurin's brother's letter, "tortures, torments, and tyrants." I do not think I have seen a copy of my deposition, or of my written evidence. The servant's name to whom the letter of the Jesuit brother was read was Eliza Connor. I saw Miss Saurin take the buttered toast which the chaplain had left after breakfast, out of the oven. She put it in a tea-cloth, and brought it to the pantry. She knew I was present. She was infirmarian, as well as housekeeper, at the time. There was one sick sister at that time. I went to the pantry ten minutes after she brought in the toast, and found her there. She may, in the interim, have been all the time in the pantry, or in other parts of the house. I am almost certain that tea or toast was not taken away to the other part of the house, where she may have been. I did not see her actually eating the toast, but I am certain she ate it. The empty cup and the plate on which the toast had been were there when she left. The sick sister had already got her breakfast. I kept these things in mind. I did not think a day might come when it would be useful to repeat them. It was in 1858 she sent five or six guimps to the wash. I found the cakes I mentioned in my deposition on the top of the cabinet, in her cell. I think she had been called out of her cell. They were not concealed, but the door was shut, which was unusual. The cakes I missed from the kitchen were made by me.

Did you make any report as to the cakes?—I did not mention it.

The Lord Chief Justice: I wish it had not been mentioned here.

Mr. Mellish: I was obliged, by the statements of the deposition, to go into cakes. (Laughter.)

The next witness was another sister, Mrs. Nelligan, who gave evidence similar in its general character. This witness, however, had been with Miss Saurin at the school, and gave evidence in particular as to the children's dinners. They had complained, she said, of missing their dinners; and on coming into the room suddenly one day she found Miss Saurin with a little paper packet in her hands in which she said were parts of the children's dinners they had left. Witness said she knew it was not so, and she took it from her and asked the children to whom the contents belonged, and the contents were claimed and consumed. This was in Miss Saurin's presence, and she looked confused. On another occasion witness said she saw Miss Saurin take from three of the children portions of their dinner. In consequence of these things witness said she made statements to Mrs. Star, and she gave certain directions about it, that is, that no one should interfere with the children's dinners. The witness being asked as to her statement on the subject to the bishop said she honestly believed that Miss Saurin on these occasions had taken the children's dinners. She went on to say that Mrs. Star's manner was always kind, but that Miss Saurin was often violent, and spoke loudly and impertinently to her. From her manner the witness said she almost thought Miss Saurin would have struck the Mother Superior. Next morning, of her own accord, she knelt at the table and confessed her violence of the previous day. Asked as to Miss Saurin's conduct to the children, the witness said it was not kind, unless strangers were present. On one occasion the witness came in and found a child crying. On asking her the reason, the child said, "Sister has struck me." Miss Saurin looked displeased, and moved towards the child; witness, turning round, saw Miss Saurin strike the child. Miss Saurin denied it, and declared she had not touched it; but the child said, "You did, Sister, you did." Witness said she was quite certain she had seen Miss Saurin strike the child. The witness went on to state that she wrote to the bishop in these terms:—

"My Lord,—You would confer a very great favour on the community by making arrangements for the removal of Sister Scholastica. The health of the Reverend Mother becomes visibly worse every day owing to the anxiety her perverse conduct, and her over great solicitude as to its effect on the community occasion her. Could your Lordship see the sad difference in our once happy community, you would not refuse our petition.

"Your Lordship's humble servant in Jesus, "SISTER MARY BERNARD."

Mr. Russell : Now, were the contents of that letter true ?—They were.

Has the community been happy since the plaintiff left ?—Yes.

Was there any other cause of uneasiness but that arising from her presence ?—None.

Is it true that the Mother Superior's health had declined in consequence of her anxiety on this account ?—It is true.

The statement sent by the witness to the bishop was read—to the same general effect as the statements of the other sisters, and to the like effect as her present evidence. It spoke of the plaintiff's spirit of deception. It stated that anything missing was sure to be found in her cell. It stated that the witness always feared and avoided her, and "dreaded being with her." Witness stated that she always knew Sister Scholastico did not speak the truth, but her falsehoods were so frequent that they were notorious.

At this point the case was adjourned.

THIRTEENTH DAY, *Wednesday, February* 17th.

Minor evidence, repeating the well-worn topics, or introducing a few trivial statements in support of the testimony given by Mrs. Star and her sister-defendant, is now bringing to its long-deferred end the case for the defence. Still the court is crowded, and still it echoes with occasional expressions of popular feeling, though the sounds have somewhat abated their loudness in proportion to the falling away of interest in the witnesses who are now bringing up the rear of the defending party. Artists who have been sketching all the heads that have been laid together, or carefully opposed, in this battle of brains, continue to bestow their impartial skill on each new face that comes forward in the field ; and the humblest lay-sister is as faithfully limned as the superior whom she obeys. The interest to-day has centered, not in the evidence, but in certain remarks of the Lord Chief Justice, who said he should hold that the moral restraint in the particular case of appointing a sister to watch over Miss Saurin was not false imprisonment; that the plaintiff had to show by what right she remained in the convent ; and that her great point was the conspiracy. This charge of conspiracy, his lordship went on to say, divided itself into two branches, one being the question, did the defendants conspire by ill-treatment to drive the plaintiff out of their community, and the second whether, having so conspired, they further resorted to false accusations, in order to induce the bishop to expel her. If the statements to the bishop were honestly though injudiciously made, the defendants were not responsible for the conduct or for the miscarriage of the commission.

The hearing of this case was resumed at the sitting of the Court.

Mrs. Nelligan was examined by Mr. C. Russell, and deposed as follows : The plaintiff frequently broke the rule of silence. She was frequently disobedient, and spoke disrespectfully of the superior. I saw Miss Saurin frequently eating between meals in the pantry between 1859 and 1860. She was not allowed to fast, and at one time I heard the reverend mother say Miss Saurin could not eat sufficient at her meals to fast. In 1859, when Mrs. Star and Mrs. Kennedy were engaged, Miss Saurin provided a private supper of hot cakes and tea in the pantry. She always said she disliked butter, but on that occasion she ate a great quantity, and in the presence of externs. We are prohibited from eating before externs. Once I saw her in the pantry before a plate of ham. She was helping herself with her fingers. She appeared very much confused. Her mouth was too full to speak, and her lips were greasy. (Laughter.) She would meet the children of the better class as they came into school, take their dinners and examine them. She could always say what they had for dinner. At another time a paper parcel was found during the dinner hour containing various pieces of food. and on examining them and showing them to the children they owned them. Miss Saurin looked confused. I saw Miss Saurin take portions of three children's dinners in the playground. She was standing in front of the children, and they gave it to her. She turned round immediately, but she had nothing in her hand. I could not see what she did with it. I believe it to have been put into her pocket. The children frequently complained of their losses. The children told me Miss Saurin asked for some of the dinner of Mrs. O'Brien's little boy. He always brought nice things for dinner. She took very special care of him. He was a very innocent child, between four and five. She held his dinner in her hand, and fed him. She told him which bit he was to eat first and which to keep till the last. (Laughter.) She was not so careful about the other children. Pastry or currant cake was what was taken. I honestly believed at that time that Miss Saurin had taken these things. Mrs. Star was very kind to the plaintiff, but Miss Saurin was often very violent to her. In 1865 I was attracted by a loud voice in the community room. I there saw Miss Saurin speaking very loud and incoherently to Mrs. Star. I could not distinguish what she said, but she appeared so excited that I thought she would strike the reverend mother. The next morning, of her own accord, she knelt at the foot of the community table and apologised. She was unkind to the children. In 1865 she beat one of the children, and then denied it. I saw it, and the child complained. I wrote to the bishop asking for Miss Saurin's removal. I had considerably more work to do than Miss Saurin, and could get it done within the time. I could take up the cocoa matting, although it was rather hard work.

The witness's deposition was here read.

Cross-examination continued : The statements

made in that deposition are true. The plaintiff, when she ceased to be a member of the community in 1866, ceased to attend the Prince-street Schools. I had to attend them. There were no complaints whatever as to the children's dinners after she left the schools. In 1865 I saw Miss Saurin try to pull the strings out of an article of clothing—a coif. She could not pull them out, and she cut them out. Mrs. Kennedy spoke to her about it, and reproved her next morning, and she denied having done it. That was during the absence of the mother superior in June or July. I noticed that she sewed two handkerchiefs together. They were a yard and a half long. At the redistribution of clothes I got the use of a skirt which had belonged to Miss Saurin. It had material for three petticoats, having six linings of material.

The Lord Chief Justice: Had it been so originally?—No, my lord. The layers were sewn one over the other, and the outer one was of a finer material than the rest, and unfit for the purpose.

To Mr. Russell: The layers were not necessary to cover holes or defects in the garment. It was taken to pieces and petticoats made out of it. I only got one of them.

To the Lord Chief Justice: I do not know how many petticoats were made out of it.

To Mr. Russell: It was not one of the petticoats which her mother gave her. I missed working material, and on one occasion a pocket-handkerchief; and from what I heard from a sister I knew Miss Saurin had the handkerchief. I asked her for it, and she said she hadn't it. I saw her using it, and knew it very well. When I lost it, it had my mark on it—three nails worked into it—and these had been removed. I did not say I had seen it with her, as I was only a novice, and it would not be respectful to say so to a sister.

To the Lord Chief Justice: I saw it at the wash, and the marks were gone.

To Mr. Russell: The penance spoken of, holding a dust-pan and wearing a duster, was not unusual. I have frequently worn things on my head. It was a general penance for sending things to the wash unmarked. We had to wear them on our heads during spiritual lecture. (A laugh.) I have had to hold boots or shoes in my hand.

The Lord Chief Justice: For what?—For having left them out of their proper places, my lord.

Examination continued: Other sisters frequently had similar penances. The penances were not at all exceptional, except that in her case they were less frequent than in ours.

The Lord Chief Justice: Did you see her wearing the duster?—I saw it on, my lord.

Were you there when she was told to take it off?—I was not.

To Mr. Russell: Mrs. Star never at any time asked me to tell her my confession. It would be a grave fault to commit. To my knowledge she has never asked any sister to state her confession. I was with Miss Saurin for some weeks—from the 12th of February, after her dismissal, to the 20th of March. She left the bath dressing-room in April. She was there only about a fortnight. Miss Saurin stated that sisters with sore legs were put into that room with her. I was the only one to whom such a thing could refer. I had sprained my knee, but it only required rest. It was untrue to say that liniment was used. No such thing

was used. There was no offensive smell. She said that the window was never opened. It was always opened whenever she went out to mass or elsewhere. There were five closets besides that used by the community, and these five were open to her, and in fact she did use some of them. It is quite untrue to say that she was not allowed to leave the room for any purpose. She left her room at least, on an average, ten times a day. There were two chairs in the bath dressing-room. One was rather beyond her reach, but the other she used every day, not for sitting on.

The Lord Chief Justice: For what, then, did she use it?—For keeping her books on. She seemed to prefer sitting on the floor; and when she did sit on the chair, she sat on it as she did on the floor. She took up her feet altogether. (Laughter.)

To Mr. Russell: Sometimes she sat on the side of the bed. I never intimated to her that she ought not to use the chair.

The Lord Chief Justice: Did she put her feet on the bar of the chair?—No, my lord; on the seat.

Mr. Russell: Like a Turk?—Yes. (A laugh.)

Was there anything peculiar in her manner?—Yes; she seemed to me to try and make herself ill.

How was that?—She used to sit up in the bed with nothing but her night-dress on; and sometimes, early in the morning, she would go out of bed—hot, of course—and put her feet in cold water.

Anything more?—She abstained from food. I sometimes saw her taking only the least scrap of bread for her dinner, and nothing else.

What else had she?—Meat and vegetables.

Was it always mutton?—No, not always; but generally.

The Lord Chief Justice: On the days when it was not mutton did she make any difference?—No. Even then she did not eat it all.

Did you dine in the same room with her?—Yes; until my knee got well.

Had you the same as she had?—I had the same quality, but I don't think I had as much as she had.

To Mr. Russell: Her food was exactly of the same quality at all times as the other sisters', and she was treated in all respects exactly like the other sisters. When I say exactly like the rest, I speak of the quality; for she had a great deal more than the others.

The Lord Chief Justice: A great deal more than the others?—Except as to dinners. I make that exception. I allude to other all meals. While the mother superior was away she took mutton every day; but when the mother superior came home she discontinued it.

To Mr. Russell: She was given less mutton than the rest, but of other meat she had much the same. It is not the fact that when going to Prince-street School she had to blacken her foot on account of a hole in her boot. Her boots were better than mine, although the soles of one or both were broken. She spoke to Mrs. Kennedy, and she gave her overshoes; but when she got into the street, she let one come off. She said they were too small, but I do not think that was the case. When the mother superior came home both of us got good boots. Hers are in existence yet, and are not broken. I think Mrs. King is wearing them. In February, 1866, when her religious dress was taken away, a new black dress and good underclothing were provided for her—all comfortable and suitable. She put some of it on after a week; but the dress she put on on the first Sunday to go to mass, and then took it off. Some first days afterwards she put it on, and kept it on. When in the attic she pinned the back of the dress up to make it smaller; and when the reverend mother heard it she said she would get her a smaller one—and she did, and sent it to her. It was made of woollen material. It looked very respectable on her. She used to go out of her room and walk about. Sometimes after mass she used to walk about the corridor for twenty minutes.

Was there, so far as you know, any restriction put upon her going or coming from or to her room?—Not the least.

Did you receive any directions on the subject?—No. I remember once when the novices were in the corridor, and I asked Miss Saurin to wait a moment, as I knew the mother superior did not wish the novices to see her.

Why?—She looked so very odd. When the novices passed she went out. With that exception, there was no restriction upon her going out or in.

Examination continued : Suitable clothes were ready for her to go away in. She knew the dress was ready, and I think the mother superior told her she had everything ready. At the end she went away hurriedly. No one knew she was going. After the order for her dismissal was made, Mrs. Dawson cleared out her room, and I did it sometimes. I do not know that Miss Saurin did not do it sometimes, but I did not see her. Mrs. Dawson is dead. In the attic there were two beds, a cabinet, a chair or two, and also a stool—I am not quite sure as to the second chair—likewise a washhand-stand. There was no lumber whatever in the room. She might have used the second chair in the bath-room as she wished. She was not prevented doing so. The sheets in the attic had been given to her clean. It is not true that they had been used to cover lottery tables. It is also untrue that the blanket came from the children's room. The bedclothing she had in the attic was the same as she had in the bath dressing-room. In April she told me to keep away from her bed, as it had vermin in it. I took the bedclothing off and examined the sheets and the blankets very carefully and found no sign of anything of the kind. Her sheets were not particularly clean, but I would not say they were much soiled. There was nothing particular upon them. She told me she had been given the blankets of the pupil-teachers upon which they had combed their hair. I knew that not to be the fact, as I had taken them up from the bath-room myself, and had charge of the bedclothing of the pupil-teachers. She stated she had not facilities for washing. She had; and washed every morning and nearly every evening. There is not the slightest pretence for saying she had not every requisite for washing. There are two lines of cells on the attic story. I sleep in one of them. They are all exactly of the same size. The room in question is occupied by a sister.

The Lord Chief Justice : Did you make any remark to her when she said she was given a pupil-teacher's blanket?—No. My superior had given me directions not to speak.

Examination continued : The bath dressing-room is considered the most comfortable sleeping room in the house, and it is the room in which sick sisters are put for that reason. The doctor recommended the mother superior to keep it as an infirmary, as it had a southern aspect, and was the only sleeping room in the house which had a fireplace.

To the Lord Chief Justice : The house was not built on purpose as a convent.

Mr. Russell : It is said there was a rope fastened to the door and to a bed in the lobby. Is that so?—It was a piece of cord or twine, not a rope.

Was it ordinary twine?—It may have been rather thick twine. While it was on the door I slept in the room and could get out readily.

The Lord Chief Justice : How was it fastened?—To the handle of the door, my lord, and to the bed in which a sister slept outside.

To Mr. Russell : It did not prevent the door opening sufficiently to let a person out, but the twine made the bed shake when the door was opened.

Why was it put there?—Because, as I understood, Miss Saurin had got up, and gone about the house.

The Lord Chief Justice : Had she done so?—I know she did so once or twice while I slept there.

To Mr. Russell : I do not think she stayed away very long, nor do I know what part of the house she went to. In April, before she went, she asked for something Mrs. Kennedy had belonging to her.

A Juror : Was it the case that hot water bottles were brought to the other sisters who were with her?—I think Mrs. Star could explain that better than I could.

The Lord Chief Justice : Is that the fact?—Yes ; I think it was for this reason—that Miss Saurin could go to the fire if she liked, but the sister who could not go.

Cross-examined by the Solicitor-General : The weather was cold then, I suppose?—Yes.

Was she terribly cross with the reverend mother?—She was a great cloud to the community.

And it affected the rev. mother's health?—Yes, very much.

And I suppose none of you liked her?—I never disliked her, never.

Disliking the effect she produced, did you not dislike the cause?—No.

But you disliked the effect?—Yes, but I had not the slightest ill-feeling towards her.

You do not mean to say you liked her?—I did.

Was she an amiable person then?—No.

Then why did you like her?—For the love of God.

In the way a Christian loves his enemy?—I did not say that.

Then you really liked her?—Yes, I liked her.

In the way you liked the rev. mother?—I cannot say I naturally had the same affection for her, but I did not dislike her. I liked her.

As a matter of duty?—All I can say is that I did not dislike, but liked her.

The same as the rest?—Yes, I think I did, but not naturally.

By an effort of duty?—Yes.

Before you had to make the effort of duty, while you were a novice, did you like her?—I had no particular affection for her one way or the other.

There was no change in your feelings?—None. I knew her as well at the first as I did at the last.

She was bad all through?—She may have made it more apparent at the end.

Cross-examination continued: She was not capable of teaching, and she did not do her best. I frequently showed her how to teach, and all to no purpose. She may have been capable of teaching the alphabet, but she did not succeed, for the children whom she taught forgot what they knew. (Laughter.) I tried to teach her repeatedly, and she would not learn.

Was she incorrigible?—I think that is too strong a way of putting it. She did not try to take advantage of the teaching. If she had tried, she would have had some success, as other sisters had. Those who did not wish to learn asked to go to her class. That was at the night school. They asked to go, but were not let. There were fourteen or fifteen sisters then in the convent. The reason why she was sent to the night school was, that at that time she did not teach in the day school. It would have been hard upon the other sisters to send them, but I do not know what the mother superior's motive in sending her was. I think she taught needlework in the day school. Those in my class in the night school who did not wish to apply their minds to their lessons, but would rather be laughing and talking, asked me to let them go to her class. At that time I did not know she was incapable of teaching, but I knew she was incapable of keeping order in a school. I speak entirely of Hull. I was never at Clifford with her. The girls who attended the night school were grown girls. My evidence as to the children's dinners, and her treatment of the children, refers to the time after she returned from Clifford, in 1864. The children spoke to me about their dinners in her presence. Complaints also came from their parents as to the loss of the dinners. The children were generally poor, but there were a good many respectable children who brought very comfortable dinners. The school is an infant school, and the children all under six years of age. There were about 100 altogether. In summer they dined in the playground, and in winter in the room. They dined about half-past twelve. The children put their dinners in a press or on a table. There was a set of children whom Miss Saurin always met, and took their dinners from them. The number might have been twenty or thirty, and some of them she met every morning. I may remark she had no business to meet them. She may have taken their dinners, but I do not know what she did with them. She may or she may not have put them in the dinner press. She looked at the dinners she took. I saw her taking them, and looking at them. She knew what they had for dinner, and I infer she suited herself, and took what she liked afterwards. My attention was directed to this, it was so very remarkable. Some dinners were brought in bags, some in paper, some in cloths, and some in baskets. She paid most attention to the baskets.

(Laughter.) I saw her untying them. I saw her go to the dinner press where the baskets were put. I may remark—it is not evidence, of course (a laugh) but it will confirm what I say—that Mary Ann Driscoll told me she saw her eating in the cloak-room.

When did she tell you this?—Within a year.

Since the action commenced?—Yes.

Pray, who told you it was not evidence?—I heard so.

Yes; but from whom?—I do not know, but I was told so.

Mr. Mellish: She may easily have picked up that much law within the last fortnight. (Laughter.)

Cross-examination continued: There were over one hundred dinners. The children, as they passed the table on which the dinners were placed, claimed their own dinner. They easily recognized their own. Sometimes, but not at all often, there was a dispute as to a dinner when two were wrapped up in pieces of newspaper; but when they were opened the matter was cleared up. Miss Saurin ate her luncheon with me in the cloak-room. That was the right place to do so, but not to eat at other times.

When do you think she ate the children's dinners?—After luncheon; she generally stayed there after me.

And did a little private refection on her own account?—That is what I suppose.

Name some persons who complained?—In 1865, or the beginning of 1866, Francis O'Brien's mother sent the servant to me to complain that Francis told his mother every day that Miss Saurin had eaten—not taken, but eaten—his dinner every day, and she said she would have to send the boy to another school. She did not, for I took the child from Miss Saurin.

What were the O'Briens?—Shopkeepers, in Cumberland-street, Hull; I think they were grocers.

Are they there now?—No; they have left. They left in 1867.

What was the servant's name?—Catherine Wallace. She is gone to work in a factory in Lancashire.

Can you give me the name of anyone now in Hull who complained?—No.

Or anywhere else whose address you can give me?—No; I only remember that one case, as Miss Saurin took particular notice of the child.

Cross-examination continued: I reported what I observed, and the conclusion I drew, to Mrs. Star. I told Miss Saurin not to interfere with Francis O'Brien's dinner, and I more than once took his dinner out of her hand. She used to get him near her and open his basket at dinner-time. I joined and was professed after her, and was her junior by six years. She was under me in the schools. I was professed in 1860. Mrs. Star put me over her, but please remember she could not manage the school. It is not at all unusual, but quite usual, to place one who can manage a school over one who cannot, and I was a certificated teacher. I mention this, as Miss Saurin has made a grievance of it.

Can you give me the name of any child whose parents reside in Hull whom you say Miss Saurin ill treated?—Yes; Jane Coulan. I saw Miss Saurin beat her, and she denied it. Her father is a bricklayer. You will remember this, that the children will not be able to give you any knowledge, for they were small infants then, and it is several years ago.

Can you give me the name of another?—Andrew Owen. I saw Miss Saurin catch him violently by the arm. He screamed out, "You have pinched me." Miss Saurin said, "No, I did not." I looked at the child's arm, and saw the mark of the finger and thumb. The child said, "Yes, you did; you nipped me." (Laughter.) Miss Saurin continued to deny it in the child's presence. She could have seen the mark of the finger and thumb had she looked, but in the face of the mark she denied she had done it. I saw Miss Saurin out of a window taking dinner. I got to the window by the gallery, but I did not go for the purpose of watching her. I saw her use the long pocket-handkerchief—there were two sewn together. It was a yard and a half long. She could not get it into her pocket, so she put it into her sleeve and kept it there. No remark was made to her about it; it would not have been polite. The sisters spoke of it afterwards. When I spoke of the petticoat which had materials for three, I did not mean that there were three petticoats stitched together. There were pieces of cashmere put over one another, and made into one petticoat. I do not know whether it was so made originally. I daresay the pieces were put on from time to time. My mark on the pocket handkerchief was three nails. Her mark was three nails and a cross.

Would not the presence or absence of the cross make all the difference between your mark and hers?—Yes, but I knew my handkerchief, not because of the mark, but because of its material and newness.

Cross-examination continued: I was three or four weeks in the bath-room with a sprained knee. Miss Saurin could not go about alone. There was always a sister with her. Her movements were not controlled in any way.

The Solicitor-General: I should think it a great restraint to have a person always following me.

The Lord Chief Justice: It would not be pleasant to have a shadow always following you; but the question is, what is the effect of the evidence as regards the count for false imprisonment?

The Solicitor-General: I have said from the beginning, my lord, that it was not a case of keeping in against will, but of turning out against will.

The Lord Chief Justice: I understood the latter part of the history to be put to the jury as a case of real physical restraint.

The Solicitor-General: I did not so intend it, my lord.

The Lord Chief Justice said that the point was well worthy of consideration. It became stronger when there was a visitor with power to remove, and who had exercised that power.

Mr. Mellish said that that was an important view, as bearing upon the length into which he should go into the evidence regarding the commission. He submitted that no court but the Court of Chancery had power to inquire into the manner in which the visitor had exercised his power.

The Lord Chief Justice said he entertained the clearest possible view that for the result of the commission the present defendants were not responsible. They might be responsible for false accusations, intentionally made for the purpose of inviting an exercise of the visitor's power. If the depositions and accusations were honestly made, the defendants were not responsible for any miscarriage of the commission. They were charged with conspiring by false accusations to procure her expulsion. The question was whether the accusations were honestly, even if mistakenly made, or made with a sinister motive.

Cross-examination continued: When my knee got well I went again to the schools. During the Easter holidays I saw a good deal of her again. I saw her in the reception-room. She was not ordered out of it. Mrs. Kennedy asked her what she wanted, and told her she had better go upstairs. The priest was about—in a room near at hand—and the reverend mother did not wish him to see her, she was so oddly dressed. I saw her once going to the library. She saw the priest's breakfast laid there, and came out of her own accord.

To the Court: It is not usual for any member of the community to be present while the priest breakfasted; and, besides, she was so oddly dressed that any one seeing her would think she was out of her mind.

Cross-examination continued: I do not know whether she succeeded in making herself ill. She said she was ill. I could not see her face; all I could see was her nose. (Laughter.) She had a shawl pinned over her face.

Her veil had been taken away?—Yes, as part of her religious dress.

Did you think she was ill?—I did not. She told me she could not walk to the church, and that day she spent two hours walking up and down the room. She lost mass, and that with us is considered a grievous sin. She did not put on the secular dress for some time. She sat on the floor and rolled her feet up in it. This occurred in April. It was not cold then. There is not a shadow of truth in her statement that she had not abundance of water. The tap was in the lobby, and I have seen her get water from the tap. I have seen her once or twice put her dinner water in the ewer, but I think now she did it on purpose. Then I thought she might have imagined the water was scarce, but it was not.

Did you bid her good-bye when she was going away?—No; I was out at the time. I should have been very glad to have bade her good-bye. (Laughter.)

To a Juror: The cord that was fastened to the handle of the door and the bed was slack. I have myself got out of a morning while it was on. The door opened inwardly, and drew the cord tight. The bed was an iron chair, and was very shaky. The object was that when the door was opened, the sister who slept outside should be awakened. There was room for egress and regress.

Re-examined: For the first week or so after her removal from the community she went about with the sheets rolled round her. Afterwards she wore the dress which was provided for her, and the shawl.

To the Lord Chief Justice: She used to go to mass with the shawl over her face.

Mrs. Hewetson, examined by Mr. Russell: My name in religion is Sister Mary Francis. I

entered as a postulant at Hull in 1858. In 1862
I was professed as a lay sister. In April, 1860,
Miss Saurin went from Hull to Clifford. I did
not see much of her until August, 1863, when I
went to Clifford. I remained there until March,
1864. In June, 1864, she came to Hull. When
I was a postulant at Hull, in 1859, I missed a
penknife, and it was found amongst some things
the mother superior had put aside for Miss Saurin
when she left the convent, and which had belonged to her. I also missed two pairs of new
gloves, which I afterwards saw Miss Saurin wearing ; one pair about a month afterwards, the other
pair about three years afterwards. I also missed
from my trunk three yards of black woollen material and some black ribbon. That material I
saw Miss Saurin wearing in the form of an apron,
and the ribbon she used as strings. In 1859 two
children were resident at the convent. They both
missed thimbles. I saw them in Miss Saurin's
work-basket. I asked her about them, and she
denied having had them. She took some pack-
ages of needles, and about a dozen spools of
cotton out of my workbox. I saw her taking
them. I did not speak to her, because she was a
professed sister, and I was only a postulant. In
October, 1859, Sister Mary Katherine died of
consumption. Plaintiff was infirmarian, and I
was her assistant. We had to prepare her body
for burial. It is our custom to bury sisters in
their entire habit—a full suit of their dress, as
they were dressed at the time of their reception.
I recollect getting out the deceased sister's habit
for that purpose. She desired me to get out
another habit of Sister Mary Katherine—a better
one than she was buried in—and to take out one
of the inside sleeves, while she herself took out
the other. The inside sleeve is tight, and attached
to the body. There are loose outside sleeves. She
told me she wanted the inside sleeves to put on
the deceased sister. She put them on. I afterwards saw her taking them off the deceased sister
and put them away with some other articles of
Sister Mary Katherine's wearing apparel. A
short time before the coffin was screwed down I
was with Miss Saurin in the chapel, where it then
was. Miss Saurin took off the outside sleeves.
She gave them to me, telling me at the same time
to put them out of sight, behind the stalls in the
chapel. I afterwards saw Miss Saurin wear those
sleeves, and six months later I saw them in her
cell. She had gone to Clifford on very short
notice. I could not be mistaken about the sleeves.
I knew them. At the time I speak of, Miss
Saurin drew the church cloak in which the sister
was to be buried over the body, so that the absence of the sleeves would not be noticed. On the
night Sister Mary Katherine died Miss Saurin
told me to get some of her guimps and coifs. I
brought four guimps and two coifs. One of each
was placed on the sister, and I was about to take
away the rest, when Miss Saurin said, "Leave
them there ; I'll wear them out." After she went
at short notice to Clifford, I found between the
mattrass and the bed a pocket-handkerchief,
coifs, and guimps, belonging to Sister Mary
Katherine. She wore shoes and stockings belonging to the deceased sister. I know she had
no permission to use those things. I was desired
to collect the deceased sister's clothes, to be given
up to the reverend mother ; but there were very
few left.

To the Lord Chief Justice : A dead sister is
buried in her full dress, inside sleeves as well as
outside sleeves.

To Mr. C. Russell : The dying sister had asked
me to sew her silver devotional medal to her scapular, and put them both on her, as she wished
them to be buried with her. I did so, and placed
the medal and scapular on her before she died. I
saw it on her when she was dead. Before the
coffin was brought down I looked at the scapular,
and saw that the medal was cut off it. No one
but Miss Saurin and myself had anything to do
with the body. I did not cut off or take the
medal. This was at Hull. I do not know that
Miss Saurin had a silver medal of her own. She
asked me in 1860 whether I had found a silver
medal—one of her own—which she said she had
lost when she left Hull for Clifford. I remember
in 1863 being sent to her cell with water for her
to bathe her feet. She said she was ill. I noticed
she had round her head a piece of flannel of very
fine texture. Sister Mary Katherine had had petticoats of the same material, and, excepting her,
no sister had. Some time after I asked the
mother superior for permission to mend my habit
with pieces of material which were in the attic.
Next morning Miss Saurin was in the attic. I
knew it by the way she ran downstairs, and all
the other sisters were at the schools. She ran
down in her usual quick way. In the course of
the morning I went to the attic to get the pieces
of black material, and they were gone. After
the commission I got a habit of the plaintiff's to
rip up, and I found what I believed to be the
black material sewn in the lining of the habit.
It was not put there to repair the habit. In
1862 or 1863 Miss Saurin was sent to the wardrobe for lining, and she took double as much
as is usually given for the purpose ; also a hand-
ful of spools of cotton and some sewing silk. I
saw her take them. I have seen Miss Saurin
eating out of meal hours frequently. I remember
that in 1859 a present of tarts was sent to the
convent. They were given to her as refectorian.
I don't know what became of them. They were
never used in the refectory. In 1863, at Clifford,
I saw Miss Saurin take charge of the children's
dinners, especially the dinner of one child, and I
saw her put part of the dinners into her work-
basket. On other occasions she put portions of
the dinners into her pocket or into a drawer. On
one occasion a child wanted to get her cake, and
Miss Saurin only gave her part of it. I do not
know what became of the rest.

To the Court : The entire cake would not
have been too much for the child ; and, besides,
it was at dismissal time, when the children were
going home.

To Mr. C. Russell : On a Saturday afternoon I
found a cake concealed in the drawer of the ros-
trum in the schoolroom. During six months at
Clifford I cooked, carved, and served the meat.
It is not true that we always had mutton. We
frequently had beef, or veal, or fowls, or bacon.
Miss Saurin frequently ate mutton when it was
boiled or fried ; and on one occasion I knew her
to take a very good breakfast of mutton-chops.
From my own observation I knew her to treat the
children severely. I knew her to strike them.
She was not very truthful, and I have known her
to commit frequent acts of disobedience. She
often murmured against the sister superior. I

can testify that Sister Mary Agnes was most kind to all the sisters, including Miss Saurin. I never at any time saw any trace of ill-will in the conduct of Mrs. Star or Mrs. Kennedy towards Miss Saurin. I never saw Miss Saurin perform a penance, and I have seen all the other sisters, including the present mother superior, performing penances. I have seen them all except Miss Saurin kiss the floor, and kiss the sisters' feet, and mine also. I have worn things on my head as a penance. That is very usual. Miss Saurin neglected Sister Mary Katherine when she was dying. She gave her salt butter when her lips and mouth were sore. There was fresh butter in the house, and I changed the salt for it, but Miss Saurin reproved me and changed it. She also gave her very poor, weak tea, nearly cold. There are other things of the same kind which I saw, but do not now remember. I saw her once put forward the clock, and two or three times putting it back. I did not write to the bishop. Sister Mary Katherine gave Miss Saurin a book, and one to me also. Mrs. Star knew this. At the distribution in January I had to give up the book, and it was given to Mrs. King. I did not complain of that. It was not mine to keep. Mrs. Kennedy wrote my deposition. I did not tell her about the clothes which had been taken from Sister Mary Katherine.

Examination continued: The statements in the depositions are all true.

Cross-examined by the Solicitor-General: Were you questioned on the subject of what you knew about Miss Saurin?—Yes.

By whom?—By Mrs. Star and Mrs. Kennedy.

Did they take down your answers?—I do not remember. There was very little about it. Mrs. Kennedy wrote out my statement. I did not make any notes.

Did she read it over to you?—I do not recollect.

Did you answer questions, or were things suggested to you?—I can't tell you. I have very little remembrance about it.

Did you never make a deposition against a sister before or since?—No.

Did you know what you had been sent for?—I cannot say I did.

Can you say you did not?—I cannot say one way or the other.

Did you go more than once?—I cannot remember more than once.

What was the attic used for in which the pieces of black material were?—I really cannot tell. (A laugh.)

In what part of the attic were they kept?—In some place about the middle.

In what?—In a parcel on the floor.

When had you last seen them?—On the evening before.

Now, how long after that did you find them in the lining of Miss Saurin's habit?—Two or three years after.

And you knew them again?—I did.

Where is the book Miss Kavanagh gave you? —It is here in London.

Was she fond of Miss Saurin?—I cannot say.

Did you see the inscription she made in the book you gave her?—No.

Did she write an inscription in yours?—No.

Now, about the medal and scapular; was it not next the body of the dead sister?—It was under some of her clothes.

And did you remove the clothes for the purpose of looking at the medal?—No; but in doing so I saw that the medal was gone.

What other purpose then?—Well, it is not necessary to tell.

The Lord Chief Justice: Oh, pray tell.

Witness: Well, my lord, it was simply to lighten the gwymp, and to draw back the habit more.

The Solicitor-General: Where was the medal? —It was under the gwymp of the habit.

You said you placed it on her body?—That was when she was alive. She wore it on her tunic.

Then it was next to her skin, except with the tunic?—Yes.

And did she so die?—Yes.

Was its position altered?—Yes; when we changed her clothes after her death. When I moved back the habit, I saw the edge of the scapular outside the habit and the tunic, and, seeing it had been cut, I pulled it out, and then the medal was gone.

You say in your deposition that you found that the medal was gone. Afterwards, when Miss Saurin asked you for the medal, you could not help thinking of Sister Mary Kavanagh. What did you mean the bishop to understand by that?—What any one would understand by it.

That is, you meant him to understand that Miss Saurin had taken it?—Yes.

Did you not think that that was a charge which would injure her for life, if known?—It would injure her, I daresay.

Then, if you made a charge that would injure her for life if known, why did you refrain from making the charge as to removing the sleeves from the dead sister because, if known, it would injure her for life?—They were more unimportant than the medal; and, besides, I saw her taking the sleeves off, and I did not see her taking the medal.

Do you think it would make any difference, if a person stole from a dead body, what was stolen?—I really do not know more than I have stated.

And you did not say a word about the sleeves although you mentioned the medal, because from conscientious motives you considered it a very serious matter, and one which would injure Miss Saurin if living. Do you mean to adhere to that answer?—I do.

Why, then, did you mention about the medal? —Because the medal was of lesser moment.

Was not the medal a sacred one? Had it not a sacred emblem on it?—Yes.

The Lord Chief Justice: What was the size of the medal?—About the size of a sixpence.

The Solicitor-General: You mean deliberately to state that you mentioned about the medal because it was of less importance, and might not injure her for life, if known?—Well, I can only say as I said before; I have told you the reason.

You must have been exceedingly shocked at this stealing from the dead body?—I was shocked.

What year did this occur in?—'59.

And you never mentioned a word about it until '65?—No.

Did you ever say a word about it to Miss

Saurin herself?—Never; I was only a postulant at the time.

To the Lord Chief Justice: I told everything else I could remember about Miss Saurin and Mrs. Kavanagh. She wrote what I said down. It is likely she read it to me before she signed it for me.

Re-examined by Mr. Mellish: I mentioned about the medal to Mrs. Star the same day as I mentioned it to Mrs. Kennedy. I asked her had she taken it, and she said she had not heard of it before.

The Lord Chief Justice: Are medals common with the sisters?—Silver ones are not; other medals are.

Had it an object of devotion on it?—Yes.

Are the objects different on the medals?—They are.

What was on this one?—The image of our Blessed Lady.

Were you educated and brought up as a lady?—Yes; I think I was.

And did you think this menial work degrading?—Not at all.

I believe you once had to wear your boots round your neck as a penance?—I had. (Laughter.)

Why?—Because I forgot to clean them at the proper time. That was when I was a novice. Since I became a professed sister I have had to wear my shoes on my head for leaving them out of their place. I am naturally very untidy.

Did you look upon these as tyrannical acts?—Oh, no; I was pleased to get the penances, and I think they have done me a great deal of good. (Laughter.) I certainly have not been so careless since. The sisters often ask for penance, and sometimes they do not get it. It is bad for a novice when she does not get plenty of penance—(a laugh)—as it is almost a sure sign she will be sent away. In July, 1861, I came suddenly into the pantry to say a visitor had come, and found Miss Saurin eating raspberries and cream.

Raspberries or strawberries?—Either; but I am sure about the cream. (A laugh.)

Examination continued: Her mouth was so full she could not speak. She put the plate away, and covered it up. In 1861 I was ill with the mumps, and could swallow only with great difficulty. Miss Saurin was the infirmarian, and she brought me, each day of the three or four I was ill, a small mug of tea, and thick bread and butter; and even that two hours after the proper time. I hold a Government certificate as a teacher. I heard complaints in 1865 about the taking of the children's dinners by Miss Saurin. I made no report of it until I had noticed it myself. When she left the schools the complaints ceased. I never entertained any ill-feeling towards her, nor did the other sisters so far as I can judge. I never heard one of them make an ill-natured remark about her, or one that could pain her. I mended the clothes of the community for several months, and had more to do for her than for anyone else. I have reason to believe she destroyed her clothes wilfully. I gave her a tunic which had no mending on it, and when it came to the wash it was only fit for the rag-bag. It is not true that the reverend mother took the thimble off. I turned to put by the bag, when I heard reverend mother say, "Do not kneel to me." When I looked round Miss Saurin was moving her hands violently, and I thought she was about to strike reverend mother. So I went over and put my arms round reverend mother, so that, if she did strike, the blow should fall upon me. Miss Saurin talked something about not stealing a farthing's worth, and something about persecution as well.

To the Lord Chief Justice: She said this while she was moving her hands about. It seemed to me that she was objecting to the change of the thimble.

To Mr. Russell: She did not say her thimble finger was sore until she got the smaller thimble. I saw her finger, and it was not sore. There was a chapped chilblain, a small one, on the knuckle of the next finger, but the thimble could not touch it. The rev. mother trembled, and seemed terrified. Next morning Miss Saurin knelt in the community room, and asked pardon for the bad example she had set us; then she went on, but I could not understand what she said. She spoke of mouldy bread and black bread, and about the sisters trying their larks on her at recreation; and she said she could get into another convent, but would not go. Mrs. Star said the acknowledgment of faults ought not to be made the opportunity by the imperfect for venting ill-feeling; that she could excuse her on the day before, as she might have erred then involuntarily; but now she had no excuse, as she was doing so deliberately.

The Lord Chief Justice: Did the plaintiff say anything about her sore finger then?—She did, my lord, but I could not understand it. She was excited, and did not speak plainly.

To Mr. Russell: Sisters frequently kneel of their own accord. Miss Saurin considered kneeling a humiliation, and the reverend mother spared her in that respect as much as possible. I was present in December when Miss Saurin says she was stripped. She asked to have her staylace mended, and Mrs. Star brought her into a room with a sister to mend it. I was called in to mend her habit. It is not true that the door was left open. It was opened once, when the portress came with a message. It is not true that Miss Saurin was stripped all but her tunic. She had on her stays and petticoat besides, and a loose sleeve over her head. It is not true that the reverend mother tore off a garment she put on her shoulders to keep her warm. There was no unnecessary delay, and she had only to remain partially undressed for a few minutes, and not for the length of time and in the condition she stated. She said to reverend mother, "This is five times you have stripped and searched me." One of the times she mentioned she was not stripped, as she said, or searched at all. I was present. Miss Saurin was unwell, and reverend mother advised her to go to bed. I was left to attend to her, and give her whatever she wanted. Rev. mother came in afterwards, and finding Miss Saurin in a great heat she had her head covered up. She took off the counterpane. It is not true that she tore off the clothes. She thought it necessary to take off the counterpane, and did so, leaving it beside the bed. I wrote to the bishop in August, begging that steps might be taken to remove Miss Saurin, as she was a heavy cross to us, and the cause of rev. mother's ill-health.

At this stage of the witness's examination, the Court adjourned. It was arranged, at the request of the jury, that the Court should not sit on Friday.

FOURTEENTH DAY.—*Thursday, Feb.* 18

A PARTIAL suspension of interest in the great convent scandal was noticeable to-day in the appearance of the Court, which, though reasonably full, was not crammed in excess of such accommodation as Horace Smith happily described in the line, "no room for standing, miscalled standing-room." Moreover, the rival attraction of the Westminster petition case was no doubt conducive to an agreeable thinning. It was remarkable that, while the avenues of the Court of Queen's Bench were almost clear of the overflow which has for days made the mere approach to the interior a difficult passage, the outside crowd in Westminster Hall found as much matter of talk in the proceedings before Baron Martin, as in those over which the Lord Chief Justice presides. There is no reason for supposing that the action, brought by Miss Saurin against Mrs. Star and Mrs. Kennedy, has lost any of its real importance in public estimation. The cause of a lessened display of curiosity is easily found in the circumstance that for two or three days the witnesses have been subordinate personages in the story. Not that they are by any means women of an ordinary or inferior stamp. Each in turn has shown remarkable powers of mind, and a still more remarkable capacity in a recluse for engaging in worldly controversies. Not Mrs. Star alone, or Mrs. Kennedy, has been a match for Mr. Solicitor-General; the several sisters who have followed suit on the side of the defence, have held their own with great tact, composure, and seeming confidence in the strength of their case; and to-day, one of the professed nuns, fully sustained the character of the convent for sagacity, prudence, and temperate firmness of statement. She resisted with quiet effect the suggestive tendency of Sir John Coleridge's questions as to her having relied on her memory, and yet having been minute in the recollection of dates. There was no surprising minuteness, she showed, in a clear and convincing reference to the few dates she had given. But she was palpably worsted in one passage of arms with her keen antagonist. It had been a great point in her evidence that Miss Saurin had made to her some disadvantageous remarks about Mrs. Star. "What were they, and when were they made?" The witness was quite ready to answer: she had been in delicate health, she said, and was travelling in company with the plaintiff, who told her that, but for her (Sister Scholastica's) intercession and earnest entreaty, Mrs. Star would have given the witness certain work to do in the kitchen, where the heat of the fire must have been hurtful to her. "Where was the disadvantageous remark in that instance?" the Solicitor-General asked. "Well," replied the witness, "I don't think it would have been very kind in the reverend mother to have put me to work that might have injured me." "But she did not," said the Solicitor-General; "on the contrary, Miss Saurin's representations of your weak health were, by her own account, listened to; and Mrs. Star, instead of giving you work in the kitchen, sent you on a journey to another convent for change of air. You see now that we have got at what you really mean by 'disadvantageous remarks,' and we put our own

construction on them." The success of this line of cross-examination, tending as it did to destroy the effect of general statements, and indeed to reverse their entire purport and transfer all their value to the other scale, was unmistakably great. At three o'clock to-day Mr. Hawkins, who has been engaged in the Westminster petition case, edged his way through the little knot of barristers at the step of the reporters' box, and bowed to the Lord Chief Justice as he took his seat by the side of Mr. Mellish. No person who has been constant in attendance during this trial can have failed to observe how these two leading counsel have been assisted by Mr. Russell, who has watched every atom of the evidence with a lynx-eye, and has never allowed a point to escape him, or to escape his chiefs. His hints and suggestions, tendered *sotto voce*, have been many and useful; and the hard work of the defence has, in short, been borne by him with consummate and imperturbable ease. The Court rose early to-day, for more than one good reason. It suited all interests that some leisure time should be snatched at this period; the Judge was anxious to review the depositions; the Attorney-General had business "in another place;" and the jury, being for the most part commercial men, were desirous of having their freedom at the time of the overland mail. So the Court at half-past three was adjourned until Saturday morning, leaving Friday a blank in the action of Saurin against Star and another.

The examination in chief of Mrs. Kerr by Mr. C. RUSSELL was resumed: I wrote the letter to the bishop of my own accord. Sister Mary Dawson spoke to me about it. Mrs. Star did not know I was writing. Mrs. Kennedy did know, as the letter was sent through her.

Witness's deposition was here read. She said she considered Sister Mary Scholastica a most dangerous person; that she was given to indulging in unfounded calumnies; and that to attract esteem, or prevent the loss of it, she resorted to falsehood; and she added that she feared intercourse with Miss Saurin, who was a great actress, would injure the foundations of religious life, from her murmurings, disobedience, and breaches of the rules of poverty, silence and charity. She resolved to shun her society, as she was a dangerous person. Many of the circumstances detailed in the witness's evidence were set forth in the "deposition."

Examination continued: I honestly believed that that deposition set forth a true statement of the case so far as my observation went. After Miss Saurin's separation from the community, I used to see her almost every day. I took up her dinner to her for about a fortnight, and sat with her. When Mrs. Neligan was with her, until her sprained knee got well, I did not sit with her. I went to Clifford in March. I returned to Hull in about a fortnight, but did not see much of Miss Saurin. The refectorian took to her what the other sisters got in the way of food. If it was meat, she got that; if it was fasting fare, she got that. Whatever we had she had—off the same dish. The library is free during the greater part of the day—from nine o'clock in the morning. She might have gone there. There was a fire in it. A message was sent by Mrs. Star to Miss Saurin by Sister Mary Dawson, to the effect that she might go to the library. Sister Mary Gonzaga —Mrs. Rafter—brought her a similar message. I was present on the 12th of February, when the rev. mother gave Miss Saurin a suit of clothes.

Was it a secular dress ?—Yes ; an entire outfit. It was entirely new ; I helped to make it.

Examination continued : It was a ladylike dress, and quite warm enough for the time of year. Miss Saurin was two or three times in my presence offered clean linen and refused to take it. The first time was about the 18th or 19th of February, while she was in the bath-room, and again the Wednesday before Easter. Mrs. Star came to inquire why she would not put it on, and tried to persuade her to do so, but she would not.

Have you ever had a penance for being impetuous? (Laughter.)

The LORD CHIEF JUSTICE : You are not bound to answer that question.

Mrs. Kerr : I think I have one now, my lord. (Renewed laughter.)

Examination continued : I was present when a bonnet and mantle were brought to her. They were quite new and ladylike. She threw them out of the room. The warm water bottles were given to the sisters who were obliged to remain in the cold because Miss Saurin choose to do so of her own accord. She was free to go to the library if she liked to do so. The reverend mother intended to have used the reception-room instead. It is not true that Miss Saurin was not free to leave her room for any purpose. She was free to go and come as she liked. There were five closets to which she had access. I have seen sister Mary Stanislaus and other sisters cleaning out Miss Saurin's room. Whoever slept in the room with her cleaned out the room. There are several rooms in the upper storey, which has been called an attic, which are used as cells. The room which she occupied is now used as a cell. It is not true that she had not facilities for washing. She had everything that is usually on a toilet table and wash-hand stand, the same as the other sisters.

Has Mrs. Star ever asked you your confession ? —Never.

Or what the priest said to you?—Never.

Would it be a proper thing to do?—I should consider it a very serious and improper thing to do.

Has she ever done so in the case of any sister to your knowledge ?—Never.

Examination continued : In March, while in the bath room, she asked reverend mother for leave to write to her brother ; or rather, not for leave exactly, but for materials—paper, pen, and ink. She got them and wrote a letter, which I took to reverend mother.

The LORD CHIEF JUSTICE : Did the reverend mother dictate what she should say ?—No, she was not in the room at all while Miss Saurin was writing.

Mr. RUSSELL : Was it closed or open ?—Open, I think.

Examination continued : After a little while reverend mother and Mrs. Kennedy came into the room with the letter, and Mrs. Star read it aloud. She had also with her two other letters. I think they were addressed by the reverend mother to Mr. Jas. Mathews and Mr. P. Mathews, uncles of the plaintiff, and brothers of Father Mathews. She told Miss Saurin that she would send those two letters a post before she sent hers, as she did not approve of something that was in Miss Saurin's letter. Miss Saurin asked her as a favour not to send them.

The LORD CHIEF JUSTICE : Did Mrs. Star read aloud the letters to the uncles ?—She did.

Examination continued : Miss Saurin said if reverend mother did not send the letters to her uncles she would write the letter to her brother over again. She did not suggest anything that Miss Saurin should say.

The LORD CHIEF JUSTICE : Did she point out the passage to which she objected ?—She read it all.

What was the passage ?—I forget. It seemed to be a very extraordinary letter altogether.

Examination continued : I do not know what has become of Miss Saurin's letter. She wrote a second letter. No one interfered with her. I do not remember that reverend mother suggested anything she should write. The only sister with a bad leg that was in Miss Saurin's room was Mrs. Neligan, and she had only a sprained knee.

Do you remember Mrs. Star destroying letters? Yes, I remember her destroying some letters she had received from Mrs. M'Keon. There was a bundle of letters, and these were amongst them.

When was that ?—In January, 1867.

After the action commenced ?—Yes.

Are you conscious of ever entertaining any ill-feeling towards Miss Saurin ?—No.

Did the reverend mother treat her unkindly ?— No ; I often heard her speak to Miss Saurin very kindly.

Cross-examined by the SOLICITOR-GENERAL : I am almost sure it was in March Miss Saurin wrote the letter I speak of. I was not present on the 18th of April when she wrote to her brother. I now remember the first letter was written on the Sunday after Ember Saturday, which was in the end of February.

Did Mrs. Star say to Miss Saurin, "If you do not write a very different letter to your brother I will write to your uncles and to your aunt too ? "— No. She said she would send the letters to her uncles a day before she sent the one Miss Saurin had written. She might have had her letter sent if she liked. (Letter produced.) This letter is, I think, in Mrs. Kennedy's handwriting. I did not know of her taking a copy of Miss Saurin's letter.

Mrs. Kennedy was asked whether she wrote the letter, and she said it was not, she thought, in her handwriting. Sister Mary Dawson wrote exactly like her. She often mistook Sister Mary Dawson's writing for her own.

The LORD CHIEF JUSTICE : I have compared the writing with your deposition. Have you any doubt that it is your handwriting ?—Mrs. Dawson's writing and mine are exactly alike.

Is there any doubt that the letter is a genuine copy?

The SOLICITOR-GENERAL : Not the least, my lord.

The LORD CHIEF JUSTICE : I think it is more likely to be your writing, Mrs. Kennedy, than Mrs. Dawson's.

Mrs. Kennedy: She has changed her handwriting since. (Laughter.) She used to copy mine at first. It is quite true. I would not hesitate a moment to say it was my handwriting if I thought it was.

The LORD CHIEF JUSTICE : As a matter of opinion I think it is yours. But so long as it is a genuine copy, it matters very little.

Cross-examination continued : Was not this letter in truth the original, and was not the letter sent to Mr. Patrick Saurin copied from that ?—Oh, no. The letter from which that was copied was written by Miss Saurin herself.

You say the first letter which was not sent was burned ?—Yes.

Why was it burned and a copy kept of the letter which was sent ?—It seems to me to be very natural. It was destroyed soon after it was written, and not with the letters of Mrs. M'Keon.

Is the fair effect of your evidence that, except that some one accompanied her, Miss Saurin was free to do whatever the other sisters could do ?—Yes.

Was she treated the same as you were as to clothes, except that she had secular clothes provided for her ?—Yes, except that she would not change her clothes as often as we did.

As to food ?—She was treated exactly as we were.

As to lodging ?—Yes, she had better lodging than we had, as the bath dressing-room is considered the most comfortable room in the house.

Had Miss Saurin the opportunity of being fed as well, lodged as well, and clothed as well as any one else in the house ?—Yes. The secular dress was fully as warm as ours was, and her food and lodging as good or better, as I have stated.

Your answer does not apply to the brown dress in which she went away ?—No ; but so far as I saw it, for the upper part was covered with her shawl, it looked very well.

Did you see the stockings she went away in ? I do not know, but I saw her taking off her stockings at night and pinning them across her face—(laughter)—and she had as good stockings as we had. We all wear our stockings while they hold together.

Now were not her stockings the veriest old rags and tatters that ever a scarecrow was dressed up in ?—Not those I saw. She had good stockings provided for her to go away in on the 13th of February. I mended all the stockings from August, 1865, to January, 1866, and they were the same as we all had. There was nothing remarkable about them. We all, as I say, wear stockings while they hold together. (A person at the back of the court here hissed.)

The LORD CHIEF JUSTICE said that if the persons at the back of the court did not behave with decency he should have that part of the court cleared.

Cross-examination continued ; I have a suspicion that Miss Saurin used to tear her stockings. My evidence, as to "hearing her tongue" in the school as I passed through, applies to the period before 1861, when I had charge of the schools. She was a great source of distraction to me at times when there should be silence. She was always laughing and talking as I passed through, and there was only a partition between her school and mine, and I heard her through it.

You heard her constantly ?—Indeed I did, and at work lesson, when there should be silence.

But may there not be a little talking during stitching time ?—No : we taught the children self-control and moderation, and how to hold their tongues. (Laughter.)

May not a teacher make a class go off pleasantly by a little speaking ?—Certainly, if she had leave.

Then speaking without leave was her fault ?—I take it both ways. Disobedience and breach of school discipline. If you were in a large school yourself——

The SOLICITOR-GENERAL : I was once.

Witness : Well, if you had my experience you would know the benefit of silence in school. We are taught to make signs.

The SOLICITOR-GENERAL : That makes work very dull.

The LORD CHIEF JUSTICE : Well, that is no business of ours.

Witness : The inspector is very strict as to having silence in the school.

The SOLICITOR-GENERAL : Well, now, as to eating the raspberries, which for her sake I hope were strawberries, do you not all sometimes eat some ?—Yes, but not with cream.

If she had leave to eat them, would not the pantry be the place ?—Yes, if she had leave to do so there.

You know the pantry is the place where the queen " eat the bread and honey." (A laugh.)

The LORD CHIEF JUSTICE : No ; it was in the parlour. (Laughter.)

The SOLICITOR-GENERAL (to witness) : Now, did you think it a very grave offence ?—Oh, I did, very bad indeed ; it was so contrary to what I had been taught.

But was it bad in itself to eat a strawberry ?—It is not a great sin ; but eating an apple is not so either, and you know what has come of eating an apple once. (Much laughter.)

The SOLICITOR-GENERAL : There the sin was not the eating of the apple, but disobedience.

Witness : Here there was disobedience also.

The SOLICITOR-GENERAL : Very well. Now, rightly or wrongly, when she spoke of persecution, did she seem to think she was persecuted ?—I suppose she did when the thimble was changed, or she would not have said it.

Did she cry ?—No ; she was very angry, but I did not see a tear on her face.

It seemed to you very unreasonable ?—It seemed the most extraordinary scene I ever witnessed.

You had your back turned when she knelt ?—Yes.

And she said something about persecution ?—She did, and of being a poor creature. She spoke incoherently.

The LORD CHIEF JUSTICE : You heard her use the words " poor creature ?"—I did, my lord.

Cross-examination continued : She said something about never having stolen a farthing. That she said frequently at different times. I did not examine her finger on the occasion of the thimble being changed. I saw it next morning, when she put her hands up. There was no sore on the thimble finger. There was a chilblain on the next finger, but it was not worth talking about. I was frightened with her manner on the previous day. I am sure her thimble finger was not sore. I do not know whether there was grease on it or on the paper; I did not see any. It was after morning lecture she knelt down and begged pardon, and spoke of the mouldy bread.

Was what she said this, that she was sorry she did not eat the mouldy bread cheerfully?—No; she complained. She spoke incoherently.

Did she say a good deal that you could not understand?—She said some things I could not understand. She said something about saving her soul either that morning or the morning before. She was greatly excited.

Was she excited at first?—No, she did not appear to be so.

Did you ever see a person who was very unhappy breaking out in lamentation suddenly?—I cannot recollect.

Do you think it possible that she had been very unhappy, and was appealing to your sympathy? Well, if it was an appeal to sympathy I did not understand it as such. I took it to be a complaint.

An incoherent complaint?—Yes.

Now, with respect to the stripping, she asked to have her staylace mended, you say?—Yes, and I thought that reverend mother was in a difficulty. If she did not have her lace mended Miss Saurin would complain of neglect, and if she did I felt sure Miss Saurin would complain that she was stripped.

Then you knew she had complained of being stripped before?—I should not have been surprised if she said so.

Cross-examination continued: While undressing she said that, as God saw her, she never had told a lie in her life. I thought how I wished I could say the same.

You saw nothing more taken off her than was necessary for the mending of her staylace and habit?—Nothing.

Cross-examination continued: On that occasion reverend mother told her her absolution from vows had been received, and she advised her to get her friends to have her admitted as a boarder into a convent in France, and that her removal would save her a great deal of suffering.

Did any one look over your deposition?—Mrs. Star looked over the rough copy. The composition was mine. Some things were struck out of the rough copy, as reverend mother said my language was too strong. She told me to be moderate in what I said.

Now, you begin by saying, "From my first acquaintance with Miss Saurin I have been impressed with the idea that she was a most dangerous person; that she was very vain, and to gratify her vanity she would spare neither sister nor superior in her invectives." You say she told "uncalled-for and positive falsehoods;" that "intercourse with her would undermine the foundations of religion;" and that she made "false and unjust representations of her superiors." What was there stronger than that which you were made to strike out?—I do not remember. I had some difficulty in retaining that about the positive falsehoods, but I had good reason for saying it.

Cross-examination continued: I had no dislike for her. I always had great sorrow and compassion for her.

You wrote more in sorrow than in anger?—I wished to let the bishop know what I thought of her.

You say you did not dislike her.—I did not. I

used to fret for her. From the day she told me she had a strong will turned to evil I always pitied her, and felt sorrow that her life should be thrown away.

Is it unknown to you that good people sometimes speak strongly of themselves. St. Paul said, "Sinners, of whom I am chief."—Oh, it was not said in that way at all. I told her if she had a strong will she ought to turn it to good. She said it was turned to evil, and she had no power to change it.

Mrs. Collingwood, examined by Mr. CHARLES RUSSELL: I am a lay sister. My name in religion is Sister May. My duties did not bring me very much in contact with the plaintiff, but I saw something of her from 1858. In that year, when I was a pupil at the day-school, Miss Saurin taught needlework. She did not observe the rule of silence. It was not about the work she spoke. She tattled of her family, and asked me about my friends. I was asked in 1865, by the rev. mother, to write what I knew of the plaintiff. She said the bishop wanted to be informed what we knew. I said I could not write it myself. I then told Mrs. Star what I recollected of Sister May Elizabeth. Mrs. Star wrote it down.

(Deposition read, in which it was stated that Sister Mary Scholastica in 1859 closely questioned witness—then at school as a pupil—on the subject of courtship; and she added that she now blushed at the things she said—that she told her mother of these conversations, and she replied that the sister had an innocent heart, and saw no harm in it. Witness added in the deposition she saw the plaintiff kneel down to a priest in the schoolroom, pull things out of his hand, and ask him to go with her.)

Mr. RUSSELL: What was the name of the clergyman?—Mr. Motler.

What year was this in?—1858 or 1859.

This was at the convent school at Hull?—Yes, I was then a pupil.

Examination continued: Mr. Motler was fastening down some desks to the floor—arranging the school. He was using a screwdriver. Breakfast and lunch were provided for him. Miss Saurin came in. Mr. Motler was on his knees. She asked him to go with her.

The LORD CHIEF JUSTICE: Go where?—She did not say.

To Mr. RUSSELL: She said, "Mr. Motler, will you come?" He did not offer to go; so she knelt down, took the tools out of his hand, and said he should not do any more until he went with her. I afterwards heard his luncheon was waiting for him. Her conduct appeared to me to be very forward, and very different from any of the other nuns, who were very grave. I only meant to imply in my deposition that she was very forward.

Cross-examined by the SOLICITOR-GENERAL: You are quite sure as to the fact about the priest?—Yes; I believe it is the truth I am telling you.

You believe. Are you not quite sure?—Yes, I am. I saw it.

Did you communicate the fact to any one?—No; except to my mother.

Who else was present?—Another sister, Mrs. Dobson.

Is she alive?—No.

Any one else?—Five or six children; the eldest seven or eight years old.

Did the circumstance produce a great impression on you?—It did.

How old were you then?—About 21.

When did you mention the fact first to anyone in the convent?—Not until I was told to write to the bishop.

Did you tell Mrs. Kerr, when she wrote your deposition, that luncheon was awaiting Mr. Motler?—I think I did.

Are you certain?—I think I did; but I am not certain.

Was it read to you?—No; I read it myself.

Did it occur to you that the fact as to the luncheon ought to have been added?—It did not.

Well; did it occur to you that people might draw very unfavourable notions from it without the addition?—I did not know any one would see it but the bishop.

Did you think that the bishop would draw unfavourable conclusions?—No.

Tell me what did you mean by this passage: "Her conversations with me were most generally and usually on such subjects as courtship. I do not think there was a single young man of my acquaintance about whom she did not question me closely. She drew me out and encouraged me to speak on such subjects. She would go any lengths with me, so that I now blush to think of many things I said." Now what do you mean by that?—She asked me whether I had any admirers; whether I thought I would be married; and the ages, employments, and residences of the young men of my acquaintance.

Surely that is not what made you blush. Is that what you meant by the lengths she made you go?—Yes.

The ages and employments of young men?—Yes.

If that is all, I think I may venture to ask you to give me a notion of what made you blush?—It was so contrary to the religious spirit.

Yes; but you were not a religious then?—It is as a nun I blush to think of it. It was scarcely a proper thing for a nun to say.

Then again I ask, was it the ages of the young men, and what they were, that you referred to, and all you referred to? Is that what you really meant to say?—Yes.

Did it occur to you that any man, or I may say any woman either, would not draw from what you stated a strong impression as to what Miss Saurin was?—No.

Was the composition of the deposition yours or Mrs. Kerr's?—It is the sense of what I gave her, but I could not compose it myself.

Were you told to use very moderate language? That is all.

To Mr. MELLISH: I entered the convent in 1861. I was not thinking of being a nun when at school in 1859.

To the LORD CHIEF JUSTICE: Other sisters attended the school. They never spoke to me of these sort of matters. Once I spoke to one of them, and she reproved me so sharply, I never attempted to do so again.

Mrs. Fearon examined: My name in religion is Sister Mary Evangelista. I entered the convent in February, 1860. I had very little acquaintance with Miss Saurin until I went to Clifford in April, 1863. I stayed there till August, 1864. I then came to Hull. I was there till after the commission. I was housekeeper and refectorian for some months at Clifford. Miss Saurin taught a junior class in the school, and a grown class needlework. I was only a short time in Clifford when I observed Miss Saurin being very disobedient to the orders of the sister superior. On two occasions I heard her give a direct refusal to obey her, which I may remark is a breach of the vow of obedience. I knew her to do work which the sister superior desired her not to do. She was given needlework to do, and was directed to do no other work till that was done. I saw her, in the absence of the sister superior, do work of her own; and, when the sister superior returned, Miss Saurin hid her own work, and took up the other, which I considered very deceitful. She also spoke to externs, contrary to express directions given to her in consequence of her frequent breach of the rule of silence. She only observed the rule whenever she could get no one to speak to. Her manner also was something remarkably noisy in the house. Her class in school was disorderly, and made a great uproar, owing to her neglect. I heard her speaking to an aspirant for the position of lay sister, just before the mass—a time of solemn silence. The aspirant cried on another occasion, in consequence, as I thought, of something Miss Saurin said. Miss Saurin denied it, but I saw it. Once I saw her at a cupboard when she ought to have been in the school, and she ran away when she saw me. Evidently from her manner she had been caught doing something wrong. I heard her deny having spoken to externs, although I had seen her do so. Of her habit of telling falsehoods I can speak positively. She also took portions of the children's dinners; I have seen her do so.

To the LORD CHIEF JUSTICE: This occurred on several occasions.

To Mr. RUSSELL: She had no business to interfere with the children's dinners. She used the children very roughly, and in some instances tyrannically, as I considered.

Give an instance.

Witness: I remember a boy named Clarke, a rough boy, almost an idiot. She took him one day by the hair tightly, and shook him. The boy screamed. I went over, and she turned to me with quite a calm and smiling countenance and said, "Sister, what do you think of this child?" I replied, "I think so much of him that I will take him from you;" and I did. She also treated the sister of that boy roughly. On one occasion, having done so, the child cried, and Miss Saurin pinned the child's pinafore over her head, put her on a high stool, and used a strange expression.

What did she say: "Now roar, you big beauty." (Laughter.)

Examination continued: Miss Saurin had not to clean the stone steps at Clifford. She did no work that the other sisters did not do. If she cleaned the stoves, it was of her own accord. She was treated in all respects as the rest were. Mrs. M'Keon never ill-treated her—quite the contrary. She appeared to be quite a dupe to Miss Saurin—not to know her as well as others did. At Hull also there were frequent complaints of portions of the children's dinners being taken while Miss Saurin was at the schools. The better class of children brought nice things, and she took charge of them, although she had no business to do so. On one occasion I saw part of a currant cake in her hand, which had been brought by a child. I observed, and often wondered at, how patient Mrs. Star was with her. In word and manner Mrs. Star was kindness itself with her. I wrote to the bishop in August, without Mrs. Star's knowledge, and afterwards wrote a deposition. (Deposition read.)

Examination continued: Mrs. Star told us to be moderate in our language, and not to exaggerate anything. I honestly believed the statement contained in my deposition. I never was conscious of any feeling of ill-will towards Miss Saurin.

Cross-examined by the SOLICITOR-GENERAL: I did not think the depositions were being prepared over several days. Mine was done in one day, and I think the others were. I may have shown mine to some one else, but I do not remember. I composed mine on a slate, and then copied it. The direction to be moderate in our language was given to three or four of us at the same time.

Did she say much about it?—No; she gave us a few general hints—that the bishop desired us to write our experiences of Miss Saurin.

Cross-examination continued: My object in writing the letter to the bishop was to have Miss Saurin removed from the convent; and that, I suppose, was also the object of the other sisters who wrote.

Did you know her at all before 1863?—Not particularly. I remember once, in 1860, travelling with her between Clifford and Hull, and she made some remarks to me in the train which were disadvantageous to her superior, and which gave me an unfavourable impression.

Who were the superiors she spoke of?—Mrs. Star and Mrs. Delany, the sister superior at Clifford.

Are you sure as to Mrs. Delany?—Not quite. I am as to Mrs. Star. I know she spoke to others to the disadvantage of Mrs. Delany.

What did she say to the disadvantage of Mrs. Star?—I was going to Clifford as I was delicate, and she told me Mrs. Star was about to have put me in the kitchen when the fire would have ruined my health, and that it was at her earnest request I was sent to Clifford.

And that is what you meant by speaking to the disadvantage of Mrs. Star?—Yes; for it would have been unkind in Mrs. Star in my then state of health, to have put me in the kitchen.

Cross-examined: She gave me an unfavourable impression also, as I thought she was unhappy, from her sighs and her apparent sorrow; and I heard her crying, or what I supposed was crying.

Do you mean to impute that she was shamming?—No; but I did not see her crying; I heard her.

What were the two instances of flat refusal of which you spoke?—Once she refused to do work —to make a dress for a child.

She did it afterward, although badly, it is said? —Yes.

What was the other instance of flat disobedience? —The sister superior, who was reading to us, told her to come to the fire, and she spoke about being watched, and refused. She had no cause for saying she was watched. No other sister to my knowledge ever disobeyed orders in that way.

But the disobedience consisted in not coming to the fire?—Yes; but there was a great deal in her manner of doing it.

To whom did you refer when you said she spoke to externs?—The mother of the children and the girls in the night-school to whom she spoke about village news and Mrs. Grimstone.

Was not Mrs. Grimstone a great benefactress of your institution?—Well; yes.

You say that in a half sort of way—was she not?—She was a very charitable lady.

And gave money to the convent?—I cannot give information as to that. I have no right to know.

Do you mean to say that the subjects on which she talked to the girls were not the subjects then being taught?—I do. She spoke of other matters; and once, when I came up and overheard her, she put her finger down on the book suddenly, and said, "Spell that."

What brought the mothers of the children to the school?—To speak something about the children.

And was there anything wrong in the person having charge of the children saying a few words to their mothers?—Not a few words, if they were on the subject of the children. Miss Saurin had no permission to stop the length of time she used to do with them.

Do you mean to say that the main body of the conversation did not relate to the children—it was unnecessary?—The conversation lasted too long. I do not refer to any short conversation. The breaches of rule in this respect were frequent. I reported her, but not on all the occasions.

Cross-examination continued: The stone steps were not washed and cleaned by two orphan girls from the village. Miss Saurin had to see to their being done, and to the school being cleaned by some one. If there was no one else to do it, it would be her duty to get it done. That would be the duty of any sister. I never saw her wash the stone steps, and I do not think she could have done it without my knowledge.

Did you like her?—I did not dislike her. I had no particular feeling one way or the other. Did you know the opinion Mrs. Star had of Miss Saurin when you wrote your deposition?— I did not. Neither Mrs. Star nor Mrs. Kennedy ever gave me the least intimation of what they thought of her.

To Mr. MELLISH: It would have been a breach of rule to have told me what they thought.

Mr. MELLISH said there was only one other sister who had made depositions, and she was in charge at Hull. He purposed to read her deposition.

The SOLICITOR-GENERAL said he had no objection to the deposition being read.

The LORD CHIEF JUSTICE said he was glad the depositions had been put in evidence. If the jury thought from their contents, viewed in the light of surrounding circumstances, they were made *malâ fide*, the count in the declaration might be sustained. On the other hand, if the jury thought that they were made *bonâ fide* and for the purpose of invoking the admitted jurisdiction of the visitors, he should tell the jury that the occasion was privileged.

The SOLICITOR-GENERAL said he should have put them in at first had he seen them. He had acted on the rule of not putting in what he had not seen.

The LORD CHIEF JUSTICE: It is very right that they should be in evidence, and we have them now.

The deposition of Sister Mary Stanislaus was then read. She said she had only been one year in the convent with Miss Saurin, and saw very little of her ; but the impression she had of her was that she was full of deceit and hypocrisy, and did not scruple to break the rules.

FIFTEENTH DAY.—*Saturday, Feb. 20.*

"I AM afraid," said one of the learned counsel, to-day, in answer to a plaintive appeal from the bench, " that this case will last all next week." There was laughter at the words of Mr. Mellish, as there possibly would be at the most doleful announcement or the most serious remark that might be made at these hilarious but lengthy sittings at Nisi Prius. Just as, in the old story, the tractable member of Parliament who had been ordered to cry "Hear, hear," whenever the leader of his party had anything to say, saluted with those approving syllables, the right hon. gentleman's statement in committee, that the speaker had just gone home in a state of the greatest anguish from a sudden attack of the gout, so there is pretty sure to be laughter at any little digression or novel incident in these proceedings before Lord Chief Justice Cockburn. The line taken by the defendants, that of putting in evidence relating to circumstances upon which Miss Saurin was not cross-examined, will, says the Solicitor-General, entail the duty on his part of bringing forward a great deal of additional evidence in reply. At this dismal representation of matters, deplored in very grave accents by the judge, and met with dismayed looks by the jury, the mysterious public in the Court of Queen's Bench "laugh consumedly." The witnesses to-day were two, the Roman Catholic bishop having authority over the convents at Hull and Clifford, and his secretary. Their examination was extended by the reading of letters ; and the impugned orthography of Sister Mary Scholastica—whose name "in religion," oddly assorts with the character bestowed on her as a secular instructress—was made a topic, first by the Solicitor-General, who could only find one little fault with his client's epistle, the spelling, that is to say, of "atone," with a double t ; then by Mr. Russell, who noted the absence of an h from the word "character ; and then by the Lord Chief Justice, who observed that "perhaps" was written with a final e, and "since" without one. These trifling lapses, he charitably added, were nothing more than might occur to anybody in the hurry of writing. Indeed, there was the excuse of agitation as well as of haste for Miss Saurin's little slips of the pen. Untidy spelling has been a weakness with great men as well as good women ; and the late Duke of Wellington, who seldom addressed a letter without putting the word "Immediate" on the cover, was accustomed to spell that word with a single m.

Dr. Robert Cornthwaite sworn, and examined by Mr. CHARLES RUSSELL : You are the Roman Catholic bishop of Beverley ?—I am.

When were you appointed?—In September, 1861.

The convents in question were under your jurisdiction ?—They were.

State the extent of your jurisdiction as ordinary in respect of the convents. —I am superior of the convents in my diocese.

The LORD CHIEF JUSTICE : What is implied in the word "superior?"—I am to see to the observance of the rules.

Mr. RUSSELL : Does your authority extend to the removal of any member of the community ?—Certainly.

For what cause and under what circumstances ? —If their conduct is such as to tend to the disunion and destruction of the community, even though in the individual there was not necessarily any grave fault.

Now, would habitual disregard of the rules be a sufficient cause ?—Certainly ; because that tends directly to the destruction of unity, and existence of the community.

Does that apply even when the acts of disobedience do not involve grave and moral faults ?—Yes.

Is there an appeal against your judgment, even if exercised erroneously, and if so, of what nature?—There is an appeal to the Archbishop, my metropolitan, and from him to the Holy See.

Does your authority extend to directing the manner in which an inquiry is to be conducted ?—Yes, I am to obtain evidence sufficient to justify action on my part.

And you are to judge of the means of obtaining it?—Yes.

The LORD CHIEF JUSTICE : I understand your answer to be that there must be evidence sufficient to justify your action, but that you can obtain that evidence in any manner you think proper?—Yes.

Mr. RUSSELL : Now, subject to the two appeals you have mentioned, are you to judge of the sufficiency, or otherwise, of a case for expulsion ? —Yes.

Has the exercise of the power of expulsion anything to do with absolution from vows ?—I feel a difficulty in using the word expulsion, because that involves necessarily penalty. I should prefer your using the word dismissal.

The SOLICITOR-GENERAL : We have had a very colourless word heretofore—the word removal.

The LORD CHIEF JUSTICE : Or you might use the old word amoval.

Mr. RUSSELL : Has that power of removal necessarily anything to do with the question of dispensation from vows?—Nothing whatever.

That is to say you have power to remove without dispensing ?—Certainly.

The LORD CHIEF JUSTICE : Leaving the party free to go into another convent ?—Yes.

Mr. RUSSELL : Would removal from a particular community necessarily deprive her of the character of a nun, if her vows were not dispensed ?—No ; it would only deprive her of the right of being in that particular house.

But practically would it not involve the impossibility of her entering any other house?—It would.

Now are the vows taken by sisters of mercy what are called simple vows ?—They are declared to be so.

The LORD CHIEF JUSTICE : What does that mean ?—There are vows solemn and simple. Absolution from solemn vows is reserved for the Holy See. A bishop can absolve from simple vows.

Mr. RUSSELL : And these are simple vows?—Yes.

The three vows are poverty, obedience, and chastity. Is there anything peculiar as to the last ?—Yes, it is reserved for the Holy See in every case.

Then, in a certain sense, it is a solemn vow?—No, it is a reserved simple vow.

As regards the vows of obedience and poverty, have you got yourself any power as to these ?—Yes, I can dispense from them for sufficient cause.

And that without any special authority or rescript from Rome, but by virtue of your office ?—Yes.

Now, in 1861 was your attention first called to the convent in question in reference to the writing of clandestine letters ?—I do not know when that first came to my knowledge.

Was that the first matter you heard of ?—The first important matter.

You remember being in communication with the Rev. Father Mathews on that question ?—He came to me in March, 1862, I think, but I do not remember his mentioning that point. Then some letters passed. He called upon me in March, and he either saw me or wrote to me in May. I set out for Rome about the 15th of May, and returned about the 15th of June.

In the interval had you been aware that negotiations were going on for the removal of Sister Scholastica to Baggot-street, Dublin?—No.

Do you remember receiving this letter from Mrs. Star, dated 4th August, 1862, stating that the negotiations for her removal to Baggot-street had failed, and making certain charges against her?—Yes.

In consequence of receiving that letter, did you reserve the making of your visitation to the convent ?—No.

Then why did you do so ?—Owing to the receipt of a letter from Sister Scholastica herself.

The SOLICITOR-GENERAL asked if the letter was to be produced.

Mr. RUSSELL said he was about to read it.

The SOLICITOR-GENERAL stated that it was the first time the letter had been mentioned. He had never heard of it, or received a copy of it.

Mr. RUSSELL then read the letter, which was as follows :

Convent of Our Lady of Mercy, Clifford,
Sept. 28, 1862.

My dear Lord,—In duty and obedience I address your lordship. I never felt anything so much. I I would willingly, as I told rev. mother, submit to any penance rather than your lordship should get any trouble by me ; and that was the reason for writing to my rev. uncle. I thought I could get quietly to Baggot-street. It is now past six years since I came to England. I entered religion shortly after our present rev. mother. From my entrance I was constantly employed with her in the schools for four years. When she came here she had some trouble with her community. She wrote several times for me. God alone knows all I went through to get here. No one in the community seemed to be able to do anything to please but me, until our numbers increased. I first perceived a change after rev. mother returned from a visit to Ireland. I think she then thought she could get enough of postulants, and that she preferred her own training, as she changed many of the old customs. Besides, I knew the circumstances of many of the sisters, some who were once under me in the House of Mercy at Baggot-street, which she did not like. Though I saw evidently reverend mother was very much changed towards me, for a long time it never struck me she wished to get rid of me until lately. Don't for a moment think, my lord, I believe I have no faults. Far, far from it ; nor do I know a member of the community who has not. I must say reverend mother has made many charges against me which are certainly false. I collected more than six from my mother (a secular). 1st. I took presents from children. Nothing could be more untrue ; as I never took a single thing from a child in my life. 2nd. I interfered with the novices. I have been down here for three years, and have had nothing whatever to do with novices ; they do not come here. 3rd. So particular about my dress, &c. I never once, since I entered religion, made a remark about my dress—I mean, to complain—though it was often very bad, so much so, when I was in Ireland two years ago, reverend mother gave me a present of a habit. Neither have I cost the community a shilling for dress, &c. since I entered. 4th. My great affection for my parents, &c. I justly esteem and respect them. I believe there never lived better or more affectionate. I used to write affectionately to them perhaps four or five times a year, but since reverend mother made some remark to me about it I have not written now for two years but three times, which pains them more than a little. 5th. My writing to my reverend uncle, which reverend mother would never have known, only I acknowledged it to her myself in my private manifestation of conscience, and which your lordship will see by our rule she had no right to make use of as she has done. She first made me put it on paper for her and sign my name to it—told two of the community and others. On the 27th of July reverend mother dictated a note for me to send my reverend uncle, begging of him to get me into his convent. She told me your lordship left all to her to settle, and out of Hull I should go. She also said your lordship asked her to write to Baggot-street to try and get them to take me back, as if any one would take a sister who she told them wrote clandestinely to my uncle. She does not know, nor do I wish she should, I had the permission of my former confessor to do so. One note I wrote I trust your lordship will see, as reverend mother has it ; the other was a few lines just to let my uncle know the sister here found a note I had to send to him. I feel I did wrong in writing, but I have tried my best to atone for it ever since. When I explain all to your lordship I think you will forgive me. During the retreat I begged most humbly, promising to undergo any penance either your lordship or she wished, only let it be settled. I could never tell you all I fretted, both night and day, until I felt my mind injured for want of sleep. After I got a letter from my uncle, who considered it would ruin my character and happiness for life to go to his convent, reverend mother told me then it was in the bishop's hand, who was quite ready to dispense me with my vows, and if I remained here it would be most miserable for me, as she was determined to punish me. I should first give up all I had, wear the cast clothes of the community, never again look on myself as a choir sister, but as the drudge of all, to which I perfectly agreed if your lordship thought proper. Then she said she had only to call the chapter, and that no bishop or any one could go against it ; that she could send me home to my parents. I said I should go to the work-house before I could go to my dear father and mother. My lord, I only regret now I did not make the use our good God intended of all my [word omitted]. Were I to commence again—I trust I shall do better in future. Forgive me, my lord, for trespassing upon your precious time. If I were only fortunate enough to see your lordship I could explain all, but can never do so in writing. I trust your lordship will forgive this untidy, un-connected letter. If you knew the way I have tried to write now and then, as I am scarcely allowed five minutes alone. I felt I was bound to make an attempt, though I begged of my uncle and Mr. Cullamore to ask you to excuse me until I could see your lordship. Will it be too great a favour to beg your lordship will let me know, through Rev. Mr. Cullamore, if you wish me to write again, and what your lordship re-quires? I feel I have not said half what I would wish. But I know not when I can write again. I shall do my best to answer any questions your lord-ship wishes to put, if I only knew. My dear lord, in your great charity I feel you will not attribute this untidy letter, full of mistakes, to any want of respect on my part, but to the real cause—want of time. No one ever saw it.—I am, my dear lord, ever your lordship's obedient and humble child in Jesus Christ,

                    Sister M. SCHOLASTICA SAURIN.

If I ever have the pleasure of seeing your lord-ship, I shall explain all to you with God's help. I feel much happier since my uncle saw your lordship.

Mr. RUSSELL remarked that several words in the letter were mis-spelt.

The SOLICITOR-GENERAL: I have looked over the original and admit that "atone" is spelt with two "t's," and "they" once written for "the."

The LORD CHIEF JUSTICE (having examined the letter) : There are some other mistakes, but nothing that may not be attributed to the hurry of writing, and the circumstances under which the letter was written.

The SOLICITOR-GENERAL : They certainly do not lessen its importance, and it is now produced for the first time.

A juror expressed a wish to see the original letter.

The LORD CHIEF JUSTICE said that the originals of all the letters should be placed before them.

Mr. RUSSELL (to witness): When did your lordship first show that letter to any one ?—Not until May, 1868.

In consequence of the receipt of the letter you determined to make a visitation of the convent ? —Yes. I made a visitation in November. I did not tell any one that I had a special object beyond the ordinary visitation. The visitation lasted one entire day and part of two others.

What is the object of a visitation ?—To ascer-tain that the community has provision for its spiritual wants, the requisites for the altar, and other sacred things ; and next the great object is to know whether the rules are kept by the whole of the sisters, and whether there are any com-plaints.

What are the means of informing your mind as to these things ?—I see every sister by herself, and hear what she has to say.

What conclusion did you come to after that visitation ?—That I had heard nothing which authorized me conscientiously to take any further steps for the present. As far as general obser-vation of the rules went, I was satisfied.

Can you recall whether you found things in a satisfactory state in the convent ?—I was satisfied on all points except the one which I wanted to hear most about.

Which was ?—In reference to Sister Mary Scholastica.

Why were you dissatisfied as to that ?—I was unable to come to any conclusion. I had hopes that possibly things might get better and im-prove.

I believe that soon after this your lordship fell into bad health ?—The following year, 1863, was a year of enormous labour. In 1864 and 1865 I was in bad health.

You recollect a question arising as to the ad-mission of Father Saurin to see his sister in July, 1864 ?—I do. I wrote to the reverend mother to give Mr. Saurin permission to see Sister Scholastica.

The letter was to the following effect :—

I have heard that you refused permission to Mr. Saurin to see his sister the second time he came. This was a grave error of judgment. You should have taken into consideration that he could have compelled you to grant his request, and you should not have run the risk of his doing so. To get you out of the difficulty, I should recommend you to write to him and say you now have per-mission, and will offer no further objection to the reasonable claims of a brother on a sister. You must believe that I have the best interests of the community at heart.

You received a reply from the rev. mother, in which she says :—

You must not imagine that our confidence is shaken by your decision in the case of Sister Scholastica. Her presence here is a heavy cross, but we respect your lordship's motives in over-ruling our wishes. And the reason for the feeling you seem to ascribe to a studied reserve, proceed-ing from want of trust in yourself, arises from her presence in our community. We regard her as an enemy living among us; she dislikes us and her superiors, and as long as she continues among us we cannot enjoy peace. We long for the day when you can say that we may send her back to Dublin. Rest satisfied that I shall do nothing without the authority of our holy rules and constitutions. The issue of the visitation gave her and her supporters an immense triumph over us, of which they show a great appreciation. If she was troublesome and exacting before, she is now so to an extreme, and will have all her rights on all occasions.

The bishop replied that he had.

Mr. RUSSELL: I believe nothing more important happened until you received from Mrs. Star the letter dated 27th April, 1865?—That is so.

The letter, which was as follows, was then read:—

Convent of Our Lady of Mercy, Hull,
April 27, 1865.

My Lord,—After many prayers for guidance, and after weighing well before God the whole matter in my mind, I have formed the resolution of resigning the office of superioress of this community, for which I beg your lordship's consent. My reasons are simply these: It is plain that either Sr. M. Scholastica or I must yield. She will not, consequently I must. It is not my intention to make any charge against her. I only wish to speak of myself and the community. I feel that I have not sufficient mental or physical strength to bear up against the anxiety she occasions me on account of the other sisters. I was obliged, as a matter of convenience, to remove her from Clifford last June. Since she has been here the whole spirit of the house has changed. We are not like the same happy community we were. Although peace is in the exterior, a settled gloom and constraint appear to have rested on us all. Recreation, which was once so joyous, is now a mere formality, and when the time of silence comes we feel relieved. There is not one of the professed sisters who does not bear an anxious and troubled look. If this tells on all as it tells on me, the consequences may be serious, for I feel as one paralysed, and without heart, mind, or spirit for anything. I do not shrink from trouble and anxiety so long as they do not go between my soul and God, for I am willing to sacrifice health, life, happiness, reputation, everything short of my salvation, for the happiness and welfare of this community, which is dearer and more precious to me than all in this world beside. I feel that my soul is in peril in my present position, and that I ought to resign for that reason and for the good of the community. I do not possess the virtue and talent to govern in trying circumstances. It is a fault of character in me, which time has rather increased than lessened, that I take things too much to heart, and am too solicitous about those who are under my care. Another may govern and effect the good I had hoped to do with more ease and merit to herself, and more fruit to others, than I could in consequence of my natural disposition. The time prescribed by our rule for the resignation of superiors is Saturday, within the octave of the Ascension, when I hope and pray that your lordship will release me from my present dangerous responsi

bility. The election should take place on the following Thursday. In giving up my charge of the sisters it makes me happy to give my testimony to their sterling goodness. They are, with that one exception, docile, simple, self-sacrificing, and laborious. They love God, love each other, love their rules, love the poor. I do not think your lordship need apprehend any unpleasantness in the community in consequence of that change. The sisters are quite prepared for it, and I expect that all will be tranquil. Hoping your lordship will accede to my request, and begging your blessing, I am, my lord, with much respect, your obedient servant in Jesus Christ,

SISTER MARY JOSEPH.

The reply of the bishop and a letter written by Mrs. Star on the 1st of May were then read:—

Dear Rev. Mother,—Your letter has caused me great anxiety, and I have taken time to consider my reply. You say that either you or Sister Scholastica must yield. I cannot admit the alternative. If it be a question of one submitting to the other, the sister must yield to you. Where is your confidence in God? As He has placed you in your position, He will support you.

" Convent of our Lady of Mercy,
" Hull, May, 1, 1865.

" My Lord,—I am sorry your lordship has not granted my petition, but I still hope you will when you hear how things are. Sister Mary Scholastica need not know that she is the cause of the change. It is a most painful duty with me to enter into the subject of her failings, so much of the past must be brought to bear upon the present. The principal points in which she errs are poverty, obedience, and truth. If I close my eyes to her faults, she perseveres in them with confidence. If admonished in all mildness and charity, she denies them, and continues to transgress. If reproached with severity, or her faults proved, she assumes a tone and manner of defiance. If given a penance, which is rarely done, she continues it longer than she was desired, to show how little she cares about it. If she seek to speak to me in private, it is merely to give vent to the bitterness she feels against me, and to reproach me with cruelty, tyranny, and persecution. Of late she has made the same accusations against me in the presence of the community. With regard to poverty, I must refer to the past. We have long suspected her of stealing. Suspicions are not proofs; therefore I have been silent on that head. Within the last year I have discovered that my suspicions were well grounded, and that her offences can be proved by different members of the community, who through a mistaken charity, kept their knowledge to themselves, until by chance I made inquiries on the subject. I believe her late conduct has been occasioned by her vexation at the precautions which have been quietly taken to guard her against indulging this propensity in the convent; but, like an incurable disease, if healed in one place it breaks out in another with greater malignity. We now fear she steals from the school children. She is so artful, so dexterous, that it will be almost impossible for any one to detect her; but the eyes of the young are piercing, and their tongues ever ready to publish the weaknesses of others, and disgrace may come upon religion and upon us before we are aware of it. This last suspicion occurred to the minds of three of the sisters almost simultaneously about different things, and without communicating with each other on the subject. When at confession a few days ago I mentioned my trouble about Sister M. Scholastica to N. N. for the first time, and told him of my fear of a coming scandal. He told me I was bound in conscience to make it known to your lordship.

Mr. RUSSELL : I believe your lordship received a letter from Father Mathews, dated the 27th of May, 1865? — Yes. (In the letter Father Mathews complained that the rev. mother prevented free communication between Sister Scholastica and her friends, and that he himself had been subjected to a cold surveillance ; and he asked the bishop to see Sister Scholastica, as he could not go over to Hull for two months.)

Examination continued : I wrote to Mrs. Star on the 5th July :—

Springfield House, Leeds, July 5, 1865.
Dear Rev. Mother—Be calm, patient, and full of trust in God. I go to Ireland on the 11th, and will take steps to settle your difficulty. What convent did S. M. S. come from in Ireland ?—Where did she spend her noviceship, and where was she professed ?—With a blessing, I am yours in Christ,
ROBT. CORNTHWAITE.

I was going to Ireland for the benefit of my health, and hoped while there to see Father Mathews, in order to arrange the matter.

The LORD CHIEF JUSTICE : In what way ?— To arrange for the removal of Sister Scholastica to another community. But I was not able to see him.

The witness's next letter to Mrs. Star and her reply were then read :—

Dear Rev. Mother,—I hope that you are quite certain about the thefts and other things, and that the facts are provable. I was unable to move efficaciously in the matter without facilities from the Holy See. I asked for them long ago. They were, unfortunately, missent, and have only reached me this morning. In case of expulsion, will Baggot-street do anything in the way of dowry ?

My dear Lord—Your direction shall be obeyed. The rev. father shall see his sister as often as he pleases. I could not give him my confidence, as your lordship thinks might be well ; but if I see him, I will urge him to obtain a change for his sister. But my reason for declining to speak frankly to any of the family is, that in 1862 Mrs. Saurin begged me, with the earnestness of a mother, to speak to her of her child's conduct. I did not suspect the snare. I felt for her, and I told her all. In consequence, she expressed gratitude, and told me I had done right, and that her daughter would have no sympathy from her. And when she had heard all she could, she distorted the case against me, with the help of her brother the priest (the Rev. Mr. Mathews)—an able, clever man of the world, who fears disgrace to his family—and her representations have been submitted to your lordship. We know the sequel.

Although her brother is a religious, yet, at the beginning of his sister's career, he helped to make her what she now is. He described her former superiors at Baggot-street as "tyrants" and "tormenters :" his letters breathed a spirit of sarcasm and contempt for the community, calculated to awaken a spirit of insubordination and uncharitableness. I cannot blame him for this, for her powers of misrepresentation would raise an edifice of falsehood on the least foundation of truth.

On the 15th of August the witness wrote :—

Dear Rev. Mother,—Bear in mind that everything will need to be fully proved, to render my powers of any avail. I send a fervent blessing to you all.

And on the 21st of August the following :—

Dear Mother Superior.—Be good enough to receive this information I now give you. Give the enclosed to the Rev. Mr. Saurin. It is an order to remove his sister from the convent. Prepare clothes. I will send absolution from her vows.
P.S.—You must still send me your papers, and let me have all the information you can.

You had before this time received letters from several of the sisters at Hull ?—Yes, from Mrs. Kennedy, Mrs. Nelligan, Mrs. Kerr, and Mrs. Dawson, who is since dead. I received them on the 9th August. I subsequently received what are called the depositions. In the postscript of the letter of the 21st August I spoke of the necessity of sending Mrs. Star's deposition, which I had not then received. The other depositions I received on the 20th August.

Did you consider the whole matter before you wrote the letter of the 21st August :—Certainly.
Gravely?—Gravely.
What was your lordship's decision?—That I should quietly arrange with her friends for her removal. I felt that I could conscientiously do so.
And if you could not, what then?—I felt that for the sake of the peace of the community I should try and do so myself.
Did you receive a letter from her Jesuit brother, Father Saurin, dated 14th September?— I did.
(The letter was read. It stated that he should have written from Bordeaux to say that he was anxious to see his poor sister, whom he had not seen for years ; that he was about to go to Hull, trusting to receive his lordship's protection against uncharitable treatment ; that he could not tell how his brethren in France sympathised with him on the fact that his mother had to leave Hull without seeing his sister twice, and he entreated his lordship's merciful care for poor Sister Scholastica, to whom he could not write even then.)
Examination continued : I did not see Father Saurin when he came to Hull.
You wrote, I believe, to Mrs. Star, enclosing a note for Father Saurin ?—I did.
The following letters were read :—

Dear Rev. Mother,—Tell the father when you give him this note, that I have told you the nature of the contents. If he refuses to remove his sister tell him I will take care to have her removed. And that on no consideration will I permit her to remain.

Rev. and dear Father,—It is a fortunate circumstance that you should be making a visit to Hull, as it has become necessary to require the removal of your sister from the community . . . I should prefer her being accompanied by you. Under the conviction that no other community will receive her, and that her religious obligations are a source of danger rather than of merit. I have thought it proper to commute them, and I will send the necessary documents. Upon application to the mother-house, your sister will receive her dower.

Examination continued: I received a letter from Mrs. Star on the 15th of September.

The letter, which was as follows, was read:—

Father Saurin is still in Hull. Upon reading your letter to him he questioned the validity of the absolution without application from the person to be absolved. He was quiet, but steadily refused to take his sister, and said he would advertise his uncle, the Rev. T. Mathews, and leave the matter to him to manage, as he had done hitherto. I do not think he would be induced to remove his sister. He said he did not wish to mix himself up with the quarrels. The family are clever, and I believe they will either try to gain time by temporising, and in the meantime take measures to give trouble, or they will come over here and cause great scandal by publicity. I think the only way is to anticipate them by sending her home at once. They cannot complain of this, as her brother refused to take her.

Mr. RUSSELL: Your lordship replied on the 17th of September in that year, 1865: "Do not be in too great a hurry. Matters are fast tending towards a commission. They are taking such a course, that a commission only will meet the case? —I did.

Had you made up your mind at that time that she should leave the community?—Yes.

Either by the voluntary action of her friends or by action on your lordship's part?—I had.

Did you receive a letter from her Jesuit brother, Father Saurin, on the 16th Sept.?—I did.

The SOLICITOR-GENERAL said that he had never seen this letter. No copy of it had been furnished. It was now produced for the first time.

Mr. RUSSELL then read the letter, which was as follows:—

Springfield, Sept. 15, '65.
My dear Lord,—I waited two days at Hull, and received your letter. Mrs. Star assured me the causes for which you absolved my darling sister were grave faults against vows and rules, as of course they should be. Of course, also, they were known to you, and from you I was to learn them; but in the uncertainty as to where I should see you, I saw my poor darling this morning, and interrogated her under the secrecy of my priestly character, when she revealed a mystery that exceeded all the horrors I ever heard or knew. Her story is equal to anything I saw in the lives of the saints, and the horrors of which she has been made the victim, far surpass anything that has entered the minds of the most fanatical enemies

of the convents. Under operation, which was repeated four times. "I hesitated for a moment," said she, "when Christ, as it were, appeared to me, bound and stript at the pillar; I raised my eyes to heaven, and the rev. mother said, "See how her eyes turn." I thought my body was falling to pieces, and I cried aloud, "Yes, my Lord, I will, I will make the sacrifice." When telling me this, my lord, I saw she was falling against me, and you may guess what was my struggle and my pain to seem unmoved. Her crimes are those of Christ my Lord, by whom she is even physically sustained. She is starved and naked (for even her covering by night and day is gone.) She has been watched lest she might eat the bread of the poor children, and though starved she made up her mind to die rather than taste a morsel of it. She has been dexterously kept from any interview with your lordship, and she knows she is dying a victim. For of course she would rather die ten thousand times than leave the convent or commit one single sin. She has been kept in absolute silence, my lord, and no one allowed to speak to her during these two years, her greatest dread being lest she might lose her reason under these horrors. The train is going, my lord, and you will pardon this scrawl. Mrs Star has two solid reasons to try and keep my poor darling sister out of Baggot-street, and she scrupled not to murder her soul and body to gain that end.—Adieu, my lord, and protect my darling saint, ever your obedient,

MATHEW SAURIN, S.G.

Mr. RUSSELL: Do you know what kind of a person this Father Saurin is?—I do not. I have never seen him.

When you read the letter, 'did you think he meant that his sister had been scourged and bound?—I thought it most absurd.

But did you think that she had been scourged? —I thought it a made-up story.

He says, "Under operation, which was repeated four times, ... She thought her body was falling to pieces;" what did that suggest to your mind?—I could not understand it.

Did your lordship do anything in consequence of that letter?—No.

What was the next step you took?—I wrote to Father Mathews.

Examination continued: I received a letter from Mrs. Star, dated 17th September. (Letter read.)

Father Saurin came again to the convent. He spoke to me in a strange way. He said that his uncle (the Rev. T. Mathews) was a wicked man, who would go any length to punish those who should displease him, and that on one occasion he had done so when the question was as to his sister's expulsion. He ascertained that a claim of damages would lie for £5,000, and that if it cost the family that sum they would not mind it. I said that if such a course were taken the sympathy would be with the community, but £20,000 would not compensate them for the public disgrace which would arise from the evidence given at the trial. I said, also, that there was no ground for a lawsuit, as his sister had not been decoyed. She had begged to be admitted, and she now remained in the community against our will; that I had applied to her family to remove her, and urged her to go elsewhere. His object, I think, was to intimidate me, and when he perceived he could not do so, he changed his tone. They might try to bring against us an action for defamation of character, if they were informed of what had been stated against her. They will try and get the information, and then take proceedings against us. There is, therefore, every reason for our being prudent. The rev. father saw his sister a long time. I do not know what he told her.

What was it that suggested the commission to your lordship's mind?—The fact that Father Saurin refused to take his sister away, and that he had partly questioned the validity of the dispensation, and also the statements he made in his strange letters.

Then it was partly in consequence of the letter of Father Saurin that the commission suggested itself?—Yes ; I should add that Father Saurin wrote another letter, returning my order to see his sister, and declining to comply with my request to take her away.

A letter of Mrs. Star's to witness was next read, dated 18th September. She stated that the commission would be very painful to them all, but that the facts would stand ; and, respecting the statements in the "deposition," she said that everything that was stated as positive could be verified in the most solemn manner if necessary.

The following letters were then read. The first, from Father Mathews, was dated 28th July, 1865 :—

My dear Lord,—Shortly before your visit to Rome I had an interview with you relative to the unpleasantness exhibited by the rev. mother towards my niece, at present at Clifford. Your lordship kindly promised me to investigate the matter by commission or otherwise. I hope by this time you are safely returned. I do not wish to say one word to influence your judgment ; but in truth, I must say that from her childhood I never knew material for a better nun than there was in her.

Sept. 15, 1865.

Dear Father Mathews,—I wished to have seen you, as I wished to speak to you as to your niece, to induce you to have her recalled home. I feel myself under the necessity of taking the initiative, and the visit of her brother is the most fitting occasion for a settlement. I have tried to follow out your wishes, but I have come to the conclusion that the best interests of the community require her removal. I will only add that her dowry will be repaid upon application to the mother house.—Your faithful servant in Christ,

R. ✠ CORNTHWAITE.

On the 20th of September the bishop wrote to the Rev. Mr. Mathews this further letter :—

I wrote you on the 15th to inform you that, being under the necessity of requiring the removal of your niece, I intended to place her under the charge of her brother, and I then expected to hear from you in reply. Her brother, however, refused to take charge of her, and he wished to see me, but I was from home. Her brother wished the whole matter to be referred to you, and I wrote to ask you if you or any of your family intend to take steps for the removal of your niece. I hope so for your sake and her's. If I have to take steps for the purpose, I shall feel bound to do so. Her brother has raised two

questions. He doubts the validity of the dispensation, and he speaks of his sister as a suffering saint, and makes a serious charge against the community. This representation has in no degree affected my first decision, and I have to request the removal of your niece. I feel I ought to endeavour to satisfy you, and therefore in this case I should appoint a commission to inquire into the whole matter, leaving you at liberty to attend. The rev. mother told me such a course would be painful, but she would be willing to agree to it, if I desired it.

On the same day, September 20, the Rev. Mr. Mathews wrote to the bishop in answer to his first letter :

My dear Lord,—Your lordship's letter of the 15th has only just come to hand, and I cannot say how distressed and afflicted I am. I have always had the most unbounded confidence in your lordship's discernment and justice, and there must have been something surely fearful to necessitate this awful step. In the absence of all knowledge as to the cause, I make no remark, as a little time must develop the whole matter. I will communicate with the parents, who must decide as to the future of poor Sister Scholastica. In the position of the case I am glad I have not that responsibility ; that responsibility rests upon the parents. I fear that their long pent-up feelings of exasperation may carry them too far. I will try to do my best as *amicus religionis* to have the matter satisfactorily adjusted.

On the 22nd of September the Rev. Mr. Mathews wrote :—

I am in receipt of your lordship's second letter. I have not been able to consult with the heads of the family. Your lordship's mode of dealing with the case appears extremely fair. If the parents desire an inquiry, an impartial tribunal such as that your lordship proposes must be satisfactory to them. It certainly would satisfy me. If the parents leave the case in my hands, as I think they will, I shall be happy to make all matters, as far as I can, and as far as justice to all parties concerned will allow, harmonize with your lordship's views. Though the course proposed will meet all the requirements of this painful case, though it is distressing to me, I trust I shall ever bow to the demands of justice, and concur in any course necessary to serve the interests of religion. If anything has been said that might annoy your lordship, you must make allowance for a natural feeling.

A letter from Mrs. Star to the witness was next read, in which she stated that she felt greatly distressed at the trouble which his lordship had in the matter. She did not think the enemy of all good would permit "such a good to us as the removal of a bad member without resistance." She added, "This is the month of Our Lady of Mercy, during which we have special devotion in her honour, all of which we are directing to have Sister Scholastica removed from the community secretly and quietly. I feel confident that the dear mother will help us." And she added, "We have had prayers six times a day for this purpose."

The SOLICITOR-GENERAL : There is a postscript to the original letter.

Mr. RUSSELL : It has not been copied in my brief.

The SOLICITOR-GENERAL : In the postcript Mrs. Star asks to have Father Porter put on the commission, and adds, "He is an able and singularly gifted man, and knows this case in all its bearings."

Mr. MELLISH : We only got extracts of the letters from the bishop at first, and afterwards the residue, and they were not therefore copied together.

Examination continued : Father Mathews called upon me at Leeds. I read to him the whole of the depositions now in Court, with the exception of about half of the short one—a part which referred to a third person.

Did Father Mathews make any remarks upon the depositions ?—As far as I remember he did not until the whole were read, then he said it was a got up conspiracy. I then intimated that we would have a commission, and it was settled that we should. He asked if he might bring one of two Irish priests as a commissioner, and he also named the Very Rev. Mr. Trappes, the priest at Hull, to which I assented. Mr. Trappes did not attend, because at the very last moment he had to be absent from Hull at the marriage of his niece.

Mrs. Star asked you to appoint the Rev. Mr. Porter?—Yes. I appointed him in consequence of my intending to allow Father Mathews to have one of the commissioners a friend of Miss Saurin.

Did Father Mathews object to the Rev. Mr. Porter and the Rev. Mr. Cullimore because the one had been and the other was confessor of the convent ?—I do not remember their names being mentioned.

Was any objection made by the Rev. Mr. Porter to the Rev. Father Mathews ?—I do not remember any.

Now, did Father Mathews ask to have the witnesses examined, and that he should be at liberty to cross-examine ?—I do not remember that the subject was ever mentioned.

Did you assent to that course being taken ?—I do not remember anything of the kind.

Did you ever tell Father Mathews he was at liberty to cross-examine ?—I do not remember a word about it.

Did anything of the kind take place ?—I think not.

Examination continued : I received a letter from Father Mathews, stating that Dr. O'Hanlan consented to act, and replied accepting him. (Letter read.)

I accept Dr. O'Hanlan, and I have already appointed Mr. Porter. I have not settled as to appointing the vicar-general. If I do, I shall appoint five. If any of the family present themselves I will not allow the commission to act, and I require a written promise that in case the decision is adverse to your niece, she shall be removed in twenty-four hours. If she is pronounced innocent, and as a necessary consequence, if a case of conspiracy is proved against the other sisters, it will be for you to consider whether you will leave her in the community.

Not receiving a reply I wrote again :

Rev. and dear Sir—I wrote on the 3rd, and you have sent me no reply and no promise. If it is not given, I shall proceed on my own responsibility. I am aware that threats have been used, but they will not deter me, as I know the well-being of the whole community is at stake.

The answer of Father Mathews was as follows :—

On the receipt of your lordship's letter, I saw the parents, and told them that your lordship promised a fair and impartial constitution of the commission, and they have authorized me to say that they are prepared to submit to the conditions imposed—that they will remove her, though it would be most painful to them, in the event of the commission finding her guilty. I should be happy if your lordship could be present at the commission, for I have every confidence in your justice.

Examination continued : I do not recollect that Father Mathews ever objected to Father Porter being on the commission. If he had there would have been no difficulty in naming another commissioner. I received a letter on the 8th of December from Miss Saurin. I did not answer it until the 1st of January, when I gave her notice of the commission, and stated that her uncle would be present with a friend whom he would bring. On the same day I wrote to Father Mathews stating that the commission was to consist of Canon Walker, President ; Canon Chadwick, Dr. O'Hanlan, the Rev. Mr. Pinnet, and the Rev. Mr. Porter, and naming the 10th of January as the day for the holding of the inquiry. I addressed a letter of instructions to Canon Walker, and also had the following order of procedure prepared :

Order of Procedure in the Commission.

The president having handed his commission to the secretary, who will read and file it, the following order of procedure will be observed :—

1. The secretary will read the case with its history and evidence so sent for investigation ; such explanation as may be needed, and such as his previous study of the case may enable him to give, may be asked of him by the president, or by the other commissioners through the president.

2. The accused shall then be called, and the charges that have been made shall be severally read to her ; she may reply to all of them in detail, in any way that best suits her. No comment will be made in her presence. She will then retire.

3. The commissioners will now confer together, and if it be found that four-fifths of their number are of opinion that the charges have been proved, then each commissioner will give his opinion in writing freely, and the reasons on which it is based.

4. The opinions of the commissioners having been read over, and again considered, the acts of the commission drawn up by the secretary are signed by the president, and with the opinions of the commissioners are forwarded to the bishop.

5. If erring from defect in the evidence, or in the number of notes, further investigation be deemed fitting or necessary, then such witnesses shall be called as the commissioners think fit to summon, and the accused shall be consulted as to those whom she may wish for.

6. Let the witnesses for the charges be examined separately, in the absence of the accused, by the president, and by the other commissioners through the president.

N.B.—1. This examination must be very accurate, but not on oath, though the witnesses, if not unwilling to do so, should assert that on fitting occasion they would be prepared to confirm their testimony on oath.

N.B.—2. This testimony may be repeated afterwards in the presence of the accused, provided that it be deemed prudent to do so, and the witnesses consent. The accused may then, through the president, interrogate the witnesses.

6. After the same manner will be examined the witnesses on the side of the accused.

7. The commissioners will here confer together, as in No. 3.   [Bishop's seal.]

Mr. RUSSELL: Did you know that any one of the commission was aware of the circumstances of the case then?—I do not think I knew. I certainly did not think of it. I must, however, have known from Mrs. Star's letters.

The following letter to Father Mathews, dated 13th January, and his reply, were then read :—

Rev. and dear Sir,—I have received the report of the commission in the case of your niece, and I claim the fulfilment of your promise to remove her. Had all gone in her favour I should have recommended this course, as it would have involved such a grave reproach upon the entire community as to require her removal. But the more important part having been proved against her, her removal becomes necessary. I will absolve her from her vows, but she must accept the dispensation before she leaves my diocese. I regret that I have no choice but to perform so painful a duty.

My dear Lord,—I never agreed to remove my niece under any circumstances. I merely stated that her parents authorized me to say that, I having assured them that your lordship had promised a full and impartial investigation, in the event of her being found guilty, they would be prepared to remove her. I consider that the late investigation was not full nor impartial, nor such as your lordship promised. I remonstrated with the commissioners, but in vain. I was most anxious that your lordship should be present. Had you been there, you would have prevented an indecent exhibition, which made it worse than a cruel and offensive farce. I have only taken part in the affair as the friend of peace. But the parents feel most intensely the cruelty of the persecutions to which their daughter has been subjected. I am persuaded that if your lordship had been present, and heard the details of the mouldy bread kept for her, and the duster put upon her head to wear even in chapel, and the ignominious strippings she had to endure before the reverend mother, and a silence never broken but by insult, your lordship would have assigned punishment in a very different quarter, where every principle of justice and religion had been so shamefully violated. All this, I presume, was without your lordship's knowledge, and I venture to say that such treatment never was dealt out to any "religious" before ; and its exposure by any legal proceedings cannot fail to bring infamy upon the superioress and discredit upon every convent in the three kingdoms. When the commissioners

inspected, as well as they could, the clothes of my niece they expressed their disgust. I presume your lordship will have heard of this. I must say I am sorry that your lordship could not discover any other mode of proceeding except the removal of my unfortunate niece, whether guilty or not. I think it would be more in accordance with religion and justice to depose and expel the fabricators of false charges than to let all punishment fall on the persecuted sister, whose greatest fault was her patience and long endurance.

Now if Miss Saurin had left the convent without dispensation, and gone into another diocese, would you have had power of absolving her from her vows should she wish to enter the world again? —No.

In considering the evidence, and coming to the conclusion you did, did you act to the best of your judgment?—Yes, certainly.

Were you conscious of any bias against Sister Scholastica?—Oh, not the slightest. Quite the contrary.

Cross-examined by the SOLICITOR-GENERAL : I understood you, bishop, to say that a person might be properly removed from a community for mere incompatibility of temper, and without moral fault on her part?—Yes.

Now when two sides are at issue, one numerous and the other standing alone, might it not happen that the latter might be right?—It might.

In such a case would you still say that the removal of the dissentient member would be a right thing to effect in the interests of the community?—There would be no attempt to force her out.

Do you mean force her out by such proceedings as have taken place?—By force.

But at the same time removal would be necessary?—It would be a case of removal from one convent to another.

Must you not get the consent of the other convent?—Certainly.

Suppose you could not?—I should leave her where she was. Some risk to the peace of the community would have to be run.

I understand you to say, bishop, that you have power of removal on sufficient evidence, but that you are the judge of the sufficiency of the evidence?—Yes.

Where is that laid down?—By the rule the bishop is the superior of the convents in his diocese.

Outside the rule is it laid down anywhere?— No.

Then it all follows from the interpretation of the word "superior?"—That and the approval of the Holy See.

The LORD CHIEF JUSTICE : It equally follows that the rest of the community cannot turn a member out without your assent?—Yes.

The SOLICITOR-GENERAL : No doubt. In 1862 they had made up their minds to get rid of her, and the bishop after visitation would not allow it.

Cross-examination continued : Removal, without consent of another convent to receive, would practically render her reception in another community impossible.

And that wholly without dispensation from vows?—Yes.

Then what was the good of forcibly dispensing

her from vows which she was so desirous of being subject to?—It had no object but to favour her.

Did you not know she was clinging to her vows with her whole soul?—I knew she said so.

You did not think she meant what she said?—I had grave doubts about it.

But you might have, as you say, protected the community, and still leave her her vows.—Dispensing was simply to favour her.

Then shall I misrepresent you, bishop, when I say that, in spite of her protest, you did that which was unnecessary to effect the object you had in view; namely, preserve the peace of the community?—I cannot say that that was present to my mind.

Why, the fact that she was protesting you must have known?—I do not know that I knew it.

Excuse me. You have just told me you did not think she was sincere. You must then have known it?—I have told you all I remember about it.

You say the Pope only can dispense with the vow of chastity?

The Bishop: It is outside the question—utterly outside the question.

The SOLICITOR-GENERAL: Pardon me, bishop, I have a right to ask you.

The Bishop: It does not concern the question.

The LORD CHIEF JUSTICE: Let me remind you that you have already answered it.

The Bishop: Well, in that way I tried, so far, to favour her.

The SOLICITOR-GENERAL: Then it was to enable you to dispense with that vow that you communicated with the court of Rome?—Certainly.

When was that?—I think about June, 1865.

Then you had made up your mind at that time, I presume?—I had made up my mind as to the probable necessity.

What do you mean by probable necessity?—Probable need.

Well, you would hardly have applied to the see of Rome for power to dispense unless you thought there were reasonable grounds for supposing that you would have to exercise that power?—Certainly not.

Did you receive a letter from Father Mathews about 7th July, 1865?—I have such a letter, but I do not know when or where I received it.

(Letter produced by the bishop's secretary and read. Father Mathews stated in it that he had received a letter from his niece asking to be removed to the convent at Drogheda, but that it had evidently been written at the dictation of some one; that she was under a system of terror, and was bound by the rule of obedience to write the letter; and he added that he had every reliance on the justice, judgment, and honesty of the bishop, and that he would not make the parents unhappy by making their daughter an outcast at the caprice of a woman of questionable prudence.)

Cross-examination continued: I do not remember answering that letter. In 1862 I visited the convent.

Did you tell Father Mathews that you had strongly reproved Mrs. Kennedy and Mrs. Star for their conduct?—If he says so I believe him, but I do not remember it.

Can you recollect that you had an interview with him on the subject?—I remember nothing about it. I have a very bad memory.

That is a misfortune. Can you remember whether you reproved them, and whether they wept?—I remember that at the end of the visitation I said nothing. I went away rather biassed against them, but I dare not tell them.

The LORD CHIEF JUSTICE: Dare not tell whom?—I remember when I left, after the dispensation, they appeared to be disappointed at what I had done or had not done, and I felt in my own mind that they reproached me that I appeared against them. I felt it a duty to the weaker party to be biassed on that side. I felt that I ought to bear the reproach of treating them unkindly.

The SOLICITOR-GENERAL: What I asked you was whether you had reproached them, and had they not been crying?—I think Mrs. Star did cry.

Perhaps Mrs. Kennedy was not so much given to the melting mood. (A laugh.) But did she cry too?—I do not remember. I remember their apparent dissatisfaction.

Was that at what you said to them? Some people think the slightest word of a bishop a heavy thing. Did they not both cry?—I remember nothing about it. I remember Mrs. Star cried.

About something you said at the visitation, and your conduct of it?—(No answer.)

The SOLICITOR-GENERAL: Well, you wave your hand. I must take that as indicating that it was so.

Did you see Mrs. Star in 1863 or 1864?—I am unable to reply. I have no note of having seen her.

Did you see Sister Scholastica after you got the letter of 27th April, 1865, from Mrs. Star?—I do not remember.

You were in Hull after the receipt of at least one letter begging and entreating of you to see her?—Yes.

Did you see Mrs. Star?—I cannot say that I did.

Can you say that you did not?—I do not remember.

Did everything pass by letter down to the issuing of the commission?—I cannot say. I think it is likely it did; but I do not remember.

Here is a letter of yours to Father Mathews, dated "Bishop's House, Leeds, 15th Sept., 1865," but bearing the Hull postmark of the 17th. Can you account for that?—I cannot.

Did you send it from Leeds to the convent for approval?—I do not remember anything about it.

You did not send it through Mrs. Star?—I cannot explain it.

Are dispensations granted by the Holy See as a matter of course, and do they act upon the judgment of a bishop?—Oh, they do not dispense themselves; they give the faculty to do so. They give the bishop power to act or not.

The LORD CHIEF JUSTICE: Do they go into the matter at all?—No.

They trust to the discretion of the bishop?—Yes.

The SOLICITOR-GENERAL: Mrs. Star was aware that you had the faculty?—Oh, yes.

Had you communicated to Sister Scholastica that you had obtained it?—I did at one period.

But at no period except by letter?—I think not.

Then, when you got this faculty, you thought it nine chances to one that you would have to hear it?—(No answer.)

Well, perhaps I ought not to talk about chances. But you thought it highly probable?—I thought it likely.

Then, let me ask you what was the use of the commission?—Merely to give her a fair and favourable chance; and to inform my own judgment with greater certainty.

You had the depositions as to matters to be laid before the commissioners?—Yes.

Did you intend to examine and cross-examine witnesses?—Yes, as in the case laid down in the code of procedure.

And in no other case?—No.

The LORD CHIEF JUSTICE: If I understand aright, the witnesses were not to be called unless the commissioners thought it necessary.

Mr. MELLISH: If four-fifths were satisfied, after the statement of Miss Saurin, there was to be no examination.

The SOLICITOR-GENERAL: That is, if they were satisfied with the depositions.

Mr. MELLISH: And the explanation of Miss Saurin.

The SOLICITOR-GENERAL: Then, if the depositions, as they are called, were held to be satisfactory, however much Miss Saurin might have desired to have the sisters examined as part of her case, that was not to be allowed anyhow?—It was only to be allowed if the commissioners did not agree, if they considered the evidence insufficient.

But no amount of desire on her part was to entitle her to have her accusers brought before her?—No; because they were not on trial.

Excuse me. If it was part of her defence that the commissioners should see the witnesses, and judge of their demeanour, should they not be called?—It could not be, considering the number of the witnesses, their credibility, and character.

The LORD CHIEF JUSTICE: What could not be?

The SOLICITOR-GENERAL: Do you mean by that, that as it was on paper 7 or 8 to 1, you were to believe that 7 or 8, to 1, you knew nothing against them?—Yes.

Then, again, I ask you, bishop, what was the use of the investigation?—To verify what she should have to say to the charges.

Your were already perfectly satisfied with the number and character of the witnesses against her?—I had been before.

And it was not to be supposed that these persons could have worked against her without being right?—I think hardly.

Then, I am sure you will tell me the truth,—you did not contemplate the possibility, or, I will say probability, of the witnesses being produced?—I did not think about it. I wished to provide for it if necessary.

They were only to be confronted with her if the commissioners thought it prudent, and, further, that the witnesses themselves consented. Is that so?—You have the document before you.

What did you mean by the word "prudent"?—I do not remember.

You say in one letter that you gave her short notice of the commission because you did not like

to have it hanging over her. You had probably well made up your mind to use the faculties you had received from Rome, without telling her of the pending investigation?—I had not made up my mind about it.

Surely, bishop, you cannot say that. There would have been no commission without the intervention of Father Mathews. Is not that so?—Yes.

And you might have dismissed her?—My anxiety was that her friends should remove her. I had resolved if her friends did not I would take steps to remove her.

The LORD CHIEF JUSTICE: To remove her if her friends did not remove her?—I was very glad to fall back upon the commission.

The SOLICITOR-GENERAL: You had made up your mind to use the faculties. Why did you not let her know about the commission sooner?—I really cannot answer you.

Now you say your memory is bad. Are you prepared to place your recollection of the conversation you had with Father Mathews against his?—Oh, certainly not. I sometimes do not remember the letters I have written.

Then if he has made a statement upon oath all you mean to say is that you do not remember that what he has stated took place?—That is what I mean.

Do you remember something being said about an objection to Father Cullamore being on the commission, on the ground that he was confessor to the convent?—It has been brought to my mind, and I now remember it.

Well, would not the same reason operate against Father Porter?—Yes, but not in the same sense.

Why?—Because Father Cullamore was constantly confessor to the convent, and Father Porter only occasionally.

Does that enable you to remember that Father Mathews objected to both?—It does not.

Father Cullamore was confessor at Clifford?—Yes.

And Father Porter conducted the retreats at Hull?—He did.

And then confessed the nuns at Hull?—Yes.

Were you aware that Mrs. Star went to Liverpool to see Father Porter?—I now hear of it for the first time.

But you advised her to write to him?—I did.

And she had recommended him?—Yes.

Did you understand that he was to be a sort of advocate for the convent?—Oh, not at all. A friend. There was to be a friend at the other side.

Now, did you, in your interview with Father Mathews, tell him anything about the charge as to the medal?—I do not remember.

Will you undertake to say that you read the whole of the depositions to him?—I did, with the exception of those I have told you.

It must have been a longish interview.—I was hoarse and tired when it concluded.

And it was then he said it was a got-up conspiracy?—Yes.

When did you receive the report of the commission?—October the 12th—the day after it closed.

Did you then communicate the result to Mrs. Star?—I do not remember.

You say there was no charge against Miss

Saurin of what is commonly called immorality?—Oh, no.

Did you consider that any serious crimes were charged against her?—Such a thing never entered my head.

You only understood them to be charges of breach of poverty, obedience, and the rule of the order?—That is all.

Did you not consider the charge of stealing a medal from a dead body a serious charge?—Well, I all along thought that her mind was not all right, and I interpreted it in that way. I thought that there was the disease called "kleptomania," and that that would account for a great many things.

Apart from kleptomania, would you have said that the stealing of the medal was a very serious thing?—Yes.

Ought you not in candour to have told her she was charged with that? You say you did not give her a copy of the charges, because they were only what she was over and over again charged with. Did she understand that she was charged with stealing a medal from a dead body?—Certainly not.

But you understood what she was charged with?—Yes ; I saw it in the depositions.

But was she not charged with it before the commission?—I do not think it was mentioned in the summary of charges.

Well, either these things were done or they were not done. Did you yourself believe about the medal?—Yes.

And you accounted for it by kleptomania?—I did not think she was sound in mind, and thought that very possibly there was no moral fault about it.

Well, if she was not of sound mind was it not hard to treat these smaller matters as breaches of poverty?—That was in my mind a charitable explanation to account for it.

Well, but either there was responsibility or there was not. Did you think there was, or did you think there was not?—I wished to account for it in that way.

Did you direct any inquiry to be made into her state of mind?—I did not. It was merely a charitable justification.

But if you thought it likely to account innocently for the charges against her, ought you not to have inquired into it?—It did not enter into my mind.

Then she was to suffer whether she was guilty or innocent?—I do not think she suffered.

Was she not to be turned out of the convent?—(No answer.)

I understand you to say that you dispensed her vows to favour her?—Yes.

Am I to take you as seriously believing that you contemplated the probability of her wishing to return to the world?—(No answer.)

Well, you had a great many of the documents connected with the case in your possession ; and we applied to you for copies, which you refused, while you gave copies to the other side. Do you think that that was quite fair?—Yes ; I acted under the general direction of their counsel. (A laugh.)

Did you think that quite fair to us?—I did, indeed.

The SOLICITOR-GENERAL: I have the greatest possible respect for my learned friend ; but I would not take the measure of my legal rights from him in this case.

The LORD CHIEF JUSTICE: His opinions are generally sounder than the advice he gave in this instance. (Laughter.)

To the LORD CHIEF JUSTICE: It is a very grave offence against the rules for a sister to correspond with externs without permission. I am not aware that letters to relatives are allowed to be sent without being handed to the superior.

The Rev. Edward Goldie, secretary to the bishop, was next examined, and produced the documents laid before the commission. He was present at the commission. Three of the commissioners, at all events, were wholly ignorant of the matters for which they were summoned to Hull. Before Father Mathews was admitted, the history of the case was read, the analysis of the charges, and the letter addressed by the bishop to the president of the commission. When Father Mathews entered the room the history of the case was again read, and the depositions were also read. He complained that his niece had not had time to prepare herself for the commission. That was not a matter that the commissioners could go into. To satisfy him that they were acting according to the bishop's directions, the greater part—perhaps the whole—of the order of procedure was read to him. The commissioners determined to proceed with the inquiry, feeling that they were bound by the order of procedure. Sister Scholastica was then sent for. The president himself rose when she entered, and conducted her to a seat near her uncle, where she remained until six o'clock of that day. By the terms of the instruction everything had to be conducted by the president, and therefore no other commissioner spoke to her. He addressed her in a kind and considerate manner, and bade her answer without fear and without constraint. Witness then read the summary of the charges. The president told her she would have liberty to reply to each item of the charges in detail as she pleased. Witness read each item of the charge, and paused, even if the charge was contained in two words only. When Sister Scholastica did not remember the charge as contained in the summary, he turned to the depositions and read the parts that referred to the charge, and sometimes read them over two or three times for greater clearness. The president required her to answer each item of each particular charge as it was read. It was witness's duty to take notes of each answer of the plaintiff, in order to draw up the report to be sent to the bishop. He drew up notes of her answers as well as time permitted. Father Mathews spoke very frequently during the whole proceeding, not merely to her, but to the president and to witness. He frequently asked that the depositions might be referred to ; thus, when one had been referred to, he asked that the other depositions might be referred to for further information. Such requests were always complied with. From time to time charges were incidentally made by her in the course of her answers against the other sisters. He did not recollect whether Sister Scholastica or Father Mathews was stopped from speaking during the whole of the inquiry. He thought that neither of them was stopped from giving any explanation they desired. Her answers were often contradictory, and again and again Father Mathews came to the rescue, and put her confused answers into intelligible form. The commission closed at six o'clock on the first day, and re-assembled at half-past nine o'clock on the following morning, all the commissioners and Father Mathews being present. Sister Scholastica was not summoned for the first half-hour. As soon as the commission reassembled Father Mathews begged that the remaining four depositions not referred to in the summary of charges might be read. They were read, and then Sister Scholastica was summoned. She sat by her uncle, as on the previous day. The first day had been occupied with inquiry into the charges of faults against the rules and against obedience. The second day was occupied with inquiry into the charges of breeches of the vow of poverty. She was again allowed to give any answer and explanation to the charges made against her. Before she left the room Father Mathews remonstrated on two or three points. He complained first of all that the two or three letters from Mrs. Star to the plaintiff's mother highly commendary of his niece had not been put in. Witness could only reply that "the bishop had not furnished me with copies of them." He complained that his niece had not received the same food as the other sisters, that her clothing had been insufficient and poor, and that she had been kept in silence for three years. Upon these points witness made notes at the time. The plaintiff did not say anything upon these points at the time. Father Mathews was told that this was not an investigation into the general state and the conduct of the sisters, and that, therefore, the matters to which he referred could not be entertained. Father Mathews then left the room, but no discussion took place upon these points in his presence. When he left the room the president reminded the commission that it was their duty to confer upon what they had heard, and that it would be necessary for them to state what were their opinions upon the charges and upon the plaintiff's statements, in order to ascertain who were of opinion that the charges had been proved or disproved. The first speaker was Dr. O'Hanlan, who said : "Mr. President, I suppose we are all agreed." Upon being asked which way, he said, "Agreed that the charges are proved;" and after him the others expressed the same opinion. Before that the order and procedure were referred to in order to see what was to be done.

A discussion then arose as to the counter-charges, and it was resolved that Father Mathews should be allowed to put questions to her upon them, which he accordingly did and witness took notes thereon, and on further questions put by the Commissioners in order to elicit further information. She then reduced her statement of silence from three years to a year and a half. She made a statement as to what is called the stripping, and I think that she confined that to two occasions only. She also spoke as to her relatives not being admitted to see her at the convent. She never mentioned her having been required to disclose her confessions, except that she said the superior had, upon taking her tablets from her, insisted upon reading the matters of confession. She spoke of the estrangement of the reverend mother, and ascribed it to the discovery of the letters (*i.e.* the letters to obtain her

removal). The main excuse which ran through the whole of her answers was that there had been no settled rules at first, and that as all was in confusion it was easy to go away, and that she had been put under special and exceptional reasons, which applied only to herself. She said she had three times as much work as any other sister. She was not checked in these statements. The Commissioners then conferred together on these counter-charges. It was discussed whether the other sisters should be summoned to give explanations ; but the conclusion arrived at was that the instructions did not allow of it.

The LORD CHIEF JUSTICE : So the commissioners could not enter into the counter-charges ? —No. This did not alter their opinions that the charges were proved, and they still adhered to it. Each commissioner wrote his opinion.

Was there any application on the part of Father Mathews or his niece to have witnesses called and examined ?

Witness.—I don't remember any.

The witness's notes of the answers made by the plaintiff to the heads of charges were here read :—

1. Disregard of rules. Answer.—Not as a habit. 2. Complaints of superiors.—Don't remember ever having done so. 3. Reading letters and talking with lay sisters.—Never remember it. 4. Talking with lay sisters on improper subjects. —Not on improper subjects ; not before charged with it, nor conscious of it, nor heard of it ; the most unfounded of all the charges. These charges have all been collected since the affair of the letter. 5. Speaking as to courtship, &c.— Never remember speaking about courtship ; certainly never about young men. 6. Speaking to externs.—Only within the last three years forbidden to speak to externs, and I had duties which rendered it necessary. 7. Speaking with priests unnecessarily in the kitchen, in the school, &c.—Acknowledge it in the kitchen ; all of them did so ; do not remember the school. 8. Neglect of school duties, time spent in talking and laughing, &c.—Never laughed or talked in school ; never curtailed the hours of school without authority. 9. Hardship to children.— Instead of hardship was more inclined to be over indulgent, and was said to have spoilt them. 10. Inflicting pain on children.—Never did so. 11. Curtailing time for spiritual exercises.—Had the charge of 19 boarders, pupil teachers. 12. Clandestine correspondence (*a*) sent by child, (*b*) found under the pillow, (*c*) sent by another child, acknowledged and afterwards denied.—Admitted the interception of the first letter ; admitted the writing of two ; made acknowledgments of them. 13. Altering clock.—It required alteration ; never altered it for my own purposes. 14. Speaking disrespectfully of superiors, taxing them with tyranny, and behaving in a violent manner,— Never spoke with deliberate disrespect. Did once use the word "cruel." Never remember to have behaved violently. 15. Murmuring and taking notes of faults of others.—Acknowledged taking notes on tablets. Reverend mother reproached her—not correct. It was matter for confessor. Her own friends, when visitors, badly treated. 16. Faults against poverty ; excess in dress ; unwillingness to part with it ; destruction of clothes ; keeping watches, &c.—Never excessive in dress ; never destroyed clothing ; was allowed by the

superior at Baggot-street to keep the watch; the other sisters were allowed to do so. 17. Thefts from the community, the book, the boots, small quantities of clothing, &c. (no mention of the medal or the other things alleged to have been taken from the dead body).—No remark was ever made to me about removing books; never heard the book was missing. Put on pair of boots; we were then allowed to borrow things until the new regulations; I procured the sister's consent. 18. Thefts from the school-children; taking their dinners.—Never took them to eat them, only to take care of them; always returned them to the children.

Such was the substance, according to the witness's notes, of the summary of charges and the answers made. The witness then read his notes of the statements made by Miss Saurin as to her ill-treatment, which were to the same general effect as those she has made in this action—that she had been badly fed and clothed; that she had had to wear rags; that she had been stripped to her chemise and searched, and that this had happened on a similar occasion before; that the sisters either would not speak to her or taunted her with her family, telling her that her father was only a horse-dealer, and that as to her sisters being in a Carmelite convent, why that six Carmelite nuns had become lunatic in one convent; that, in fact, she had been systematically ill-treated and insulted, and that the superior told her that the longer she remained the more painful her martyrs dom would be. Such was the substance of the witness's evidence.

He was cross-examined by the SOLICITOR-GENERAL whether Father Porter, one of the commissioners, had not more than once contradicted the plaintiff, and he admitted that he had rather warmly intimated more than once that what she said was not correct, but he denied that this could be considered contradicting her. Pressed as to whether Mr. Mathews had not asked that the sisters should be produced to substantiate their statements, he said he had not, but admitted that he had made some complaint about it, and that the mother superior had a message sent to her from the commissioners to furnish some dates, &c.

Sixteenth Day, *Monday, February 22.*

The wretched weather to-day made Westminster Hall a refuge for many idlers who in other cases would have been following in the open air their enviable occupation of doing nothing, with plenty of able assistance. The snow and the biting winter wind actually made it seem that this interminable suit of "Saurin versus Star and Another" had already lasted through more than one season, and that the Lord Chief Justice, who, " never flitting, still is sitting, still is sitting," has become a living fixture, like the famous raven that contrived, by some remarkable disposition of lamp-light, which has always been a grievous puzzle and stumbling-block to artists attempting the pictorial illustration of Poe's sonorous lines, to cast his shadow from the top of a plaster cast over a door, right into the middle of the room. His lordship, though he declared his regret, last Saturday, at seeing fresh matter imported into the proceedings, was the first this morning to reopen a discussion on the new point raised by the Solicitor-General, as to the true reading of the legend, "Sing a Song of Sixpence." The end of the convent case, however, seems dimly visible, the evidence for the defence having been brought to a conclusion this day. The witnesses were priests who had sat on the commission to investigate the charges against Miss Saurin, and to report thereon to the bishop having jurisdiction over the convents of Hull and Clifford. The Solicitor-General recalled the plaintiff to contradict certain statements, and said he should have to bring forward six witnesses on the morrow. After their examination public interest in the case will take a fresh lease of life, the addresses of counsel on either side and the summing-up by the Lord Chief Justice having been for days looked forward to with a curiosity that has rather been stimulated than diminished by the long and tedious extension of evidence. The conversation around the court, touching every matter that relates, nearly or remotely, to the question at issue, is of course the same that may be heard all over England at this time. One very general topic is the payment of costs. These on both sides are immense, and can hardly be borne by the persons ostensibly concerned. Indeed, it is not supposed by any one that the plaintiff and her immediate friends stand unsupported in a contest which makes so urgent a call on the sinews of war.

The hearing of this case was resumed at the sitting of the Court.

The Lord Chief Justice said that some person who did not agree with a quotation which had been incidentally made from a nursery rhyme, had written to him questioning his version of it. It appeared to be a letter sent to some newspaper.

A Juror: *The Daily Telegraph.*

The Solicitor-General: It appears that my version has been questioned too, my lord.

The Lord Chief Justice: It is said that neither of us quoted correctly from the " Four-and twenty blackbirds." (A laugh.) I said that it was in the parlour that the Queen eat the bread and honey, and you said it was in the pantry.

The Solicitor-General: The subject of the moment was the pantry. I admit I knew it was not the pantry. (Laughter.)

The Lord Chief Justice: This gentleman makes out that the King was in the parlour counting out the money, and the Queen in the kitchen eating bread and honey. (A laugh.)

The Solicitor-General: The King was certainly in the counting-house—(laughter)—the proper place for the purpose of counting the money.

The Lord Chief Justice: And the Queen was in the parlour. Those who set themselves to correct others should be sure that they are correct themselves—especially on so grave a matter. (Laughter.)

Mr. C. Russell: I am in a position, from the fact of having heard several little authorities on the subject, to say that your lordship's version was undoubtedly the correct one.

The Very Rev. Canon Walker sworn and examined by Mr. Charles Russell : My first connection with the matter was getting a letter from the bishop as to the commission. I knew nothing whatsoever about the matter before. I summoned the other commissioners. The commission met at Hull. I heard the account Mr. Goldie gave of the course of procedure. I believe it to be very correct. When the plaintiff came before us and was placed in a chair on my right, and Father Matthews on her right, with Dr. O'Hanlon in front of her, so that she should be as much as possible in the presence of her friends, I told her to have no fear about the case ; that she should receive kindness and consideration at all sides. I never heard Father Matthews making any objection to Father Porter. I did not hear him asking for the letter "postulating" Father Porter's attendance.

Was the plaintiff stopped in any explanation she desired to make ?—She may have been stopped to secure order, as her remarks were desultory, but never for the purpose of embarrassment.

Did Father Matthews say, in reference to the order of proceedings, "These are a violation of the engagement the bishop made with me."—I never heard anything about it. I was not aware any communication had passed between the bishop and Father Matthews.

Did Father Matthews apply to have Mrs. Grimstone examined ?—I never heard her named.

The Lord Chief Justice : Was any application made by Father Matthews to have any witness examined ?—I do not remember anything of the sort.

Mr. Russell : Did he ask to have any witness examined for the purpose of exculpating his niece ? —I do not know whether towards the end he may not have complained of the hardship on his niece in not having these things.

What things ?—Witnesses. But that could not be entertained. The crisis had passed ; that is, the occasion contemplated in the instructions had not arisen.

The Lord Chief Justice : That would apply to witnesses against her, but did he apply to have witnesses examined for her?—When the commission was closed or closing he may have complained of the hardship of his niece's position in not having witnesses examined ; but if it happened—and I do not recollect that it did—it must have been just before we went into deliberation.

To Mr Russell : I cannot remember what commissioner spoke in the deliberation. The conversation turned upon statements we received from the plaintiff—how far they affected the depositions of the sisters, and the credibility and manner of the plaintiff. There was a general and unanimous assent that the charges had been substantially proved, but that if the witness was to be believed there were circumstances which would go to extenuate the complaints which had been made against the sister.

Were these the counter-charges ?—Charges of cruelty.

Were these entered into before the first deliberation ?—Yes.

The Lord Chief Justice : What did you determine to do in respect of them ?—Oh, we considered what weight should be given to them, and we then proceeded to write our opinions.

Was she examined about these counter-char-

ges ?—Oh ! quite sufficiently, my lord. She represented herself as having suffered from wanton cruelty, and if that was true——

The Lord Chief Justice : Well, everything depends upon the "if."

Mr. Russell : Did you inquire into the truth of her statement beyond her own evidence ?—No ; we heard what she had to say.

Cross-examined by the Solicitor-General : I am a little deaf, but I heard her statement sufficiently. I am sure I did not hear Mrs. Grimstone's name mentioned. I heard the depositions read by the secretary. I did not hear Mrs. Grimstone's name mentioned except in the depositions. I state confidently I never heard her name mentioned in connection with her being called as a witness. I never heard a desire expressed in any shape that reference should be made to her. Father Matthews did not, I think, mention her name.

When the commissioners wrote out their opinions, did not one or two of them say that as they were twelve to one, and as no further testimony could be had, they should decide in favour of the twelve ?—I did not hear that.

Did any of them say that if the counter-charges were true she had been guilty of no fault ?—Not that I heard.

Well, that if so there was no case against her ? —I did not hear any such statement. It was said that in that case there would be an extenuation..

You did not interrupt her ?—No, except for the purpose I have mentioned.

Did any one else ?—She was called to order, for it was hard to keep her from wandering from one track to another. That was the prevailing reason for interrupting her.

Was she often called to order ?—I think I might say often during the two days.

Did you ask her questions?—Yes.

Did you pursue an examination with her to clear her statements ?—No, she had perfect liberty to pursue her statement if it were not inconsistent or varying.

Then you called her to order?—She was called to order.

By more than one of you ?—By one at a time.

Was Mr. Porter a little active in keeping her to the line ?—On one occasion he used more urgency and persistency in bringing her to order than most of us—I would not say than all. Dr. O'Hanlon was equally urgent, but in a gentler way than Mr. Porter was at one special time.

The Lord Chief Justice : Do you limit what you say as to Mr. Porter to one occasion ?—I do.

The Solicitor General : Was he unkind with her ?—I think not.

Well, was he warm ?—I do not know what you call warm.

Was he warm according to what you call warm ?—Well, I think he was. He was urgent to get at the truth of the case.

Used he to say, "That's impossible ; I know to the contrary "?—I do not remember.

What was the particular instance to which you refer ?—I do not distinctly remember.

Do you know what it was about ?—I don't.

Did he not bring his own knowledge of the convent to bear against her statements?—No ; so far from that I did not know he was a friend of the convent more than others.

Did you know that he had been appointed at the instance of Mrs. Star ?—I did not ; but Dr.

O'Hanlon was, you know, appointed at the instance of Father Matthews.

Examination continued: On one occasion the secretary objected to a statement of Miss Saurin, which he said was not admissible in point of form. I ruled that as they were explanations of previous statements of hers they might be "transplanted." I used that very word to her former statements.

Then you overruled an objection made by the bishop's secretary to the reception of a statement of Miss Saurin in point of form?—I allowed it to be received.

Was there any allusion to the fact that there were twelve to one?—Oh! that was obvious.

Was any question raised as to the credibility of the sisters in reference to their depositions?—No. They were unimpeached. They were taken as conscientious, deliberate, and faithful statements of eye-witnesses—witnesses who had experienced and seen what they stated.

Then they were twelve to one, and taking one from twelve eleven remained. So there were eleven unanswered?—That was obvious.

And had it any effect?—It operated. (Laughter.)

It operated, you say?—It is a mathematical fact.

To Mr. Mellish: There was no opportunity given to the sisters as to whom counter-charges were made to answer them.

Canon Walker's deposition was then read. It stated that he was of opinion that the charges bgainst the accused had been abundantly proved, tsut that some of her explanations, if true, might tie justly admitted as greatly mitigating some portion of the complaints against her. He added teat he found it impossible to resist the concurrent aostitnony of so many deponents, and that he could not place much confidence in the hesitating, varying, and indecisive replies of the accused.

The Rev. Mr. Porter examined: I am a member of the Society of Jesus, and live at Liverpool. I gave the annual retreat at the Hull Convent in August, 1861. That was an eight days' retreat.

To the Lord Chief Justice: A retreat is a period of seclusion, during which people, either religious or in the world, withdraw.

It is not confined to religious people technically so called?—Not at all. They withdraw themselves from the world, more or less to devote themselves to prayer, self-examination, reading of ascetical works, and other pious exercises. The time is spent more or less completely in silence.

To Mr. C. Russell: The director of the retreat meets the nuns in chapel, and explains to them the points of meditation, and each day gives them instruction on some virtue, or some duty of religious life. He receives ordinarily the confessions of those in retreat, and should be accessible to them for advice out of the confessional.

If they desire it?—Yes.

Examination continued: I also gave a retreat in December, 1861, at Hull, which lasted three days, and again in August, 1862, which lasted eight days, ending on the morning of the 15th, the Assumption of Our Lady. I never went to Hull from August, 1862, until the commission in 1866. I never was connected with the convent at Hull except in the way I have mentioned, and in having had occasional correspondence with the superior, Mrs. Star, and receiving one or two letters from Mrs. Kennedy. In December, 1865,

Mrs. Star called on me at Liverpool with Sister Mary Stanislaus, who was about to pass an examination in Liverpool, to get a certificate under the Privy Council. I was not well at the time. I cannot speak as to the length of the interview. The principal point upon my mind is that I learned then in fuller detail what I had previously known slightly as to what had taken place at the convent since 1862. It is not true that she "precognosed" me. I learned in detail the series of events in reference to Sister Scholastica. I have never in my life known Mrs. Star to exhibit any ill-will towards Sister Scholastica. She regretted her conduct, and wished her removal, but I never saw any symptom of bitterness whatever. I received a letter from Mrs. Star asking me to sit on the commission.

What has become of the letter?—I have destroyed it.

What do you do with such letters?—I invariably destroy letters when I have answered them. She stated in her letter that the bishop had authorized her to write that he would be glad if I acted as a commissioner, and that she and the community would be pleased also if I accepted the post. I received no instructions or suggestions from her. I may say, that up to five minutes before the inquiry commenced, neither Mrs. Star, Mrs. Kennedy, nor myself knew what form the inquiry would take, further than that we knew it was about Sister Scholastica and her leaving the community. I saw Mrs. Star and Mrs. Kennedy, and the other sisters, on the question. There was nothing particular in the conversation.

Did she give you instructions on certain points?—Nothing whatever. I was already in possession of these events, up to the time of the commission.

Mrs. Star had told you?—Yes. I never heard one word of objection to my acting falling from the lips of Father Matthews, nor did I hear him express a desire to see Mrs. Star's letter to me. I corroborate what was stated by the two previous witnesses, that the plaintiff during the inquiry was never interrupted in any way to embarrass or trouble her. I can testify that she spoke at her ease throughout, and even at the worst charges betrayed no emotion. Questions were asked by the commissioners, and the Rev. Mr. Matthews assisted her throughout, putting the answers in form, as has been stated. When the Rev. Mr. Matthews and Sister Scholastica withdrew, the commissioners conferred together, and all expressed themselves satisfied that the charges were substantially proved. Then followed a discussion whether Father Matthews's request to go into the charges against the community should be gone into. When Sister Scholastica had gone into her statement, he had asked that the charges against the convent should be taken into account.

Mr. Russell: Do you mean examined into?—I say "taken into account," and that he should be allowed to question his niece upon them.

The Lord Chief Justice: What was done then?—Nothing.

Was he overruled?—Well, the explanations continued. It was like an observation he threw in. No answer was given to it. He continued to get the explanations from his niece.

Was he allowed to go into the counter-charges? —I think he was prevented going into counter-charges. The commissioners objected, because we were limited to hearing the charges and the explanations to them. When he attempted to go into the counter-charges he was checked, and stopped for the time.

Examination continued : When they had withdrawn, a debate arose upon whether Father Matthews or Sister Scholastica should be allowed to go into the counter-charges, and I urged that our instructions did not allow it, and I was overruled. Then Father Matthews and Sister Scholastica were re-introduced into the room, and the counter-charges were brought forward seriatim. On several occasions after their return I interposed ; and I remember once saying, " Such a charge was impossible in a religious house."

The Lord Chief Justice : Which was that ?—I cannot remember, my lord, which it was ; but it was one of three. Either that she had been condemned to two or three years' silence, or that she was treated exceptionally in point of food for a length of time. The third was, that she was treated exceptionally in being made to wear old tattered clothes.

Examination continued : I may have interposed with some warmth because I could not see how these counter-charges at all exonerated the plaintiff from the charges brought against her. I may explain. The charges against her were pilfering, untruthfulness, and habitual disregard of rule. She had denied the pilfering, I may say, in toto ; she denied the untruthfulness in toto, and substantially denied the disregard of rule. It seemed to me that no severity on the part of Mrs. Star or the others affected the charge of pilfering or untruthfulness ; and I may add the imputation of a conspiracy on the part of twelve ladies cruelly and unfairly to drive Sister Scholastica from the convent, was a most odious one. All my personal knowledge of those ladies satisfied me it was utterly false, and I may add the charge was absurd. An active and a useful sister in a community, especially of sisters of mercy, is too valuable to be wantonly and wickedly thrown away.

Examination continued : The counter-charges were stated at great length—for two or three hours. I never heard Father Matthews mention Mrs. Grimstone's name. I have professed and taught dogmatic theology.

Moral theology also ?—No. The question of the bishop's powers is a question of moral theology. I have heard the bishop's statement as to his power, and I entirely agree with it. Removal and dispensing are altogether different matters. The bishop can remove a nun and refuse to dispense her.

The Lord Chief Justice said he hoped that before the case closed some light would be thrown upon the legal rights and liabilities of a community of this kind.

Examination continued : I did not hear Father Matthews ask to examine any witness, or to cross-examine any of the sisters.

The Lord Chief Justice : Father Matthews says that he submitted to the commissioners that the statements ought not to be taken as proved without cross-examination. Do you recollect his doing so ?—I do not recollect that he did.

The witness's report was then read. He stated that after reading the evidence brought in support of the charges, and the answers made to them, he thought that the greater and more important charges were proved ; he thought it fair to add, that as to some of the minor charges sufficient evidence had not been adduced to sustain them. In coming to that conclusion he took into account the moderation of tone and unanimity of the witnesses in support of the charges, and the hesitating and unsatisfactory character of the verbal statements of the accused.

Cross-examination continued : You will find information as to the power of the bishop in " Feraris," and the works of " Bouix." Simple vows can be dispensed by the bishop. There are five vows reserved for the Pope.

The bishop in one letter says he could not act " efficaciously" in the matter without reference to the Holy See?—I presume his lordship referred to the power to dispense from the vow of chastity.

Can he dispense whether the party likes it or not ?—Yes.

Then a party can be, in effect, released from vows by which she desires to be bound ?—Yes.

By the fulfilment of conditions which she cannot help fulfilling ?—Yes.

What constitutes the difference between a solemn and a simple vow ?—A vow is made solemn by the word of the Pontiff.

The Lord Chief Justice : Vows are solemn that the Pope only can dispense from ?—Yes, such as the vow of chastity taken by sisters of mercy.

Cross-examination continued : Some vows are simple for a time, and become solemn on being again taken after a certain time. I had had an outline of the facts connected with Miss Saurin in Mrs. Star's letters. When she called upon me in 1865 she filled up the outline. She called on me twice in that year. I knew from her letter the community wished me to act.

Did she ever vary in her letters as to Miss Saurin's conduct, and as to wishing her dismissal ? —Well, in her letters she only spoke generally. I cannot say whether that extended over the whole period.

Well, latterly ?—Yes, latterly she wished her removal.

How many letters had you from Mrs. Star and Mrs. Kennedy?—Well, twenty would be the outside, and there were intervals of several months sometimes.

The Lord Chief Justice : Had they all reference to Sister Scholastica?—Oh, not at all. She was mentioned in four of them—certainly in not more than six.

To the Solicitor-General : I had about three letters from Mrs. Kennedy. I knew that she and Mrs. Star did not know the form the commission would take, because I was speaking to them on the subject two or three minutes before the commission sat. I saw them for about an hour on the day before the inquiry.

The Solicitor-General : You say the outline was given to you in the letters, and that the picture was filled in when she called at Liverpool. Were the light and shade, the finishing touches, given at Hull?—No ; the picture was just left as it was.

The subject of the commission was not spoken of ?—It was—generally.

Was it not the principal topic of conversation ? —Oh, not at all.

Then Father Matthews did not call for Mrs. Star's letter ?—I did not hear it.

And Miss Saurin was not interrupted?—I would not call that an interruption the object of which was to make a statement more intelligible and more clear.

Did you not interrupt her?—I made very few remarks. There were some questions asked for explanation in the first part, but nothing that embarrassed her in the slightest degree.

And you say she showed no emotion?—I say it was painful to see the unmoved manner in which she heard herself charged with what I call very odious and hateful charges against any woman, any lady, and, above all, a religious lady.

Were these things about the priests mentioned before her?—If you allude to the charges of levity of conduct, I do not recollect.

Was she interrupted whenever her explanation involved a counter-charge?—I think not. The counter-charges were gone into.

You state three charges, one of which was pilfering. What was the pilfering?—Of food. If she said she had not had sufficient food and took some, that would have been, not a counter-charge, but a matter of exculpation.

What charges did you think serious and odious of which you thought she was guilty?—The best substantiated charges were those of untruthfulness and deceit.

Would not instances of untruthfulness very much have depended upon the circumstances connected with the statements?—If the charge had turned upon the particular instances, yes; but not when there are twelve deponents, and when the charges are stated quite generally and do not turn upon particular instances.

Well, but the charges being, as you say, general, how on earth could she have answered them except by general denial?—I do not complain of her answer, but it at once shut me out from taking the counter-charge as a sufficient reply. I take it, that if twelve ladies who devote themselves to the poor, all say seriously that they have found a sister frequently telling falsehoods, deceiving them, and conducting herself, as I think more than one of them says, as a hypocrite, I cannot resist such evidence.

You mean that you must assume it to be true? Yes.

Well, but you knew all that before you went into the inquiry?—Yes; but I did not know the number of depositions.

You knew the complaints?—Yes; but nothing of the proofs.

But the proofs, as you call them, were only assertions?—Yes; but twelve such assertions coming from such ladies and with such moderation.

Did you not think it natural to see what the charges might come to in particular instances on cross examination?—The plaintiff denied them. She said, if I remember rightly, that she had never told a lie in her life.

Well, no doubt that was a little exaggeration. But would it not have tended to elicit the facts if you had found out what the ladies meant by untruthfulness, and the particular instances of it?—I could not doubt what they meant. I supposed they meant what I meant myself. I had no objection to cross-examine, but I had no option to call for it.

You say your personal knowledge of the ladies satisfied you that her charges against them were untrue?—I could not say that.

Well, substantially?—Yes.

Did you know anything of Sister Scholastica?—Yes; in the retreats.

You think that in a community where twelve were at one side and one at the other, the twelve would be right?—I do.

Was there ever a nun unjustly treated in a convent?—A sister might be unjustly treated by a superior, but not in a community of twelve or fourteen. There would always be some to represent such injustice to the bishop.

Have you known instances of sisters being unjustly treated?—I have known some instances of their being hardly treated. I am not speaking of this community.

I mean unfairly and cruelly treated?—I have known instances.

Have they complained?—Yes.

The Lord Chief Justice: What was done?—I have known an instance where the superior, through ignorance, took a prejudice against a nun, and the nun was rendered unhappy, and she applied to the bishop, and, through his mediation, was received at once into another community; and I have known instances in which the bishop has interfered, and inquired into the case, and checked the superior for her treatment of the particular sister.

The Solicitor-General: Are cases of that sort frequent?—Not within my knowledge. They have too much to do from morning until night to have time for these little affairs, as a rule.

Is not care taken during the noviciate to see that the parties are, in all respects, fit for the life they embrace? Now, in Roman Catholic religious societies would not expulsion be considered a very grave stigma?—The gravity of the stigma would depend upon the gravity of the charges. I think charges of pilfering and theft are very grave indeed.

Was the suggestion of the bishop that she was not quite responsible for what she did, suggested before?—Is that a fair question, my lord?

The Solicitor-General: Why is it not?—Witness: Of course my acquaintance with Miss Saurin up to a certain time was confined to confession and confidential communications. I next saw her while on the commission. I was very much drawn to the reason that both intellectually and morally she was warped.

To the Lord Chief Justice: What do you mean by warped?—Assuming those instances of pilfering and gluttony to be true, I considered that a person yielding to that habit, unless it be mania (and I would not go the length of saying it was) would be morally warped.

The Solicitor-General: The bishop spoke of kleptomania. Was that conveyed to your mind?—Not so strongly as he conveyed.

Was it at all?—Oh, it entered my mind certainly.

Did you prosecute the inquiry at all?—I had no business or power to prosecute it.

If you came to that opinion would you not have stated in your report that she was irresponsible?—I should still have been of opinion that the charges were proved, and that she was most unfit to be in a community, and charged with the education of young children.

But surely you would not have been a party to her expulsion with ignominy?—Then the expulsion would not be with ignominy.

But would you not have suggested to the bishop that the moral aspect of the case had changed?—There was no question of moral aspect before us. The question was one of fact? The other would be a question for his lordship the bishop.

You say you considered the depositions moderate in tone?—Yes.

Then were the conversations of Mrs. Star and Mrs. Kennedy stronger than the depositions?—I cannot say they were. They also spoke about Miss Saurin very moderately. My judgment was that their action also was moderate — always strictly within rule under great provocation.

All which you knew from them?—Yes.

And from them only?—From them only.

The Lord Chief Justice: Did you form any general opinion as to her state of mind?—There are degrees of responsibility, my lord, as you have observed, and it is exceedingly difficult to judge. I was inclined to think that she had arrived at what I should call the beginning of loss of responsibility, such as I have too often the opportunity of seeing in drunkards. I have seen persons whom I consider perfectly irresponsible before God after they take one glass of spirits. I used the word warped for that reason. I did not form a definite judgment. I thought there was a distortion of nature—less power of seeing truth, and less power of using liberty.

The Lord Chief Justice: What becomes of nuns who lose their reason?—There are institutions for them in different parts of Europe—asylums kept by religious persons where nuns who lose their reason are cared for.

Are there such asylums in this country?—There is one in Ireland, and one is I understand about to be established near London.

Have you known nuns removed to such asylums?—I have known several removed.

Mr. Mellish said he had now to put in the reports of the other commissioners.

The Solicitor-General: Do you not call Dr. O'Hanlon?

Mr. Mellish: You wished to summon him, and complained he had gone out of the way.

The Solicitor-General: All I know is that he is now here. He went away for the most natural of all reasons—not desiring to be mixed up in this case.

The Lord Chief Justice: I thought he had intended to go away upon business previously.

The Solicitor-General: It is no reflection upon any man to endeavour to keep out of a case like this.

The Lord Chief Justice: I cannot altogether agree with you. It would depend upon the circumstances. I think he should be called.

Mr. Mellish: Then I will put him in the box.

The Rev. Dr. O'Hanlon was next sworn and his deposition read. He stated that he was not satisfied that the charges relating to the period from 1862 to the time of the commission had been sufficiently proved. The sisters might not have been aware of the extraordinary and unexampled severity with which Sister Scholastica said she was treated by the mother superior, and if so, would not have known that many of the violations of rule which they charged her with were involuntary and inevitable.

Cross-examined by the Solicitor-General: I am librarian of Maynooth, and am prefect of the Dunboyne Institution.

What is that?—It is a religious institute founded by Lord Dunboyne, who had been Roman Catholic Bishop of Cork, then became a Protestant, and afterwards relapsed into Popery. (Laughter.)

Cross-examination continued: I have studied the canon law for twenty-five years. In Roman Catholic countries dispensation from vows from which the Pope only can absolve can only be obtained on the oath of two credible witnesses making out a grave charge. The bishop in this country cannot have an oath administered; but he can apply to the Pope, as the American bishops have done, for the substitution of a solemn declaration in place of the oath.

But for purposes of admonition he may appoint four or five gentlemen to make inquiry without oath or solemn declaration?—Yes.

Cross-examination continued: I have been consulted as to questions arising in convents in this and other countries. Assuming the penances or punishments inflicted on Sister Scholastica to be rightly described, I never heard of the like of them being inflicted before in any convent. They totally exceeded the power of the mother superior to inflict. Such as stripping her, and keeping her in the cold.

Mr. Mellish: That is a matter in dispute.

Dr. O'Hanlon: I am assuming it to be true. Also the putting of a wet duster on her for six hours; also making her eat tainted meat.

The Lord Chief Justice: That has not been mentioned before.

Cross-examination continued: I never saw Miss Saurin until the time of the commission. Father Matthews and I were fellow students. He wrote to me saying that the bishop had agreed to appoint me. I met him in Dublin, and we travelled to Hull together. We went from Dublin to Holyhead by steamer. I had very little conversation with him. He told me there were charges made against his niece, but I don't recollect that he particularised any of them. When the commission had met, and the order of proceedings were read, Father Matthews complained that the bishop had violated a promise he made to him as to the cross-examination of the nuns. I recollect that distinctly. The commissioners replied that they could not go beyond the bishop's instructions. I am disposed to think that Father Matthews also spoke about calling witnesses on his niece's behalf, but I don't so clearly recollect it as to swear it. During Sister Scholastica's examination Father Matthews came to her assistance occasionally, to make what she had said clear. She was interrogated by the president and the other commissioners.

To the Lord Chief Justice: I put questions to her myself.

The Solicitor-General: Was she interrupted when making statements?—I have no recollection of any interruption. She was allowed to make her statements. Sometimes Father Matthews was stopped when he was asking questions which were held to be outside the inquiry. The same course was pursued on the second day of the investigation. Her stockings were looked at on the second day. I must confess I never saw such things in my life. I did not know what they were composed of. I have never seen such stockings on a sister of mercy before or since. (Much laughter.) They were unfit for any human being.

To the Lord Chief Justice: The rest of the dress appeared to be tolerably decent.

To the Solicitor-General: She said that the stockings which were at the wash were worse than those she had on, and some of the commission spoke about seeing them, but we had seen enough of the stockings. (Laughter.) I think she asked that the dress she had been wearing up to the commission should be sent for. Although Father Matthews was continually checked, he did continue to go beyond the limits of the inquiry. (Renewed laughter.) The reports were written on the evening of the second day. I was astonished at the statement of the bishop's secretary here, that I said I supposed the commissions were all unanimous. I never said any such thing, and my report will refute it. I understood that I was there to hear the depositions, and to hear Miss Saurin's explanation. I looked upon it as a useless investigation, and I should not have taken part in it had I known what it was to be.

The Lord Chief Justice: Useless as an investigation of truth?—Yes, my lord, and also useless for the bishop's purpose—namely, expulsion.

To the Solicitor-General: The testimony of the twelve outweighed the testimony of one, and in that way I held that the charges were established; but I subjoined the observation that I was not to be understood as saying that they were juridically established. She said, as an instance, that she had been told to remain at work until such an hour that it was physically impossible for her to go to mass in proper time. The sisters, not knowing that, and seeing her come in late from mass, would naturally think that that was culpable which was inevitable. I said that the charges collectively had not been proved.

The Lord Chief Justice: But the individual charges, such as stealing food?—It did not apply to that. I took the charges collectively, and said that they had not been proved to my satisfaction. As, if nine charges were made and evidence given as to only three of them, the charges collectively would not have been proved.

The Solicitor-General: Now, as to the taking of food; did you understand there to have been a positive statement in the depositions that she stole food?—No, that they had been told so-and-so. They inferred it, and she denied it.

Mr. Mellish: It is mentioned positively in at least one of the depositions.

Re-examined by Mr. Mellish: I do not think that the investigation gave the bishop power to expel, the witnesses not having been sworn. A bishop cannot inflict a severe penalty on any one, priest or layman, unless the charges are sufficient, and are canonically or juridically proved.

Could he not remove a nun from a convent if her removal were necessary for the peace of the community?—Yes, but not expel, which is a severe punishment. I could tell you of a case in Ireland in which a parish priest had been misco..ducting himself. The Archbishop sent down the Vicar-General, and he said, "My good people, I cannot administer an oath; and, without an oath, your testimony will be of no avail." He then left the room, and in his absence an oath was administered. (Laughter.) He then returned and took evidence, but he subsequently got a

letter from the priest's attorney threatening him with a prosecution. (Renewed laughter.)

The Lord Chief Justice: This evidence raises a new question. If Dr. O'Hanlon is right, there was no expulsion at all.

Dr. O'Hanlon (to the Lord Chief Justice): I think the sentence of the bishop is null and of no effect.

The Solicitor-General: She was expelled in fact, rightly or wrongly. In any case, the conspiracy is not affected in any degree.

The Lord Chief Justice: Not in one point of view.

Dr. O'Hanlon (to Mr. Mellish): I objected to the sisters being examined in reference to the counter-charges. We had no power to go into them at all. I do not think the charges brought against Sister Scholastica were such as to warrant expulsion.

The Lord Chief Justice: Not the charge of theft?—It is not serious theft.

Not serious theft to steal portions of children's dinners?—It is not a grievous sin.

Would it not be if it left the children without their proper sustenance?—If it materially injured the children it might be a grievous sin.

Mr. Mellish: Would not habitual untruth be?—There is no case for expulsion unless for grievous sin that affects the interests of the community. Even the stealing of 18s. has been held not to be a grievous sin.

The Lord Chief Justice: Suppose it was the last 18s. a poor person had?—There, my lord, another point is introduced. If you take a needle from a tailor and keep him a fortnight out of work, you commit a grievous sin. (Much laughter.)

Mr. Mellish: Would not habitual untruth be a sufficient cause for expulsion?—It would not justify removal by the bishop, unless it caused public scandal.

Would all these things together?—Yes; taken together and juridically proved. But, singly, they would not have injured the community seriously.

The Lord Chief Justice: Take the case of stealing a medal from the dead body of a sister who had expressed a wish that it should be buried with her?

Dr. O'Hanlon: That would be exactly as if one sister in a family took the medal of her sister. These are sisters in one family, the superior being their spiritual mother. I do not think that in common estimation that would be regarded as a very heinous crime. Then, again, taking the boots. Suppose a young woman in a family took her sisters boots and wore them, I do not think would be regarded as a very grave matter.

The Lord Chief Justice: Perhaps you would extend the same principle to the taking of garments off a dead body in the chapel?—I think there would be something unnatural in that proceeding, my lord.

Unnatural?—And improper.

Mr. Mellish: There was nothing about that in the deposition.

The Solicitor-General: Not a word.

The Lord Chief Justice: I am aware of that, but I wanted to know how far the principle was to be applied.

Mr. Collins, examined by Mr. Russell: I recollect being at Clifford on the occasion spoken of. My wife was with me. I believe Mrs. M'Keon was the sister superior. I brought my wife to Clifford as she was in bad health, and that she might be near the nuns. I brought her to see the convent, and she wished to see the convent garden. We saw Mrs. M'Keon, and passed through the school where Miss Saurin was. The tower is a small fanciful building not higher than the court, and no more than the length of West-minster Hall from the convent. My wife, Mrs. M'Keon, and I went to the top of the tower. Mrs. M'Keon wished to go away immediately; but I asked her to remain, as I then understood the tower was outside the convent grounds, and we might be regarded as trespassers. We re-mained about twenty minutes or half-an-hour.

Cross-examined by the Solicitor-General : It was a beautiful day, and the time passed quickly. We endeavoured to see the Towers of York Ca-thedral.

I hope you succeeded.—We did not.

Mrs. Kennedy was then recalled, and, in re-ply to the Lord Chief Justice, stated that, by the rules of their order, no member of that community could hold property. At first they had been very poor, and the house which the commu-nity had used as a convent was obtained for them by some members of the congregation, who made themselves liable for its cost. For some time they made use of the school revenue for their mainte-nance by permission of the bishop, using the residue for charitable purposes. Subsequently, after the sisters came into the community they paid off the sum of £2,000 by degrees. A deed, which in equity was called a trust, was executed to seven or eight members of the community.

Mr. Russell said the conveyance was in court; that no trust was declared in it, but that it was well understood what its uses were. The three names of the parties were those of the plaintiff and the two defendants.

Mrs. Star was recalled, and in reply to the Lord Chief Justice, stated that the " leaves " were taken from the plaintiff after her return from Hull in 1864. She told her she was not to lend them or borrow, but from herself, who would give her anything she required. She had never given her any directions as to taking away the leaves at Clifford.

This closed the defendants' case.

A rebutting case on behalf of the plaintiff was then entered upon.

Miss Saurin, plaintiff, recalled.

Solicitor-General : It has been said that you have been unhappy and wretched in Baggot-street? —I never was unhappy there.

Is it true that you spoke harshly of the mother and sister superiors of the convent?—I am quite certain I never did.

Did you never mention to any one of your family the nature of the duties you had there?— I may have spoken of the schools, nothing more.

How many sisters were there?—Thirty or forty, if not more.

Something has been said about a letter of your brother's in which he represented you had made complaints of the superior and sisters at Baggot-street?—I never saw such a letter.

Mrs. King stated you read a letter from your brother and your sisters, to postulants or nuns. Did you?—I am positive I never did such a thing in my life. I remember Mrs. Star reading edify-ing letters from my sisters, and of my brother to a member of the community, and that was done at Clifford also by the mother superior.

Did you ever complain of being employed in the laundry in Baggot-street?—No. I was never employed to wash there. I used to keep the ac-counts, and received messages.

Did you ever cut the ham in the pantry, as was stated ?—Never.

Were you caught with your mouth full of ham, and your face greasy?—Never. I heard the charge here for the first time.

Now, as to the raspberries or strawberries and cream ; were you ever caught eating any ?—I am positive I never was. I remember Mrs. Grim-stone bringing a few occasionally for Mrs. Star, but she always kept them herself. (Laughter.)

Were they ever in the pantry?—Never.

Had you cream there?—No ; I do not think I ever saw cream in the house.

Examination continued : It was in 1860 Mrs. Kennedy and Mrs. Star withdrew from recrea-tion. The mother superior (Mrs. Morris) of Bag-got-street was there at the time. She was also there in 1857 or 1859 upon a ceremony of recep-tion.

Mrs. Star (recalled) : Mrs. Morris was never there after 1859.

Miss Saurin's cross-examination continued : I do not know what time of year it was. The book called " Devotions to Jesus," was given to me by Mrs. Star in Baggot-street. I do not know that it was given by her to Mrs. M'Keon. (Book produced.) This is the book. I never saw it after I gave it to Mrs. Star. Mrs. Delaney is, I have heard, in Belfast. I was on affectionate terms with her while she was sister superior at Clifford. I recollect the retreat of 1862. It was at that retreat I was first, I think, reproved by Mrs. Star. I did not com-plain about the reproof, or murmur about it. I never murmured against any reproof I got. I am quite certain as to that. I never requested Mrs. M'Keon to send for the extraordinary confessor of the convent. He came about once a quarter. I did confess to him, but that was the week he ought to come. His coming was nothing out of the regular course of practice. My letter to my uncle was not written on the night of the day I confessed, nor for a considerable time after. I wrote a copy of the intercepted letter, or all I could remember of it, and sent it to my uncle, to show him that there was nothing objectionable in it.

To the Lord Chief Justice : That is one of the two letters I acknowledged. I sent it to the post by a girl.

To the Solicitor-General : I am certain I made no admission of having written that letter before I went to Hull. Mrs. M'Keon conversed with me several times on the subject.

The Lord Chief Justice : Did you deny it?— I avoided the question. She asked me had I sent a letter by a little girl, and I said I had not. I had not done so then.

To the Solicitor-General : When she asked me afterwards about it, I said I had made a vow before the blessed sacrament not to speak about it, and I had.

The Lord Chief Justice : An ingenious mode of evading a troublesome question.

To the Solicitor-General : I had no conversation with Mrs. Star about the letters until the retreat. I did not make admissions about them, and afterwards withdraw them. I never said I had told lies about them to Mrs. M'Keon, or anything to that effect. I never said that the letter I sent by the girl was a letter to a Mrs. Watson, at Leeds, which had been sent to me to read. After acknowledging having written the letter, I never denied it. I never took a child's dinner.

The Lord Chief Justice : Or a child's cake?—Never, my lord. I never took a particle of any child's food ; of that I am perfectly certain.

To the Solicitor-General : I never ill-treated Lizzie Wilson. I never told Bridget Conolly to put on the clock, or any other of the pupil-teachers. I never refused to examine a class before Father Lynch. Nothing of the kind ever occurred. I recollect Margaret M'Cutchen and Charlotte Needom. They swept out the night-school, and sometimes on Saturdays washed the steps. They were engaged all day at a factory, except on the Saturday. I, as a matter of fact, did it on other days frequently, and swept the school twice a day sometimes. There was no request put upon the chapel door for prayer after my brother died.

Did you ever sew two pocket-handkerchiefs of yours together?—There is not the shadow of foundation for it. The only thing that could have led to it was that two handkerchiefs were tacked together to carry some underclothing to Clifford, the bundle being too big for one.

Examination continued : I never sewed thicknesses of garments together ; the only thing I did was to make one good garment out of two bad ones. I never took the marks—nails—out of a handkerchief. I would not in any case use any handkerchief but my own. It was the duty of the pupil-teachers to put the children's dinners by. I never ill-treated Jane Conolly or Andrew Owen. I was in attendance on Sister Mary Catharine when she died. She died of consumption. I never neglected her. I did not take a medal from her. I never did such a thing. It is utterly untrue that I took her sleeves. I never heard a word of it until I heard it in court here. I lost a medal myself, and may have asked a sister about it. I had got it on leaving Baggot-street.

The Lord Chief Justice : You are wearing one now?—I am, my lord. (Medal handed up.) The medal I lost was silver ; this is not.

At this point the case was adjourned, and it was arranged that the evidence in reply would be probably completed before mid-day to-morrow, and that Mr. Mellish should at once proceed to sum up the evidence ; that on Wednesday the Solicitor-General should reply on the whole case ; and that on Thursday the Lord Chief Justice should sum up the case to the jury.

SEVENTEENTH DAY, *Tuesday, February 23rd.*

To the agreeable surprise of all in the Court of Queen's Bench to-day, the witnesses called by the plaintiff's counsel, to rebut the supplementary evidence which had been unexpectedly introduced by the defence, were rattled so briskly through their examination, that Mr. Mellish was able in the forenoon to begin his address to the jury. Several young persons, who were younger a few years ago, and who were, in point of fact, the scholars from whom Miss Saurin was said to have taken food brought by them to the school-room for their dinners, utterly denied the story told by the nuns. The opportunity of extracting from the juvenile witnesses, while on the subject of bodily nourishment, some fresh and valuable testimony in settlement of the question where it was that the king "totted up" the contents of the privy purse, and in what other apartment of the royal palace the queen ate the bread and honey, was strangely neglected ; and we may conclude that no more will now be heard of the four-and-twenty blackbirds baked in a pie. When Mr. Mellish rose to speak, he and the Solicitor-General were the only occupants of the front row of seats allotted to leading counsel ; Mr Hawkins on the one side, and Mr. Digby Seymour on the other, being absent. The learned gentleman on whom had devolved the heavy duty of the day was seen to limp painfully as he entered the court ; and after he had been on his legs for about five hours, his suffering was so apparent that the Judge considerately suggested the adjournment of the Court at the hour of four. Mr. Mellish, however, went on half-an-hour longer, with the laudable intention of leaving as little as possible for the close of his speech next day. The court was more crowded than it has been since the early stage of the action ; and the heat, notwithstanding the low temperature outside, was oppressive ; a hoop of gas jets, like that which ordinarily illumines a country-circus, aiding in the vitiation of the atmosphere. To-day, the number of ladies was greater than ever, the front seats being almost exclusively taken up by them ; and there were two or three among the privileged spectators in the vicinity of the beach. The course taken by Mr. Mellish was that of a powerful appeal to common-sense, and the valuable impression left by his eloquence was, that the advocate felt the force of his advocacy, and was resting with perfect confidence on the strength of his case. He was watchfully helped by Mr. Charles Russell, but in so unobtrusive a way that the even tenour of the address—and Mr. Mellish has a very even and fluent, though not rapid, delivery—was never materially broken. Could it be supposed, the defending counsel asked, that nine ladies of unimpeached and unimpeachable character had united in the fabrication of a long and elaborate tissue of falsehoods? The main question, he observed, actually was the plaintiff's truthfulness ; and, if the jury saw that she was in the habit of inventing and altering her statements of facts to suit her own purpose—as he undertook to show that her three several narratives given at different times were totally irreconcilable one with another—the whole case tumbled to the ground. During the early and perhaps most effective passage of his address Mr. Mellish was closely pursued by the attention of the Solicitor-General, who made copious notes, but who gradually slackened his vigilance, and, when the Court rose for mid-day refreshment, went away, for good and all. It was owing to Mr. Russell's complete mastery of facts and dates, and to his surprising and unerring readiness of information, which almost anticipated the want of it, and yet never seemed to suggest an idea of any want at all, that the speech of Mr. Mellish was so thoroughly exhaustive, and — till the reply shall be heard—so convincing. The sturdiness of a second, whose first thought is that of seizing every possible advantage for his principal, and whose last is that of throwing up the sponge, was characteristic of Mr. Russell's calmly anxious mode of prompting. Miss Saurin, argued Mr. Mellish, had not the conventual mind. If a woman were not able to conform to ascetic and mortifying rules, she was not fit for a convent, and a convent was no place for her. However strange it may seem to externs, there was a certain view taken in conventual life, according to which the practice of checking natural affection towards relatives is necessary to the attainment of a highly-religious state. Grant that hypothesis, and it follows that means to check those exuberant affections would be justifiable in a convent, though not elsewhere. So argued Mr. Mellish with respect to the keeping back of letters written to Miss Saurin by her friends; and he took occasion to say that Mrs. Star and Mrs. Kennedy had the misfortune to be represented by perhaps as Protestant a counsel as could be found. But, said he, these sisters all start with a theory and they are bound to go on with it. What you have to see is that they honestly and fairly act up to their professions. The manufactured grievances of Miss Saurin are not those which a nun has any right to bring before the world. Instead of having had more penances imposed on her, she has had considerably less; and in fact, she has been humoured because it was seen that her worldly temper could not support the trials of an austere religious life. For a nun vowed to a life of mortification, her love of warm clothes, blazing fires, and mutton-chops, is certainly remarkable, and, one would think, inappropriate. This was the thread of Mr. Mellish's address, and the court was hushed and attentive while he was speaking.

The re-examination of Miss Saurin, in support of the rebutting case, was resumed. In reply to Mr. Wills, she said : I never took any article of clothing belonging to Sister Mary Catherine—guimp, coif, sleeves, medal, or anything else. I never took a penknife belonging to Mrs. Hewetson. I had a broken penknife, which was taken from me by Mrs. Star. I never took any gloves or any article of clothing belonging to Mrs. Hewitson, nor any black silk ribbon or black woollen material from the attic at Clifford. I never took a thimble from a school-child.

Or any needles or spools of thread belonging to Mrs. Hewetson ?—Never.

In 1862 or 1863 did you take any lining or other articles from the press ?—No.

Did you talk to Mrs. Collingwood about courtship ?—Never.

Or about what she has stated here—about young men, their ages, and so on ?—No.

Did you take tools out of the Rev. Mr. Motler's hand when he was screwing down a desk ?—I never did anything of the kind.

Mr. Wills said he had gone through everything he could possibly remember that had been stated by the defendants. If he had omitted anything it was unintentional.

Mr. Mellish : I shall not say that my learned friends have been afraid to ask Miss Saurin any question.

Witness (to Mr. Mellish): The time I speak of that the defendants retired from recreation, Mrs. Norris, the mother superioress of Baggot-street, came alone. I do not remember about there being a reception of a nun on that occasion.

(Book produced.)

Mr. Wills said that they had called for the chapter book, and it had not been produced.

Mr. Mellish said the book produced was not the chapter book. It was a note book in which the dates of the receptions were registered. It appeared that at the time stated Sister Mary Dixon was received.

The Lord Chief Justice (to plaintiff) : Now listen to this letter, and answer me truly the question I shall ask you ; and, remember, do not "avoid the question."

Leeds, Springfield, Sept. 16, 1865.

My Lord,—I waited two days at Hull, and received your letter. Mrs. Star assures me the causes of which you absolved my darling sister were grave faults, against vows and rules, as, of course, they should be. Of course, also, they were known to you, and from you I was to learn them ; but in the uncertainty as to whether I should see you, I saw my poor darling, and interrogated her under the secrecy of my priestly character, when she revealed a mystery that exceeded all the horrors I ever heard or knew. Her story is equal to anything I saw in the lives of the saints, and the horrors of which she has been made the victim far surpass anything that has entered the mind of the most fanatical enemies of the convents. Under one operation, which was repeated four times, " I hesitated for a moment," said she, "when Christ, as it were, appeared to me, bound and stripped at the pillar. I raised my eyes to heaven, and the rev. mother said, 'See how her eyes turn.' I thought my body was falling in pieces, and I cried aloud, 'Yes, Lord, I will—I will make any sacrifice.'" While telling me this, my lord, I saw she was falling against me, and you may guess what was my struggle and my pain to seem unmoved. Her crimes are those of Christ, my lord, by whom she is ever physically sustained. She is starved and naked, for her covering by night and by day is gone. She has been watched lest she might eat the bread of the poor children, and, although starved, she made up her mind to die rather than taste a morsel of it. She has been dexterously kept from any interview with your lordship, and she knows she is dying, for of course she would rather die ten thousand times than leave the convent or commit one single sin. She has been kept in absolute silence, my lord, and no one allowed to speak to her during two years, her greatest dread being that she should lose her reason under this cross. The train is going on, my lord, and you will pardon this scrawl. Mrs. Star has too solid reasons to try and keep poor darling sister out of Baggot-street, and she scrupled not to murder her soul and body to gain that end. Adieu, my lord; protect my poor darling saint.—Ever yours truly,

MATTHEW SAURIN, S.J.

What does that letter refer to?—It refers to the stripping on the 31st of May, my lord, when rev. mother obliged me to take off all my clothes to my tunic.

Is that what he here writes about?—That was the first time I had ever mentioned it.

And that was what he says surpassed all the horrors he had read in the lives of the saints?— I believe so, my lord. I never heard of it until it was read in court.

Did you tell him you had seen a vision of our Lord—that you had seen Christ bound to the pillar?—No, my lord ; what I said was this——

Attend to the question. Did you say you had seen a vision of our Lord bound to the pillar— that you raised your eyes and said, "I will, Lord; I will make the sacrifice." Did you tell him that?—No, my lord.

Is it his invention ?—No.

Did you tell him then ?—I said that I was dreadfully shocked, and that I remembered all that our Lord had suffered.

Did you say anything about a vision ?—I did not mention anything about a vision.

And that is what he means by something that exceeded all the horrors he had read of in the lives of the saints?—I told him more than that, my lord.

What more?—I told him what I had been obliged to submit to.

What did you tell him ?—About stripping, my lord—the stripping off of my clothes.

Anything more ?—I do not remember, my lord.

The following additional evidence was then given.

Mary Ellen Margaret Swales called and sworn. In reply to Mr. Wills, she said : I live now at Darlington. My parents live at Clifford. I was a scholar at the convent school (St. Elizabeth's) at Clifford. I first went in 1861, and remained until 1863. My brother went with me. We were in the habit of taking our dinners to the school.

Did you or your brother ever lose your dinner? —No.

Or any portion of it ?—No.

Were you under Sister Scholastica ?— For work.

Did she ever take any part of your dinner ?— No.

To Mr. Mellish : I am now fourteen years of age. In 1861 I was six years of age. My brother is sixteen months younger.

Have you much recollection of what your dinners were when you were six years old ?—No, sir.

Mr. Wills : But she would have recollected losing them if she had lost them.

Elizabeth Copeland called.

Mr. Mellish said he did not recollect any charge coming from Elizabeth Copeland.

Mr. Wills : It was stated that her cake and dinners were taken.

The Lord Chief Justice : Her name occurs, I believe, in one of my early volumes of notes. (Laughter.)

A juror said the name was certainly mentioned.

Mr. Mellish : Mrs. Hewetson spoke of an infant between one and two years of age.

Mr. Wills : This is the only person of the name of Copeland in the schools.

Witness sworn and examined by Mr. Wills : I always took my nephews to school—always. There are no other Copelands in Clifford. We were under Sister Scholastica all the time I was at school.

Did you ever know your little nephew's cake or eatables to be taken from him by Sister Scholastica ?—No, sir.

Did you ever know her do anything of the kind ?—No.

Now, what was the conduct of Sister Scholastica to the children ?—Very kind and very good.

Did you ever know her to beat or punish the children? I never knew her to do it.

Or anything of the kind?—No.

Cross-examined by Mr. Mellish : I went to the schools when I was three or four years of age, and remained until I was sixteen. Sister Scholastica was only there some part of the time I was there. My nephew was in a different room from me. We were not both under Sister Scholastica. My nephew was. I was under Sister Mary Agnes (Mrs. M'Keon), but Sister Scholastica taught us sewing in the day school. My nephew's dinner was never brought to the school at all. He always went home. Occasionally he might have been taken to school by some one else. He went home to dinner, but brought some cake to eat between times. I do not know where it used to be put. I did not take care of it. He brought cake both in the morning and afternoon. He was three years old at the time.

The Lord Chief Justice : Who took care of him in the other school ?—He took care of himself. (A laugh.)

Re-examined : Miss Saurin taught us sewing every day from one till two. The dinner hour was twelve o'clock. I never heard any complaint from my nephew that he had lost a cake, or any part of a cake.

Elizabeth Amoss called. When the child entered the box, her appearance—her head was scarcely visible above the desk—caused much laughter.

The Solicitor General : This child's size causes some amusement ?—But what are we to do?

The child, who, at the request of a juror, was placed on the bench, was examined.

In reply to the Lord Chief Justice, she said she would be ten years of age next April.

To Mr. Wills : I went to the school at Clifford, and remained until the nuns left. I was under Sister Scholastica. She took care of me. I used to take my dinner on wet days in a basket.

Did Sister Scholastica ever take your dinner, or any part of it ?—No, sir.

Cross-examined : Our dinners were put in a cupboard.

What become of them ?—We ate them. (A laugh.)

Elizabeth Wilson, also a child of ten years of age, examined : I went to school at Clifford, and was under Sister Scholastica. She was kind to me and to all the children. She never took any of my dinner.

Cross-examined by Mr. Mellish : Two men came to me about coming here. I do not know who they were.

What did they tell you?—I do not remember.

The Lord Chief Justice : Try and remember. Try and remember.

Witness : They told me they came about Sister Mary Scholastica taking my dinner.

And you said she had not ?—Yes.

What else did they say?—About her beating me.

Did you tell them she had not?—I did.

Were you always a good child at school? (A laugh.) (No answer.)

The Lord Chief Justice: When you were naughty, what did the nuns do?—Slapped me.

With what?—With a stick on the arm.

Mr. Mellish: Were you under Sister Scholastica?—No.

Who, then?—Sister Mary Agnes.

The Lord Chief Justice: Was it Sister Scholastica slapped you with the stick on the arm?—No, sir.

Who was it?—Sister Mary Agnes. (Laughter.)

A Juror: Does she know the nature of an oath?

The Lord Chief Justice: Why did you kiss the book just now?—To tell the truth, sir.

Were you out of the infant school, and in the other school, at five years of age?—I was, sir.

Mary Margaret Clarke, also ten years of age, sworn. In reply to Mr. Wills she said: I was at the convent schools at Clifford till the nuns went away. I had my brother with me. I was under Sister Scholastica sometimes, and sometimes Sister Mary Agnes. My brother was in the gallery, and was taught by Sister Mary Josepha.

Was Sister Mary Scholastica kind or unkind to you or your brother?—Very kind, sir.

Did you ever know her to be unkind to any child?—No, sir.

Or take their dinners?—I never did, sir.

To Mr. Mellish: I never was put on the stool.

[The charge was that plaintiff put her on a stool, and said to her, " Now roar, you big bully."]

Mr. Wills: Did Sister Mary Scholastica ever put you on a stool and say, " Now roar, you big bully"?—No, sir.

Miss Bridget Conolly, examined by Mr. Wills: I was pupil-teacher at Cannon-street, and at the convent school, Hull. My apprenticeship lasted five years, and during that time I was in one or other of the schools. Sister Scholastica taught at times at both schools.

Did she ever tell you to put back the clock or put it on?—No.

The Lord Chief Justice: Have you ever done it?—Yes, I have.

Mr. Wills: But did she ever give you directions on the subject?—I never remember anything about it.

Examination continued: When I did put forward the clock she was not at the school.

Did you ever tell Mrs. Kennedy that Sister Scholastica had told you to put on the clock?—No; I never did.

Mr. Wills: You know what her conduct was towards the children?

Mr. Mellish objected.

Cross-examined by Mr. Mellish: The schools were under the management of Mrs. Kennedy when I put on the clock. Before the sisters came to Hull at all I was at the schools, and was blamed for putting on the clock.

Did you ever put on the clock after the sisters came to Hull?—If I did it was of my own accord.

But did you?—I really cannot tell positively.

Mr. Mellish: Did Mrs. Kennedy ever blame you for putting on the clock?—Never.

Did she complain of irregularity in the school hours?—No. The sisters had watches to appeal to. There was a clock in the room, but it did not regulate the time, as the sisters went by their watches.

Julia O'Brien, examined by the Solicitor-General: I am the wife of Daniel O'Brien, of Hull. I have two children, one of them named Francis Joseph, who is turned seven years old. When he was about eighteen months old I sent him to the Prime-street infant-school.

Have you any reason for recollecting the three first birthdays you kept of his and the fourth?—No; he was at school on his fourth birthday, as he had been on his third and second. (A laugh.)

Did you ever complain of his dinner being taken?—I never heard any complaint on the subject, except from the servant on one occasion. I heard the servant asking the child why he had not got his dinner on that day. I said it was very likely the school children had got it from him. That was after his fourth birthday, as I thought he was getting old enough to take his dinner with him and get it himself. He left school in December, 1866. In the February following he was five years old. No complaint was ever made to me connected with the name of Sister Scholastica. I never sent a servant or anyone to the convent to make a complaint against Sister Scholastica or anyone else.

Mr. Mellish: There was no complaint made of that sort?

Mr. Wills: Indeed there was. Mrs. Nelligan in her evidence said that Mrs. O'Brien's servant, Catherine Wallace, came to the convent and " complained that Sister Mary Scholastica had eaten, not taken, the child's dinner every day. I promised it should not happen again, and took the child away."

The Lord Chief Justice read his notes of the evidence to the same effect.

Witness, cross-examined by Mr. Mellish: I had a servant named Catherine Wallace. She left my service last March. She is now in Preston. She used to go with the child to school in the morning. If the servant heard any complaints she did not tell me anything about it. I have no reason to believe she ever heard any complaints. On the one day I refer to Catherine Wallace told me that the child had not got his dinner. I said it was likely one of the children took it from him. She then spoke to one of the sisters, and the sister said she would give him the dinner herself. The child told the servant that one of the sisters had given him some bread and cheese out of the dinner, and put the rest on the chimney-piece, and that it was taken away.

Was the sister's name mentioned who did that?—Yes, sir.

Who was it?—Sister Mary Bernard.

Jane Conlin, aged ten and a half years, examined by Mr. Wills: I was at Prime-street school and the convent school also at Hull under Sister Scholastica. She never beat me or ill-treated me. She was always very kind to me. I never saw her beat any of the children.

Mr. Wills: The statement was, " I saw her beat Jane Conlin, and afterwards she denied it."

Not cross-examined.

Andrew Owen called.

Mr. MELLISH: I am told this is not the boy.

Mr. WILLES: This is the only Andrew Owen I can find.

Mr. MELLISH: I understand that the Andrew Owen had red hair.

Mrs. Nelligan (to the Lord Chief Justice): This child was never in the school.

Did you not give his name as Andrew?—His name is Alexander.

The SOLICITOR-GENERAL: She said it was Andrew.

Mr. RUSSELL: She said she was not sure.

Mr. WILLES: The charge was that the plaintiff pulled his hair and pinched him, and that he screamed.

The SOLICITOR-GENERAL: We can do no more than produce those who were named.

Anne Bailey called and examined: I had a little girl at the Cannon-street Convent School. She is now in a reformatory. She was in the school seven years. I had other children in the school also. They used to take their dinners with them. I never heard any complaint from any of them of having lost their dinners.

Mrs. Fearon called: I named Bailey or Watson. The child I spoke of was not the child of this witness.

The SOLICITOR-GENERAL: We have done our utmost to find the Watsons, but without effect.

This closed the rebutting case.

Mrs. Kennedy, in reply to a juror, said that the convent in Clifford was closed on or about December, 1867.

To the Lord Chief Justice: The plaintiff came to this country in May, 1856, from Baggot-street.

The LORD CHIEF JUSTICE: The plaintiff, I have no doubt unintentionally, said she came over in 1857.

Mr. MELLISH then said that, before he proceeded to address the jury, he had to draw his lordship's attention to the pleadings. The first count was for assault and imprisonment. Now, the first assault was what was called the stripping, in May, 1865, at which Mrs. Kennedy no doubt was present. He could not deny that, on that occasion, Mrs. Star put her hand into the plaintiff's pocket, and that in law would, if unexplained, amount to an assault. The defence was that the plaintiff, being a voluntary member of the society, licensed Mrs. Star to deal with her according to the rules of the society.

The LORD CHIEF JUSTICE: She made no resistance. She seems to have admitted that it was part of her duty to obey; even if the jury came to the conclusion that some force was used, I think it would come under your plea of leave and license.

Mr. MELLISH: As long as she remained a member of the society she was bound by its rules, and she might at any moment claim her liberty. But as long as she insists on remaining, she licenses the superior to carry out the rules. Then there is a count in trover as to which we have lodged a small amount in Court, and there is no question about it.

The LORD CHIEF JUSTICE: Even if you have not, I should have held that while she was a member of the community she could have no property. But as, when she ceased to be a member, the property may have reverted, you acted wisely in lodging money in Court. There remains the libel.

The SOLICITOR-GENERAL: That count was framed from the best information we could obtain of the commission. Since, however, we have seen the depositions, and your lordship has already intimated you would allow us to amend.

The LORD CHIEF JUSTICE: Mr. Mellish objected, unless you amended at once. You are too late now.

The SOLICITOR-GENERAL: Very well, my lord. I think the libel is sufficiently and substantially stated.

The LORD CHIEF JUSTICE said that if the writing of the letters, and the framing of the depositions were done honestly, he should hold that the occasion was privileged.

The SOLICITOR-GENERAL: In that view I concur.

The LORD CHIEF JUSTICE: And that would apply equally to the libel.

The SOLICITOR-GENERAL said he should contend that the count as it stood was sustained by the depositions.

The LORD CHIEF JUSTICE: That I doubt very much. Now, as to the imprisonment, you have heard all the evidence. I do not know whether you intend to ask the jury to say that she could not leave the house or her room if she had desired to do so.

The SOLICITOR-GENERAL: I do not mean to suggest that she could not have left the house if she had submitted to the putting on of the secular dress.

The LORD CHIEF JUSTICE: What about being confined to her room?

The SOLICITOR-GENERAL: Suppose I dismiss a servant who will not leave the house, and that I do not wish to try conclusions with him—if I lock him in a particular room it is imprisonment, even though I tell him that if he wishes to leave, the door will be opened.

The LORD CHIEF JUSTICE: The question here is whether there was any such restraint. You say there was.

The SOLICITOR-GENERAL: I do, my lord.

The LORD CHIEF JUSTICE: Very well, then it must go to the jury.

Mr. MELLISH said he should contend that even confinement to one room—if the party knew he or she could get out of the house at any moment —would not be imprisonment.

The LORD CHIEF JUSTICE said it was matter of law, as to which question should be reserved if the jury were of opinion that restraint was used.

Mr. MELLISH: The next count is as to the conspiracy.

The LORD CHIEF JUSTICE: There are two distinct charges—conspiring to expel by ill-treatment, and conspiring to procure expulsion by false charges.

Mr. MELLISH: What is the nature of the contract between the parties?

The LORD CHIEF JUSTICE: I think there was no contract at all. The plaintiff never gave any consideration to the community. Her dower was paid to Baggot-street convent. As at present advised I am of opinion that the action cannot be sustained, inasmuch as the consideration in respect of which she would be entitled to the advantages set forth in the declaration was never paid. It may be that she has rights elsewhere; but she could remain in the Hull convent, as it appears to me, only so long as they wished to keep her. Of course I will reserve that point for you.

Mr. MELLISH submitted that if there was a contract it was like a contract in a trades' union society, with a variety of clauses in restraint of trade. If there was a contract at all, it was that the parties should remain in the community for life, and was, therefore, one in restraint of natural liberty, of marriage, and of the accumulation of wealth. The contract, therefore, if there was one, was opposed to the policy of the law and could not be sued upon.

The LORD CHIEF JUSTICE: That objection also is a very grave one, and you are entitled to have it reserved.

Mr. MELLISH: Then, as to the conspiracy. If two parties combine to procure a legal object by legal means it is not an actionable conspiracy. If the thing to be effected is not of itself actionable, there is no conspiracy.

The LORD CHIEF JUSTICE: My impression is that your objections are well founded, and I will reserve them should the jury find against the defendants.

Mr. MELLISH then proceeded to address the jury on behalf of the defendants. He said he had to congratulate them upon at length nearing the conclusion of that protracted case. From the observations which the Lord Chief Justice had let fall, they would see that the question they had to try was not so much the character of Miss Saurin, although incidentally that might be involved in their decision, as the character of Mrs. Star and Mrs. Kennedy. The charge against them was that, from wrong and malicious motives, they had conspired together, by cruel actions and by false representations to the bishop, to procure the dismissal of Miss Saurin from the convent. They had seen the witnesses who had been examined for the defendants, and who belonged to the convent, and they must have arrived at the conclusion that they were ladies by birth and by education. They were ladies who had given up their time and devoted their lives for the purpose of charity and relief of distress and the education of the poor; and he was entitled to say that, after a fortnight or three weeks' examination, they had had, with the exception of the matters relating to Miss Saurin, nothing whatever which in any way could bear against the character of any one of these ladies. As far as they knew, putting aside the present case, these ladies had passed their lives in strict conformity with the rules and professions they had made; and the gross scandal that had been produced against them was that trumpery affair about Mrs. M'Keon going up to the tower with Mr. Collins, and, as it afterwards appeared, with Mrs. Collins also. Did they not believe that, if any charge could have been brought against Mrs. Star or Mrs. Kennedy of cruelty towards a single nun, towards any novice or postulant or child, during the last ten years, the hand that noted down the circumstances of the tower would have noted down that charge also? He was therefore entitled to say that there was no imputation against them, except with respect to this matter of Miss Saurin. That was a fact which he thought ought to weigh very much

with them. And now let them look at what the charges against them were. They were not merely that Mrs. Star and Mrs. Kennedy, but that the whole of these ladies had agreed together to invent false charges against Miss Saurin. Was it really likely that this was the case? Could anybody suppose that ladies who had devoted their lives to such purposes, whose characters were utterly untarnished, had united together, and for what cause and for what purpose, against one of the sisterhood—one who, according to her own account, was liked by them during several years—who, according to her own account, had given them no cause whatever of offence, and who, according to the opinions of society, must have been just as agreeable, if not more agreeable, than any of the others. Could any one believe that these ladies would have united wickedly to effect the ruin of a sister by false charges, or that, by cruelties they would endeavour to get one of themselves expelled from the nunnery? The first thing they should ask themselves was, what was the cause of the state of the feelings that arose respecting Miss Saurin? One thing was plain, that Miss Saurin had no partisan in the convent. It might be said that perhaps Mrs. Star had got a spite against her, and was able, by her influence over the others, to induce them to join against her. But he did not think that they could possibly come to any such conclusion. He had seen all the witnesses in the box, and he thought that they would be of opinion that their distaste towards Miss Saurin, their wish to have her removed, arose from feelings of their own, and was not in any way inculcated upon them by Mrs. Star. Surely there must have been something in Miss Saurin herself to have caused this feeling. Otherwise, how could this same unanimous opinion have actuated this number of ladies? Let them consider the evidence of even those who were novices under her, and who said that she was constantly talking of worldly things, and acting in an un-nunlike spirit. They all knew something of the conventual spirit, and therefore such things as took them all at first—the opening of letters, having restrictions on interviews with relatives, having penances to perform—were in accordance with that which those ladies believed would lead to a holy life. They might not agree with them; they might think them absurd; but they were, and Miss Saurin knew them to be, in accordance with the rules by which she voluntarily bound herself. It was important to remember the origin of the state of feeling which arose in the convent, and Miss Saurin gave three different accounts of it on three different occasions. The first was in a letter to the bishop of the 23rd Sept., 1863, in which she attributed it to something that had occurred during a visit of Mrs. Star to Ireland. "I first found a change after she returned from Ireland. I think she then thought she could get enough of postulants, and that she preferred her own training, as she changed many of the old customs. Besides, I knew the circumstances of many of the sisters, some of whom were under me in the house of mercy in Baggot-street, which she did not like." There was not, in point of fact, any truth in that the first ground of the change of feeling alleged. When she was called before the commissioners she gave another version of it, and attributed it to the discovery of the concealed letters in 1862. What was the account she gave during her evidence in this case? She then introduced an entirely new charge, namely, that some time in the year 1860 Mrs. Star asked her to tell her her confession, which she declined to; and also asked her what the priest had said, which she also declined to state. Was there any truth in that statement? Could any one of them believe it? She had already given two other versions of the origin of the ill-feeling which she said Mrs. Star entertained towards her; and when she came to this Court, she gave another and a different one, which Mrs. Star swore to be untrue, and which was opposed to, and and would, if it happened, be a violation of obligations held in the Roman Catholic Church to be most sacred. He thought they would have no difficulty in arriving at the conclusion that this third version of the cause of alienation was a pure invention, and if it was, what became of the plaintiff's case? He did not ask them to weigh the testimony of witnesses against that, but he asked them, if they thought this matter was an invention, could they believe the story of the plaintiff? But, even if the three versions were true, and that they accounted for the feeling of Mrs. Star towards her, how could they account for the feeling of Mrs. Kennedy and of all the other nuns towards her? Their evidence made matter clear. They saw from the first that she had mistaken her vocation. Whatever they all thought of conventual life, it was only a certain class of minds that was suited to it. However they might disapprove of it, they could not fail to see that these ladies thought that they could obtain holy perfection only by breaking the will to absolute obedience to the will of another. The mind of Miss Saurin was not so constituted, and to one like her a convent must be intolerable, and she must have made the convent intolerable to herself and to every one else. If the fact were that she habitually disobeyed rules in matters trifling in themselves, but serious in the aggregate, it would surely account for the feelings of the other nuns towards her. That was the view which commended itself to his mind. The story of the plaintiff was altogether inconsistent, and they should pause before they came to the conclusion that it was out of some wicked hatred on the part of Mrs. Star, which she contrived somehow to instil into the minds of the others, that all the unpleasantness which took place in the convent had arisen. If they could not trust her, there was an end of the case. She was contradicted not only by nine credible witnesses, but on this point she was convicted of falsehood out of her own mouth, and if they could not believe her, her case fell to the ground. Again, the plaintiff said that in 1860 she was sent to Clifford because Mrs. Kennedy thought she was better fitted than any one else to get schools there into a state of efficiency. Mrs. Star stated that that was not the case, and that the reason for her being sent to Clifford was because the novices and postulants were at Hull, and that her example was disedifying to them. Her own letters were evidences against her in this respect, and supported Mrs. Star's statement, as they were full of errors of spelling, and showed that she was unfit to promote the efficiency of schools. She complained, too, that she had been made to rise earlier in the morning than the other sisters, but this was subsequently explained by the fact that all the sisters on one occasion, when they wished to finish some shirts, asked to get up earlier than usual; and, in fact, it was shown by the evidence for the defence that this was a manufactured grievance to make out a case of persecution. She stated in the most positive manner that up to March, 1862, she never had been reproved for any breach of rule, while the fact appeared to be abundantly proved by the defendants that at the retreat of 1861 she was publicly reproved by Mrs. Star for insincerity. It was said that Mrs. Star in her deposition made a malicious statement as to the sending of a letter by Miss Saurin to the post by a girl, and the denial of it by plaintiff when about to take the sacrament. Now the question was not what were the charges against the plaintiff, but what were the charges against the defendants. They, not she, were on their trial now. They had the evidence of Mrs. King, Mrs. M'Keon, and Mrs. Star on the subject, and he confidently asked them could they believe they had conspired to tell an untruth about the matter? Mrs. Star had received the reports of Mrs. King and of Mrs. M'Keon, who had questioned the girl Mary Murphy on the subject of the posting of the letter, so that Mrs. Star had abundant evidence to satisfy her as to that fact, and that fact she stated in her depositions, as she was bound to do. From that time—from the discovery of the intercepted letter—Mrs. Star became desirous of having Miss Saurin removed, and she wrote to Father Mathews on the subject. The wish of Mrs. Star and Mrs. Kennedy was to have her removed quietly, and without confusion or exposure. On the 27th of July, 1862, Miss Saurin wrote a letter to her uncle on the subject of her removal to Drogheda. Her statement was that Mrs. Star dictated it, but he submitted that the letter bore natural evidence that the letter was her own. " Unless you settle with the community to remove me, my dearest uncle, I know not what to do.' They knew what Mrs. Star had said in reference to the expression of too great affection for relations, and would she be likely to have interjected the words " my dearest uncle" into the middle of the letter. Mrs. Star stated that she dictated one sentence only of the letter, namely, on the subject of steps being about to be taken for the removal of the plaintiff; but she denied that she had dictated it all. They would observe in the middle of the letter the words, "the horrid writing." Again: "For God's sake, do not say a word to any of my friends—not even to mamma—I know she would feel it so." It was beyond question that the letter—with the exception stated by Mrs. Star—was the plaintiff's; and that the story of the writing of it first on a slate from the dictation of the rev. mother was a story. It was a small matter, but not unimportant in considering, as they should do, which of the parties was to be believed. In August, 1862, Mrs. Star wrote to the bishop, applying that Miss Saurin should be released from her vows and dismissed from the community for writing letters to her uncle, an extern, and for habitual disobedience. That letter served to show that the statement of the plaintiff that up to August, 1862, she had not been reproved, could not be relied on. It was clear that these things having been going on for some time she must have been, as in fact she had been, reproved for them more than once before that time. To that letter Miss Saurin replied in a letter to the bishop, in which she made a grave counter-charge against the reverend mother. She said that Mrs. Star would never have known about the sending of the letters, but that she had herself revealed the fact to her in her private manifestation of conscience, a thing she said Mrs. Star had no right to make use of, and that her doing so was against rule. Now it was a direct untruth that Mrs. Star would not have known about the letters but for the acknowledgement of the plaintiff. One letter had been found by Mrs. King under her bed; the sending of the other she had been frequently charged with by Mrs. M'Keon, and she knew that the strongest possible circumstantial evidence existed as to the sending of it. It was therefore altogether the contrary of the fact that Mrs. Star only knew of the sending of the letter by the plaintiff's acknowledgment in her private manifestation of conscience. In the following October or November the bishop held a visitation, and, no doubt, inquired into these matters. His own account of it was that he determined to take no action, in the hope that matters would mend. Then plaintiff went to Clifford, and here she made various charges of acts of severity against Mrs. M'Keon as the delegate of Mrs. Star. Amongst them was the keeping back of a letter, announcing the death of a brother, for three weeks. Was that true? It appeared to be a very cruel act when the case was opened. But did they think three or four ladies had invented the statement they had heard with respect to it, namely, that the letter was put to the plaintiff within three hours of its arrival, and that a notice was put up in the chapel that very evening requesting that the brother's soul might be prayed for? Now here there could be no mistake: one party or the other was telling a direct untruth. Was it the plaintiff, or was it Mrs. M'Keon and the ladies who spoke positively in direct contradiction to the story of the plaintiff? Let them determine that single question, and they determined the whole case. It was said that some of the letters of her Jesuit brother had been held back. Well, judging from the tone of the letter from that gentleman, which had been read that day, it was not improbable that they were. There was nothing, so far as they could judge, in the character of her Jesuit brother which could lead them to doubt the statement of the defendants' witnesses, that he had written and she read aloud letters in which there were most disrespectful remarks as to the superiors of Baggot-street. Right or wrong, the checking of natural affections towards relations was a part of the conventual system. They thought that the affections should be placed on higher objects, and that towards all earthly things they should be limited. Granting their hypothesis for the sake of argument—granting that a life of mortification and works of charity was the life most pleasing to God, it followed that checking exuberant affections towards relations might be a necessary part of it. It was not for him to argue whether that was right or not. Perhaps one of the hardships under which Mrs. Star laboured in this case was that she had the misfortune to be represented by as Protestant a counsel as could be found. But, if they meant

to do justice, they must bring their minds to believe, for the purpose of the case, the defendants' theory of what constituted the most holy life. They believe it can only be attained by the means they adopt. That was the theory they started with, and on which they acted, and it was for the jury to say whether they acted on it honestly; and it was perfectly consistent with acting on it honestly to keep back letters from relations. He would not go into the matters complained of by the plaintiff as to the domestic duties she had to perform. They had the evidence of the defendants before them, which clearly showed that Miss Saurin did nothing, and was asked to do nothing, that the other sisters had not to do. The taking of the watch and the taking of some bedding one night at Clifford had been fully explained, and the explanation demonstrated that the facts had been greatly exaggerated, and had been put forward in support of trumped-up grievances. The circumstance that on one occasion no fewer than five pockets had been found on her went to support the bishop's view, that she really could not keep her hands off anything, however trifling. After this, no doubt, Miss Saurin was not trusted; it was thought necessary to watch her. Mrs. M'Keon could not keep her in order, and wrote to Mrs. Star that she would rather beg her bread from door to door than have further charge of her. Everything she stated she exaggerated; everything she was charged with she denied; and many things which appeared strange at the opening—such as the wearing of the duster—now towards the close of the case, and with the light that had been thrown upon conventual life, appeared to be matters of ordinary occurrence. She had not penances inflicted on her that others had not to endure—on the contrary she had less, because, owing to her temper, she was indulged. The plaintiff swore in the most positive manner that she never on any occasion ate between meals without leave, but as against that statement there was not a sister who had not seen her eating ham, or strawberries, or gooseberries, or cake. These might be considered trumpery matters, but they were important in considering which side was telling the truth. For a person who undertook to lead a life of mortification Miss Saurin appeared to have strange tastes. She disliked mutton when roast or cold, and she had a great love of warmth, and, to acquire it, wore a number of petticoats, or made her ordinary petticoats heavy. She complained of having had bad clothes to wear, but they now knew that nuns wore their clothes for years. Mrs. Star told them that she had had but one veil for ten years, and Mrs. Kennedy that she had never had but one habit. Miss Saurin's stockings may have been bad, but they had evidence which showed that she was in the habit of destroying her wearing apparel wilfully, and stockings were part of a nun's dress which no one ever saw.

The LORD CHIEF JUSTICE: There is an error in the report of Dr. O'Hanlon's evidence which he may wish to have corrected. What he said was not that he had never seen such stockings on a nun before or since—(laughter)—but that he had never seen a nun's stockings before or since. (Renewed laughter.)

Mr. MELLISH next referred to what was called the thimble affair, and called on the jury to believe that the plaintiff had grossly exaggerated what took place, and that the evidence on the subject given for the defence was correct. The circumstances as to the stripping also had been greatly exaggerated, and with respect to the taking of children's dinners, no fewer than four sisters swore positively that with more or less certainty they had reason to suspect that Miss Saurin was in the habit of taking the children's food. The facts were reported to Mrs. Star. She believed them, and it became her imperative duty to ascertain how the facts were ; and with that view, although leaving Miss Saurin to believe that it was to look after a staylace, she directed her to undress immediately on returning from the school. The learned gentleman then read the letter of Mrs. Star to the bishop offering her resignation as mother superior. Was that a genuine letter? Was it true that from the time the plaintiff came from Clifford to Hull the whole spirit of the community had changed? They all said so. Miss Saurin was too much for them. She would break through the rule. They had no command over her, and they were miserable. It might be that Miss Saurin was also miserable ; but the fact was she was not suited for the life she undertook to lead. If the real state of things was set forth in that letter, what injustice would be done if the plaintiff succeeded in this action ! He begged of them not to allow popular prejudice to get hold of their minds and prevent them forming their own judgment. Let them decide for themselves upon the evidence. They knew what the popular feeling had been, and how they had had to struggle against it. He asked them as honest, truth-loving men, to form their own judgment, and to see whether the account Mrs. Star gave in that letter was the real truth— that, with one exception, the sisters were "docile, simple, self-sacrificing, and loving. They love God, love each other, love the rules, and love the poor." If that were true, what monstrous injustice would be done if there were a verdict for the plaintiff in this case ! Here were nine women, simple, self-sacrificing, who loved each other, loved God, and loved the poor ; what injustice it would be if, because one woman came among them of a different kind, who had a temper unfit for the position, and became the cause of this unhappy dispute—what injustice if, having rendered them unhappy in the convent, she succeeded against them, owing to popular prejudice, in a court of law ? He could not and did not believe that such would be the case. The learned gentlemen then read the letters of the sisters to the bishop, appealing to him to remove the plaintiff. He then referred to Mrs. Star's deposition, the gravest charge in which, he said, related to the sending of the clandestine letters, as to which she said, "She did not scruple to make use of the Holy Sacrament to cover her deceit." But it was the strict and natural inference from what she had heard from Mrs. M'Keon and Mrs. King, and was made in good faith, and in the firm belief that it was true. The words relating to familiarity with a priest would, no doubt, be strongly relied on, but they had the evidence of Mrs. Star that she did not mean to impute immorality ; and of the bishop, that he did not gather any such charge from it ; and of Father Mathews to a like effect. He called on the jury to believe that Mrs. Star *bonâ fide* thought that the charges she made were true, that she was really acting in the conscientious discharge of what she believed to be her duty towards the community. With respect to the proceedings before the commission, he thought they had nothing whatever to do with them. The question was, had Mrs. Star and Mrs. Kennedy combined together by cruelties and false charges to procure the plaintiff's dismissal from the convent. When they made their depositions they had done with the matter. How the bishop acted was no part of this inquiry. As to whether he was right or wrong they had nothing whatever to do. They had been yesterday invited to a consideration of the canon law ; but into that subject either he would not enter further than to say that he had before him a copy of a rescript from the present Pope, dated 19th March, 1857, in clause 5 of which it was laid down that the question of dismissal of monks or nuns from simple vows was not to be done according to the strictness of the canon law, but according to the rules of substantial justice. Observations had been made on the fact that the sisters were not produced before the commissioners for cross-examination. Well ; cross-examination in the hands of a skilful artist led sometimes to very valuable results, but in the hands of one who was unused to it there was no more certain way he believed of proving the case against the cross-examiner. Father Mathews was no doubt a shrewd, clever man ; but, judging from the demeanour of the sisters examined during the present trial, and the manner in which they had come out of the cross-examination of the Solicitor-General, he believed that if Father Mathews had had his way the result would have been a unanimous report not only that the charge had been proved, but that the counter-charges were disproved. In fact, if injustice were done at all, it was to the sisters who had not been called before the commissioners.

EIGHTEENTH DAY.—*Wednesday, Feb.* 24.

IN a searching though temperate mode of argument Mr. Mellish proceeded this morning with the address which he left unfinished yesterday. He made light of the evidence given by the young children, or at least advised the jury to receive it with caution, and asked what would have been said if these small witnesses had been called by the nuns. He did not blame the plaintiff for producing such testimony ; and, indeed, he made a great point of treating her with certain ostensible leniency and consideration throughout the concluding half of his speech. The extraordinary letter written by her brother to the Bishop of Beverley ought not, said Mr. Mellish, to be foisted on her. No mortal man could tell how much of it was the invention of the writer. When the Lord Chief Justice suggested that it might have been their joint production, Mr. Mellish magnanimously waived the question, and intimated his desire to abstain entirely from making the charge against Miss Saurin. But he adroitly seized on the opportunity of enforcing his former proposition that Mrs. Star had good warrant in keeping back letters from Miss Saurin that were written to her by "this man." Repeating his effective phrase "manufactured grievances," Mr. Mellish pointed out the fact that Miss Saurin might, if she had so pleased, have appealed from the bishop's decision to Archbishop Manning, a gentleman of high honour, a most learned and great man, and afterwards, if she had been dissatisfied with his judgment, to the Pope himself. Finally, the counsel for the defence insisted that, if Mrs. Star and Mrs. Kennedy had conspired, the guilt of conspiracy extended to the whole of the convent. The reply of the Solicitor-General, on the whole case, commenced with an iteration of what everybody has been thinking and saying for days past—that never before was so much valuable time taken up in the investigation of details so mean, petty, and contemptible as those which for three weeks have been before this Court. Nevertheless, the learned gentleman left off speaking at a point of his reply which did not seem to be near the end of it; and there is yet reason to apprehend that the prediction of Mr. Hawkins will be verified, and that the case will swallow up the whole of this week to the last scrap of its working time.

Mr. Mellish continued his address to the jury. He said no doubt the Solicitor-General would lay great stress on the two commendatory letters in favour of Miss Saurin written by Mrs. Star, but which had been lost. Their effect entirely depended on the period they were written, because Mrs. Star was the last to form an unfavourable opinion of her conduct. Stress would no doubt be laid upon the taking away the papers and pictures, but it was done to prevent clandestine letters, and no doubt it would have been more prudent if she had made an examination of them, and a selection of such as she thought it was desirable to retain. The question with regard to the children's food was not so much that Miss Saurin took the food, but that the sisters informed Mrs. Star she did, and that the latter believed it. The sisters spoke strongly to circumstances which led them to believe Miss Saurin did take it. The evidence of the young children called yesterday in contradiction should be received with caution. They did not speak to particular facts, but only that they did not recollect being slapped five years ago, or that they had lost any food. What would have been said if the defendants had called them? Would they not have been laughed at, and would they not have been told that the nuns had gone to them, and instructed them what to say? He did not blame the plaintiff for producing such evidence, but he submitted it was not to be relied on. The last stripping was said to have taken place in December, 1865, and at that time the depositions had been sent in, and the bishop had expressed an opinion, though he afterwards decided on a commission, and it was known if the commission considered the charges proved she would be discharged. What was the use of Mrs. Star further prejudicing the plaintiff's case? Was it not a manufactured grievance? The brother's letter was a most extraordinary document, and it was equally extraordinary that he, a confessor and a Jesuit, could have acted in such a manner. What an enormous exaggeration it was, and could they for a moment believe that he had obtained information in his priestly character, and then have made it public. One assertion, he said, had been repeated four times, and any one reading it would have concluded that she had been scourged. She was, he said, physically supported by God; and that would lead to the inference that she was being starved. It would be wrong to make the plaintiff answerable for that letter. No mortal man could say how much of that letter was the invention of the man who wrote it.

The Lord Chief Justice: It might have been their joint production.

Mr. Mellish: I don't make that charge, but it shows beyond all possible doubt that Mrs. Star might have had excellent reasons for keeping the letters of this man from his sister, as being unfit for her to read. I shall not go into the proceedings before the commission, because it is immaterial in my view of the case whether the bishop acted in that respect right or wrong. Mrs. Star and Mrs. Kennedy were ready to be examined before the commission, and they had prepared themselves for that purpose. It is an undisputed question that there was an appeal from the bishop to the archbishop, and that Miss Saurin might have pursued that course. That is material as to the law of the case. It has been held that in the case of an expulsion from a college where there was a visitor, the court would not inquire into the circumstances, but left the party to appeal to the visitor. The bishop in this case was the proper person to remove, and this court will not inquire into the question whether he acted according to the Roman Catholic law or not. If he mistook that law, Miss Saurin had a remedy in appeal to the archbishop. This action is brought to vindicate her character in the eyes of the Roman Catholic world, in order that she might resume her conventual life; but your verdict will not have the slightest effect with regard to the latter, because she had an appeal to the archbishop. What reason was there to suppose that perfect justice would not have been done her if she had appealed. Archbishop Manning is a gentleman of high honour, a most learned and just man, and if the plaintiff was dissatisfied with his decision, she had an appeal to the Holy See. There is nothing we know of in the private character of his holiness to lead us to believe that in a matter of this kind, that he also would not have done perfect justice in her case. Now with reference to the decision of the commission and the 12th of February, there was no doubt she was treated as not belonging to the convent, because no one could doubt that defendant believed she had been legally dismissed. Assuming she was dismissed properly, what were the defendants to do? Ample opportunity was given to her to go, but she would not, and the sisters were placed in a most difficult position, and what they did was to prevent public scandal in Hull. When it came to this, that the brother said to Mrs. Star, "Just put your hand upon her," and thereby commit what in law amounts to an assault, if I had been asked about the matter I should have advised them to run the risk and just tap her on the shoulder. (Laughter.)

The LORD CHIEF JUSTICE: I think I should have done the same. (Renewed laughter.)

Mr. MELLISH: The bishop's letter requested Mrs. Star not to use force, because it might give rise to an action. What, therefore, was she to do? and I think it was a great act of kindness when the bishop directed that she should not leave the convent alone. I now come to the question of imprisonment.

The LORD CHIEF JUSTICE: I must take every possible precaution to prevent the chance of this case ever having to be tried again.

Mr. MELLISH: It seems to me physically impossible to try it over again.

The LORD CHIEF JUSTICE: Or that the result should prove abortive. If the jury should think physical restraint was employed, I shall ask them to assess the damages, and give you leave to move. Heaven forbid that we should have to try it over again.

Mr. MELLISH: I hope we shall not. I have now gone through the whole of the evidence, and I will make no further observations except once more to remind you that the question you have to try is whether Mrs. Star and Mrs. Kennedy did form this wicked conspiracy. The sisters of the convent are ladies of unimpeachable character, and if the defendants have entered into this conspiracy, the whole of the members of the community must have joined them. Is there, then, anything in the lives and conduct of these ladies to induce you to believe they have committed such a wicked act.

The SOLICITOR-GENERAL then proceeded to reply on behalf of the plaintiff. He said: May it please your lordship and gentlemen of the jury —There is one remark amongst the many I have heard and read in the very remarkable address of my learned friend in which I can entirely and cordially concur. I heartily agree with him that it must be matter of sincere congratulation to all of us, and especially to you, gentlemen, that we are at last coming step by step somewhat nearer to the end of what at one time appeared to be an interminable case. I suppose that never before has so much time been taken up with an inquiry into details so mean, so petty, so paltry, so utterly contemptible, than those which have formed, I do not say the whole, but the main staple of this protracted inquiry. Whether or not a nun's veil was honestly torn; whether her clothes, internally and externally, were worn out or not; whether her stay-laces were broken too soon; whether too many bits of calico and silk, pins, needles, and cotton were in her pocket; whether she put a pair of boots on her feet belonging to another sister; whether a great man visited the convent; whether she ate too much ham in the pantry when she ought to have been eating mutton in the parlour; whether she talked a little to externs—these and other matters of an equally grave and important character have chiefly occupied the time for the last three weeks of twelve gentlemen of the county of Middlesex, and of the Lord Chief Justice of England, in the first court of common law in the country. Perhaps, however, when you come to reflect upon the matter, you will think that the time thus consumed has been anything but wasted. Certainly, so far as

the plaintiff is concerned, it has not been wasted, for however trivial and contemptible the details of the case may appear to be, and may be in fact to a great extent, the issue to her is of the most momentous character. It is my duty to tell you now, though I had no right to say so before, that it is in truth and fact an issue to her of social life or death. It is a question whether she is to be permitted to continue in a life to which she has devoted herself, to which she is virtually wedded and passionately attached; whether her desire to consecrate what may be vouchsafed to her of health, and life, and strength, to the cause she has espoused is to be permitted; or whether she is to be flung back upon the world she believed she had left for ever, and for which she is now utterly unsuited, with a stain upon her character which no lapse of time can efface, and be exposed to the dislike and the contempt of every well-regulated member of the Roman Catholic community. I think, therefore, gentlemen, that no time is wasted which is spent in an attempt to do justice to a subject of the queen who has been outraged—if her story be true—by an ingenious system of cruelty and oppression. Neither has time been altogether wasted in exposing to public view what convent life in England in the nineteenth century really is. I cannot help hoping that this trial will do good in two points of view —first, by showing that it is at least possible to try a case of the kind, and to lay bare the interior of a convent, without the faintest trace— with absolutely no trace—of what is commonly called immorality or scandal; and, in the next place, I think it will do good if it strips off the veil of sentiment and removes the halo of holiness which the devoted and heated imagination of some people are fond of thinking surrounds a so-called religious life. With the essence, the substance, and the reality of a religious life no Christian man, to whatever sect or body of Christians he may belong, can possibly object. To feed the hungry, to clothe the naked, to teach the ignorant, to watch by the sick, to comfort the mourner, to pray night and day to Almighty God, to live simply and by rule, and, in short, to use this world as not abusing it—these are things which, probably, Roman Catholics and Protestants alike are bound by the precepts of their religion to practise; and if they do not practise them themselves, they are at least bound to respect and reverence those who do. But I cannot help thinking that this trial will have this effect— that it will point out what common sense might have done without the expense and tiresome process of so long a trial, that in order to do this it is not necessary to go into a convent, and that if you do go into a convent and shut yourself up from mankind, you by no means get rid of temptations, but that you subject yourself to temptations far baser and more contemptible than any to be encountered out of doors; and that, dragged into the light of day, and judged by common human understanding, this conventual life loses all its romantic character, and turns out, on inspection, to be a very poor and ordinary affair indeed. We have little sins created by petty rules, childish penances imposed for childish faults, boots worn round the neck, dusters on the head, pins and needles watched and counted as a miser guards and counts his gold— all naturalness and simplicity of character destroyed by a perpetual petty self-watchfulness, and all independence of mind destroyed by an abject humility, which is a very different thing from true humility. This is what convent life has come down to in the 19th century; at all events, as it is seen in the convent of Our Lady of Mercy at Hull, and under the rule of the two defendants in this action. And I do hope that one of the good results of this trial may be to show men and women throughout the length and breadth of the land what thorough rubbish all this is; what a parody it is of the true simplicity and manly sense of the teaching, to use no higher or holier names, of St. Peter and St. Paul; how dull, how unattractive, how prosaic, how utterly unsuited to all the great and crying needs of the world that surrounds us. Gentlemen, speaking for Roman Catholics, I may say that in the older and sterner times, when the world was harder, and when men were even rougher, if they were more simple than they are now, I can imagine that the great monastic system of the middle ages might have its recommendations as well as its faults, and that in such a state of things its virtues and vices, its good and evil, might have been nicely balanced. I cannot, however, help thinking that those who have devoted themselves to it have imitated far too much, and remembered far too exclusively one part of the life of our Divine Lord, and forgotten the other—that they have remembered and imitated as best they might the forty days in the wilderness and the lonely nights on the mountain, and have forgotten the marriage in Cana and the feast in Bethlehem. Not that I wish here or anywhere else to make an attack on a life of self-denial and self-devotion, or to deny that there are persons to whom such a life may be acceptable. There may be men and women, for aught I know, who feel it to be their duty to separate themselves entirely from the world, and who may find some kind of serene satisfaction in treading their lonely path, if kept refreshed by Christian charity, and lighted by Christian faith; they may try to outwear the temptations of passions, and outlive the asperities of the temper; and they may find that a life begun and ended under such influences has a beauty and a purity of its own. If that be so the system should be simple and intelligible, founded on the necessities of human nature and administered with a due regard for them. But I cannot help thinking that the miserable and paltry system which has been disclosed in this case is a travesty upon the religion of antiquity, and is altogether unsuited to the people of this time, or adapted to the wants of the world we live in. Nevertheless, I agree that the question is not whether this life is in itself good or bad, wise or unwise, but whether the system, such as it is, was, in the case of Miss Saurin, fairly and honestly worked out. If so, having submitted herself to it, she must fail. But if, on the other hand, the system was unfairly and dishonestly perverted to her disadvantage, administered in a spirit of private hostility, and used against good faith to drive her from the convent where she had a right to live, and out of an order to which she had a right to belong, then, I say, she must, as she ought to, succeed. Before I proceed to touch upon the questions you have to try and the evidence given on the one side and on the other, I

think I ought to refer to the suggestion which has been thrown out that as there was no contract between the parties the plaintiff could not maintain her action. Now, I am prepared to contend that there was a contract.

The LORD CHIEF JUSTICE said that that was a difficulty which had suggested itself to him at an early stage of the case, but he did not mean to direct as to it. It should be reserved for future consideration.

The SOLICITOR-GENERAL said that the conspiracy charged was one to drive Miss Saurin from the order as well as from that particular house. The rule showed that the order had a number of houses affiliated in it. The bursar was directed by the rule not to take from any member of the order "the food and raiment promised to the religious on their embracing that congregation." It was with the order or congregation, which had many houses or offshoots, that the contract was entered into. In a case like the present evidence was necessarily difficult to procure, and could only be obtained under great disadvantage. The whole matter took place within the walls of a convent, and the only witnesses that could be called were nuns, who had been trained to strict obedience to the opinion and will of the mother superior, and were bound to see with her eyes, to judge with her judgment, and to act according to her directions. They should bear in mind that the very trial of that case was of necessity a great scandal to the order, whether Miss Saurin was right or wrong—a scandal which every member of the order was naturally desirous to avoid, and would use every effort to defeat. In considering the evidence for the defendants, and weighing it, they should not lose sight of the rule by which they were all bound to surrender their will to the will of the mother superior. They were to "submit their will and their judgment also to the will and judgment of the superior." "To this end they shall teach them to behold God in their superior, and to be as firmly convinced that God spoke to them in their superior as if an angel spoke, Jesus Christ having said, He that heareth you heareth Me." Now that was not rhetoric, but simple fact; and Mrs. Star to the fullest extent admitted that that rule was binding on the conscience of each member of the community. He need not point out the enormous difficulty which such a state of things threw in the way of any one who questioned the will of the superior, and came before a lay tribunal to assert that the mother superior had done wrong, because all the instincts of the religious, all her duties, all her views, would be at once arrayed against the person so acting; and it would not be only a temporal, but an eternal, a sacred, a conscience-binding duty to defeat her object. The evidence, therefore, was, so to say, poisoned at its very source. Evidence could not be offered by a plaintiff from a member of the order without some amount of violation of solemn obligations, which, to do her justice, Mrs. Star admitted to be binding on the conscience of the whole of them. He had, therefore, been perfectly prepared for the effect which the giving of evidence day after day by nun after nun of necessity created. He had never for a moment been led astray by the temporary sympathy which the statement of Miss Saurin's case by herself in the witness-box had elicited, because he knew that the whole convent was to be arrayed against her, and that if she took three days to tell one story, the nuns would take three times three days to tell another. Miss Saurin knew that too, and was as well aware as her counsel of the inevitable result of bringing the action, namely the coming forward of the whole sisterhood against her. He did not, therefore, of course, ask them to believe her story; but, in reason and common sense, he asked them to remember the fact that she was undeterred by that fact from appealing to a court of justice for redress. It was making a mountain of a molehill to say that the plaintiff had given three different versions of the origin of the coldness which had led to the unhappy results which followed. It was, after all, a matter of opinion, and the argument which had been spent upon it was like the breaking of a butterfly upon a wheel. The fact had been relied upon that there were a number of witnesses on the one side against one on the other; but, he asked, were witnesses to be numbered, or was their evidence not rather to be weighed with all the surrounding circumstances? They should remember what he had already stated as to the rules, and this further fact, that the evidence of the witnesses was not concentrated upon any one point, and that to the various points there was, after all, but witness against witness. He made no observation on the fact that the letters of Mrs. Star, which Father Mathews brought to the bishop with a view to show the high opinion she had had of Miss Saurin up to a then recent period, were not forthcoming. It was unfortunate; but of course letters will get mislaid, and he made no imputation, nor did he mean to make any, as to these letters having disappeared. What he did complain of was that, the bishop having lost the letters, the version which Father Mathews gave of them should have been questioned. They should not lose sight of the fact that in 1862 the cause of complaint against Miss Saurin had been complete. Every act which was alleged against her, even to the most serious of all the charges, namely, the writing clandestine letters to her uncle, the parish priest, had been committed and were set forth in the letters of Mrs. Star to the bishop, written in August, 1862, in which she called on the bishop to release the plaintiff from her vows and dismiss her from the community. These matters were inquired into by the bishop in his visitation in November, 1862; and yet the bishop, as he stated in the witness-box, found he could not conscientiously take action against the accused sister. Strong observations had been made on the fact that, to avoid examination as to the letters she had written, she made a vow before the sacrament not to speak further to Mrs. M'Keon on the subject. Well, whatever might be thought of that fact, she had frankly admitted it. If they thought it told against her, so it should be; but when they considered all the surrounding circumstances, he did not think they would allow it to weigh against her. Whatever the heinousness of the crime of writing what was called the clandestine letters. She confessed the fact to the mother superior. She was admonished for it. She repented of it, and had reason for a time to think it was forgiven. But it was not. It was reserved to be raked up against her, and used to bring about her ruin. He could not help

thinking that if these ladies had acted more as sisters in the wicked world did when offences were acknowledged and forgiven, they would have been spared all the scandal. But all her offences were known and charged against her in 1862. The bishop was besought to inquire and to dismiss. He did inquire, but he found no cause for dismissal.

The LORD CHIEF JUSTICE: He took the oddest way possible of inquiring. It was his ordinary visitation, and he did not let them know he had any special object in view.

The SOLICITOR-GENERAL: That was no doubt the case, but the subject uppermost in his mind, and in the minds of the sisters, was all that related to Miss Saurin, whom they were anxious to have dismissed; and was it to be believed or imagined that these ladies—who knew what's what as well as any one—who are not shut up within four walls, but hold intercourse with the outer world—who are sharp, shrewd, and intelligent, and resolutely bent on accomplishing the object they had in view, left anything undone so far as the bishop was concerned that was at all calculated to effect it? They were mortified at their failure, and in 1864 Mrs. Star wrote to the bishop speaking of his decision as having overruled their wishes, and adding: "The issue of the visitation had given her and her supporters immense triumph, of which they have shown a full appreciation whenever they have had an opportunity." When asked for an explanation while under cross-examination as to what she meant by the plaintiff's supporters, she said she alluded to Miss Saurin's relations. Now, the visitation took place in 1862; the letter in question was written by her in 1864. In the interval four visits of relations only had been made, and on not one occasion had anything taken place that could, even by the ingenuity of the defendants, be pointed to as a manifestation of triumph, much less an immense triumph. Was the statement in the letter true? If it was not—and they could not resist the conclusion that it was not—then they were afforded a standard by which they might measure the value of the defendant's testimony. The learned Solicitor-General, having referred at some length to the evidence bearing on this and other points, proceeded to say he had next to refer to the letters written monthly by the plaintiff to Mrs. Star, and he should like to have heard what his learned friend Mr. Mellish had said about them.

Mr. RUSSELL: He did not allude to them.

The SOLICITOR-GENERAL thought his learned friend had shown his wisdom by passing them over. They afforded conclusive evidence in support of Miss Saurin's case. He should read but one of them, but it was a fair sample of them all:

Convent of our Lady of Mercy, Clifford.

My dearest Reverend Mother,—I feel really very sorry that I had not my letter with the others; still I think it was not the will of God the long letter I had should have gone. Sister Mary Agnes seemed very much displeased I closed it without her telling me to do so. It was one sheet of note-paper put up in a little silver paper, which I had to open again as sister wished it. I also crossed it a little, which I gave you my reason for. I am always, I believe, to be doing things wrong. I did feel very much indeed, dear reverend mother, to come back to Clifford with Sister Mary Agnes. I knew she looked on me as such a cross—I could not help seeing her feelings towards me. I went, as Father Landes told me, on my knees, begged pardon, and made the most humble apology I could. I well felt how she received it. First she said, "You cannot say now, as you did before, it was unkindness to you." I only said I did not deserve, nor did I expect, kindness from any one. If I were dying, dear rev. mother, I could not remember one act of her kindness. I did not say a word when Father Landes told me all the trouble I gave Sister Mary Agnes. All I will say, I tried my best to please and obey her, though I often failed. Dear rev. mother, when I said sister was not the same at Clifford, I did not mean to complain in the least. It was only of what she herself and iester Mary Evangelist said the Sunday after we returned. I could not help thinking, dear reverend mother, in my heart, of when you were last at Clifford. You said I would never be able to bear all I had to go through. I could never have as much as I have gone through. I can bear so much more now. Much of that horrid pride is broken down. I had a long list written in retreat to read for you, but could not do so. Human respect overcame me. How much I wished, when in the train, I had done so, or that you could have seen all that happened for the past year with your own eyes; but God knows all. Sister said, I did not mind. Little she knew, when sound asleep, my many wakeful nights. If I had only wet as many handkerchiefs for my sins as for other things, I would have a little off my Purgatory. I must say, dear reverend mother, I never felt so happy after a confession in my life as I did after my last to Father Landes. I did my best, both in confession and out of it, to let him see the real state of my soul. I do not remember to have even once mentioned any one, or to have excused a fault. I really tried to make him think me as bad as I did myself. I could not tell you how bad he thought me. Some of the questions he asked me quite shocked me, but I felt glad if it proved to me the light he looked on me; and still he told me he could not account for it; but still felt, notwithstanding all he heard and knew gave him but little hope. Still he felt that if I only kept to my rule and to things marked out to me, he felt I would persevere and be good yet. I hope God will never let me live to disappoint him; and see, dear rev. mother, how soon I fell the day I was leaving Hull. Sister Mary Agnes left the paper for Clifford. I took a sheet, intending to leave a note for you to send mamma; then I had no ink or pens; and, instead of going to you as soon as I could to acknowledge the fault which I saw, I said I will just leave it back with Sister Mary Agnes when I go to Clifford, which I did; but what I suffered after I did so I shall never forget. I thought lecture would never end. I went to sister, told her all about it, how sorry I felt, &c. I do feel, rev. mother, I shall never do so again. All my promises to both you and Father Landes rushed to my mind. I thought was this the way I was to acknowledge every fault. I stayed longer than I had leave several minutes with a person in the school, also spoke to a little girl unnecessarily, and allowed her to

speak during school-time, rang the bells a few minutes late, did not eat all my food, though I did not get half what others did. I have been sick every day. I even dread dinner coming; but, please God, next time you will see I will be better. I did so long without I feel is the whole cause. Out of the past twelve months I spent, nine I never tasted meat. I often thought then, though I did not seem to mind, how unkind sister was not to get other meat besides mutton. Now dear, reverend mother, I feel so ashamed, and think it far too good. I also see how wrong and contrary to poverty I have acted. Still, only think, Sister Mary Agnes has just told me all the trouble I gave her for the past two days. All I can say, I never intended it. I knew she would feel my want of confidence in closing my note. I trust God will reward the charity of Mother Magdalene, M.M. of Mercy, and M.M. Clare, after you asked them to forgive me. May I beg a little cotton and wool to mend our stockings— a little black and white cotton? I did not know whether dear, reverend mother, you meant to get my winter habit. The other is in complete rags; but Sister Mary Agnes said one was enough. I felt the cold very much for the past winter. I often had to get M.M. Clare to tie my bonnet and coif strings; but if you wish me to have but one, all right. It is well patched, but looks badly. Dear reverend mother, I have suffered very much from constant pain in my back. If any message is coming I shall feel grateful for something. I have so much more to say, dear reverend mother, but I have to finish. The box is going to be shut. Forgive me, dear reverend mother, this once, for this untidy letter. I shall write the next, please God. With love to all, your ever attached and obedient child in J. C.

Sister M. SCHOLASTICA.

I have no time to read.

Comment upon that letter was needless. It spoke eloquently for itself, and was the letter of a poor, crushed, broken-down, persecuted, scared, and, to use an old word, "despaired" woman. The Solicitor-General then referred to what was called the thimble transaction, and contended that the evidence, even for the defendants, in which it was admitted that the plaintiff spoke of herself as a "poor persecuted creature," and complained of a sore finger, sustained her version of it. Then, again, humiliation and indignity were inflicted on her in depriving her of every scrap of paper and every object of devotion which she possessed. Religious pictures—relics she regarded as sacred —were taken from her, and the only explanation that Mrs. Star could give of it was that she did not wish Miss Saurin to have anything upon which she could write. Was that the real reason? Was that the truth? Could she write on the relic case? Could she make notes on the pictures? Could she jot down her observations on the bit of the true cross, as she regarded it, although he might be pardoned for questioning the fact? She believed it to be so, and she revered it. Why was she deprived of it? Did they believe Mrs. Star's explanation of the matter, or did they not rather believe that the only object was to carry out the system of petty tyranny and persecution which Miss Saurin had to endure? This brought him to one of the most romantic parts of the case. He had read the examination which the Lord Chief Justice thought it right to administer to the plaintiff on the subject of the strange letter of her brother the Jesuit priest, and he only regretted that he was not in a position to place him in the box, and elicit from him his explanation of what he had written. He was a Jesuit, and while he respected that great body he could not forget that its discipline was proverbial, and that perhaps accounted for the fact that he had disappeared, and that his whereabouts could not be traced. But was it not somewhat hard that an excited and heated letter written by a gentleman belonging to a foreign order, and who had spent seven or eight years abroad, should be hurled at Miss Saurin's head; that when she heard of it for the first time she should be suddenly called upon for an explanation, and that with the direct imputation that she had been guilty of trumping up the story.

The LORD CHIEF JUSTICE: You are quite wrong. What I desired to elicit was whether the letter was the spontaneous production of the brother, or whether she had authorized the statements it contained. It was absolutely necessary for the purposes of this cause that she should be solemnly interrogated on the subject.

The SOLICITOR-GENERAL: It was certainly one of the strangest incidents in this strange case.

The LORD CHIEF JUSTICE: There can be but one of two alternatives. Either she endeavoured to impose on her brother, or he endeavoured to impose upon the bishop.

The SOLICITOR-GENERAL submitted that there was a third view and one which he ventured to think was the true one. He hoped his clients would forgive him for saying that Father Saurin was an Irishman. He saw his sister in a wretched state; he heard her state the humiliations she had undergone, and the indignities to which she had been subjected—that once she thought of resisting, when the thought of our Lord's sufferings occurred to her and she submitted; and then the brother—an Irishman, a foreign Irishman—ardently affectionate, and writing of one whom he called his darling sister, wrote this heated and exaggerated letter. But he asked again, in what was Miss Saurin responsible for it? Surely, knowing nothing whatever of the letter until its production by the bishop in the course of the trial, it ought not to be hurled at her. But to pass on, he came to the commission, and with regard to the commission he had little to say. The defendants were not responsible for the acts of the bishop further than for having brought about his action. The inquiry had been styled a farce by Father Mathews, and could they regard it in any other light? The sentence was already prepared. It had been forwarded to the Jesuit brother before the commission was thought of, with a request to take his sister away, but he had returned it. He (the Solicitor-General) understood that his learned friend had gravely stated that the plaintiff ought to have appealed from the decision of the bishop to the archbishop, and if he decided against her, from the archbishop to the Pope. Sydney Smith once said that to tell a curate to appeal to the bench of bishops was like telling a delinquent frog to appeal to the Zoological Society. (Laughter.) Miss Saurin ought to have appealed to the archbishop, and then, if necessary, to the Pope! As well might it be said that she ought to have appealed to the man in the moon.

At this stage of the learned Solicitor-General's address the Court rose.

NINETEENTH DAY, *Thursday, February 25th.*

Day after day, for three weeks, the scene in the Court of Queen's Bench has been extraordinary, but it has never been so striking and so full of memorable incident as to-day. There were the same figures, now so familiar, in that reserved area, between the bar and bench where parties to the suit, with their friends and solicitors, are accommodated with seats; there were the nuns, still as statues, and seemingly as cold, like the time-worn monumental image of Patience, passively resigned to possible persecution, though not exactly smiling at grief; there was the plaintiff, in her half-secular and half-religious dress of plain black, and the long, thick veil hanging from the drawn bonnet, of old fashioned shape and size; there was her sister, not of the cloister, but of the hearth—her sister in the flesh, and of the sinful world—sitting by her side; there was the Drogheda parish priest, their uncle, with that venerably comfortable air which one is apt to associate with parish priests in general, not only of Drogheda, but all over the Ireland of fact and fiction; there were the Roman Catholic bishop and canons, with their priestly secretaries at their elbows; there were the father and mother of Miss Saurin, looking on from a corner of the gallery. The usual space and positions of the court were in fact filled by the usual groups; and the usual groups had nothing very unusual in their appearance, except an increased nervousness and a heightened attention, which last was common to all present. But the general aspect of this peculiarly incommodious hall of justice had undergone a change. It would not have been possible to crowd the public part of the court more closely than it had been crowded in the first days of the trial; but the desire to obtain sitting or standing room had evidently moved scores of persons to exert all their influence to that end. There was, in some measure, a different class of audience; there were more known faces, and there was a feminine invasion of the seats properly apportioned to the bar. So, too, looking towards the bench, great augmentation of interest was to be perceived; for this is a part of the court which had not till to-day been positively full. At the clerk's table sat many ladies, who now and then exchanged looks and signs of recognition with their acquaintance facing them in the barristers' benches, where needlework was strangely plied. When the short half-hour allowed for luncheon came to check the flow of the Solicitor-General's eloquence, there was little dispersion of the crowd in the court. Those only of the barristers who, being engaged in the case, were sure of regaining their seats, ventured to leave them. The rest kept the places they had managed to get, and handed coffee to the ladies, who bartered the friendly sandwich that is seldom eatable but when home-made. Among the company admitted to the bench was the young Duke of Norfolk, who has been present during some part of the former hearings. If, as may be justly allowed, the jury have cause to think themselves injured men, suffering the aggravation of insult in being paid at the rate of a shilling a day for their loss of time, they have at least the consolation of knowing that hundreds of persons would compete for the privilege of paying any money to take their place. The struggle to get into court this morning was desperate ; and the attempts to win over the officers at the doors, by persuasion more eloquent than words, were many and unavailing. Of the Solicitor-General's speech, and its effect on those who heard it, the full report which follows will give a fair, but not a perfect idea. Printed oratory is, to the freshly spoken words, what a careful engraving is to a picture, the life and colour of which are missed in the coldly accurate rendering. Still, this masterly appeal may be left with little preface to speak for itself. There was a depth of feeling in the advocate's tone, which often stirred the whole court, as when, after discoursing of the narrowness of conventual life, and of the spites and meannesses hidden by its false or imperfect piety, he quoted John Bunyan's terrible words : "I now saw that there was a bye-way to Hell, even from the gates of Paradise." When Sir John Coleridge ended his speech, with the declaration that he left his client and her social life or death in the hands of the jury, there was a burst of applause, which was checked by the officers and rebuked by the Chief Justice, who threatened with committal any one who should again dare to turn the court into a theatre.

The Solicitor-General resumed his address to the jury. He said :—This is a case the like of which I was never before engaged in, and the like of which I hope never again to be connected with. The great length and the immense complication of this case make it almost beyond the possibility of condensation, but I will endeavour to be as short as I can. Many things I have deliberately omitted, and I shall not touch on more points than are absolutely necessary. Miss Saurin was not aware of the object of the stripping in 1865, and it was not to be wondered at that she thought it an indignity. I admit, on consideration, that Mrs. Star's statement of that occurrence is a correct one, to the extent it went—the actual truth probably lies between the two—but I ask you to consider whether Mrs. Star's conduct was not harsh, unkind, unfeeling, and illegal on that occasion, and if you believe it was unkind—I was going to say indecent—I submit that nominal damages will not be a sufficient compensation for Miss Saurin. The defendant's case necessarily is that Miss Saurin was unfit for the state of life to which she had devoted herself—that she had no vocation for it—and that from her conduct they were compelled, for the benefit of the community, to put her out of the convent. But how do you account that every document and every incident in her conduct shows that so far as she was concerned she did not agree with them, that she disliked or was unfit for a conventual life. For two and a half years she was a novice, during which time her temper was tried, penances were inflicted,

and a number of things were done to test her fitness to go on in the life she had undertaken. Up to 1851 no one doubted she was fitted for the life she had undertaken, and is there any reasonable doubt that down to May, 1856, when she joined the community at Clifford, those who were interested in the foundation and well being of the community entertained the same opinion ? Up to that period, then, to use the words of Father Matthews, "she had all the materials in her for making an excellent nun." In their depositions and evidence the defendants say there was that in Miss Saurin's conduct previous to this time, and the evidence is incredible unless a change came over her, both in mind and temper, between 1860 and 1865. The whole of the defence is want of vocation, but there was no force in that part of the defence, for there was no want of vocation discovered until 1860 or 1861. And that is very remarkable, because if she gave trouble after that time and none before, why did they not discover it sooner? The necessary foundation of the defence, when we come fairly to look at the case, must fail altogether. They have to start with the singular circumstance that Miss Saurin was unsuited for a life which, against the wish of her parents, she has devoted herself to. Now, down to 1860 there was no thought of turning Miss Saurin out of the convent, for it appeared, that in July, 1860, a deed of trust was made out for the fabric of the convent, and on it her name appears as one of the persons to whom the legal estate is conveyed, and yet for years they say they had found out that she was unfit for her vocation. The case, however, is further put on a breach of rules, and Mr. Hawkins scorned to put it as a breach of morality. Now, the plaintiff never heard of the worst charges that were put forward until this trial, and, more than that, it only came out in Miss Saurin's cross-examination. We were aware of the depositions that had been sent to the bishop, and when we applied to the bishop for copies, he thought it fair not to supply the plaintiff with them, but that it was to give them to the defendants, and that he did, he said, under the advice of counsel. Episcopal minds are sometimes of a peculiar kind, and episcopal justice, if it be measured by episcopal rule, would be of a peculiar kind also. I should have thought that a visitor and a reverend father in God, would have been indifferent between them, and let each side see these documents, but he did not do so. The defendant's counsel at first tried hard to prevent my seeing these depositions, and when they were produced, Mr. Mellish thought it right to say that his real objection to his producing them was that they contained charges that would convey to the world more than was really intended. These depositions contained not merely the charge of misconduct with the priest, but a charge of stealing a medal from the dead body of a sister, respecting which not a single question was put to her in cross-examination, and of which I never heard until then. Now, what is the answer or explanation of this part of the case? They are two. Either my learned friends did not believe a word of those charges, or, believing them because they could not help believing them from their having heard of it from their clients, they did not think you would believe them. I now come to the children's dinners, a most disgraceful and abominable thing ; but **the gravamen of the** charge was never put to the plaintiff or opened by her counsel, which showed that they have no confidence in this part of the case. The real force of Mrs. Star's statements in these depositions is that Miss Saurin "was in the habit," "she was always," "she was perpetually," and so on. Well, now, I don't suppose Miss Saurin is perfect. I am not one who believes that she is that wonder the world never saw—a perfect person—for I believe that she, and women generally, like men, have faults. I don't contend such nonsense that she has no faults, and when the defendants were asked to explain them, I appeal to you whether the explanations given were not the most childish. Mrs. Star, in the language she has used in these depositions, was creating a false impression in the bishop's mind with reference to Miss Saurin, and what right has Mrs. Star to say after that she wished to give Miss Saurin the kiss of peace? Mrs. Star described the incident with respect to the watch as a deposit of an extern, and a want on the part of Miss Saurin by wishing to retain it to defraud the congregation: but can you believe otherwise than that Mrs. Star has told a tremendous lie about the watch? Then again there is the statement about her stratagem to obtain clothes, and the loss of the gloves ; but who, as the Lord Chief Justice observed, has not lost a pair of gloves ?

The Lord Chief Justice : I have had a number of abusive letters sent to me on this and other matters, from both sides. In that respect I have been fairly dealt with. I hope I have done neither injustice, for I do not intend to do it.

The Solicitor-General : Some one wrote me an unpaid abusive letter, and in consequence I have since refused all unpaid letters. (Laughter.)

The Lord Chief Justice: I can't say that. I have some comfort in knowing that my anonymous correspondents have paid the postage.

The Solicitor-General—Mrs. Star, in her deposition in referring to the loss of Miss Saurin's gloves, disbelieves her statement, and says it is a lie. Now see, gentlemen, how these Christian people love one another. (Laughter.) There is in almost every institution a cat, and the excuse is, "I didn't do it ; it was the cat." (Laughter.) I have no doubt that after a time poor Miss Saurin became the cat of the convent—(laughter)—and whatever was done, whether great or small, it was laid on Miss Saurin—her excuses being considered immaterial. Referring to the passage about the priest, I must say my learned friends struggled hard to keep that out, and they took care to explain that it should not be considered by men of the world as meaning something wrong. Mrs. Star in the witness-box said it meant only to infer that her speaking to the priest was wrong. But, gentlemen, was it meant to mean nothing more? She says—"And although I could not say positively there was anything wrong beyond disobedience, yet an undefinable feeling pervaded my mind that all was not right on her side. I felt very uncomfortable, and I sent her to Clifford for that reason and others combined." I ask you—do you believe that all she meant by that statement was a breach of the rules of obedience and silence in talking to a person she ought not to speak to, and that she was more forward in talking to this gentleman than she ought to have been? There could have been no more wrong in talking to the priest than there was in talking to a sister, yet that

was the reason why she was sent to Hull. Can you doubt that Mrs. Star did not mean that Miss Saurin had committed an impropriety? She has sworn she did not, and if you believe her evidence in the box, she has sworn deliberately to what every one believes to be untrue. She made the charge to the bishop in unmistakeable language, on which men of common sense can form but one opinion. When Mrs. Star is asked—with the statement in her deposition staring her in the face—she cannot deny that she wrote it, but if you believe her evidence on oath, she says she never meant it. She does not say it is true. She dare not say so, or whisper, or suggest an impropriety, on her oath in the box, against a person of whom she could write that with regard to a gentleman she had an undefinable feeling that all was right on her side, and that she sent her away that she might be out of his way for that and for other reasons. If you don't believe her, Mrs. Star has committed perjury. And this is the way my client has been treated ; and Mrs. Star now admits that she made a charge against Miss Saurin for which there was not a shadow of foundation. Mrs. Star charges her with innumerable falsehoods ; that she was absent from meditations ; that she conversed with externs—her uncle. The latter was no doubt true to the card, but could any one imagine the extern meant her uncle when she saw him with the quarter-hour glass in her hand. Mrs. Star charges Miss Saurin with duplicity, falsehood, and fraud in reference to the clandestine correspondence, and she says she knew Miss Saurin made a false statement to the bishop in 1862, because his lordship had mentioned it to her. The bishop hears the statements of both and communicates them one to the other, yet, if you believe her in the face of the depositions, she never told the bishop when he came to inquire what, if true, was the most crushing and overwhelming part of the case against her. In another part of her deposition she says, "I never knew the depth of her malice until then. She appeared to be a spy, and the poor unsuspecting sisters' words, acts, and actions appeared to be carefully noted, if there was anything in them that could be turned against them in the slightest degree." Now, these are general statements, and when she was asked in the witness-box for an explanation of what she meant by the depth of her malice, the only one she could give was the entry about Mrs. M'Keon and the tower—of which too much has been made: "Visit of the sister—mutton-chops." Now I ask you is the description Mrs. Star has given of Miss Saurin a fair, honest, kind-hearted description, which one nun ought to give of another? In 1865 matters came to a head. Mrs. Star was extremely anxious to get Miss Saurin dismissed from the convent, and the bishop was ready to act, provided he was furnished with charges on which to act. One might take it that at all events the worst Mrs. Star knew of the plaintiff she would be sure to have stated in her depositions in 1865. She then stated there were suspicions of Miss Saurin having taken the food of the children, but that Sister Scholastica would never acknowledge these things. Mrs. Star, however, swears upon her oath in the box that the plaintiff admitted having taken the food of the Swales. Is that true? If so, why did she not state it to the bishop in her letter, and if she did not mention it then, why did she not do it when she made her deposition which was to justify the dismissal of Miss Saurin? If it stood alone, the cogent and probable answer was that she did not, because she never heard it, and that it is not true. She was challenged with the names of the children whose food Miss Saurin was said to have taken; and she gave the name of Swales. They were produced, and you will recollect they said that no food was ever taken from them by Miss Saurin. I can perfectly well understand why she did not state it in 1865 in the letter to the bishop, because she did not know it—that it was not true; yet she has been represented to you as a paragon of virtue, who can have no possible interest in misleading you, and whose slightest words are to be taken as Gospel truth when they are opposed by Miss Saurin; yet I think I have broadly convicted Mrs. Star, partly out of her own mouth and partly out of her deposition. Mrs. Kennedy describes Miss Saurin's conduct as being composed of the grossest falsehood, deceit, and trickery. She was requested to write her opinion of Miss Saurin in moderate language; but I can't say much of her moderation; and when she admitted, and she stated she did not think Miss Saurin had a vocation, she had a pretty good idea of the defence. I think Mrs. Kennedy drew very largely when she spoke in her deposition of Miss Saurin's conduct to gratify her love of dress, because I think there are many more attractive to any one who has an eye for colour than black and white; and if she had such a love for dress as Mrs Kennedy states, it is strange she should have gone into a nunnery. (Laughter.) I have never been in Ireland. I am told the hospitality of that country is proverbial, and that the inhabitants of that country are never so happy as when they are dispensing it; and if Miss Saurin wished to gratify her love of food, it would have been far better for her if she had remained at home. If she was fond of made dishes, it was not likely she would find them in a convent; and if she liked champagne—and some ladies not improperly are fond of it—I should think a convent was the last place in which to find it. (Laughter.) And certainly if she wanted the affections and attentions of externs, she had nothing to do but keep outside a convent. (Laughter.) I cannot imagine a person fond of gratifying her love for dress, food, and externs, going into a convent, where you get nothing the best part of the year but mutton, and where you are cut down to the primitive but trying form of dress to a female as that worn by nuns, and where you cannot hold communication with externs without committing a breach of the rules. Mrs. Kennedy, no doubt, gave admirable evidence. A more thoroughly self-possessed lady I never saw; and when she sat down to write her deposition they had seen the charitable way in which she had viewed a sister. Every word she has said Mr. Hawkins would have you treat as Gospel truth. Now, in treating of abstinence from food, Mrs. Kennedy says in her deposition —it was a curious thing that her life seemed a miracle, for none could make out how she got her food. In her evidence in the box she said Miss Saurin habitually resided in the pantry, and if that were so, there was no great miracle how she got her food; and if Mrs. Kennedy knew that crime, it is a curious thing she did not mention it in her deposition. I don't want, however, to go into the details of her evidence. You recollect, I

have no doubt, the character both of her evidence and her deposition; and I don't mean to say that they were both of the same character. Her evidence was plausible and extremely well delivered, with great aplomb, self-confidence, ability of language, and perfect calmness and contentedness of behaviour. Her evidence was of a general kind; and of all the witnesses that came into the box she was the only one who least condescended to particularise. She, however, does condescend in one particular; and I am reminded that she stated that Bridget Connolly was the pupil teacher, who put back the clock. We called her before you, and the result is that she flatly contradicts Mrs. Kennedy that she did it at Miss Saurin's request. Again, I say, why is it to be supposed that Mrs. Kennedy tells the truth, and Bridget Connolly an untruth? I now come, gentlemen, to the deposition of Mrs. Collingwood. She says very little but about the priest, and you will remember that it was written by Mrs. Kerr and passed through the hands or was touched up by Mrs. Star. She said, "When I was at school I noticed that her manner was very familiar with one of the priests. I once saw her on her knees beside him, pulling the things out of his hand that he was using, and entreating him to go with her. At this same period her conversation with me was most worldly, and was usually on such subjects as courtship. I do not think there was a single young man of my acquaintance about whom she did not question me closely. She drew me out and encouraged me to speak on such subjects, and never seemed weary of listening, but would go any lengths with me, so that I now blush to think of many things I said. But then I did not think it any harm as I was speaking to a nun." Now look at the connection in which this is put. On her knees beside a priest—pulling things out of his hand—entreating him to go with her—always talking of courtship—going any lengths, and bearing things that made the other blush to think of. My learned friend said with great gravity that there were things in the depositions from which men of the world would draw different inferences from those which nuns would draw. But there is a statement to the bishop—a statement which he believed to be true, and therefore acted on—a statement upon which the commissioners, assuming its truth, convicted her. Now they disavow the plain and obvious and only inference which men of the world, or nuns, or bishops could draw from it, and they say that it only meant that she wished to convey to the priest that her luncheon was ready. Well it is, to say the least, a very unworldly way of doing so. To the pure all things are pure, and kneeling down beside a priest pulling things out of his hand, and begging him to go with her, on the part of one who was constantly talking of young men, going any lengths on the subject of courtship, and making a young woman say things which made her blush, is, to my mind, rather an odd way of conveying intelligence that luncheon was waiting for a priest. (Laughter.) Gentlemen, it is a scandalous thing if that is all that is meant, because I utterly deny that these women, who came after a reasonably mature life into the convent, and who had not—at all events it was so in the case of Mrs. Collingwood—contemplated taking vows, did not know perfectly well what was intended to be conveyed. Do not tell me such nonsense. It is not consistent with common sense or the plain and obvious meaning of language. But Mrs. Collingwood said it was not intended to convey an imputation to the mind of the listener. I asked her, "But if that is so, what was it that made you blush?" The reply was, "She said she asked me if I was going to be married." Why should she not marry? She was not then contemplating conventual life. I asked her what were the lengths to which Miss Saurin had driven her. She hesitated, but after a time said that it was the ages and occupations of young men about which she was speaking. Gentlemen, do you think that that was what was meant on the part of these women who seemed to have searched the dictionary for language in which to convey their thoughts? If they meant nothing that was inconsistent with pure and unspotted morality, is the English language so poor that they could only express it in the words they used? My learned friend knew what you would gather from it, and admitted that there was not the smallest shadow or pretence for gathering that, and yet here are nuns writing in a religious spirit about a sister, and saying what you have heard. Mrs. Collingwood tells it to Mrs. Kerr, who writes it, and to Mrs. Star and Mrs. Kennedy who read it; and all these three women combined to send letters to the bishop which any woman of common sense must have known conveyed a particular imputation which they dare not now reiterate, because they are aware it is without foundation. I now come to the depositions of Mrs. Hewetson. She was told to write down what she knew about Miss Saurin, and she was aware that the object was to have her dismissed from the community. I beseech you to remember that until this lady got into the box, charges which she prepared were not so much as hinted at. She states in her depositions that she and Miss Saurin had charge of a sick sister, Mary Kavanagh; that, when she was laid out after death a silver medal was about her neck, and that some months afterwards Miss Saurin asked her if she had found a silver medal. She adds that she then thought of the silver medal of Mary Kavanagh, and she frankly admitted in the box that she meant to convey to the bishop that Miss Saurin had stolen the medal. Mark the date of these transactions. Mary Kavanagh died in October, 1859, and this charge was made in the depositions in 1865, but a charge of a much more odious and much graver nature was suppressed, viz., the stealing of the grave-clothes. After she entered the witness-box she told a horrible story—a story of an abominable perversity of mind, viz., that a nun, with no reason for it, against natural affection, against religious principle, against devotional feeling, against the common reverence which, thank God, all Christians entertain for the body which God has sanctified, that a sister while the body lay in the chapel awaiting burial stole a portion of the grave-clothes, hid them under the chancel, and some months afterwards put them on their own wretched person. There are two persons in the world who know whether this is true—Mrs. Hewetson and Miss Saurin. The one asserts it, the other positively denies it; but Mrs. Hewetson, in writing her depositions in 1865, although she was told to state all she knew of Miss Saurin for the purpose of her being driven from the convent, suppresses it. Is it credible. Do you believe that this woman would day by day, and week by

week, have associated with another whom she knew was the actor in so horrible a story. I questioned her on the subject, and the reason she gave for suppressing it was that it would injure Miss Saurin for life. At the same time she admitted she knew the story of the medal would injure her for life; and that the sending of the depositions, the object of which was to drive her from the convent, would injure her for life also. She put into her deposition a charge upon mere suspicion; but here was a fact suppressed as to which, if her story were true, she had absolute proof. We are dealing with women, with conventual women, with whom it would appear any course of conduct may be justified by some strange religious twist or warp. But then you have the solemn and indignant oath of Miss Saurin, on the other hand, that the story is not only repulsive to an extraordinary degree, but absolutely untrue. It is bad enough to steal children's dinners, but to steal the grave-clothes of your most intimate and dearest friend! Why, good heavens, do you suppose, if such a thing had happened that it would have remained locked in the breast of a member of the religious society so long, or that Miss Saurin would have been allowed to leave the witness-box without the least intimation, or having the least suspicion of such an odious charge being about to be made against her. My answer is that it was not put in my learned friend's instructions because it was known that it would be received by everybody with loathing and horror. It is horrible. It is inherently incredible, and I ask you to disbelieve it. If you do, what becomes of the evidence of this woman? what becomes of the evidence of Mrs. Star and Mrs. Kennedy, who back her up? what becomes of the whole case, which is supported by the evidence of people of this description, whom it is impossible to believe? Well, then comes the matter about the dinners. Remember that in the depositions there is no direct statement that any one saw her taking a child's dinner, or eating it. Mrs. Nelligan is the great witness to this part of the case, and she tells stories which, if they be true, leave no doubt that from time to time the plaintiff did take the children's food to gratify her own gluttonous appetite. Now the only way the charge can be met is first of all by the denial of Miss Saurin, and she says it is untrue, and next by getting from the witnesses the names of all those to whom the charges refer. Well, we accepted the challenge, and every one whose name was mentioned, and whom it was possible to produce we produced, and they one and all told you that the charges were utterly untrue. But it does not stop there. There is one case in which I hope you will be able to pass a lenient judgment. Mrs. Nelligan said that a child named O'Brien lost his dinner, and that a complaint was made, and a threat to take him from the school. Well, the child's mother was produced, and she said it could not be true, because the complaint was made after the fourth birthday of the child— that is, after February, 1866, or, in other words, after Miss Saurin had been dismissed from the order, and of course from the schools. It could not therefore refer to him. But suppose the mother was even wrong about the date. To whom did the complaint refer? Mrs. O'Brien says, that the complaint, rightly or wrongly, was made of Sister Mary Bernard—Mrs. Nelligan herself. She stated in her evidence that a complaint had been made. That was true. That it was made in relation to the child O'Brien. That also was true. But she fixed it upon poor Miss Saurin, it being true of herself. Gentlemen, I have nearly concluded the observations I have to make. It has been urged that these atrocious charges were honestly put forward. I ask you whether there was any bonâ fide inquiry, any real desire on the part of the two defendants to arrive at the truth, or whether the charges were not put forward recklessly without sufficient consideration—without due thought of the effect they must of necessity have upon the character of the plaintiff, and therefore whether you must not associate the two defendants in the guilt of having coloured them and put them forward? If you disbelieve these stories, is it worth while going into contradictions upon small matters? If these people do not hesitate to tell you such stories about matters of serious import, do you think they would hesitate upon such trifling and petty things as pots of jam, half-pints of gooseberries, buttered toast, and tea in the pantry? The man who is guilty in a little thing may be guilty in a great thing, but the man who is guilty in a great thing will seldom stick at a small thing. Sweeping accusations are here reduced to nothing when they are asked to state particulars. I cannot help thinking that when you recollect what I told you yesterday about the habits and obligations and duties of persons in a religious community, and recollect the condition to which Miss Saurin was reduced, and the conduct that for a series of years was pursued towards her, you will see the solution of a great deal of the more important matter in this case. For observe, without a single exception, almost every person about whom evidence is given—every class of persons outside the walls of the convent formed, as appears from the evidence of the nuns themselves, a different opinion about this unhappy sister to what they did. She was popular with the girls, with the villagers, with Mrs. Grimstone, whose patronage of the convent at Clifford was withdrawn, or transferred, owing to her removal. Father Cullamore was, they said, entirely blinded by her, and thought her a suffering saint—at least a person entitled to the greatest admiration. Father Motler the same. The bishop thought well of her. All these persons, whenever admitted to personal communion and intercourse with Miss Saurin apart from the other nuns, took a totally different view of her from that by which they were actuated. That is a matter worthy of your observation. And on the other hand, observe there is not a single person connected with Miss Saurin—not one of her family, or friends, or supporters, as they called them, who either directly or indirectly, in the course of the letters, or depositions, or evidence, is not injuriously commented upon by Mrs. Star or the other nuns. Miss Saurin's family have given pledges of their devoted attachment to the Church to which they belong — a son a Jesuit priest, two daughters Carmelite nuns, the plaintiff a sister of mercy, Father Matthews a parish priest. The whole family are spoken of as wily, dangerous people ; the two sisters' letters contain exaggerations, as they are called, and they are withheld ; the Jesuit brother is a man not to be trusted. Father Matthews, whom it does not become me to praise, but whom you have seen and heard, whose letters are before you, whose whole conduct has been laid bare to you—he is described as a clever man of the world—a man without much religious feeling—a man whom the Jesuit brother is made to represent as a wicked man—a man who would spare no pains to ruin anyone who opposed him. Mr. Saurin is disbelieved, Mrs. Saurin is disbelieved, the brother, the uncle, the sisters, all are made the subject of attack. It is said, gentlemen, that all this is consistent with the kindness and Christian charity which ought to animate people of this description ; but I say that it is in these things you can distinguish and find out the real spirit that has animated Mrs. Star and Mrs. Kennedy. You cannot fail, in the depositions they sent to the bishop, in the letters they had previously written to him, in the evidence they gave here, to see a deep-seated dislike of Miss Saurin—an earnest desire, by any means to get rid of her, and a total disregard of all those principles and that good feeling which, even if they were not religious, ought to have actuated their conduct. The greatest of living Roman Catholics, a man of whom, neither here nor elsewhere, can I ever speak without respect and veneration—Dr. Newman, has said :

> " Nature amid the spheres hath sway—
> Ladies rule where hearts obey."

But that, like other propositions, cannot be accepted simply. You cannot say that hearts always obey where ladies rule. And in these pieces of petty malignity and spite you will see that the system pursued towards Miss Saurin has been a system calculated, it was so intolerable, to fret the temper of any one who had a temper to be fretted—to crush to pieces any one who had any independence of mind left to be crushed, or whose nerve and power of will was not entirely broken down. And, give me leave to say, that when you recollect that all this was done towards her in the name of God, and possibly, let us hope, disguised from those who did it under the forms of religion and devotion, you have a proof, if proof be needed, of the awful truth of those two sublime passages in that solemn book of Bunyan's, where he says he saw there was a bye-way to hell from the very gates of Paradise itself. Gentlemen, with one closing word I will now release you. You were told finely and impressively by my learned friend that you ought to beware of the danger of doing anything wrong, because of prejudice and prepossession. Considering, gentlemen, that Miss Saurin is a Roman Catholic nun, and desirous of remaining one, that neither she herself nor her counsel on her behalf have said one single word against conventual institutions in general, but only against the perversion of them in this particular case, considering that her whole family are Roman Catholics to the core, the warning, fine and impressive as it was, was not, I think, needed. But I will take the liberty of giving you a warning upon another matter. Do not you be afraid of doing what is right and just because it chances to be popular. That is a danger to which sensitive and high-minded men are much more liable than to coarser and commoner forms of temptation. But, gentlemen, there is an old and a grand distinction—a distinction drawn first by perhaps the very greatest man who ever filled the seat that my lord now so worthily occupies, I mean Lord Mansfield—the distinction between the popularity which follows and the popularity which is followed after—a distinction which I earnestly entreat you carefully and inflexibly during this case to remember. Remember, also, that not in the language of rhetoric or declamation, but in the language of sense, and truth, and soberness, you are Miss Saurin's sole refuge. Through you alone can she obtain reparation or any compensation for the wrongs which she has suffered. My learned friend told you that anything you might do could have no effect upon Miss Saurin's future. Do not believe it. It is not so. His opinion is nothing. My opinion is nothing. The opinion of the Lord Chief Justice is a very great deal, but your verdict is everything. Clear away then from her, if you can, the dark cloud with which the defendants have overshadowed her. Set her back, if you can, in the bright light from which

they have shut her out. Give her such a verdict as not passion, or prejudice, or bias, or partiality, but such as sense, and truth, and honour, and justice demand. She asks for nothing more at your hands. She ought to be, and will be, content with nothing less. She asks to have what any honourable and high-minded man will say she ought to have, and in the hands of twelve such men I leave her. (Applause.)

The Lord Chief Justice : Let there be no more of that. The court is not to be turned into a theatre.

Addressing the jury, his lordship said : It is now two o'clock, gentlemen, and as I could not conclude my summing up this evening, it is better it should be commenced to-morrow. I shall, however, conclude at such an hour as will give you ample time to consider your verdict.

The Court then adjourned till ten o'clock to-morrow.

Twentieth Day, *Friday, Feb. 26.*

This, the twentieth and last day of this remarkable, extraordinary action, was the most exciting of the whole trial—first, because the public mind was stimulated by the knowledge that the Lord Chief Justice was to sum up the evidence, and secondly, because of the anxiety of the people of every denomination and class to know what the verdict of the jury might be—whether they would agree or disagree : and in the event of their agreeing what amount of damages they would give.

Westminster Hall at an early hour presented a large mass of people waiting for the court doors to be thrown open ; and when open a rush took place, and the court became almost immediately crowded in all parts. A large proportion of the audience was composed of ladies, many of whom were accommodated with seats in the " Masters' " tier, immediately below the judicial bench. On the bench a considerable number of noblemen and members of Parliament were accommodated with standing room, the limited proportion at either side of the judicial chair not admitting of better accommodation. For such a trial—a trial upon which the public appetite has been feeding from its commencement—the area of the court was far too small. The scene might well have been laid in the great hall—a most appropriate site for such an action ; and had the court been constituted in that vast space, with the judicial bench at its utmost end, beneath the stained-glass window, at the head of the steps, judging from the excitement and the anxiety to be present, the Great Hall would be crowded throughout.

The Lord Chief Justice addressed the jury as

follows :—I congratulate you most heartily on having arrived at the closing day of what I may call this monster case. I regret, at the same time, that you should have been kept so long from your vocations, and that your valuable time should have been occupied to a wearisome length in a case of this kind. On public grounds I regret that the time of this Court, when so many causes of importance are waiting for trial, should have been occupied for nearly a month with a matter arising out of the miserable squabbles of a convent, which might, I think, much better have been disposed of, and ought to have been disposed of, by the visitorial power, which, according to the constitution of their convent, had authority over it. There can be no question, however, that the case is one of great and vital importance to the parties concerned, and we must deal with it according as the interests of justice require, to do what is right between the parties, and endeavour to ascertain to the best of our power and ability on which side the truth lies. Again, however uninteresting to you and me the case may be, there can be no doubt that in consequence of its being connected with a religious association, and of having afforded a revelation of what passes in convent life, this trial has acquired factitious importance, which, if it had related to disputes arising in any other form of association, it certainly would not have presented. And we must take care that neither party derives any undue advantage from the religious element that is mixed up with the consideration of the question. The plaintiff has what the defendants may deem an advantage to her, the fact that they are upon their trial before a Protestant jury. I must warn you, and I trust you will forgive me for doing so, not to allow any religious preferences, or what the defendants may think religious preferences, to operate to the advantage of the one party and to the disadvantage of the other. I believe I am addressing twelve gentlemen who belong to our great Protestant community, and as such, and perhaps also as thinking men, you may look on convent life as an object of dislike ; but I warn you that no such considerations must for a single moment influence your decision. You may think that the withdrawing of women from the sphere for which they were destined—that of being wives and mothers, and thus forming and cementing the ties upon which, in the main, human happiness rests—that this attempt to obliterate human instincts, and to chill human affection, or at all events to repress them within the narrower bounds and limits of an artificial, cold, and unnatural life, is contrary to the voice of nature and to the ordinance of God. We may also think that although man's object through his passage here should be to look forward to eternity and prepare for it, yet that the passage to Heaven lies through the world in which we are placed, and that man's service to God is never wholly and entirely fulfilled except when he discharges those duties, domestic and social, which are incident to the life which he is called upon to pass through. You may think, too, as the Solicitor-General the other day so well expressed it, that the more generous emotions, and finer sentiments and perceptions of the human soul, as also the religious sentiment itself, must lose rather than gain by this life of monotonous observance of trivialities — petty, pitiful observances—which you have observed described. But, gentlemen, we have nothing to do, as I have said before, with these considerations. This is not a case in which Protestant parents complain that their daughter has been inveigled into a convent, and subjected to restraint when she wished to leave it and had experienced other ill-treatment. You are dealing with a case in which parents do not complain, and in which the plaintiff does not complain of having entered a convent. I listened, and I dare say you did, to the observations of the learned Solicitor-General at the outset of his address to you upon the subject of convent life, with all the satisfaction that one feels when one hears one's own opinions supported by cogent reasoning, and expressed in eloquent language ; but I own to you that his observations sounded to me startling, as coming from one who was the

advocate of the plaintiff, who so far from seeking to decry this convent life, declared that her aspirations from the beginning was, and now is, and will be to the end, to be and continue a nun—in the words of our great poet, to

> "Endure the livery of a nun,
> For aye to be in shady cloister mew'd,
> To live a barren sister all her life."

It therefore would certainly be improper if in a case of this kind any religious feeling should mix itself up as a disturbing element in the consideration of the rights of the parties. To try this case properly, you must try it justly ; you must try it as though you were twelve right-minded Catholics, members of the Roman Catholic Church, accepting as a common *datum*, common to both parties, the convent, and especially accepting it with unlimited powers in the superior and unqualified subjection in the subordinates ; in short, with all those incidents we have heard described. Unless you do that, unless you put both parties on a common ground, you cannot do justice to them. I am sure you are anxiously, earnestly seeking to take from the consideration of the question anything that has the slightest approach to religious sentiment or opinion on the subject of the convent. Now, let us see what it is of which the plaintiff complains, of which it is most essential that you should have a clear and definite view. In the first place she complains of having been assaulted ; in the next she complains of having been imprisoned ; she further complains of articles belonging to her having been taken from her and converted to the defendants' use ; she complains, fourthly, of having been libelled by the statements written by the defendants in their letters to the bishop, and in the depositions which they submitted to his consideration ; and lastly, and most important of all, the plaintiff complains that there has been a conspiracy against her on the part of the defendants, which assumed a twofold shape ; first, that they conspired by ill-treatment—I think the language of the declaration is "indignities and persecutions," but that substantially means, by ill-treatment, to force her to leave the convent ; and secondly, that there was conspiracy by false accusations to induce the bishop to expel her from the convent, and that by means of those false accusations he was induced to take that step, and so she was compelled to leave the convent. In all these matters the defendants, in the first place, denied the truth of the charge ; and they further put upon record a plea, which in this case is of great importance ; it is a plea which, technically, no lawyers call a plea of leave and licence. Its effect is practically thus, that it alleges that the plaintiff gave her consent to those acts of which she complains. Now, nothing can be better settled than this, that where a person invites or consents to an action that would otherwise be wrongful, it cannot be complained of. We lawyers know the maxim in the Latin form, *Voluntas non fit injuriam*—no wrong is done to him who consents to a wrong. The application of the plea here is this, and that is the main statement of the defendants. They say that we were members of a common association, you joined it voluntarily, the association is based on certain principles, you assented to the principles upon which it is based, you assented to the terms by which we all bound ourselves to one another, you have taken certain vows, you have engaged to assent to certain rules, you have joined the community upon that understanding, and all that has been done has been within the powers conferred upon us ; and you cannot, therefore, be heard to complain of that which has been the result of your own voluntary will. If you should be of opinion in the result that what is alleged under this plea is true, it may be an answer to a considerable portion, but not to the whole of the matters complained of. There is nothing, so far as I can gather from the rules and customs of this association, that would warrant personal violence. There is nothing that would warrant restraint of person against the will of the individual. There is nothing that would warrant a conspiracy such as that which is set forth in this declaration. If, therefore, by-and-bye, you should be of opinion that a conspiracy is made out, and that the acts complained of have been done in furtherance of it, that will justify a verdict for the plaintiff. But it may be an answer to acts which would be un-justifiable in point of law if you should be of opinion that these acts have been done under the power given to the superior by the voluntary sub_mission of the plaintiff, and have been submitted to by her, not against her legal will, but simply as a part of the obedience to which she had volun-tarily bound herself. In the first place, the one of the vows to which I shall call your attention, the party who enters into that association re-nounces all rights of poverty whatsoever, and therefore is not in a position to complain that any-thing is taken from her, because, *ex concessione*, she has nothing of her own. The defendants were, however, in this difficulty. They allege that by the sentence of expulsion she ceased to be a member of the community ; and as to whether, under this circumstance, the right of property

would not arise, to meet that difficulty they paid a sum of money into court. I heard with much satisfaction from the Solicitor-General in his address to you that it was not to be contended, but that the sum paid into the court was suffi-cient to cover those small, unimportant value-less articles which had been taken from her, and which, either by accident or otherwise, had not been restored to her. We, therefore, put entirely out of consideration all the matters com-plained of which relate to property. As regards the assault I own that I was a little pained to hear that that part of the case was to be insisted upon ; because if the defendant fails to get a verdict upon the great matter she has brought before you, the getting a verdict for an assault, which would carry perhaps a shilling damages, does not matter a moment. The only point of the case, I understand, in which it is possible to allege any-thing, relates to the so-called stripping of the 1st of May, 1865. The plaintiff alleges that upon that occasion her articles of dress, if she did not take them off with sufficient celerity, were rudely torn from her by Mrs. Star and Mrs. Kennedy. All this is denied. That is the only part of the case, as it seems to me, in which there is the slightest shadow of an assault. Next we have the case of imprisonment. My object now is to clear the case of these outlying parts of it, and to come to that which is real substantial matter. As regards imprisonment, nothing was complained of except what took place after the commission, and upon that there is a conflict of evidence upon which you may have to decide. There, again, I would point out to you that, with the exception of that particular part of the case, there can be no pre-tence whatever for saying that any imprisonment was imposed on the plaintiff. Now I come to that which is the real gravamen of this complaint, and upon which it seems to me the plaintiff must have a verdict or fail in having a verdict at your hands. I will call your attention to the main and leading facts of the case from its beginning to its close, and I propose to divide it into several epochs. This course will keep your attention more fixed on that which is material, and assist in giving clearness and precision to the points which arise in the case. We have a history extending, I am sorry to say, over fifteen years, and almost every year of the time is pregnant with some fact or other of impor-tance to the decision of this case ; I have di-vided it thus :—Beginning with the outset of the plaintiff's convent life in the year 1859, I will bring her down to the time at which she alleged that a change in the manner of the defendants towards her in their treatment of her took place, and that will carry us over a period from 1850 to 1861. The next epoch will be from 1861 to 1864, when she was transferred from Clifford to Hull; and I take that period because, as it appears to me, it is from that period that the matter of the alleged conspiracy and acts done under it commenced. We then have another period, beginning with the transfer to Hull in 1864, extending to the close of 1865, when the commission was issued. Next we have to turn our attention to what took place under the commission; and then we have the last and closing chapter in the history of this painful case, namely, the matters of which she complains during the period which intervenes between the bishop's sentence of expulsion and her finally leaving the convent. You will, perhaps, say why do I go back to so remote a period, seeing that the real matters complained of are comprised in the materials beginning in the year 1864? Why take us back to the commencement of this history? I will tell you why. It seems to me very important to ascertain what may be the origin of the differences which arose between these parties. I think it is impossible not to believe that after 1864 the plaintiff was treated with great severity and great harshness; and, unless there were circumstances that could at all account for the excessive harshness with which she was treated, she has great reason for complaint. But, on the other hand, if we find that her own conduct in resisting the authority to which she had sworn obedience, and in resisting the discipline to which she ought to have submitted, and in resisting the regulations, then the case becomes very infinitesimal. If, on the other hand, you can see any base or sinister motives in the defendants for treating her as they had done, that would be matter of great importance, for your attentive, serious consideration, and in leading you to the conclusion you may finally arrive at; and inasmuch as the origin of those differences dates back to so remote a period, and inasmuch as, in tracing the history of those painful events from the commencement we may have some light thrown on the case, and will be enabled the better to understand on which side the truth lies. I will therefore, begin with the beginning. First let me tell you what is the case which the plaintiff lays before you : She says—At a very early age my vocation was to be a nun. She desired to enter a convent, notwithstanding that her friends declined at first to allow their then last daughter to be consigned to a conventual life. She, however, at last obtained their consent to enter the convent at Baggot-street,

Dublin. She says she was there perfectly happy that she had there formed an intimacy with the defendants, one of whom (Mrs. Star) was her senior by a few months, while the other (Mrs. Kennedy), was her junior by about the same time. In 1855, Mrs. Star came to England, a new convent at Clifford, in Yorkshire, having been founded, to which she was transferred. In 1856 she found that she needed the assistance of another sister at Clifford, and having communicated that to the superior of the convent at Baggot-street, she says the plaintiff wrote several letters to her requesting that she might be chosen as one of the additional sisters, and she accordingly came to Clifford. From that time, May 1856 to 1860, the plaintiff says nothing could have passed more happily than my life passed. I gave full and unbounded satisfaction—I seemed to be the person upon whom Mrs. Star principally rested the management. Everything I did was right. In 1860 Mrs. Star took me to Ireland, where I had the opportunity of seeing my friends. We returned the best possible friends ; and then an incident arose which disturbed this happy, harmonious state, and formed the source of all those events of which I complain. That incident was this :—She called upon me to communicate to her what had passed between myself and the priest in the confessional. I said, "No; I cannot do anything so wrong as that. It would be contrary to honour, and contrary to all rule." Then, she said, "Perhaps you'll think." There is something characteristic in that. I said I could not remember what had passed, for I tried, upon which Mrs. Star told me to take time to remember ; and upon a second occasion, and a third occasion, she pressed me again, and told me there was no other sister in the community, she knew, who had refused. Mrs. Ryan, she said, had often communicated to her what passed between her and her confessor. Now, from that moment, she changed her manners towards me, and her treatment, which before had been all friendship, assumed a harshness and a severity which at last culminated in the indignities and treatment to which I was subjected in 1864 and 1865. Now, this is a simple, plain, and consistent statement. The question is whether it be a truthful one. It appears to me a matter of very considerable moment, if true, for enabling us to judge upon which side the truth really lies. To ascertain whether the statement is true or false, it is evidence of a very cogent character, so cogent, that in his address to you, the Solicitor-General the other day, to get out of the difficulty, and, to my astonishment, had departed from his own words and the words of his client.

The Solicitor-General said that his client had intended to write and to indicate, that after those circumstances there was a change, without at all wishing it to be understood that the circumstance was the cause of the change. Now, I was startled when I heard that statement, as this is a point of cardinal importance. I have some confidence in the notes of evidence which I took myself; but I would not trust myself on this occasion, and I asked for the shorthand writer's notes, but unfortunately no transcript had been taken of the Solicitor-General's speech, it being very common not to take shorthand notes of the speeches of counsel, but simply to confine the operation to notes of evidence. I have before me a report in a morning paper, which I find in accordance with my distinct recollection of the Solicitor-General's opening statement. [His lordship here read the newspaper report confirming his own impression of what the Solicitor-General stated. He also read the plaintiff's evidence in corroboration of the same view, to indicate that it was intended that the jury should draw the inference that it was on account of her refusing to reveal what passed in the confessional that caused Mrs. Star to alter her demeanour towards her, withdraw her friendship, and subject her to cause of annoyance and ill-treatment.] I think it is impossible not to say that both the learned counsel in the opening and conduct of this case, and the plaintiff intended to convey, and did convey to your minds that what was meant was this, that in consequence of this refusal on the part of the plaintiff to communicate the matter of her confession, the defendant Mrs. Star conceived towards her an antipathy and a resentment, and evinced it in her conduct by from that hour changing her demeanour towards her. Now, I cannot allow this playing fast and loose with you and me. That is the case they presented to you ; that is the case the plaintiff is prepared to stand on, that is the case she swore to, and it is impossible to put any other construction upon it. If what she has said was true, she succeeds in establishing that the motive of Mrs. Star in altering her conduct was odious and detestable ; that her conduct arose out of most unworthy motives ; and, on the other hand, if she fails to prove it, if you are of opinion that that is proved, this was — that in order to avoid the matters of which she complained being traced back to their actual source and origin, she has, with a view to conceal what might affect herself prejudicially, with a view to foster a prejudice upon the defendants, has told you a story which is not true. Now, let us see by what evidence the story of the plaintiff is met, and then form your judgment as to circumstances. They say it is true that they were at Baggot-street together, but to say that there was no unpleasantness there was untrue. Mrs. Kennedy never was in a large establishment engaged in several avocations, and that there was little or nothing to bring them together. Mrs. Saurin, whose family was more or less entitled to certain considerations in the convent, was dissatisfied with the position in which her daughter was placed, and said that she had not been sent to the nunnery for the purpose of superintending washing. Mrs. Kennedy says—"I saw her very often crying, and I wondered to myself how she could be so silly as to remain there when she was so unhappy." Mrs. M'Keon also observed her discontent. Mrs. Star says that when she went over to Ireland in 1856 she saw Mrs. Saurin, who adverted in strong terms to the manner in which her daughter had been treated at Baggot-street, observing that nothing would ever induce her to send her to Baggot-street again. We have it also in evidence —I do not know whether you believe it or not— that the Jesuit brother, whose extraordinary letter excited so much attention the other day, in writing to his sister a letter, adverted in strong language to the manner in which she had been treated in Baggot-street, speaking of her superiors as torturers and tyrants. That brother seems to be gifted with a fiery and ardent imagination. I do not suppose there was anything to warrant such language, but it shows this, at all events— that there was in the family considerable dissatisfaction at the way in which she had been treated in Baggot-street. Then she says she was induced to come to England at the pressing instance and renewed solicitations of Mrs. Star ; but she says, "Not a bit of it. I wanted an assistant sister, and, knowing there was a great number of nuns and sisters at Baggot-street, I wrote there to know if they could send one, and I mentioned three or four names, amongst others Miss Saurin being mentioned." Accordingly she came, and, having come, things went on with tolerable smoothness until 1860, but by no means in the way Miss Saurin has described. She has said there were complaints ; but that was not so. Then comes evidence to which it is necessary to call your attention—as to what did in point of fact, take place during the years 1857, 1858, 1859, and 1866, when Miss Saurin was at the convent at Hull or Clifford, prior to what has been supposed to be the rupture between the parties. Let me call your attention to these earlier years and to the evidence there is

M

upon this subject. Of course it is all put before you subject to the observations which have been made upon the sufficiency of the evidence, and upon the credibility of the witnesses. Mrs. Kennedy said she had charge from February, 1857, during the time Mrs. Star was at Clifford, and she says Miss Saurin was very irregular, especially at meals, and that she was constantly obliged to wait, and to postpone saying grace, at which it is expected every sister should be present. She was constantly breaking the rule as to silence, gossiping with the young women in the night-school. [The Lord Chief Justice here went through the evidence of Mrs. Kennedy on this point, and also Mrs. King's.] Those are small matters, but still there appears to have been at this time a considerable amount of complaint ; and it is brought forward to show that there was not this total absence of dissatisfaction as stated. We come now to another matter. Plaintiff has alleged that she went in 1860 to Clifford, and that she was sent there for the purpose of getting up the schools, they having at that time fallen into decay in consequence of neglect ; and that she succeeded in the course of the first two months in effecting the object, and so giving great satisfaction to the superior. Defendant met that by saying that there was not a word of truth in it, except that she did go to the infant school. It was in consequence of a want of more nuns at Hull that it was desired to withdraw the sisters from Clifford, and with that view they proposed to give up the school. But it was represented to the bishop that the school being in so flourishing a condition, it would not be advisable to give it up, and it was agreed that the plaintiff should go and assist in the school. As to her being sent to restore the school to a state of efficiency, that was an utter misrepresentation. We now come to the summer of 1860, when plaintiff and Mrs. Star go to Ireland, where the plaintiff has an opportunity of seeing her friends. In November, 1860, they return to England, and plaintiff went again to Clifford. The case Mrs. Star puts forward is this—That although there had been complaints up to that time, there had been nothing to cause a direct breach between them, but that she found that the plaintiff required more discipline and obedience. Out of that arose a stern and more determined course of conduct on the part of her as superior who was bound to enforce obedience and observance of the rules. I will read you one or more pieces of the evidence as to the conduct of the plaintiff up to this time. In addition to what I was calling your attention to

just now, I should mention that Mrs. Star's account of her prior to going to Hull is this—Mrs. Star says she was very irregular and unpunctual —did not observe the rule of silence, and held conversations with externs. She frequently showed a want of sincerity, and was in the habit of taking calico and working materials, and also took a book and secreted it. Mrs. Kennedy also said she had to report the plaintiff for being very disobedient and frequently absent from duty. I have called your attention to this evidence, in order to show you what was the state of things between them down to the year 1860. We know that in 1860 she returned to Ireland ; and now it is, she says, that the difference between her and Mrs. Star first happened. I have already called your attention to it. Mrs. Star says there was nothing of the kind, and she positively and absolutely denies that anything of what passed in the confessional had ever taken place between them. You have, therefore, oath against oath, and the question is, which will you believe. Mrs. Star swears as positively in the negative as the plaintiff swears in the affirmative ; but it is necessary to look at the several circumstances of the case. In the first place, was there anything in the condut of the plaintiff, as alleged by Mrs. Star, which led to greater dissatisfaction with the plaintiff than she had previously exhibited towards her. That Mrs. Star had not treated things that had happened up to that time, of any serious moment appears, as she did not profess, when she saw the mother of the plaintiff in 1860, that she had any complaint to make ; and we have also the fact that two letters of hers, which certainly were at one time in existence, in which she spoke of plaintiff in terms of satisfaction and regard. You must judge whether the fact of those letters having been written, and of their being written, whether their reported tenour confirms the statement that, although there had been no very serious matters up to that time, still there were matters of complaint. Unfortunately we have not those letters. They were given up by Father Matthews to the bishop, and the bishop lost them. But we have this fact, that Father Matthews certainly when the complaints were made to the bishop about Sister Scholastica in 1862, produced those letters to the bishop by way of answer to the charges made by Mrs. Star to show that up to a recent period she had been satisfied and content with the conduct of Sister Scholastica. I do not know that it is conclusive, even if you suppose the date to have been 1860, because it may be that the defendant, Mrs. Star, in writing to the mother of the plaintiff, thought that although Sister Scholastica was not the best nun in the world as regards regularity and discipline and obedience to the rules of the convent, yet she would in time become all that she could desire. You must judge of that for yourself. Mrs. Star says that plaintiff, in 1861, became more regardless than before of the rules by which she ought to have been governed—a circumstance which Mrs. Star attributed to the intercourse plaintiff had had with her relations in Ireland. Is that likely? Of that you must judge from the correspondence and the other circumstances that have been brought to your knowledge in respect to the Saurin family. There are some letters from the mother in 1861 which I think will rather lead to the notion that, although they had been willing to let their daughter go into a convent, and although they might have known of the rules of the convent, they were by no means prepared to interpret those rules and put upon them the construction they had done. They seem to have entertained high notions about their daughter's rights, notions which perhaps you may think inconsistent with the implicit obedience on the one hand, and absolute power on the other, which were to exist by the terms of the association. At all events, according to Mrs. Star, the plaintiff had gained nothing in the way of humility by the intercourse with her relations. She goes back to Clifford in the year 1860. In the spring or the summer of 1861 Mrs. Star goes over to Clifford with Mrs. Kerr. [His lordship then read the evidence of Mrs. Kerr and Mrs. Star, about putting the hands of the clock backward, the making of the shirts, and the partial conduct of the plaintiff in the refectory in giving the juniors smaller portions than they should have had.] Now, the plaintiff says Mrs. Star had become more severe, and that there was nothing to account for it but the refusal to reveal what had passed in confession. The plaintiff sought Mrs. Star's cell one evening, and says, "I can do nothing to please you." Mrs. Star sternly answered, "I have given you too much liberty, and I will pull you down." This defendant Mrs. Star denies. She says, "I certainly did put her under more restraint at this time, but that was simply to compel her to place herself on the same footing of equality with the rest of the sisters. They obeyed all the rules and regulations; the plaintiff more or less set them at defiance. I felt it my duty to bring her down to the same level; but I used no such treatment as that described. Something of the kind may have passed." In 1861 there was on the part of the defendant the commencement of the course which she certainly had pursued, of applying a severer and a stricter rule to Sister Scholastica than she had done before. To what cause is this to be ascribed? Is it, as plaintiff originally represented it to be, dissatisfaction and resentment in not having revealed her confession? Or is it, as Mrs. Star suggests, in consequence of the conduct of plaintiff from the commencement compared with that of other sisters, and because at that time she showed far greater irregularity and disobedience, calling for the exercise of her authority as superior in a sterner manner in order to compel obedience? Upon this the two parties are at issue, and it seems to me important at starting to traverse the rest of these incidents to say which you believe. Now, your attention is called to three or four circumstances which, as defendants say, show that the plaintiff's statement must necessarily be wrong, and if wrong, it is impossible that the other can be false. It is remarkable that this statement about the confession was never brought forward at the commission; and it is a circumstance so remarkable that it is not possible to suppose that if it really existed it would not have been prominently brought forward. We know that in 1865 Miss Saurin wrote to the bishop a statement of her grievances, and that she narrated how all things had gone on smoothly up to 1860 or 1861, when a change took place. To what did she ascribe the change? She ascribes it to the fact that in the meanwhile Mrs. Star had got fresh postulants, who had entered the convent at Hull, and who were now prepared to be novices and nuns; that she preferred those who were of her own teaching, because they submitted to the customs which were not conformable to the old practice of the convent. She suggests as another reason—and it is a very significant one—that she knew all about the nuns that had originally come from Baggot-street. "I knew their circumstances," said she, "and Mrs. Star did not like that." Now, what was meant by that covert allusion? I am sure I do not know. Something, I presume, not favourable to Mrs. Star. She says, on account of those reasons, Mrs. Star wanted to get rid of her. We find the plaintiff's statement was patiently listened to by the commission. They determined to hear what she had to lay before them as to the counter charges against the sisters, and did hear them. We have notes taken at the time by the bishop's secretary, and we have the evidence of Dr. O'Hanlon, a friend of the family, who was disposed to say what he could in support of the plaintiff. There was no trace, so far as I am aware, of any complaint of this sort. But I will tell you something far more important as regards that, that in 1862, and again in 1863, Father Matthews came forward for her protection; that he interposed and communicated with the bishop. We know he saw his niece, and that he had an opportunity of conversing with her upon those matters, especially questioning her about the issue of the commission. In every inquiry which he made he says she made no complaint and no counter-charges against the sisters. I ask you as reasonable men is it possible to believe that if she had in her mind at that time that all this treatment to which she was subjected had its origin in this refusal to communicate what had passed in confession, she would not have made the circumstance known. Why should she not? She looked to him as her natural protector. If she had so communicated to him either on those visits, or when about to appear before the commission, do you for one moment believe that Father Matthews would not have communicated the statement to his bishop, or brought it prominently forward as one of the charges to be made against the defendants. What a lever would it not have proved for Father Matthews to use with the view of overthrowing the conduct and authority of his superior. Do you think he would not have used it to the bishop, when spoken to with reference to the complaints his niece had to make against the superioress, if such matters, indeed, existed in reality? Under these circumstances you have an oath against an oath, and it is for you to say what do you believe. Is it true that there was this endeavour on the part of the defendant, Mrs. Star, to extract, or rather I should say, to extort, from this reluctant sister what had passed between her and her confessor. If it be from that sprung this aversion and determination to subject her to the indignity and ill-treatment with a view to induce you to think that it was not out of her own conduct that their harsh dealing arose, but out of an unworthy and sinister motive on the part of the defendant. Is it true that this story was told? If you disbelieve it, it is a most inauspicious point from which to start in considering how the rest of the plaintiff's story arose. It is of the most material moment to satisfy oneself how this alleged treatment of the plaintiff arose; what was its source and origin, and what was the motive under which the defendant, Mrs. Star, acted. If it is as the plaintiff suggests, Mrs. Star's conduct was almost too abominable

to be considered with patience and endurance. If on the other hand the story has been invented for the purpose of this case, of course when you have these parties in conflict afterwards, this circumstance ought to leave its influence on your judgment as to the credit to be given to the one or the other. It is for you naturally to form your own judgment. It is the first point in the case on which you should make up your minds one way or the other. I now pass from what happened in 1861 to the more material incidents of 1862. In the year 1862, an event happened which is one of the many incidents of the history of this very remarkable case. You remember that it was in the month of February, 1862, that a letter was found under the Sister Scholastica's bed. It appears that Mrs. King, who at that time was a sister at Clifford, had received instruction to see that the cells were in proper order, going one day in the course of that month to Sister Scholastica's room, she saw with amazement partly protruding from under the pillow an ink-bottle, which had been removed from the school, and which nobody expected to find there. What was Mrs. King's evidence? She said her curiosity was aroused, and she determined to search further, looked under the mattress, and there found in a book a letter concealed. The plaintiff was called about this. She denies it. If Mrs. King be right, we have here the plaintiff denying a part of the story, which, if true, I think she must have known. That letter indicates clearly dissatisfaction at not having been allowed to go to Ireland in the winter, and expresses a desire to get to Ireland somehow. I will call your attention to the letters which passed, to show what was at that time the feeling of Mrs. Saurin with regard to her daughter's position. The defendant said there were circumstances which she could more fully particularize which prevented her giving her consent to the plaintiff's leaving Clifford and going to Ireland, and then comes this characteristic letter from Mrs. Saurin. [His lordship here read the letter.] By the terms of the association the power of the superior was to be unlimited, and her voice was to be as the voice of God. Obedience was to be absolute and entire; and, therefore, to assent that the nun had a right to leave her conven˜ without the consent of the superior was certainly to join issue with the authorities of that conventional association upon one of the main points which were involved in the authority so constituted. It seems Mrs. Star had one view and Mrs. Saurin another, and the result was that Mrs.

Star resolutely maintained her own, and refused to let Sister Scholastica go over to Dublin. There might have been another reason. It is quite clear at the time that Mrs. Star refused to let her go, and the argument of the Solicitor-General on it is well founded; for he shows that at that time there was no disposition on the part of Mrs. Star to get rid of her. The plaintiff herself admitted that she intended to send secretly the letter found in 1861. One of the rules rigorously adhered to is that no correspondence shall pass a between a member of the sisterhood and any one, no matter who, not even to her natural mother, without its passing under the eye of the mother superior, and that there is in the mother superior a most absolute, unqualified, unconditional authority to prevent any letter going forth from the convent. Of course, if there be such a rule—I think, after the evidence we have heard, we cannot help believing there was—to attempt to send a letter clandestinely is a species of high treason against the defendant's authority. Mrs. Star wrote to the plaintiff on the subject, but it was simply a letter of remonstrance and expostulation, pointing out the impropriety of such a breach of rules, and also telling her that if she had applied to her for permission to go to Ireland, she would have received such permission, as well as every facility for the journey. Mrs. M'Keon also said she had ascertained that Miss Saurin had employed a school-girl to take another to the post, but Miss Saurin said it was a letter which the mother of the girl asked her to read over before she sent it away. Upon this point the evidence was altogether very unsatisfactory. Then the mother superior wrote to the uncle, telling him that his niece had committed very grave offences, and that the best thing to be done was to remove her to a convent in Ireland. The uncle came over and saw the bishop, and asked for a visitation of the convent. He also got permission to see his niece. Afterwards there was the following letter, which Mrs. Star dictated to Miss Saurin, entreating her uncle, to get her admitted into a convent at Drogheda :—

"MY DEAREST UNCLE,—The community are determined I shall not remain. You know the archbishop and reverend mother at Baggot-street are determined I shall not return there. Unless you settle with your community to receive me, my dearest uncle, I know not what to do. The greatest act of charity you could do towards me is to settle it at once if you can. If you write to say I can get to Drogheda, even for a while, rev. mother will send me. May I beg, as a great favour, you will not go to bishops or anyone else

about it? but do let me know by next post, as rev. mother says the community here will wait no longer, as they are determined to take measures without delay for my removal. If the community in Drogheda consent to my going there, rev. mother says they need never know why I leave here, only you wish it for the sake of my father and mother. You will be greatly surprised at this letter altogether—the horrid writing. For God's sake do not say a word to any of my friends, not even mamma—I know she would feel it so—if you possibly can. I feel it is the will of God. He has some wise design in all. How can I ever forgive all the trouble, &c., I am giving you, and worse than the trouble? I again and again beg you will settle it for me, in charity, as soon as possible, and without any more fuss. Won't you write by next post?

"Believe me, your ever faithful niece in J. C.
"SR. M. SCHOLASTICA."

You will consider that statement on the one side and the other. She said the latter was dictated to her by the mother superior. Mr. Mellish, in his most able address, pointed out and criticised the terms in the language of that letter. He pointed out to you that it was more like the sensational style of Sister Scholastica—her interjections, and a sort of jerking style, and unlike the grave style of the mother superior. I don't know that it signifies very much except that it would make out if it is the spontaneous effusion of the plaintiff herself, that she was at the time desirous for her removal from the convent as much as the convent was desirous that her removal should take place. The uncle sent the letter to the bishop, and adverted to it as having been written under the immediate dictation of the mother superior. These letters were important, as being contemporaneous and written under the influence of the feelings at the time. His lordship then referred to Mrs. Star's letter, calling upon the bishop to remove Miss Saurin, and observing that the negative for removing her to St. Mary's, Drogheda, had failed, and reflecting on the plaintiff's conduct in reference to the clandestine correspondence, and that, in fact, her character was irretrievably damaged. Why Father Matthew refused to take her to Drogheda is not for me to question, but I must, in all sincerity, say that he regretted she was not removed. Had he done so, he would have been spared all that afterwards took place, and his niece from undergoing the degradation and misery she had undergone, and last, though not the least, we should have been spared this protracted and most tiresome inquiry. There was no doubt the convent was weary of the plaintiff's presence. Whose fault it was he would not stop to inquire, but they did get upon terms anything but harmonious was as clear as the sun at noonday, but plaintiff pertinaciously persisted in refusing to leave. The uncle afterwards asked the bishop to hold a visitation, and inquire into the case and ascertain the truth of the charges, suggesting at the same time that the fault lay not with the plaintiff but with the mother superior, with whom the bishop was to administer a smart admonition, to mind what she was about for the future. The bishop found himself in a position of difficulty, and to settle the matter he had recourse to a most ineffectual mode for that purpose. He held a visitation and not a judicial inquiry, and instead of giving all the parties notice of his intended investigation, the bishop took the greatest care not to let them know what he was about. He saw each sister separately, heard what she had to say, and then what the plaintiff had to state to him. The poor bishop was then in the greatest possible difficulty and hesitation, and then, like many other people in the world, he thought the best way was to let things go on, and perhaps they would right themselves. It was far from him to say anything severe or disrespectful of a high dignitary of the Roman Catholic Church, but he could only ascribe it to his lordship's weakness, which he (the Lord Chief Justice) regretted, because if the bishop had interfered with a vigorous hand and investigated the matter, and if he had found the plaintiff in the wrong, have prescribed the course to pursue, and if the superior had been in the wrong, to have rebuked her, and then to have brought the parties together, the matter might have been ended there. But a more lame and impotent conclusion than that to which the bishop had come could hardly be arrived at. His lordship then went minutely through the various incidents of complaint about the watch, the food, breach of rules, etc. He next called their attention to the monthly letters written in 1864, observing that they were of more importance than mere acknowledgments of faults. From them there might possibly gain an insight into the plaintiff's character. On the one hand, her language was put forward as the simplicity and truth of a woman who was describing what was passing in her mind with manifest humility, and who desired to do what was right ; on the other hand, they must look at them and see if there was a great amount of acknowledgments of faults, but a constant attempt to justify what she was compelled to admit—a sort of vacillating, ill-conditioned, ill-regulated, ill-balanced mind ; one minute self-condemning, another self-approving, and always desirous of taking every opportunity of saying something in disparagement of those in the convent. It was for them to form their judgments upon these letters ; he had assigned none, but he had put forward two views by which they might be understood. In one of the letters she says, " I do not know how it is, dear reverend brother, I am always doing wrong, though I do my best to improve." Now, what was the meaning of that? Was it that she was conscious of her imperfections, or was it that, though she tried to do her best, she was always found fault with? Agan, she says, " I hope God will not spare me here, or you either, that I may be spared hereafter . . . that God will let me remain in his holy house." Then, stepping from the sublime to the ridiculous, she asks for a new sweeping-brush for the school-room. In another letter she expresses this hope—" that I may to my dying day be looked on with the same contempt that I am at present. I said the office of the dead so badly that Sister Mary Evangelista must have been disedified. I have been often unkind and impatient with the little children, and have rung the bells late, and she asked leave that the new brush might be used in sweeping the school, saying, ' I have been so long sweeping out the large school on my knees with that small brush.' " There was in all the letters confessions of faults, self-abasement, and an anxiety to implicate others, between self-condemnation and self-laudation. That brought him down to the month of June, 1864, when she was removed to Hull. She complained that on the night before bedding was taken from her without necessity, to be given to others, when it might have been given to Mrs. Grimstone. The explanation given by the defendants was that some sisters had arrived who wanted to stay for one night only, and that every one in the house did their best to accommodate them under the circumstances. Again, she complained that she got short notice of removal to Clifford; that clothes she was folding up were taken from her ; that her boots were rudely forced on, and that she was herself pushed down the steps by Mrs. Kennedy. Mrs. Star and Mrs. Kennedy state that that never took place ; that she got short notice in order that the villagers might not come to bid her good-bye, as they had done to some other sisters. They thought it desirable, perhaps, to prevent an ovation as she was then in disgrace. She also gave a graphic account of what took place on the way to the train ; that she was obliged to carry a basket, and hold an umbrella over the mother superior, who walked along in the stately dignity of her position. Mrs. Star stated that she, too, had a basket, and that it was not true that she had an undue share of the umbrella. Now, he came to the time when the plaintiff, having been taken to Hull, the series of circumstances were said to take place of which the plaintiff complained. He could not help remembering that Miss Saurin had had in this case a great advantage. She had had the advantage of having her case stated by one of the ablest men at the bar, and of proving it in her own way, and the effect had been to produce on every mind a powerful and painful impression. If the circumstances she detailed were true—if the matters she spoke of took place under the circumstances she described, and were incapable of being softened or explained away by the defendants, her case was no doubt a very grievous one. So it appeared to everyone at first. She had since had the advantage not only of having made the first impression, but of having had the last appeal made on her behalf, and made in one of the most able and eloquent speeches that he remembered in the whole course of his experience, which now extended, he was sorry to say, to a remote period, and which treasured up the experience of some of the greatest men the Bar of England ever produced, and that being so he thought he ought to go through the details of the case, bringing each matter to their attention, and contrast the evidence on the one side and the other. But he trusted that from the beginning to the end he should do nothing or say nothing that would leave them less free and unfettered than they ought to be, to exercise their own judgment upon the entire case.

After a short adjournment for luncheon,

The Lord Chief Justice proceeded with his summing-up, referring particularly to the grievances alleged by the plaintiff in reference to the taking of tablets, papers, and clothes from the plaintiff, the thimble transaction, and the first stripping of the plaintiff on the 30th May, 1865; on her arriving at the convent from the school, drawing attention to the evidence given by the plaintiff and the evidence given in reference to these transactions by the defendant Mrs. Star, on the occasion of taking the tablet advising Miss Saurin to go to Dublin with a sister, and endeavour to go into the convent in Baggot-street, promising that if she failed she should come again to Hull. He could not help regarding that as an insidious proposal, as she knew the plaintiff would not be received, and it turned out on further examination that she could only be received

again at Hull as a visitor—a visitor being liable to be turned out at any moment. He left them to judge how long she would be allowed to remain in the convent as a visitor. The stripping constituted the assault which was complained of, the plaintiff stating that the defendant pulled off her clothes; they, on the other hand, swore that she took them off on being desired to do so, and handed them to the mother superior. Unexplained this would appear to be a most abominable and uncalled-for act. Was it merely for the purpose of mortifying and humiliating this poor creature, by making her feel her abject condition, and the extent to which she was in the power of the lady superior? To make her take off every article of dress, and leave her in a cold place for hours, was an act than which he could conceive nothing more tyrannical or oppressive. What was the explanation? It was said that she was in the habit of taking the children's food; that they were afraid some scandal would arise from it, and Mrs. Kennedy advised the sister superior to try and detect her; that she was seen from the window to take some food from a child, wrap it up in a piece of paper, and put it in her pocket. Accordingly, she was asked to take off her dress, but nothing was found upon her. The Solicitor-General said this showed there was no reality in the tale, not a single crumb being discovered in her pocket. The question was whether they believed that Mrs. Star and Mrs. Kennedy had received such reports and honestly acted upon them with the object of putting an end to a detestable practice. In the same year there was another grievance respecting a stay lace. Miss Saurin's story was that she was called into Mrs. Star's cell and made to take off her dress—that she was stripped in the cold and kept without her habit from ten until twelve, the door of the cell being open all the time, and the sisters and others passing along the corridor seeing her in this state of semi-nudity and humiliation. If that was true, it was a cruel act of oppression. The explanation was this. A few days after she had received a new staylace she asked for another, saying the other was torn. Mrs. Dawson asked her to take off her dress, and then she found that besides the staylace the band of the dress was torn. Mrs. Kerr mended the habit, while Mrs. Dawson mended the staylace; the whole operation occupying not more than half-an-hour. They said not a single minute was wasted unnecessarily, and that after Sister Scholastica was dressed they all went to dinner. It was for the jury to say which was the most probable story. The learned judge then referred to the charge about her being deprived of bed-clothes, and the answer of the defendants. In the same manner he dealt with the complaint about her clothes and robes, observing that one of the sisters said she had the dress she had on fourteen years, and that in accordance with the vow of poverty the whole of the community wore their clothes as long as they would hold together. There was also evidence to the effect that Sister Scholastica's clothes were not so old or so worn as those of other sisters. Another grievance was that the household duties were unduly forced upon her, that she had to wash, scrub, and shake mats, and do other degrading work, which she had not strength to perform, and from which other sisters were relieved. But Mrs. Kennedy said she was not put on different work from that of the rest of the sisters, that they, at all events, did these things in turn, and that hard work was the characteristic of their order. Mrs. Star, who appeared to have been born and bred a lady, said she did the same work as the plaintiff after she left the convent, and that she helped the lay sisters in cleaning rooms, scouring floors, and washing saucepans. She added that she never thought household duties humiliating, as they were part of the practice of the order. Mrs. Collingwood, another lay sister, said that most of the professed nuns showed the same wish as the plaintiff. He next came to the article of food. The plaintiff complained that she got mutton continually, although her aversion to it was known, and the other sisters were supplied with different meat ; that sometimes the meat which she left on the previous day was brought back to her ; that she was once compelled to eat mouldy bread. Mrs. Kennedy, on the other hand, denied that she was treated differently from the rest, and explained that it was the custom of the order to waste nothing ; but when the plaintiff complained of having the remains of her previous day's dinner returned, she ordered that not to be repeated. With regard to the bread, she said that they baked all their own bread, and that on one occasion it turned out mouldy ; but that, having no other, they were all obliged to eat it. Another ground of complaint was perhaps more just. The plaintiff said it was an act of cruelty to prevent her mending her clothes by taking away all her working materials. There could be no doubt that, whatever view the jury took of the case in the whole, an unnecessary amount of rigour which no one could justify—and everyone must look upon with pain—had been exercised in certain instances. Granted that it was inexpedient she should have writing materials, lest she should write calumny against the sisters, what harm could there be in allowing her to occupy spare time in mending her clothes? With regard to the plaintiff having, as penances, to wear a dirty duster on her head and kiss the floor, his lordship observed that these were lamentable disclosures, and he hoped the public exposure of these things would prevent their repetition. But faults which looked very petty when viewed in the face of day appeared in very magnified proportions when seen through the medium of dim convent light. Surely better and more appropriate penances might be found for educated women, but they were common to all, and every sister was bound to pay implicit obedience to the commands of the mother superior. That which struck them at first as an abominable iniquity turned out to be nothing more than an everyday occurrence in the convent. One young lady, with a *naivetté* which charmed them all, said she wore her shoes round her neck for some very small offence, and thought she was better for the punishment. That the answer came from her heart he had no more doubt than that he sat on that bench. His lordship next alluded to the charge that the plaintiff, by way of indignity and hardship, was placed below younger sisters in the school, and said the defendants replied that she was only capable of teaching the infant and the lower classes. Upon that they had something to assist them in the letters of the plaintiff. Those letters contained many instances of bad spelling, such as "altogether" with two l's, "possibly" with one s, "apology" with two p's, and "please" without the final e, "annoy," with one n, "copy" with two p's, "tawlk" for talk, "compleate" for complete, and other mistakes which could hardly be the result of accident. In almost all her letters she referred to her bad spelling, and spoke of writing without a dictionary, and it seemed she was hardly capable of writing an English letter without one by her side. He had now gone through the whole matter of complaint relating to the period from the middle of 1864 when she went from Hull to Clifford until the issuing of the commission, and it was these matters explained, contradicted, or qualified, which formed the materials upon which the charge of conspiracy was founded. The plaintiff says there was a conspiracy to drive her from the convent. Now, in order to make out a charge of conspiracy two persons must be involved, and the jury must be satisfied before they come to a verdict for the plaintiff that the defendants conspired between them to drive her from the convent. They must be satisfied there was a combination between them to effect that common object. It was not necessary that each act should be done by both ; it was enough if the act of one was in the furtherance of that object. If, however, they thought that the course pursued by Mrs. Star originated in the rebellious conduct of the plaintiff, and that Mrs. Star felt she was bound to adopt, in order to maintain discipline and order in the convent, that would be an answer to the case, provided she acted within the legitimate scope of her authority. What was the authority to which the plaintiff voluntarily submitted herself? There were three vows which each individual on entering the convent took, but they were only concerned with two of them. First, there was the vow of poverty, which was not only a renunciation of all the rights to property possessed at the time, but an abnegation of all capacity to acquire property. Therefore, Mrs. Star said that when she took away anything from a sister she only exercised that power to which she was indisputably entitled. But then arose the question—Did she exercise in this case that authority honestly, or with the object of driving plaintiff from the convent? Sister Scholastica, like the other sisters, had sworn unlimited obedience to the voice of the mother superior, as if it were the voice of God. To his mind, nothing could be more shocking than that ; but they had nothing to do with it here. He did not make the remark as a matter of reproach to any, and he ought almost to apologize for being betrayed into a genuine expression of feeling on the subject. He took it, however, that the obedience imposed by such emphatic terms must be reasonably construed, that the superior should command nothing to be done contrary to the law of man; and, moreover, that the obedience must be within the rules and customs of the community, whether written or recognized. They could not fail to be struck with the fact, that the plaintiff stands alone in this matter, but needs must be so in the nature of things; and it was her misfortune to have twelve witnesses against her, eight of whom had given such evidence, that if they believed it her case must be demolished. He quite agreed with the Solicitor-General that the fact of her being unsupported was by no means a reason why she should not be believed. Evidence was not to be taken by numbers, but by its intrinsic weight—weight rather than by tale; and if they believed, though she stood alone, that she told the truth, they would give due weight to it. It was the practice in English courts of justice to hear the witnesses as well as see them, and in hearing how they deliver their evidence. It might be that his ear, from long practice, got accustomed to these things, but the manner and mode in which replies were made afforded a sufficient indication whether a person was telling the truth or not; but more important still was the demeanour of a witness in the box; and he must say that he never heard witnesses give their evidence in a manner to claim the respect of the judge, than had the sisters who had been called in this case. They all concurred that Mrs. Star was by no means arbitrary or unjust to any one, and that she had acquired the esteem and the affectionate regard of the whole community except the plaintiff. Whilst they all spoke of Mrs. Star in terms of unmixed respect, they all spoke of the plaintiff as one for whom they entertained no personal dislike, but as one they could not help wishing to have removed from amongst them. That evidence was by no means conclusive that she might not have taken a strong dislike to the plaintiff, and that she should be expelled from the convent. One thing, however, was certain—that if Mrs. Star had been of an arbitrary disposition, that fact would have been known to her and the other sisters. It was the same as with a commander. If he was a kind man, it was generally well known, and if severe, that was known also. It was well known to comrades what was the conduct of each other; and if there was one worse than the other, it was not likely to escape their attention. Following him to that point, could they say whether a course of systematic persecution had been pursued towards the plaintiff, or that the defendant's conduct resulted from the plaintiff's own course of conduct. If they were of opinion that she did continually violate the rules of the convent, and that, in consequence of her doing so, the defendants, and more especially the superior, put her plenary power into exercise for the purpose of mending her disposition, with a view to her own good, and if the convent, however much mistaken, thought she acted rightly it was an answer to the case. There were parts of Mrs. Star's deposition which would have been better had they been couched in different language. They must give her credit for not intending to convey unusual conduct against the plaintiff with the priest; and so it was believed by the bishop. Yet it was open to that supposition, and to say the least of it it was couched in very ambiguous language. It was, however, for them to judge in this or in other matters between the parties. He next came to the alleged stealing of the deceased nun's medal and her grave-clothes. Mrs. Hewitson had made a most startling statement with reference to it. They all remembered her description of what took place when the body was lying in the coffin in the chapel awaiting interment. The scene as described by her almost took away one's breath. Her charge was, that the plaintiff, with an unhallowed and sacrilegious hand despoiled a dead sister of these things. If, however, they were to look at that circumstance by the light of the common law, as they were told they must the other day, and that stealing from the dead was no worse than stealing from the living—that it amounted in morality to nothing, no one could doubt that it shocked every sentiment of our better nature, and all those feelings of reverence and respect for the dead with which it was our nature to surround them. From the circumstance of its having been withheld until this trial, therefore, it would be well to hesitate before they placed implicit confidence in it, and he cautioned them how they came to a judgment upon it. The circumstance tended to cast a doubt about it—first, from the horror of the thing itself, and secondly, the improbability that if the plaintiff intended to do it she should have done it in the presence of a second party. There was another instance only to be exceeded by the horrible story of stealing from the dead, and that was stealing the dinners from the children. Having referred to the evidence in support of the charge, his lordship went on to state that the Solicitor-General had very fairly stated he had done all in his power to meet the case by the production of the parties named. They were little children and might have forgotten what occurred, but certainly had either negatived nor did not remember the particular circumstances stated, and that calculated to excite a reasonable degree of suspicion as to the facts. On the other hand, several spoke to the facts, and to a certain degree they were corroborated by the circumstance that after the superior had received reports as to the stealing, not perhaps of dinners, but of the cakes and tit-bits from the children. She directed the plaintiff to undress, and search to find whether she could find any trace of food to confirm the report. If it were true, and if they thought there was foundation for the charge, then it was no wonder that the rest of the sisters felt indignant; because, although they were nuns, they could not divest themselves of womanly nature in their love for little children. If it was false, he did not see how the plaintiff could be sufficiently compensated for being made the victim of so atrocious a charge. With respect to the commission, he should be sorry to say a disrespectful word towards the bishop, who from his position was entitled to veneration and respect. But he could not help saying that anything more lamentable than the course of the commission he had never heard of in the administration of justice. There was no reason to doubt the accuracy of Father Matthew's statement that the bishop undertook to him that the nuns should be produced instead of their depositions being taken as evidence. They were not, and it is all nonsense to talk about the common law, and that under the common law witnesses could not be examined in this country. It was an inquiry which was taking place in this country of England, where justice was administered with regard to those means by which long experience had shown truth could alone be elicited and innocence protected, and there ought to have been no hesitation in keeping the undertaking that had been given Father Matthew, so that it might be seen whether they would stand his possibly rough, but, he did not doubt his effectual cross-examination. They had seen the manner in which they had stood the cross-examination of one of the most subtle of cross-examiners. It did not follow that they would not own they had been handled in such a manner as might have induced the court to come to a different conclusion than that at which they arrived. It was no fault of the commissioners that the inquiry should be so limited as it had been, but in one respect Father Matthew had not treated their family in that case. That he could not help saying, with all respect for the manly way in which he had stood up in his defence of the interest of his niece. He would not say he was not entitled to their respect as a bold man, acting under a conscientious sense of duty towards one whom, he believed, required his protection. But with regard to what occurred before the commissioners, he had not dealt quite fairly with them. He distinctly stated that he had not been allowed to go into the countercharge, whereas it appeared, from the evidence of Dr. O'Hanlon, that not only were the counter-charges not gone into, but that, on Miss Saurin's evidence in respect of them, was founded his report that the charges against her from 1862 were not proved. He now came to the question whether they believed that the charges conveyed in the depositions were falsely made to the knowledge of the parties with the intention to induce the commission to unjustly expel the plaintiff from the convent. If they were of that opinion the plaintiff was entitled to their verdict. On the other hand, if they thought the statements, though highly coloured, were made honestly and with an intention to do what was right and just as regarded the interests of the community, not overlooking what was just and reasonably fair towards the plaintiff, they would find a verdict for the defendants. The communications by the defendants to the bishop, he was bound to them, were privileged, if they were made with an honest intention and not with the object of doing a wrong or injury to the plaintiff. Then there was the alleged imprisonment of the plaintiff after the decision of the commission had been made known. Whatever the result of the case there was one thing on which the mother superior could not be commended. The bishop having sent a letter to the mother superior stating that he wished Miss Saurin to be removed by her parents—a letter which was not equivalent to actual removal—the mother superior took from her finger the ring, which to a nun was the mystic symbol of her union with Christ. That was a harsh and cruel act, and much to be lamented, because at the time the bishop had passed no sentence of expulsion upon the plaintiff, although he probably would have passed such a sentence if

the brother had not come to take her away. It was within her power to take away from the plaintiff everything she possessed, but it was a harsh and cruel proceeding, as it divested her of the character of a nun. It might not, however, have been done from any unworthy motive. The habit of the plaintiff was also taken off, but then Mrs. Star probably felt that as she no longer belonged to the community she ought not to be allowed to wear the dress of the order; and it was to be recollected that other dresses were prepared for her. If they were of opinion there was actual restraint which prevented her from leaving her room, then their verdict would be for the plaintiff; and if they were of that opinion, he should ask them to find that specially, and award damages for it irrespective of any other part of the case. They had now to reconcile two conflicting statements that had been laid before them. It was, as he had said, a painful inquiry. If the plaintiff was wrong she could not be acquitted of having made a statement which she must have known to have been untrue—she could not be acquitted of having been guilty of the grossest exaggeration. If, on the other hand, the defendants were wrong, then all of the witnesses they had called to speak to matters in the convent had been guilty of wilful and corrupt perjury. Before coming to that conclusion, they ought to take into account not only the manner in which they had given evidence, but their position in the world. They were women who had devoted themselves to a virtuous and religious life, and against whom nothing could be induced beyond this wicked conspiracy of them. There was nothing otherwise to detract from their right and title to have their evidence considered with respect. If, however, they entered into this conspiracy, and had supported it by perjury, one could not consider anything more black. Judging from what he had seen, he had not seen or heard anything to disentitle them to perfect respect and reverence at their hands. Unless the plaintiff's evidence had impressed them as being the more creditable story, and her voice had carried to their breasts the conviction of truth, he saw nothing that disentitled the defendants' witnesses, who had devoted their life to visiting the sick, instructing the poor, and other acts of piety, to disentitle them to belief. It was the duty of the mother superior to exercise a reasonable amount of authority and good faith. She had kept back some letters, and she had obliterated portions of others, and of that she had given her explanation. An extraordinary letter from the brother to the bishop had been produced, and from its extraordinary character it was reasonable to infer that the mother superior had some excuse for keeping back the brother's letters. The brother's absence had been attributed to the stern rule of obedience, he being a member of the order of Jesus; but he (the Lord Chief Justice) attributed it to a different course—that his sister had been guilty of the grossest exaggerations. After reading that exciting letter of F. Saurin, they could not wonder that some of his letters had been withheld from his sister. It had been suggested that the evidence of the defendants' witnesses was unreliable, inasmuch as they were bound by their vows to strict obedience, that they were in subjection to one whose service they were to regard as the voice of God, and that they were under a solemn obligation to state that and that only which it was the first interest of their order to do. I have been pestered with publications and extracts from books on this subject. I do not now believe in their statements, or the extent to which they were carried. At all events, there may in bygone days have been all sorts of Jesuitical works, all sorts of suggestions and reservations in statement, and here and there such doctrines were laid down, with extracts which, much to his annoyance, had been submitted to his notice. It might be that in the matter of judgment of opinion the vow of obedience which bound the persons to work, and to hear the voice of God in the voice of the superior, might make them passive instruments in the hands of those who had thus the direction of their conscience. But when a number of persons came to speak deliberately to a series of facts which were no longer matter of opinion, are we to suppose that in the age in which we live, the obligations of truth could be obliterated from the conscience of persons addicted to the practice of religion, and upon whom no taint of infamy can be fixed. Still less can we believe that individuals who come forward with such stories could stand the test of cross-examination, and that the truthfulness of their story would not in some way or other be made to appear. You have seen the witnesses in question, and have heard them submit to a cross-examination of the most able and searching character possible, You are to form a judgment for yourself as to their credibility, and judge by what you have seen and heard. Let no false impression and undue and unworthy prejudice influence you in considering the question, should this body of evidence be rejected because it comes from a convent. What is just for the one side is just for the other. I am, however, extremely sorry that my observations have been extended to such length. All that I ask of you is this. As I said in the beginning, so say I now. Let no prepossession or prejudice influence you. The current of popular feeling, the echoes of which have been heard even within these walls—the cries of the unthinking populace—the cheering of one party, the hootings of another, without a knowledge of the real merits or demerits of the case—ought to find, and will find no response in the breasts of twelve honest and intelligent men who have come to discharge one of the most solemn duties which men could be called upon to perform according to their sense of right and truth and the dictates of their own free and unfettered consciences. All I ask of you is to hold, as I on my part have endeavoured to hold, the scales of justice evenly, as right and truth and justice shall require, not to let them incline to the one side or the other. (Approbation, which quickly suppressed.)

The jury were about to retire, when

The Lord Chief Justice said he had intended to state on the subject of damages, if they believed that, whatever might have been the provocation given by the petitioner, the defendants had combined for the purpose of getting rid of her by undue severity, and to procure her expulsion by charges not founded on justice or honesty, that the plaintiff had lost the benefit of dower, and had been deprived of the opportunity of continuing the life she had entered upon, for it was all nonsense to say that she could re-commence it in another community. In the event, he had stated, she would be entitled to substantial damages. On the other hand, if they were of opinion that her conduct was calculated to provoke honest and just resentment—that she had given great occasion of provocation—then, if they still thought that she was entitled to a verdict, the amount of the damages should be regulated by their view of her conduct.

The Foreman of the jury asked his Lordship to ascertain for them how many professed nuns were in the convent at the time Miss Saurin was there.

Mrs. Star having conferred with Mrs. Kennedy, said, in reply to his Lordship, that there were seven or eight.

The jury then requested to be furnished with the depositions and principal documents.

The Lord Chief Justice said, " Certainly," and they were accordingly placed in the hands of the foreman.

The jury then retired, it being twenty minutes past five o'clock. After an absence of nearly three hours, they returned into court, and there being great anxiety manifested by the audience to hear the verdict, the Lord Chief Justice expressed his desire that there should be no exhibition of feeling after the verdict had been returned.

The Foreman of the jury then handed a written paper to his lordship, stating—" The jury find for the plaintiff on the counts for assault (the stripping and imprisonment) ; they also find for the plaintiff on the counts for libel and conspiracy, with damages £500; that is to say, £300, the dowry paid in by her, and £200."

The Lord Chief Justice: Do you mean by that, gentlemen, that the damages are to be £200 in the event of the £300 being returned?

The Foreman: Yes ; that was our meaning in the event. If not, £500.

The Lord Chief Justice: I understand that the Baggot-street Convent is ready to give back the £300.

The Foreman : In that case, the damages are to be £200.

The Lord Chief Justice thanked the jury for the attention they had bestowed on the case, and at the same time expressed his regret that he could not award them full compensation for their services. He trusted the law on that subject would be altered. He also thanked the officers of the police for the valuable and efficient services they had rendered in keeping order under circumstances of very great difficulty ; and he hoped that his opinion on the subject would be communicated to the chief commissioner.

Although on the delivery of the verdict silence was preserved in court in conformity with his lordship's request, when it became known outside the court the dense crowd there congregated gave expression to their gratification in a loud and long-continued and right hearty English cheer.

APPENDIX.

Writ of Summons.

Victoria, by the grace of God, of the United Kingdom of Great Britain and Ireland, Queen, Defender of the Faith, to Mary Ann Star and Julia Kennedy, of the town and county of Kingston-upon-Hull. We command you, that within eight days after the service of this Writ on you, inclusive of the day of such service, you do cause an appearance to be entered for you in our Court of Queen's Bench, in an action at the suit of Susan Saurin. And take notice, that in default of your so doing, the said Susan Saurin may proceed therein to judgment and execution. Witness, Sir Alexander James Edmund Cockburn, Baronet, at Westminster, the tenth day of November, in the year of Our Lord, one thousand eight hundred and sixty-six.

N.B.—This Writ is to be served within six calendar months from the date thereof or, if renewed, from the date of such renewal, including the day of such date, and not afterwards.

Endorsement.

This Writ was issued by Francis William Blake, of No. 5, Serle Street, Lincoln's Inn, in the county of Middlesex, agent for John England, John Saxelbye, and George Christopher Roberts, of the town and county of Kingston-upon-Hull, attorneys for the said plaintiff.

In the Queen's Bench, the 22nd day of November, 1866.

Middlesex (to wit).—*First Count.*—Susan Saurin, by George Christopher Roberts, her attorney, sues Mary Ann Star and Julia Kennedy, who have been summoned to answer the said Susan Saurin by virtue of a Writ issued on the 10th day of November, in the year of Our Lord 1866, out of Her Majesty's Court of Queen's Bench, for that the defendants on divers occasions assaulted and beat the plaintiff, and took her clothes and other property from her, and imprisoned the plaintiff and kept her imprisoned for a long space of time, whereby the plaintiff was rendered sick and ill and greatly distressed in mind and body.

Second Count.—And the plaintiff further sues the defendants for that the defendants converted to their own use, or wrongfully deprived the plaintiff of the use and possession of, the goods of the plaintiff, that is to say, a watch, wearing apparel, books, and papers.

Third Count.—And the plaintiff further sues the defendants for that the plaintiff was a member of a certain religious order of Roman Catholic women called the Sisters of Mercy, and of a certain house or religious establishment of such Sisters of Mercy, and the defendants were members of the same order and of the same house or establishment, and the defendant, Mary Ann Star, was the superioress of the said house or establishment, and the plaintiff, as such member of the said house or establishment was lawfully entitled to certain privileges and advantages, and amongst others, to board, lodging, clothing, and maintenance at the expense of the said order, and not at her own expense, and to the right of attending certain services of the Roman Catholic Church in a certain building attached to the said house or establishment, and the defendants wrongfully and maliciously conspired together to compel the plaintiff to cease to be a member of the said house or establishment by wrongfully subjecting the plaintiff to various indignities, persecutions, and annoyances, and by depriving the plaintiff of the food and clothing to which, as a member of the said order, and of the said house or establishment she was lawfully entitled, and by imprisoning the plaintiff and keeping her imprisoned, and by preventing her from attending the said services of the said Roman Catholic Church, and further unlawfully and maliciously conspired to procure the expulsion of the plaintiff from the said house or establishment, and from the said order of Sisters of Mercy by making false charges of disobedience, contempt of authority, neglect of duty, and other misconduct to the Roman Catholic Bishop, having, by the rules and constitutions of the said order, lawful authority to act in that behalf, and to expel the plaintiff as aforesaid. And the plaintiff says that in pursuance of the said conspiracy, the defendants did subject the plaintiff to a long series of the said indignities, persecutions, and annoyances, and did deprive the plaintiff of the said food and clothing, and of divers articles of her property, and did imprison and keep imprisoned the plaintiff, and did prevent her from attending the said services, and did make the said false charges, and did thereby procure the said Bishop to expel the plaintiff from the said order and the said house or establishment, whereby the plaintiff lost all the benefits of being such member of the said house or establishment, and was deprived of the board, lodging, clothing, and maintenance to which, as such member, she was lawfully entitled, and was prevented from attending the said services in the said building, and was greatly injured in health, peace of mind, credit, and reputation.

Fourth Count.—And the plaintiff further sues the defendants for that the matters in the introductory part of the third count mentioned are true, and by the rules, constitutions, and practices of the said order all the matters contained in the libel hereinafter mentioned were and are offences and breaches of duty; and the same were and are regarded by the members of the said order, and by the Roman Catholics generally, as discreditable and disgraceful to a person who is a member of the said order; and thereupon the defendants falsely and maliciously wrote and published of and concerning the plaintiff, in a set of charges presented by the said defendant, Mary Ann Star, to the Roman Catholic Bishop in the said third count mentioned, then having such authority as therein mentioned, the words following, that is to say: "She is dissatisfied with and complains of her boots and shoes, and the food given to her, and her veil. She is late at her duties. She eats during hours during which eating is prohibited. She has spoken privately to a priest. She has contradicted the superioress and spoken disrespectfully to her. She met the priest in the convent, in disobedience to orders. She converses with externs; she does not scruple to approach the sacraments for the purpose of deception. After being guilty of the aforesaid acts she sent for the Reverend Mr. Armt, and made false statements to him." In consequence whereof the plaintiff was expelled from the said order and the said house as mentioned in the third count, and lost the benefits and advantages in that count mentioned.

And the plaintiff claims £5,000.

PLEA.

The 24th day of January, in the year of Our Lord 1867.

THE said defendants, by THOMAS JAMES ROOKE, their attorney, as to the first and second counts of the declaration, so far as the same relate to so much of the clothes, property, and goods in these counts mentioned, to which the sum of five pounds, parcel of the plaintiff's claim relates, bring into Court here the sum of five pounds, and say that the said sum is enough to satisfy the claim of the plaintiff in respect of the matter herein pleaded to.

2. And for a second plea to the residue of the causes of action in the first and second counts of the declaration, the defendants say that they are not guilty, as therein in that behalf alleged.

3. And for a third plea to the residue of the causes of action in the first and second counts of the declaration, in respect of the clothes, property, and goods not pleaded to by the first plea, the defendants say that the said clothes, property, and goods in these counts mentioned, except as by the first plea pleaded to, were not the clothes, property, or goods of the plaintiff as alleged.

4. And for a fourth plea to the third count of the declaration the defendants say that they are not guilty, as therein alleged.

5. And for a fifth plea to the third count of the declaration the defendants say that at the time of the alleged grievances in that count mentioned, the plaintiff was not a member of the said religious order or of the said house or religious establishment; nor as such member of such house or establishment lawfully entitled to the said privileges and advantages as in the third count alleged.

6. And for a sixth plea to the third count of the declaration so far as the same relates to the defendants having as alleged deprived the plaintiff of divers articles of her property, the defendants say that the said articles were not the property of the plaintiff as alleged.

7. And for a seventh plea to the last count of the declaration, the defendants say that they are not guilty as therein alleged.

8. And for an eighth plea, except as to the matters pleaded to by the first plea, the defendants say that except as aforesaid they did what is complained of by the plaintiff's leave.

9. And for a ninth plea, except as the matters pleaded to by the first plea, the defendants say that after the accruing of the said matters of complaint and causes of action in the declaration, except as aforesaid, certain differences respecting the same were depending between the plaintiff and the defendants, and, thereupon it was agreed by and between the plaintiff and the defendants that the said alleged matters of complaint, causes of action, and all matters in difference respecting the same should be, and the same then were, referred to arbitration of one Robert Cornthwaite, and the said Robert Cornthwaite took upon himself the said arbitration, and duly made and published his award respecting the said matters referred, and thereby awarded that the alleged matters of complaint and causes of action had not, nor had any of them accrued and did not nor did any of them exist.

REPLICATION.

The 29th day of April, in the year of Our Lord 1868.

THE plaintiff as to the first plea of the defendants says that the said sum is not sufficient to satisfy the claim of the plaintiff in respect of the matters to which the said plea is pleaded.

And as to the rest of the pleas of the defendants the plaintiff takes and joins issue upon them respectively.

Therefore let a jury come, &c.

In the QUEEN'S BENCH,

Between SUSAN SAURIN......... *Plaintiff,*

and

MARY ANN STAR and } *Defendants.*
JULIA KENNEDY ...... }

THE following are the particulars asked for by the defendants. Under the first count the plaintiff gives the following particulars :—That the defendants on or about the 31st day of May, 1865, stripped the plaintiff of many articles of her clothing, searched her pockets, and took away the contents thereof, a reliquary, two medals, a tablet, a needle-book, a rosary, and a silver ring. Also that upon another occasion during the plaintiff's residence at Hull, of which she cannot give the specific date (under this count the plaintiff confines herself to the assaults and imprisonment, and treats the abstraction of the contents of her pockets as mere matter of aggravation), she was searched, and portions of her clothing and of the contents of her pockets taken from her by the defendants. Also, that the defendants kept the plaintiff imprisoned in certain rooms and cells of the convent at Hull, from the latter part of January till the early part of May, 1866.

Under the second count the plaintiff gives the following particulars :—That on several occasions during the time of the imprisonment abovementioned, the defendants took from the plaintiff all her articles of dress as a nun, namely, her beads, cincture, flannel skirt, night veil, stays, cap, flannel body, habit veil, black stuff skirt, coif, guim, also an examine book, a book of resolutions, a reliquary, a tablet, a needle-book, a rosary, a silver ring, also certain papers and memoranda which were in the plaintiff's pocket at the times of the respective searches hereinbefore mentioned, and also an office book, and certain other devotional books. Also certain letters from the Roman Catholic Bishop of Beverley to the plaintiff, and letters from her friends. Also, that during the latter part of the plaintiff's residence at Hull the defendants took possession of letters addressed to the plaintiff, before they reached the plaintiff, and kept them. The plaintiff cannot more particularly specify the letter taken from her. Also, that the defendants took away the plaintiff's watch some time towards the latter end of 1865.

Under the third count the plaintiff gives the following particulars :—The defendants commenced a series of persecutions against the plaintiff in the latter part of 1862, and continued the same both at Clifford and at Hull from 1862 till the plaintiff's removal from the convent at Hull, in May, 1866. The plaintiff was systematically exposed to humiliation and degradation before the sisters, before the scholars, and before strangers. The instruction at the school was taken out of her hands, and novices and other persons placed over her. She was forbidden to speak to any person who should come to the schools or the convent, or to the other nuns, except when it should be a matter of necessity ; was kept to menial and degrading tasks ; was supplied with food differing from that given to the other nuns, both in quantity and quality ; was required to do more work than any of the other nuns, and more than her strength would allow ; was subjected to constant and unusual penances, such as having to go about the convent with a dirty duster round her head, or to hold a dirty dust-box in her hands during spiritual lectures ; was placed under the constant surveillance of one or other of the inmates of the convent ; was deprived of the use of books and writing materials ; was deprived of good and sufficient clothing, and furnished with old, worn-out, and dilapidated articles ; was deprived of the clean linen and under-clothing allowed to the other nuns ; was ordered in private to do things which were publicly forbidden, and then publicly held up to reproach for so doing,— for instance, it was publicly forbidden for the sisters to carry water along a certain passage, the plaintiff was privately ordered to carry water along this passage, and then held up to reproach before the other sisters for her disobedience of orders.

The above matters are to be taken as specimens of the kind of ill-treatment and persecution to which the plaintiff was subjected. As the matters in question extended over several years, the plaintiff cannot give more specific information as to dates. The plaintiff charges that this system began at Clifford in 1862, was continued, whether she was at Clifford or at Hull, till June, 1864, when she removed to Hull, that it was there continued, and that at length, in or about December 1865, the defendants made a set of charges of misconduct against the plaintiff to the Roman Catholic Bishop of Beverley. The plaintiff was never supplied with a copy of those charges, and therefore cannot give the particulars ; but she refers to the charges which were the subject of a so-called investigation by certain commissioners appointed by the said Bishop, at an inquiry held at the convent at Hull in January, 1866.

The plaintiff charges that after the said investigation, the defendants continued the same system of persecution as before, with greatly increased severity, and inflicted upon her the imprisonment hereinbefore referred to, during the course of which they prevented her from attending the usual Divine services and offices of the Roman Catholic religion, in the chapel of the convent at Hull. And the plaintiff says that as a consequence of her expulsion in the third count mentioned, she was deprived, amongst other things, of the right of attending the regular Divine service and offices of the Church in the said chapel of the said convent.

Dated the 14th day of January, 1867.

Yours, &c.,

FRANCIS WILLIAM BLAKE,

5, Serle Street, Lincoln's Inn,

Plaintiff's agent.

To Messrs, Parker, Rooke, and Parker,

Defendants' attorneys or agents.

In the QUEEN'S BENCH—

SAURIN *v.* STAR AND ANOTHER.

SPECIAL JURY :—

DAVID WEBSTER, 4, Norfolk Road, Merchant.
JOSIAH STANTON, 12, Bridge Road, Marylebone, Merchant.
WILLIAM LOVEJOY, 37, Russell Square, Merchant.
GEORGE WILLIAM WOODMAN, 48, Grosvenor Road, Merchant.
JOSEPH WYKES, 136, Richmond Road, Hackney, Merchant.
EDWARD TUCKEY, Sudbury, Merchant.
CHARLES ROBINSON, 7, Besborough Road, Merchant.
HARVEY RANKING, 16, James Street, Buckingham Gate, Merchant.
WALTER FAITHFUL, 19, Milner Square, Merchant.
JOHN EDWARDS, 157, Richmond Road, Hackney, Merchant.

Common Jurors {THOMAS PARKER.
{GEORGE PETERS.

CPSIA information can be obtained at www.ICGtesting.com
Printed in the USA
BVOW02s1456110416

443791BV00017B/154/P